va

D23

# ANCIENT RIGHTS
## AND FUTURE COMFORT

Centre of South Asian Studies,
School of Oriental and African Studies,
University of London

# LONDON STUDIES ON SOUTH ASIA

LONDON STUDIES ON SOUTH ASIA NO. 13

# Ancient Rights and Future Comfort

## Bihar, the Bengal Tenancy Act of 1885, and British Rule in India

P.G. Robb

School of Oriental and African Studies, London

CURZON

First published in 1997
by Curzon Press
15 The Quadrant, Richmond
Surrey, TW9 1BP

© 1997 Peter Robb

Printed in Great Britain by
TJ International Ltd., Padstow, Cornwall

*British Library Cataloguing in Publication Data*
A catalogue record for this book is available from the British Library

*Library of Congress in Publication Data*
A catalogue record for this book has been requested

ISBN 0–7007–0625–9

FOR ELIZABETH

# *Contents*

# Preface

Many obligations have been incurred while this work was in preparation. First and last, I must thank my wife, Elizabeth, who gave up her own concerns to work as my research assistant in India for almost a year, greatly increasing the material I was able to collect. Her support over the long period during which the work subsequently evolved was exceeded only by her determination in the final stages that I should finish it off once and for all. Also to Benjamin and Thomas, my two sons, my thanks: this project is about as old as they are. It too (unexpectedly and after last-minute discovery) will turn out to be twins.

The work owes a debt to Clive Dewey, for his studies of British agrarian policy and the social and intellectual history of officialdom, and for his keen comments on my own efforts. I am pleased to note also the special contributions of 'Tom' Tomlinson, who (with his wife, Caroline) shared a period of research in New Delhi, and of Walter Hauser for invaluable advice on researching in Patna and on other matters. To Binay Chaudhuri's work too I have had repeatedly to return; once he summed up my own conclusions for me in ways which made me understand them better. In SOAS, K.N. Chaudhuri and John Harrison were always encouraging; more recently Terry Byres' themes and interests suggested lines of inquiry; at the end David Arnold pointed out some typographical errors and encouraged me to keep to the overall plan of the work. Five who have sadly since died played a part—three close colleagues at SOAS, Kenneth Ballhatchet, Nigel Crook and Burton Stein; Neil Charlesworth for his great ability to think in wider contexts and against current fashion; and Eric Stokes who was an inspiring example though an enigmatic critic.

Many other colleagues and students in classes and seminars have helped and criticised my ideas. For the middle phases of the work, I remember particularly warmly discussions with three of my research students—Sanjay Nigam, Bindeshwar Ram and I.G. Khan—whose interests lay closest to those of this book, and also with Chitta Panda while he was carrying out his research at Oxford, and with Rajat Datta on his many visits to SOAS from King's College London. More recently, while the appearance of this work was delayed because of my chairmanship of the SOAS Centre of South Asian Studies and other research and publishing projects, I had the chance to benefit from exchanges of views with another generation of my students, namely

Sanjoy Bhattacharya, Andrew Grout, Shompa Lahiri, Alex McKay, Pragati Mohapatra, Subhajyoti Ray, and Sanjay Sharma. Very late in the day, Suhit Sen helped by embarking on a project which at first looked quite akin to this one, on zamindari abolition. The recent period saw an expansion of some of the concerns of this project, particularly a stronger orientation towards the study of policy in the broader context of the growth and development of the state. It is thus related to other work, on law, labour and identity, which preoccupied me during this interval.

Personal or intellectual debts should also be noticed to the published work and contributions in seminars and/or private discussions of others too numerous to list; but most of them are included among the participants, of whom mention must be made, in the conferences in London in 1980 on the 'external dimension' in South Asia, the workshop on 'arrested development in India' under Dietmar Rothermund and Clive Dewey in Heidelberg in 1984, the 'peasant consciousness' conference at Bellagio organised by Majid Siddiqi in 1987, and the three associated workshops at SOAS on agriculture and economic organisation, organised by me, Kaoru Sugihara, Utsa Patnaik, Burton Stein, and Sanjay Subrahmanyam, in July 1992. In the late stages of writing I have benefited particularly from editing two books from these workshops, on Indian agriculture, where I found methodologies congenial to my own, and (jointly) of Japanese contributions to South Asian rural studies, where contrasting perspectives helped clarify my thinking. For similar reasons, I am indebted also to the London third-world economic history group, and especially to a long, fruitful series of informal three-man seminars held with David Anderson and Ian Brown on peasants in the colonial world.

Versions of parts of the present volume or its counterpart were read at several venues in SOAS, and also at the Centre of South Asian Studies, Cambridge, St. Antony's College, Oxford, at the Imperial History seminar at the Institute of Historical Research, London, at the British Association of South Asian Studies' meeting in Sussex, at the Economic History Society's conference at Exeter, at an informal seminar on 'stratification' at Leicester, at the Canadian conference on India and the National Congress in Montreal, at Professor Ravinder Kumar's seminar at the Nehru Memorial Library, New Delhi, at the Department of History and the British Council in Calcutta, at Osaka City University, and at the New Zealand Asian Studies conference in Auckland. All these occasions produced helpful comments. The editors and readers of several journals and collections of essays have commented on articles which foreshadowed or have been incorporated in parts of the book.[1] One article has been revised for inclusion in chapter ten. It is 'In search of dominant peasants. Notes on the implementation in Bihar of the Bengal Tenancy Act of 1885' in Clive Dewey (ed.), *Arrested Development in India. The historical dimension* (Manohar Publications, New Delhi 1988), pp. 188-222. Some shorter extracts or paraphrases, cited in footnotes, have also been included, notably from 'Law and agrarian society in India. The case of Bihar and the nineteenth-century tenancy debate', *Modern Asian Studies* 22, 2 (Cambridge University Press, 1988), pp. 319-54, and 'Ideas in agrarian history. Some observations on the British and nineteenth-century Bihar', Professor Eric Stokes Memorial Lecture (May 1989), *Journal of the Royal Asiatic Society* 1 (1990), pp.17-43.

I have depended greatly on the riches of the Library of the School of Oriental and African Studies, the India Office Library and Records (now the Oriental and India Office Collections of the British Library), the manuscripts and reading rooms of the British Library, the National Archives of India, the Bihar State Record Office, Patna, and the Bodleian Library, Oxford. Janet Marks, formerly executive officer in the SOAS Centre of South Asian Studies, helped with the preparation of the manuscript. Finally, I have received financial assistance on more than one occasion from the Research Committee at the School of Oriental and African Studies. My thanks to all of these.

Peter Robb, London, 1995

## Sources and abbreviations

With exceptions included separately in the footnotes, this work is based mainly upon the records of the Government of India, especially the Revenue and Agriculture Department (or its equivalent), consulted in the Oriental and India Office Collections of the British Library, London, and the National Archives, New Delhi; upon the Ripon papers in the British Library; and upon the records of the Commissioner of Patna Division, held in the Bihar State Archives, Patna. A full bibliography of

[1] Advance indications of the arguments of volume two may be gleaned from 'Bihar, the colonial state and agricultural development in India, 1880-1920', *IESHR* 25, 2 (1988), pp.205-35; and 'Peasants' choices? Indian agriculture and the limits of commercialization in nineteenth-century Bihar', *Economic History Review* XLV, 1 (1992), pp.97-119.

these and secondary works will be included in a second volume. The departmental records are cited as 'R&A Rev B 7-8 (January 1897)' or the equivalent, showing (in order) the department, branch, series ('A' to 'D' or Deposit), proceeding number, and its date. The citations include 'keep-withs' and are mainly to the 'file' rather than 'proceedings' volumes, held only in the National Archives, New Delhi; however A-series documents, without 'keep-withs', have also been consulted in London. The Ripon papers are cited as Additional Manuscripts (Add.Mss.) of the British Library. The Patna Commissioners' records are cited with *basta* number, collection and file numbers (when available) and year. Where documents appear in more than one of these collections, only one is cited.

The abbreviations used are:

| | |
|---|---|
| Agric | Agriculture (Branch) |
| Be | Bengal |
| *CEHI* | Dharma Kumar, ed., *The Cambridge Economic History of India*, vol.2 (Cambridge 1983) |
| CO | *Circular Orders of the Sudder Board of Revenue at the Presidency of Fort William*, edited by William Peters (1788 to the end of August 1837; Calcutta 1838), by G.H. Poole (September 1837 to the end of 1838; Calcutta 1839), and by W.H. Jones (September 1837 to the end of 1850; Calcutta 1851) |
| Coll | Collector |
| G/ | Government of |
| H | Home (Department, Government of India; proceedings of) |
| I | India |
| *IESHR* | *Indian Economic and Social History Review* |
| IOL | Oriental and India Office Collections, British Library |
| LG | Lieutenant-Governor |
| NAI | National Archives of India |
| NWP | North-Western Provinces |
| *MAS* | *Modern Asian Studies* |
| PC | Commissioner of Patna Division |
| PCR | Records of the Commissioner of Patna Division |
| PSV | Private Secretary to the Viceroy |
| R&A | Revenue and Agriculture (Department, Government of India; proceedings of) |
| Rev | Land Revenue (Branch) |
| SR | Settlement Report |
| S/S | Secretary of State for India |
| V | Viceroy |

# Introduction

This is a book about agrarian policies in colonial India, what they tell us about the state, and something of their consequences. These are important subjects, for the history of the colonial state and India. Two great themes—the evolution of the state and the deployment of a 'science' of political economy—came together in the colonial debates over tenancy law. To consider them in combination offers some new perspectives, on subjects often discussed separately in the past. This introduction will begin with a brief consideration of the relation of land and political systems, especially as mediated through theories and rhetoric, and go on to consider the validity of approaching socio-economic questions by examining political ideas and policies, with particular regard to the imperfect transition in nineteenth-century India between the local and the general, between land-based and market systems.

Obviously there is nothing remarkable about looking to the land in order to understand the state. Political systems *may* be defined by the manner of control over people or in relation to a community (including democratic forms), or with regard to fluid resources such as capital and technology: developing polities, in multi-national unions or conversely in new city-states such as Singapore, are still territorial but shaped more by commerce and information than by interests in fixed property; they are late stages in a long changing emphasis. But otherwise the people have usually been led to the promised land, into formal territorial states; and for much of human history states have been forged and differentiated by the manner in which land is controlled—that is, in accordance with local power, rural property or taxation, and agriculture. Ultimately, in more complex political and economic systems, the role of land becomes symbolic, for example as the nation-state, a form defined by a demarcated territory and by the sovereign law, people and interests existing within it. Thus political historians take the importance of landed interests for granted. The link is obvious in feudal and quasi-feudal structures, but also in representative or elective systems focused around land and other immoveable property. In colonial India, land-based hierarchies, local communities and systems of rural production were central to the government, politics and economy.

Through many changes the continuing importance of the land has been reflected, though its character and influence evolved. This was why, for example, political and moral messages were implied in the developing evocations of landscape in European art—in the snatches of countryside glimpsed from Italian towns as depicted in the Renaissance, in the heroic imaginary worlds of Poussin or Claude Lorrain, in the seventeenth-century Dutch masters and much later in the Hague School, in Gainsborough, Constable and Turner, in Caspar David Friedrich, in the nineteenth-century French of several schools, in the neoclassical, picturesque, romantic and impressionist movements generally. To a similar degree, land questions help describe the political system and how it evolved; considering them is one way of describing political change. We will find in the Indian case that, at the level of policy-making, intellectual contexts were of vital importance, and that political rather than economic goals often provided motive force. But we will also see, for example, what Clive Dewey has shown, that the 'essentially *historical* study...of the village community pullulated with contemporary relevance':[1] how theories on the manner in which land was held and agrarian production arranged gave birth to important policies and helped define the functions of the state. In nineteenth-century India, whether or not 'modes of power' (to adopt Partha Chatterjee's phrase) were ultimately more significant than modes of production, both politics and economics coalesced around questions of land. Chatterjee, following Marx, discusses the impact of different forms of property; similarly Brenner's influential arguments about feudalism rely on the varying dispositions of local power on the land.[2] Land relations and policies consistently affect the exercise and purposes of power, and their importance persists when much else seems to be changing.

It follows that any changes in land-holding or its taxation might foster wider transformations. The Henrician and Cromwellian revolution in sixteenth-century England has been attributed to the diffusion of the Church's wealth (mainly land) among the middle and upper classes, as that transfer in turn demanded new laws which altered the nature and relations of parliament and the state. By the same token, patterns of land-holding tended to remain a bedrock of political systems. The Elizabethan parliament, as Neale pointed out, was not constructed to

[1] C.J. Dewey, 'Images of the village community: a study of Anglo-Indian ideology', *MAS* 6, 3 (1972), p.292. Dewey's work allows this book to limit its consideration of the European background to the ideas being deployed in India.

[2] Partha Chatterjee, 'More on modes of power and the peasantry', in Ranajit Guha, ed., *Subaltern Studies* II (Delhi 1983).

represent local interests, and thus indicated a move towards the enunciation of broader or national concerns; but those local interests—the
sheriffs, justices, and all the gentry, with their factions and patronage—
still constituted the bulk of political life. The wealth of the country was
in agriculture, and the state had little direct contact with individuals,
even during the push for religious conformity. Accordingly, it was
largely land disputes that fuelled the development of the legal and court
systems, and helped define the public role of the gentry: litigation grew
greatly, and did so in parallel with development of the state.[3] Similar
points might be made about nineteenth-century India.

The concentration upon land was not incompatible with the growth
of commerce and other political interests. A persistence of local and
seigneurial power had characterised the resurgent Spain of Ferdinand
and Isabella.[4] Despite its significant class of artisans, the small town in
sixteenth-century France—Romans—described by Le Roy Ladurie was
shaped politically by a profound involvement with agriculture and
landed property, not just through its nobility but through the lending
and trading of merchants and the bulk of the work undertaken by town-
resident labourers. When the town's lawyers and professionals sought
change, marking a political transition, they demanded an equalisation
of liabilities and political power; but by that they meant an allocation
which was proportionate to the shares held in land and other fixed
property, not to income or capital.[5] In colonial India, a superficially
modern colonial administration and policy, and the market-oriented
capitalist enterprise, both were shaped chiefly by the need to compre-
hend, pacify and demarcate the countryside, to extract land revenue or
produce, to maintain social and political control through landed intermediaries, and to encourage rural production and consumption as
essential components of imperial trade. Therefore, a basic premise of
this book is that any significant changes in the role of the state will
have been expressed (and may be discerned) in policies towards land.

It might be argued (with the physiocrats) that land became *more*
important in the early modern period, despite or because of the growth
of trade, and because of the acquisition and demarcation of territory by
and on behalf of states. India seems to be a case in point in this respect
too. For Europe the process occurred externally, as new lands were

[3] J.E. Neale, *The Elizabethan House of Commons* (1949; Harmondsworth
1963).

[4] J.H. Elliott, *Imperial Spain 1649-1716* (London 1963), p.72 and passim.

[5] Emmanuel Le Roy Ladurie, *Carnival. A People's Uprising at Romans,
1579-1580* (tr. Mary Feeney; London 1980), especially chs. I and XIV.

conquered and settled or dominated, and it occurred internally, through enclosures and other state-regulated private property, and through territorial administration and representation, which helped promote a bureaucratic and legal centralisation, state claims to a monopoly of force, and unqualified sovereignty of state law—features which characterised the mature phase of land-related states, and which were also evident in colonial India. But the process was often slow or partial. In India, the advent of 'private' landed property, whether or not wholly an innovation of Western law, developed alongside as well as superseding more communal forms of land control. Similarly, in seventeenth-century England, there were claims for individual rights, but it has been claimed that the Commons and the law continued chiefly to recognise communities—little commonwealths. Gradually, the middle-classes, in growing comfort and more frequently in voluntary, individual association with others, began to outgrow the broader, compulsory, hierarchical communities of parish and village.[6] By the eighteenth century, these local societies, concentrated by the power of landed property, were clearly beginning to break up or becoming ancillary to a new commercial order in the towns. But even this did not remove the importance of land questions. Local communities did not just disappear in Britain, let alone the attitudes they fostered, and the state was not set loose to re-form around wholly different principles. In England at least, the continuing economic and political power of landed wealth and social hierarchy has been repeatedly demonstrated, through every crisis of the gentry, and territorial principles remain embedded in the constitution and in law. One is reminded also of Fernand Braudel's eloquent celebration of the diversity of France and its *pays*,[7] or of Jürgen Habermas's demonstration of the importance of property ownership to the development of a bourgeois public sphere (*bürgerliche Öffentlichkeit*).[8]

Of course the role of land issues changed over time, and the centrality of land policies and landed power has diminished. However in India the links remained less tenuous: even by 1900 the colonial state had not

---

[6] See Christopher Hill, *Society and Puritanism in Pre-revolutionary England* (London 1964).

[7] F. Braudel, *The Identity of France*, vol. 1, *History and Environment* (tr. Sian Reynolds; London 1988), pp.37-41 and passim. Braudel stresses the limitations (and imperfect relationship) of national and political as opposed to ecological, cultural and historical boundaries, which seems (however) another way of making the same point, on a broader definition of the state.

[8] Jürgen Habermas, *The Structural Transformation of the Public Sphere. An Inquiry into a Category of Bourgeois Society* (1962; tr. Thomas Burger with the assistance of Frederick Lawrence; Cambridge 1992), p.56 and passim.

reached the stage of political or economic development of late eighteenth-century England. The growth of cities showed the trend, and some areas and activities were more commercialised or socially-mobile than others. But, with every sign of change, the rhetoric and political priorities for the colonial rulers became increasingly protective of a supposedly old, stable rural order. Their stance was like that of the conservative Jane Austen facing England's transformations in her day: Elizabeth Bennet's family was saved from disgrace, not by the often-vilified new money, but by the noble intervention of landed wealth. The East India Company often faced similar prejudice, and, though trade was clearly a valuable ally of property, it would long remain bereft of romance and fineness in the British imagination—not least, ironically, in India, an empire founded by commerce. Thus the Indian colonial state, in its relation to landed power, was partly protective, seeking to continue indigenous forms, particularly political and property rights. In the later nineteenth century, British nostalgia for 'older' forms of landed property became a luxury that flourished especially in the subject territories of the empire.

On the other hand, most of all when the colonial state sought reform, its vocabulary and expectations followed those of the European experience. It continually lamented the lack in India of the local agency of propertied individuals and of the assumptions of civil society on which it believed government could rest in Europe. Officials disagreed about the preferred form of that agency—aristocratic and peasant-proprietary models vying against one another—and they continually tried to create a centralised bureaucracy and law. But they also harnessed the collaboration of the locally-powerful, or sought to create effective local structures, as in the permanent settlement of Bengal, the use of headmen and district boards, and appeals to the village community or to communal and caste leadership. Even the army, that chief bastion and preoccupation of the rulers, could not escape territorial linkages, through its recruitment, pensioners' land-grants, and strategic thinking.

By the nineteenth century, moreover, the land impinged not only in terms of economy, power and taxation, but as a quantifiable and measurable object of knowledge, and a resource to be controlled and improved. As phenomenologists have asserted (from Husserl to Heidegger) the natural sciences aim at knowledge of the object in order to obtain mastery over it, and this attitude (which we will see here in terms of tenurial and other categorisation) was adopted in the social sciences also. Added components during the colonial era thus included the rise of scientific investigation and, specifically, changing notions of political economy. We shall see in this book how state interventions over landed property sought to reach ever-lower social or tenurial strata, and how this attempt was a part of an ever-extending categorisation, the attribution (as it were) of 'properties' defining a wider range of people and institutions. Thus the land was also a metaphor.

The changes implied, contrary to the implications of a static objectification, that land 'control' no longer was enough; land 'use' was necessary. This brings us to our second element, after land: ideas of the proper role of the state, operating within a bounded territory. Important to the issues to be discussed in this book were first the Scottish philosophers' concern with social and not individual man, as a corollary to humanist individualism and several property rights, and an answer to such pessimism as that of the acute fifteenth-century observer, Aeneas Sylvius Piccolomini, who could see nothing good in prospect in 1454, since 'Every *civitas* (city state) has its king and there are as many princes as there are households'.[9] Important secondly was the emphasis (as in Hume) on observation and experience as the basis of scientific knowledge. Together these began to impose new duties on the state. Alexander Pope (in a note to the *Essay on Man*): traced the 'Origine of true RELIGION and GOVERNMENT from the Principle of LOVE: and of SUPERSTITION and TYRANNY, from that of FEAR'; and, generally following Aristotle's *Politics*, he attributed happiness, as the human goal, to collective or social will, which the state expressed:

> So drives Self-love, thro' just and thro' unjust,
> To one man's pow'r, ambition, lucre, lust:
> The same Self-love, in all, becomes the cause
> Of what restrains him, Government and Laws (III, 269-72).

Such contrary influences of self-interest, through the individual and the collectivity, in private and public, will prove a continual refrain of this book. So will the role of government in expressing and resolving the tension.

In England, Blackstone had relied on natural principles, such as an original contract between man and the state, which minimised the state's duty; but Bentham retorted in favour of the principle of utility— he too judged the commands of law not on the basis of an abstract moral order but in terms of what was most conducive to human happiness. Adam Smith tended to offer both of these: he believed in a need to balance the selfish and social propensities of man in order to produce propriety, useful to happiness. In ways analogous to Hume's

---

[9] Pius II, *Opera omnia* (Basle 1871), 656, quoted in Myron P. Gilmore, *The World of Humanism, 1453-1517* (New York 1952), p.1.

distinction between natural and artificial virtues—the latter being those which, without necessarily pleasing, *tended* towards pleasure—Smith held that some controls over human action were 'natural' or self-imposed, or attributable to a human tendency to approve what was proper or beneficial and that which would punish transgressors; these influences went beyond deliberate motivation so as to work indirectly, by invisible hand. But Smith also argued that there remained a need for sanctions which would ensure justice between individuals. He argued too for an evolutionary or historical model of economic and social growth, moving from hunting to pasturage to agronomy to commerce. Both his moral and his historical perceptions necessitated a role for the state. Civil government, including relations of authority and subordination, was needed in later stages of development to promote the security of private property. Where land was the principal form of property, landed estates would be the origin and focus of political power; but, though commerce, manufacturing and urbanisation created alternative sources and styles of power—independent republics—and loosened the control of landed elites over their dependents, yet they also increased the motivation of the landed to secure control over land and produce, if only to match their purchasing and political power with the new range of goods and opportunities available. Thus, by Smith's account, even to promote commercial wealth, it was necessary for the state to record and protect property, and to arbitrate between different interests in society. Such efforts inevitably implied intervention in landholding rather than in the practice of trade.

Bentham too stressed individuality, but wanted to make law standardised and universal. His was a scientific approach to *morality* (as also in J.S. Mill's *System of Logic*, 1843).[10] Just as causation was a major issue of empirical investigation, so laws were considered to be instrumental, and judged by their utility. These ideas embodied several distinct messages for the state: that it and not a natural order should provide commands and sanctions, and that these had to be chosen with a view to producing specific effects. Individual happiness was the goal, but it had to be promoted by general measures, as contained in universal standardised law. Some argued that ends, being unascertainable, could not be a sufficient measure to judge particular means. John Stuart Mill pointed out that it was necessary and sufficient to identity a *tendency* towards good. Thus Mill, while lauding individual freedom of conscience and action, also endorsed the need for laws, assessed

[10] This point is made by Mary Warnock in her introduction to Mill's *Utilitarianism*; see note 11 below.

according to their propensity for good. Moreover, utility consisted in the 'permanent interests of man as a progressive being'.[11] The state's role, in short, was to promote progress.

These are well-known ideas of political economy which were even better known to nineteenth-century colonial officials. Together they implied that the state, as a good husbandman, had a responsibility to define, protect and improve. Other branches of Western science provided methodologies, and stressed man's ability to control nature. Policy was invoked in order to achieve social ends, and judged by probable results as ascertained after empirical investigation. Because of the importance of land relations, the agrarian sphere was one in which such ideas were particularly applied in India. Accordingly, in the Western knowledge of India, one finds some continuities of political interpretation and official ambition from the late eighteenth to the twentieth century, a period in which it has been more usual to see marked change. Our task therefore becomes first to identify the varying means by which such constant ideas were expressed and accepted in policy, and secondly to assess their appropriateness and influence on India. This study will examine a working-out of Smith's insights, as furthered also by J.S. Mill, in the debates over Bengal tenancy law. In addition, as said, a conflict between utility and history was implied in Bentham's differences with Blackstone. It was not resolved by that eighteenth-century debate. India's colonial land laws provide notable instances in which the dispute continued: in this book it will be characterised as a difference between 'future comfort' and 'ancient rights'.

By assessing colonial impact, we discover how differences of understanding matter. In colonial policy, a distinct complexity was created by the perennial struggle between the power of precedent (here the legitimacy of the past) and the attraction of the new (here prospects of improvement). Thus the development of tenancy law was not a straightforward, unilinear modernisation. Yet it *was* part of the construction of 'modern' classifications, of capitalist production and markets, and of nations on the Western model. Though changes in agrarian structure were framed, as changes often are, in customary or traditional form, they were always regarded as necessary and inevitable. It mattered that *property*—that is, a concept of definite, unequal shares of the common stock of land and production—was identified and reinforced by the state as the basis of its criminal and civil law. Rights of such a kind also

[11] J.S. Mill, *Utilitarianism, On Liberty* and *Essay on Bentham* with selected writings of Jeremy Bentham and John Austin (ed. Mary Warnock; London 1964).

implied social *classes*. These rights were partly new, because India's previous forms and institutions were never so bound up with discrete, individual possession, or with the associated morality of rights. India had conceived differently of property and hence of classification; even under the Mughals, its legal and social norms, for example, were more fluid, interdependent and collective—there were local systems in which the state and people could not be wholly differentiated, systems which might be called a 'moral economy', if the term did not often imply a golden past of social equity, and focus attention too much on right and wrong, and too little on rights and relations and the means of securing them.

There were interesting parallels as well as differences between the circumstances of the British state, law and local power and those to be observed in nineteenth-century India. The land was at issue in at least four ways: from interpretations of what was legitimate in India, from the colonial power's pragmatic need for support and revenue, from habits and policies imported from Britain, and from intellectual ideas. Modern state methods and goals developed in India. But they did so within a frame of rhetoric and calculation which were sometimes inappropriate. Part of the incongruity was peculiarly colonial. For example, it has been noted by environmental historians, who increasingly provide another perspective on the different ways in which states relate to land, that because India is diverse, ecologically-speaking, its political formations necessarily infringe ecological priorities and diverge from or conflict in some degree with the interests of the bulk of the population. The same disparity could be observed, worsening, in colonial times, whether or not it really originated then.[12] Nineteenth-century India too was an artificial construction: it contained a complex state which was created according to the demands of commerce and the dictates of information, introducing elements of the idea of the nation, but which remained pragmatically embroiled with the interests of the land, its proprietors, local hierarchies and production. This book will illustrate one example of this anomaly.

[12] See, for example, Madhav Gadgil and Ramachandra Guha, *Ecology and Equity. The Use and Abuse of Nature in Contemporary India* (London and New York 1995); see also their *This Fissured Land. An Ecological History of India* (Delhi 1993). The *political* implication of this is presumably in favour of localised governments or regions of economic interest under a minimal new world order, of the kind being predicted by a wide range of late twentieth-century commentators, including free-market technocrats such as Kenichi Ohmae.

## II

The agenda just foreshadowed must imply a study of how economic or political practice and success are affected by ideological contexts. Interest is increasing in that question, among historians assessing the impact of colonial rule, and also among political economists. It is not a straightforward matter. We make a convenient dichotomy between ideas and experience, but nowadays it seems a major task to distinguish the one from the other, given that the only 'experience' we have is pre-judged and pre-arranged. Accordingly, Michel Foucault's influence has led to many an attempt to identify the 'epistemes' or 'discursive practices' which define particular historical periods and situations. Of particular relevance here, it has been said that 'all academic knowledge of India' is (and must be) 'tinged and impressed with, violated by, the gross political fact' of conquest and Western hegemony.[13] But, perversely, this has tended to discourage serious study of the mentality of colonial officialdom. Such a study has to go beyond easy typing and slogans. It implies subtle problems of observation and definition. Above all, our premise does not need to be that ways of thinking are wholly determined by power, thus rendered impotent and uninteresting in themselves.[14] This book, about a region and a legislative enactment, emphasises the ideas of the historical record, as have earlier, rightly

[13] Edward W. Said, *Orientalism* (London 1985), p.11, and 45: 'I mean to ask whether there is any way of avoiding the hostility expressed by the division, say, of men into "us" (Westerners) and "they" (Orientals).' For this Hegelian reference see also Ronald Inden, 'Orientalist constructions of India', *Modern Asian Studies* 20, 3, (1986), including, at p.433, a view that 'there is a single reality, a single human nature'. Inden's critique of modern writers, especially Dumont, is focused on their Utilitarian and Hegelian inheritance—see also Inden, *Imagining India* (Oxford 1990)—and especially the 'old Hegelian proposition that caste...ever had the upper hand'; Inden himself refers to caste, after the thirteenth century, as the 'distinctive institution of Indian civilisation', but he wants something as generic as 'human' thoughts and acts to be the 'real center of attention', presumably at the expense of collectivities and localism ('Constructions', pp.438-40). It is not clear why exposing 'objectivity' as a universal conceit should render valid, *a priori*, any particular interpretation, such as the salience of power or the sameness of individuals.

[14] Compare Irfan Habib, 'Problems of Marxist historiography' (from *Social Scientist* 16, 12, 1988) in *Essays in Indian History. Towards a Marxist Perspective* (New Delhi 1995), arguing against historical determinism, and that, when Marx said 'that "ideas become a material force once they have gripped the masses", he surely meant that consciousness once generalized delimits the range of ideas of individuals and social action', a consequence in the capitalist era being that 'the role of ideas...has been substantially enlarged' (pp.3-4).

celebrated works of Indian history. That the ideas are actors in the drama is shown in the book's two objects of attention: reality as well as representations. It is possible to approach reality because the fact that there are systems of interpretation and historical assumptions does not mean that findings are non-verifiable. They may be both defensible and subject to challenge.

In this book the perceptions by the state and in the records provide a route into distinct interpretations of the society. Is it justifiable to concentrate on the state? In regard to the matters of property and tenancy to be discussed in this book, even indigenous accounts were often permeated by the constructs of colonial law and administration. But this did not signify a 'hegemony' of 'colonial' ideas, for the intellectual assumptions brought from outside had also been formed or were modified by the experience, within India, of particular problems and circumstances. Thus, interest in state ideology is needed to define its influence, but also ultimately to reduce the assumptions about its instrumentality or uniqueness. Paradoxically, history from below may be (as mostly it has to be) achieved by examination from above. To define the vantage-point on which we stand is to help reveal the different perspectives of the peoples and times we observe. Here rural conditions are measured against criteria external to the countryside and inherited from the past. Local variations of context and response are contrasted with, and viewed in the interstices of, the ideological constructions put upon them. From this beginning we can make some assessment of agrarian structure and the ways it was changing. It will be shown that the state was enlarging its capacity and to an extent its aims, but that its policies failed from weaknesses of conception and execution. What may appear state-centred here is mainly a focus on the gaps between colonial perceptions and Indian norms, a study of the officials' ideas and their consequences.

The Bengal Tenancy Act of 1885 had characteristics which marked the modern era, but this book does not endorse either of the usual versions of modernisation theory—not the one in which changes occur by mimicry (as of Britain by India) nor its antithesis in which 'natural' developments are impeded by the distortions and dependency of colonial dominion. Here we will treat the evolution of events and concepts as the outcome of a dialogue between various, changing, mutually-influenced voices.[15] The amalgam which was the Act was pro-

---

[15] Hence the book has something in common with other studies which base their explanations on mixtures of influence, on cultural accommodations, on 'traditions', imported ideas *and* new exigencies, on processes of continual

duced in both Europe and India, from (to mention a few components) long-term changes in the structures of power in the Indian countryside, a history of state attempts to acquire and order knowledge and to harness rural resources, and theories of property, society and government evolving over more than a hundred years. The context of the Act also matters, even at the specific level, because expansions of the state's responsibilities and capacity ensured that it would have an impact outside the legislative chamber. Tenancy reform was actively prosecuted through administration, law courts, surveys and the record of rights—measures which contributed to the operational aspect of a revolution in government. Interventions shaped by the Tenancy Act helped re-define agrarian structures. Actual changes reflected its own misapprehensions, and also transformed the state's relations to the society. There was another dialogue, between colonial power, representing generalising theory, and indigenous practice, marked by contingent variety or a different logic.

Contemporaries were far from unaware of these discrepancies. They were often central to the debates, in India and indeed in Britain. A balance repeatedly had to be struck between models of change through competition, and of continuity through preservation. The elements to be resolved, as Dewey has shown,[16] included still-competing attitudes to property: was it a bulwark against royal and feudal privilege, or a weapon of inequality? The Indian tenancy debates were deeply embroiled in the struggle between these two positions, sharpened on one side by the fears among the entrenched landed interest (especially after the Irish Land Act, 1881-2), and on the other side by the popular or socialist demand that private privilege be regulated in the public interest. The argument was fierce because self-interested but also because of its broad implications. It expressed a struggle between opposing tendencies of political economy: was citizenship best expressed in access to common resources, or by a guarantee of private property? And which of these forms was more progressive? On one hand there was a belief in the superiority of interdependent communities, a conservative stance still extant in leftist endorsement of the 'moral economy', and generally in nostalgia for more equitable, past ages. It encouraged measures to preserve essentialised communities—on the land, it meant establishing original rights and excluding 'outsiders'; it meant favouring collective institutions. On the other hand, there were the assertions of laissez-faire

---

negotiation. See for example Douglas Haynes, *Rhetoric and Ritual in Colonial India. The Shaping of Public Culture in Surat City, 1852-1928* (Berkeley 1991).

[16] Dewey, 'Images of the village community'.

orthodoxy that progress, which was necessary and beneficial, would best be secured by the economic freedom of individuals. Following Ricardo, it was assumed that individual effort would secure economic development through the deployment of capital: applied to land, this argument meant definite rights and unfettered ownership, including free transfer. We will see in the Bengal Tenancy Act of 1885 an attempt to marry these perennial, opposing impulses.

Another theme too will keep recurring: how the impact of law and administration (the role of the state) and that of communications, capital and trade (the role of the market) were qualified or diverted because of the mismatch between them, as forces for change or instruments of generalisation, and the multifarious continuities of circumstance and practice, environment and culture within India. It is possible to regard this mismatch as a failure of transition. How to protect the weak and adjudicate between selfish interests had been debated (as said) by moral and political philosophers for hundreds of years, while the actual means of protection were in flux through social changes. In Europe the effect of regimes of exclusive private property had naturally been to undermine notions of contingent possession, that is of social obligations as a qualification of ownership, just as shareholders came to be regarded as the sole beneficiaries of modern companies; the social functions of private ownership were gradually lost or transferred to the state. In nineteenth-century India the legal system adopted the European norms of individual property, but the state's responsibility was even more feebly developed than in contemporary Britain. Laws and social practices were at variance, both between and within themselves. From time to time, there were attempts to counter the individualistic tenor of British law by imposing collective responsibilities on landlords or social leaders or communities (indeed these remained an important strategy of colonial rule); but generally the political and social requirements made of private ownership were diminished by colonialism and the growth of the state.

Again, in Europe local-community sanctions gradually became less significant than public ones, of state, policy, law, education and income redistribution. In India, where issues of equity had also been considered, and the British were attuned once more by the later nineteenth century to what they thought to be Indian solutions, yet the colonial period (building on changes over several centuries) certainly impaired *local* sanctions and accommodations, and gave preference to *general* forces, institutions and categories. Increasingly those rich in property and rights had them protected by distant, overarching forces, even in absentia and without personal exertion; indeed such privileges were drawn from ever-wider sources and expressed in ever-wider realms. Equally-general measures began to be introduced to provide for equity, to mediate between selfish individual interests or to offer a safety-net for those under stress: one thinks of famine relief, state involvement in irrigation or communications, and legal reforms designed to protect rights. Thus even the colonial state began to claim a responsibility for the happiness of men. But because its measures remained partial, confused and contradictory, they fell far short of providing protection for the community at all levels. The public sphere broadened and deepened, while its content and operation remained contingent and various.

Habermas's conceptualisation of this important facet of modernisation is helpful to the explanation of what occurred in colonial India. The intrusion of law and the state, into property-holding, tenancy and eventually labour, and generally into production and exchange, can readily be described as an extension of the public sphere: it opened these areas of life to external scrutiny and regulation; it attempted to objectify and standardise them; and it tried to separate them out as distinct forms and functions. Where landholding rights and practices had reflected a multiplicity of relations that were neither wholly of the state nor the household, neither public nor private, or alternatively both of these at once, now the colonial government and law tried to reduce landholding to simple, definite and uniform categories that expressed relationships in property alone rather than any broader, personal, ritual or moral connections. Where rent had been multiple, various, contingent and ambiguous, the law treated it as fixed and contractual, and as subject to objective rules and judicial interpretation; where rent had denoted social conditions and standing, it now indicated the terms of a purely economic relationship. Similar measures were eventually to be extended to the rights of under-tenants and labourers; parallel understandings were applied very much more generally. There is no doubt that these were *changes*, for they were different from what had gone before and they moved Indian practice and perceptions in the directions which they indicated.

But they did not do so at once; they did so only very gradually; and the great, lingering if transitional discrepancies between the state's understandings and the manner and arrangements of Indian life were the origin of much of the damage done to India's peoples over the last hundred years or so of colonial rule. Habermas has identified the creation of the bourgeois public sphere as a particular moment of history. It occurred in western Europe from a long process of change and adjustment, which did not remove all anomalies and survivals but established prevailing or distinctive forms of institution and behaviour. In India many of the lessons and assumptions of European civil society and the public sphere were applied, as in tenancy law, axiomatically to a country in which these adjustments had yet to occur, to places and peoples with their own genius which, if they approached European forms at all, did so at the stage of what Habermas called 'representative publicness' (*repräsentative Öffentlichkeit*).[17]

The elaboration of a public-private dichotomy was one way in which the resolution of debate represented by the Bengal Tenancy Act of 1885 marked a political evolution: it widened the terms and range of state intervention, the categories within a *putative* public sphere. There was a progression, in the period under review, from official attention to structures to attempted manipulation of processes of agrarian life. The progression is reflected in this book, which considers agrarian structure and the Act of 1885, and in a proposed second volume which will discuss agricultural production and the state in Bihar.[18] On the other hand, as said, official measures were often inappropriate or half-hearted; by the 1880s they were again hesitant, restricted by fears of disturbance in India, and by theories of Indian society and the Indian past. (The failure has some relevance at the end of the twentieth century when political and economic systems, and means of social protection or equity, show the strain of yet-further generalisations, of globalisation.) In colonial India private property was offered as a boon to colla-borators, often freeing them from local responsibility; while the short-comings of countervailing general forces for the protection of the weak exaggerated the disparities of entitlement and status which existed between rich and poor, landed and landless. This broad lack of synchro-nisation had impact in addition to the fact that many of the colonial policies were anyway inappropriate to India.

A profile will be attempted here of the complex changes which resulted from the interventions of the state, and from its failure to intervene. It is necessary to map with some precision the areas of local

---

[17] Habermas, *Public Sphere*, pp.5-14.

[18] See also Eugene F. Irshick, *Dialogue and History. Constructing South India, 1795-1895* (Berkeley 1994), for some striking parallels (though also some differences) on the influence of law and policy, interacting with indige-nous forms, constituting 'sacred' land (like that of America!). Unfortunately I did not discover Irshick's work until after this book was written, but see especi-ally his chapter 2, on the importance of constructed past, and his Conclusion, on the connection between such change and citizenship or identity.

resilience and autonomy, and alternatively where change was felt—because, as this study emphasises in regard to rural Bihar, India was very disparate, with a range of influential connections between the locality and the outside world of trade and power.[19] The tenancy law altered the balance of resources and also reacted with an already-differentiated society.[20] Its rational construction of the countryside through British colonial understandings (and hence actions) was significantly at variance with existing, indigenous ways in which agrarian conditions might have been perceived.

By examining the disjunction of policy and practice, ideas and reality, this book (finally) will assess an evolutionary theory—the changes from hunting-and-gathering to factory-farming—which has dominated thinking in regard to land use. It was a theory which found settled cultivation in all respects superior to nomadism. It meant that social justice was sought in legal protection of land rights; that supposedly optimal tenurial forms (especially secure freeholding) were necessary to sustained agricultural investment; that technological control and political sovereignty over land seemed the *sine quâ non* of progress. Tenurial reform took precedence over agricultural reform, security of property over attempts to improve production methods, credit or marketing. The evolutionary theory also meant that earlier (in our case pre-colonial) land systems were assessed negatively, as inefficient and irrational, lacking the potential for development. Allegedly they had no individual ownership, little differentiation and capital accumulation, few technological or other means of increasing output. As 'careless' and communal modes of production, they produced social stagnation and environmental degradation, for want of an individual interest in maximisation or conservation. Thus, in forests, slash-and-burn cultivation was more damaging and less rational than logging; thus pastoralists were bound (if population grew) to over-exploit common land; thus farmers were unwilling to invest in agricultural improvements while collective obligations and interdependent practices were vested in their landholding. On the other hand colonial experience and insecurity also made social and economic conservatives of many a bureaucrat; the past and the

---

[19] For this argument see Peter Robb (ed.), *Rural South Asia. Linkages, Change and Development* and *Rural India. Land, Power and Society under British Rule*, Collected Papers on South Asia, nos 5 and 6 (London 1983), or the second edition of *Rural India* (Delhi 1992).

[20] Similarly, in the second volume it will be argued that the relations of production and exchange were not merely an imposition by the extractors of surplus—the rentiers and creditors—but also a necessary response by them to persistent local practice, related to environment, social norms, beliefs and values.

indigenous were also specially valued.[21] Thus it was, in Western assessments of non-Western regimes, that respect for historical rights and custom competed with the demands of economic efficiency.

It is increasingly being realised that this may have been an unnecessary opposition. As this book demonstrates, in a major Indian example, the Western assessments of custom and pre-colonial practice were often merely projections of European concepts and expectations.[22] It is not obvious that several property and capitalist agriculture offered the only formula for securing the well-being of large populations: even if particular forms of landholding were lacking, it was possible for pre-colonial societies to achieve improvements or protect environments through communal regulation, cooperation and self-denial. Land could be artificially rationed, even where it was in surplus, in order to preserve social and political hierarchies or to distribute risk, and because of the costs of reclamation or the variability of soils and water-supply. It was partly through ignoring such appropriate and evolving expedients, that European interventions produced neither equity nor prosperity for the majority in tropical countries. What they did produce, even when supporting custom and history, was reduced flexibility, a paternalist 'protection' and control, and a preference for commercial over subsistence goals. These are specific and important changes, indicative especially of the growth of the state, but not necessarily 'progress'.

---

[21] It is instructive to compare this with the rise of environmental worries through colonial observations of damage in tropical and island locations, and Western encounters with non-Western knowledge and practice, as argued in Richard Grove, *Green Imperialism. Colonial Expansion, Tropical Island Edens and the Origins of Environmentalism, 1600-1860* (Cambridge 1995). The desire to conserve Indian social institutions had some similar origins, and limits.

[22] The African literature has been richer in these arguments; the colonial debates on Africa echoed those on India over a later and shorter timespan. A useful starting pont is the introduction by Thomas J. Bassett, in Bassett and Donald E. Crummey, eds., *Land in African Agrarian Systems* (Wisconsin 1993), pp.3-31. See also David Arnold and Ramachandra Guha, eds., *Nature, Culture, Imperialism. Essays on the Environmental History of South Asia* (Delhi 1995).

Chapter One

# Property, classes and the state

He [Sir Ashley Eden, Lieutenant-Governor of Bengal] would like to see the
Bengal ryots, as a class, secured in the enjoyment of those rights which the
ancient land law and custom of the country intended them to have, protected
against arbitrary eviction, left in the enjoyment of a reasonable proportion of the
profits of cultivation, and, in short, placed in a position of substantial comfort,
calculated to resist successfully the occasional pressure of bad times.[1]

These 'ancient rights' and this 'future comfort' were like talismans of
one aspect of British thinking about agrarian policy in India during the
nineteenth century. They were the professed goals and the guiding
principles not only for the Bengal tenancy law to which Eden was
referring, but also across a wide range of other initiatives. They should
not be taken at face value, but do suggest clusters of issues or routes of
inquiry by means of which it is possible to assess the ideas and impact
of the British and to approach the realities of conditions in the Indian
countryside. On such a basis (and though much has had to be left out),[2]
this study seeks ultimately to relate agrarian structure to a critique of
colonialism, and indirectly of theories of modernisation and development. It has two main characters: rural Bihar as seen in agrarian
structure and the relations of production, and the British as revealed in
their intellectual assumptions and policies towards India. Change in
Bihar is explained by means of an analysis of British perceptions. The
intention is not to give a comprehensive account of agrarian conditions.
Rather the attempt is to uncover the object through the categories and
ideas imposed upon it, the veil both of the past and of the present.

It is also argued that perceptions themselves produced intended and
unintended effects. Through the enormous elaboration of Indian law, an

---

[1] Government of Bengal (Alexander Mackenzie, Chief Secretary) to Government of India, 15 July 1880, R&A Rev A 16-46 (July 1883).

[2] I have dealt briefly with some other aspects elsewhere, for example in *Evolution of British Policy towards Indian Politics* (New Delhi 1992), (ed.), *Society
and Ideology. Essays in South Asian History* (Delhi 1993) and *Dalit Movements
and the Meanings of Labour in India* (Delhi 1993). For background see also
Sugata Bose, *Peasant Labour and Colonial Capital: Rural Bengal since 1770*
(Cambridge 1993), Burton Stein, ed., *The Making of Agrarian Policy in British
India, 1770-1900* (Delhi 1992), Dietmar Rothermund, *Government, Landlord
and Peasant in India* (Wiesbaden 1978), and (less directly) Thomas R. Metcalf,
*Ideologies of the Raj* (Cambridge 1994).

apparent effort to close all eventualities and to fix all interpretations, the executive power of British rule was striving (in part) to legitimise and facilitate interventions by the officers of the state, to a degree beyond what was thought possible or desirable in a society such as Britain, with its organised and recognised private interests. Indian resistance to the state existed alongside opportunistic co-operation or expectations of state intervention, and Indian protest was sometimes admitted and even feared—indeed British policies helped define a range of political interests—but Indian opinion was not allowed the same voice as supposedly legitimate interests within Britain. The ideas of officials were thus peculiarly important in the colonial setting.

In this volume, the centrepiece is the Bengal Tenancy Act of 1885 and its attempt to 'reinstate' the original privileges of agricultural producers in the form of occupancy tenants. The ideas which it embodied, about societies and India in particular, and about the proper goal of British rule, were of wider significance than would be supposed from a consideration of tenancy alone. The Act was particularly important for Bihar, then administratively part of the Lower Provinces of Bengal, because the tenancy reform owed much to certain officials with Bihari experience, and because aspects of the legislation were conceived with particular reference to the needs of Bihar. It will be shown, however, that it fitted them peculiarly badly. In due course, a second volume will consider the promise of British reformers to improve the physical and economic conditions of the people of Bihar, through state action and the virtues of trade; that study will be centred on the production of commercial and other crops but, again, will be informed by an assessment of policies and the ideas which lay behind them. Thus, if the first theme is a specific one about rural Bihar, a second major thread of the discussion traces the nature and development of British rule in India. The period chosen, though not appropriate in all respects, is convenient for one important variable, the state's land policy. The starting-point is the permanent settlement of Bengal land revenues in 1793, and the effective cut-off the provincial economic, banking and agricultural inquiries of the 1920s.

It is hoped that the findings of this study may range wider than the place and period to which they are applied. However, it should be emphasised that the detailed examples are mainly confined to Bihar's old Patna Division of Champaran, Darbhanga, Muzaffarpur, Saran, Shahabad, Patna and Gaya, and to the last few decades before 1900. The concentration upon Bihar needs no excuse, given that Patna Division was more populous than the Bombay presidency, but Bihar also provides valuable illustrations both as the extreme case it was claimed to be at the time, and because it was nonetheless extremely various. The concentration on the latter part of the nineteenth century follows from the attention paid to the debates and implementation of the Tenancy Act of 1885, and is partly justified too by an argument (to be developed below) that the passage of the Act advanced and epitomised aspects of the making of the nation state in India. It marked an important step in a *general* expansion of state responsibilities. This of course was a long-term process, deriving (as Foucault and others have observed) from political and scientific developments that permitted or required the state to optimise and transform rather than to control and exploit the society which it governed: a *continuity* in such aims and in the terms of understanding will be stressed in this book.[3] Nonetheless, in these matters, as contemporaries recognised, the 1880s in particular were years of radical reform and ambition, despite the many instances of continuity or temporising. Focused under Ripon, as far as government was concerned, and also exemplified by the Famine Commission and the Local Self-Government Act, this period was analogous to other significant forward-looking decades such as the 1790s and 1830s.[4] Not just landlords' self-interest, officials' ambition and lawyers' arrogance, but a larger struggle about the purpose and role of the state, explain the length and vehemence of the debate over Bengal tenancy.

Why a piece of legislation was passed is a question admitting of many different answers. Many statutes in colonial India, and not least the 1885 Act, were derived from a peculiarly wide range of traditions and pressures, internal and external—because of colonialism and its idea of India as *tabula rasa* in legal terms, and in contrast with laws evolved largely within 'national' jurisdictions. Policy was affected by political considerations, in both India and Britain, and by legal and other precedents internationally and over time. However in this study the aim is quite restricted: it is not so much to elucidate the politics and policy-decisions as to set out the main ideas popularised by the tenancy debate, and to assess their impact. Those questions are quite complex enough. Surrounding the 1885 Act was rhetoric—properly so called because of the arguments' particular stylised forms—which encapsulated changes occurring over a long period, in the understandings of property, economy and the tasks of government. The legislation matters

---

[3] See especially M. Foucault, *The Order of Things. An Archæology of the Human Sciences* (tr. of *Les mots et les choses*; London 1970).
[4] See Briton Martin, *New India, 1885* (Berkeley and Los Angeles 1969).

partly because colonial India was so bound by rules, and increasingly focused on the state. (Again, this was a by-product of colonialism and its experiments in building institutions so as to retain and extend executive authority.) The debate helped create a picture of rural society that continues to have influence. Explaining the intellectual frame of the Tenancy Act provides a way to investigate its consequences.[5]

Intellectually what is possible and what desired for governments are constituted through perceptions, ideologies and moral imperatives. In operation as in the records, colonial policy was affected by priorities as they were then thought to be (not what we may now think they were). Decisions were taken within limits or along lines determined by a series of different but overlapping agenda. These were ideational (in the Platonic sense) as well as pragmatic, existing independently as ideal constructs, though they also shaped perceptions, categorisation, and reality itself. The absolute principles included notions of duty and arguments about 'individuality', 'progress' and 'equity'. (We might compare the case for action against slavery or *sati*.) Specific concepts related to the laissez-faire state, and to theories of property, rent and exchange. Overarching ideas included rationalist or Benthamite views of law and government, classical economic doctrines, and a historicism which was ultimately Augustinian in its view of the origin of human institutions.

Among the practical calculations were included career development for officials, and the enthusiasms which arose from their expertise or experience. Individual careers were influenced by fashion, as for example among Indian civil servants, when (at a time of worries about famine and social change and property rights) Antony MacDonnell made his mark through his Bihar food supply report or his minute on Bengal tenancy, or Denzil Ibbetson sealed his career by masterly exegesis of revenue, social forms and land transfer.[6] Obviously impor-

---

[5] It follows that, though official ideas are the core of this work, it is not a study of ICS mentality. Clive Dewey, *Anglo-Indian Attitudes. The Mind of the Indian Civil Service* (London 1994), has argued that such a study requires attention to commonplace as well as philosophical ideas, and also to the conditioning which produced the ideas, and to their consequences in practice (pp.7-10). Dewey's answer to the resulting complexity was to take two contrasting examples, on whom sufficient information was available and whom he held to be typical; his subject was the nature of the ICS. This book will cover the 'repetition of simple axioms', their application in practice, and the consequences, in one area of policy; it assumes that Indian conditions as well as British conditioning affected policy, but it will not be concerned to illustrate either. Its subject is Bihar and the developing role of government.

[6] See A.P. MacDonnell, *Report on the Food-Grain Supply and Statistical Re-*

tant were political goals—the need to protect, accommodate and co-opt Indian institutions, the safeguarding of governments and budgets, and the partisanship of colonial economic and strategic policy. For much of this book, the state is imagined to operate within a web of such goals and strategies, in combinations which changed from person to person, issue to issue, and time to time. The suggestion is (as said) that by studying the main features of British policy, in these terms, and in parallel with an understanding of Bihar conditions, it will be possible to define the nature of colonial errors and impact.

## II

The 1885 Act's categorisations and prescriptions represented those of a 'modern' state—definite categories with rights located within them, as species of property; categories and rights defined by function, and justified by use. The state intervened to regulate and encourage these rights, and thus reflected changing ideas about government. Coming together were strands of Western theory and of Indian conditions and statecraft. The British exported many of their attitudes and systems, and incorporated much into standard forms in the empire as they had within Britain. Their views and debates about India undoubtedly often reflected agenda for Britain. In addition suitable priorities *for India* also influenced institutions and the expectations of the state—arguably in both countries, just as imperial experience helped define British identities and concerns. Some practices of expanding government— bureaucracy, rules, departments, inquiries, precedent, records—were developed in tandem at home and abroad, with mutual influences.[7] Eric

---

*view of the Relief Operations in the Distressed Districts of Behar and Bengal during the Famine of 1873-4* (Calcutta 1876) and Denzil Ibbetson, 'Memorandum on the restriction of the power to alienate interests in land', an exposition incorporating some minor amendments by Alexander Mackenzie, in *Selection of Papers on Agricultural Indebtedness and the Restriction of the Power to Alienate Interests in Land* (Calcutta 1898), pp.1-253 and 304-445. Perceptions are not important only for understanding an alien state and its records. Rather, as a second volume will demonstrate, a chart of inhibitions and imperatives can be drawn equally for peasant decision-making: a deconstruction of the record will be equally necessary to uncover the ultimate subject of that volume, the choices of the peasants.

[7] Possible consequential Indian impact on the *conduct* of British affairs, especially in the civil services, and to a lesser degree on the *roles* of institutions (the Crown, church, army, parliament, law, business, finance, classes and eventually citizenship), would be a subject worthy of examination by a British historian.

Stokes's pioneering work alerted us to these possibilities.[8] The cross-currents were assisted by the fact that, more than the French, the British tempered their universalism, at least after the loss of the American colonies and the acquisition of an 'alien' India, with a partial sense of exclusivity (keeping Britishness and British institutions to themselves) and a corresponding image of India (for example) as needing the invention of special measures, especially in governance. Such inventions and distinctions were never wholly achieved, yet they were required by Indian as well as imperial expectations, priorities and conditions. The two strands of policy-making were internal reasons and imported doctrines. They came together in India to produce a growing acceptance of the duties of government and a consensus on the likely course of social development. Thus conservative debates about historical legitimacy and India's special needs were accompanied by a radical willingness to act, in order to 'put things right'.

At this time, the role of history, which had been a prominent device for legitimating policy since East India Company days, was given an added importance. Obviously, too, the state evolved along the same trajectory as a particular view of history.[9] There was a general intellectual tendency related to the development of theoretical and organised (as opposed to practical or mimetic) knowledge. This was not a wholly sceptical system: it debated with but also depended upon authorities, of Christian revelation, ancient knowledge, Indian precedents. Indeed, ideas of essential categories and rational causation inevitably privileged supposedly original forms—that is, the past. But other developments compounded this effect, not least the increased salience of texts as a result of modern languages and printing. A text standardised, fixed and recorded; by lasting and duplicating, it was predictive of the future, the very role which theory attributed to the past, through essentialism. Accordingly, in matters of land and tenancy, we find an increased emphasis on the written record and the distinct type, and a priority given to 'original' rights.

More pragmatically, too, though within the same ideas of causation, history mattered more and more because policy was being developed in response to supposed failures and inadequacies, including errors of previous administration. By the later nineteenth century it was thought

---

[8] E.T. Stokes, *The English Utilitarians and India* (Oxford 1959).

[9] See Prasenjit Duara, *Rescuing History from the Nation. Questioning Narratives of Modern China* (Chicago 1995), which relates ideas of the objectified nation-state to Hegelian, linear, evolutionary history, in contrast to complex, rival models of community and of history, in India as well as China.

that losses and disruption (literally breaches of category, and a lack of historical progression) were resulting from what had been assumed to be progress, whether of trade or law. Contrary to what is sometimes claimed, this did not subsume everything in a single, Eurocentric line of evolution. Doctrines of specificity (as in race theory) had undermined the earlier search for universal principles, a search which had included Indian examples.[10] As a result whatever was proposed had to be 'appropriate', producing fierce debate about India's past and India's supposedly inherent qualities, as clinching arguments.

At the same time there was a scarcely-concealed eagerness to reforge India, allegedly in the interests of its future. In the late nineteenth century there was a severe crisis of confidence, certainly, but it was unlike those which preceded it (from fear, weakness and ignorance) or those which were to follow (from disillusion and cynicism). In the sphere of agrarian policy, the spirit was still that of James Mill who believed in the socio-economic benefits attainable through law and administration. Among its prophets were Richard Jones and John Stuart Mill, revisionists and critics who nonetheless accepted that remedies could be found through further interventions. To a greater degree than in the past, all sides of the argument—autocrats as well as liberals—endorsed rationality and knowledge, and expressed confidence in improvement. In short, the colonial government of the 1870s and 1880s, in these respects at least, seemed the very model of a modern administration—that is, of the kind of state that has had its heyday between that era and the 1970s. At the end of that period, in the face of international corporatism and environmental threats, and with the collapse of centralised states which had taken bureaucratic command to an extreme, a new transition began, born of doubts about science, reason, meaning, and about state probity, intervention and competence; formerly, it was just those elements which had been held dear, and in which confidence had been reinforced, after a struggle, through the advocacy of the 1885 Tenancy Act.

More specifically the Act was framed by common features of

[10] See, for example, C.A. Bayly, 'British orientalism and the Indian "rational tradition", c.1780-1820', *South Asia Research* 14, 1 (1994), which describes British attempts to mine and incorporate Indian knowledge. The rational tradition of *nyaya* (among those discussed) also was not a system of scepticism but one based on the authority of the sastras (p.8). See also Nicholas Dirks, 'Colonial histories and native information: biography of an archive' in Carol A. Breckenridge and Peter van der Veer, *Orientalism and the Postcolonial Predicament* (Delhi 1994) and B.S. Cohn, 'The command of language and the language of command' in Ranajit Guha, ed., *Subaltern Studies* IV (Delhi 1985).

classical political economy. These were first the central role attributed to individualistic property and capital as engines of economic progress, and second the insistence upon social classifications as the means of deciding by whom such capital might best be deployed. If there was to be development, in the form of increased productivity in agriculture, then (it was agreed) within society there had to be concentrations of property, and its gainful employment. This implied social differentiation as well as, or prior to, efficient divisions of labour. In regard to tenancy, the dominant ideas explained how possession or ownership should be attributed to rural classes. Official analyses were based on macrostructures and generalisations, produced from ideology and experience. Differences of opinion arose largely over the class which might best manage the accumulation, which class would best promote social order and the productive use of capital. In India at least it was also apparent that the state would have to intervene in order to help produce whatever conditions were thought to be conducive to progress.

The preferred means of regeneration fluctuated between its being socially-led, for example by landlords or proprietary peasants, or being dependant on law and government (under James Mill's influence), or being focused on production and trade (developed through capital works). But by the later nineteenth century there was not much argument about the underlying processes to be expected in any of these cases. The tenancy debate was part of an extended though sometimes undeclared assault on collective property and custom, illustrated by an assertion of Henry Maine, that 'Nobody is at liberty to attack several property and to say...that he values civilisation'.[11] The tenancy issue is useful for embodying one of the most extensive of all applications of this socio-economic theory to India.

There were two theatres of debate. The first expressed the divide between advocates of radical change and supporters of appropriate law —or, in a sense, between individual and collective property. Advocates of the latter saw to it that the notion of the village community in particular ran through agrarian laws and policies as a repeated theme, from the eighteenth into the twentieth century. It appeared in early surveys of village boundaries, in the village police law (Bengal Act VI of 1870), in the Punjab Alienation of Land Act with its idea of properly 'agricultural' castes, in the co-operative societies, in union boards, and

---

[11] Sir H.S. Maine, *Village-Communities in the East and West* (London 1876), p.230. Maine claimed that civilisation was 'a name for the old order of the Aryan world', which, though perpetually dissolving and reconstituting itself, yet slowly and unevenly 'substituted several property for collective ownership'.

so on. In the 1885 Tenancy Act it surfaced when 'prevailing' rent-rates were debated, and when local custom was allowed to determine whether or not tenants had the right to alienate land.

But these gestures to 'appropriateness' were very inconclusive, and in the cases of rent-rates and land transfer irrelevant in the long run. The reason was a function of legal culture, that colonial laws did not—could not—respect custom. To be recognised effectively the village community had to be subsumed within some unit of revenue or general administration: much was written on the conflation of the estate and the village, the *mahal* and the *mauza*. As we shall see, a 'prevailing' rent-rate simply could not be found under strict definitions of legal consistency. Custom (being contingent, ambiguous, evolving) could not be endorsed by a system of law that depended upon rules and precedents. In such a system, what purported to be custom, or indeed indigenous law, survived only as definite provisions indistinguishable (except in rhetoric and supposed origin) from other aspects of the formal law. Custom survived outside the colonial spheres, of course, but, within them, did so only when codified. (This applied, in official discourse, to social constructs such as caste and religion as well as to village community and land rights.) When not codified, not reproduced in rational categories on the Western model, as was the case for the landlord's customary right to forbid the transfer of tenants' holdings, custom tended to wither away under the scrutiny of laws of evidence and of courts predisposed to respect statutory instruments. Gandhi's sentimental non-materialist village economy would founder against some similar rocks.

This being the case, the real field of battle in the tenancy debate was a second one, which concerned the type of individual in whom property should be vested. Everyone did not agree that the best means of achieving 'civilisation' had been enunciated by Sir Ashley Eden. Conflict between appropriate and analytical jurisprudence was important, but central to the tenancy debate was a closely-fought contest between pro-peasant radical conservatives and pro-landlord conservative radicals. The landlords' party advocated 'universal' social and legal rules, as embodied in the new precedents and rights which had been created in India. The peasant lobby supposedly privileged 'tradition' while seeking social reform. But both in fact supported the universal validity of several property, as good students of Maine. In some ways this was a replay of the situation 70 or 80 years earlier, when pro-raiyatwari critics of the permanent settlement disputed the social level at which private property should be granted, and purported to defend Indian traditions against aristocratic arrogance, while leaving largely unheard a more fundamental debate about Indian practice, between collective and individual, contingent and fixed property rights.[12]

If choosing the class on which individual property should be concentrated was *the* issue in 1885, it was also fundamental to the nature of colonial interventions in Indian society. It explains why a tenancy act was thought necessary in the first place. The East India Company had had to construct methods of rule distinct from existing Indian and British practice, though informed by both. Its chief dilemma was that it needed agents and brokers whom it distrusted. Intermediaries were attacked and dispossessed in the interests of generalised authority, but also recruited and favoured (intentionally or inadvertently) in the construction of working systems of rule. The British had to reconcile their allies' demands and expectations with their own assumptions and priorities. Europe supplied principles and regulations, but India required pragmatism and flexibility. Through all this, the state constituted people as subjects for whom it admitted responsibility, according to definitions of what was public and what private.

## III

The definitions were influenced by Indian demands and expectations, by special conditions, and by the very idea of state responsibility. A state might favour settled populations and road-building, as the Company did in India. It would do so from calculations of its own advantage—revenue, security and so on—but also from theories about how economies or societies worked best, in this case the benefits identified from increased production, information, and trade. Such ideas were not fixed or unrelated to influences and demands upon the state. Experiences in India, often expressed as pressure from Indians on officials, from local to higher levels of government, and from younger to older members, certainly caused modifications in policy. Thus, in a famine, the public task would be temporarily enlarged to include the providing of work and food; in an epidemic, health too would become a public matter. After each crisis, such tasks might once again be left to private enterprise; but enlarged expectations, continuing discussions, and new institutions and rules often remained to facilitate state involvement in future.

In these circumstances, different voices were heard at different

[12] See Burton Stein, 'Idiom and ideology in early nineteenth-century south India' in Peter Robb, ed., *Rural India. Land, Power and Society under British rule* (London 1983 and Delhi 1992).

levels of government, and outside it, because many read Indian conditions and state responsibilities differently. In the 1830s the Company, under James Mill's influence, was concerned to build institutions of government, law and taxation. At the same time, and with added emphasis from the 1850s, it was willing also to develop infrastructure. Material improvement (unlike moral interference) was relatively uncontroversial, and in any case was thought to be, like the reform of government, a way to achieve moral as well as economic regeneration. Trade, by this account, was an unqualified boon, as was order. Improved and safer communications would promote civilisation. There were, as at all times, contrary voices, cautioning against, say, the minor disadvantages of metalled roads,[13] or the major dangers of disrupting Indian custom. But the prevailing mood was optimistic: Indians were susceptible of improvement.

The public good of road construction, for example, was constantly held out by Company officials for strategic and revenue reasons as well as for the encouragement of trade and the prevention of famine.[14] Because in the 1830s the state's responsibility tended to be limited to infrastructure, famine conditions were regarded primarily as a good opportunity to improve the roads and other facilities by flushing out labour. Only later did such improvements, by providing work, become more of an excuse for the relief of famine distress. It follows that at this time the Company mostly sought to provide the instruments for improvement, and not to intervene directly as so to further the economic well-being of the population as a whole; laissez-faire doctrines made this limit upon policy seem obvious. Thus there were road-building, Ferry Fund committees, attacks on local tolls, and attempted suppression of Pindaris, *thagi* and dacoits, and so on—all in the Company's and the public interest.

However, from the first in isolated respects, and later more generally, more extensive interference also took place. Disagreements about this trend underlay the tenancy debate. Indian state interference and

[13] Perceived disadvantages suggested to me by Sanjay Sharma from his work on the NWP in the 1830s include the short-term losses to banjaras and other traders dependant on pack animals, and the effect of metalled roads on barefoot pilgrims. Only later came arguments that trade itself could be disadvantageous, for example by diverting producers from subsistence to commercial crops. I am also indebted to Sharma for the evidence on which I base my characterisation of famine relief-work in the next paragraph. Such evidence will be presented by him in a forthcoming London PhD dissertation.

[14] On roads and civilisation, see also Peter Robb, 'The impact of British rule on religious community' in Robb, *Society and Ideology*, pp.157-65.

responsibility paralleled that in Britain, as in sanitation, labour regulation or education, where they were prompted partly by the impact of—that is, to further or to mitigate—industrialisation and urbanisation. Similar arguments were heard for India as a more distant sufferer from the same processes. Trade, law and other changes were no longer assumed always to be mutually beneficial for imperial ruler and Indian subject. Within these changes, romantic and historicist reactions gave an added emphasis to the need to respect community and custom.[15]

As the nineteenth century wore on, more extended reforms were sought for India also because stereotypes and, frequently, racist assumptions portrayed the problems of India in bolder tones. Intervention became greater partly because of a growing pessimism about India. Further regulation had ever been encouraged by suspicion of Indian alternatives, from courts to culture, magnates to clerks, with *sati* and *thagi*, and so on; the greater the suspicion, the more need there was to intervene. At the same time, by the later nineteenth century, external models of government and infrastructure, their benefits already questioned by some in Europe, seemed even less suitable to India, which was more clearly conceived as a radically different and even unknowable society. But this too implied that fundamental, whole-society change was necessary if things were to improve.

For all the racism of the age, few agreed that India was ultimately irredeemable. To have conceded that would have been to destroy much of the rationale of British rule, and greatly to reduce the covenanted civilians' flattering image of themselves. It would have left them with few roles to play, other than those of exploiter and policeman. Some unsentimental men were attracted by this, as by authoritarian elements in Utilitarian and Liberal thought. But even these people, such as James Stephen, assumed that the British purpose in India was still to faciliate its development, albeit along idiosyncratic lines. The remainder of the British in India asserted in one way or another that they had more to offer than the force of arms. As a result, the major thrust of policy, for want of imagination if for no other reason, never followed the genius of a peculiarly Indian way, as Maine's attack on abstract universal theorising might have suggested. Though measures had to be taken to moderate the effect of the 'dissolving force' of Western civilisation, yet that force could hardly be removed or its supposed benefits denied to Indians. So much was implied by Maine's comparative method, and also demanded by the most articulate among those Indians audible to

---

[15] See Clive Dewey, 'Images of the village community', *MAS* 6, 3 (1972).

the British.[16]

One branch of British thinking in this era held on to the filtration model whereby civilisation would be inculcated through elites operating within a system of law and capitalism. This was the burden of the pro-zamindari arguments, which extolled the landlords' social and economic role and their benign treatment of their tenants. Another branch of thinking, though not analytically contradictory of the first, was diametrically opposed in its political agenda. This second line produced arguments for the greater involvement of Indians in their own government. As an avowedly educative process, these proposals could still appeal to those who called for appropriate development; some officials discovered Indian democratic traditions as a riposte to theories of Asiatic despotism. In practice proto-democratic gestures remained hesitant and grudging, even among some Indians, as they risked diluting British authority in the executive sphere (which it had been decided to retain inviolate), and led ultimately to a validation of Indian demands for self-determination and independence.

A third, and in large part triumphant, branch of thinking directed the British towards social engineering, in various aspects, of which the Bengal Tenancy Act was one. We will be tracing the course and limits of this victory. At the most basic level, it occurred because almost everyone assumed that India needed to be and could be improved, and because British rule itself was subject to its own order in which categories were not to be breached or confused. The state was required to respect individual property, and not to act out of character as defined in prevailing doctrines. Thus the idea of free trade demanded distinct spheres for merchants and rulers, and treated (for example) the fixing of prices even in times of scarcity as a confiscation of property. In this manner doctrinal differences fuelled the tenancy debate, even though the disagreements often seemed diagnostic rather than fundamental. But by the same token, being in possession of an empire, the British in India were required to demonstrate its morality by action, by making of it a type of earned rather than idle property. Law and order were not enough; empire had to be put to work. The British perceived their rule as being active in contrast with a passive India.

The Bengal Tenancy Act concerned the properties of individual classes as well as of the state. In the end, of course, the two could not be reconciled. Any act of protection had to involve a complementary act of confiscation or restriction. This was the level at which specific

---

[16] See Stokes, *Utilitarians*, esp. pp.277-322, to some of which this paragraph offers a slight qualification; 'dissolving force' is a phrase of Sir Alfred Lyall's.

doctrine mattered. In the tenancy debate the choices were expressed in
a distinctive conception of individual rights and agrarian classes, both
purporting to be justified by history. They continued the long struggle
between indigenous and imported understandings of rural society,
between aristocratic models, capitalist reformations and cultivators'
property, all regarded as having their proper sphere and function. Now
the idea of the peasantry was in the ascendant, and since then has often
framed academic studies of agrarian societies and colonial impact. Yet
the pro-peasant revolution was (and is) incomplete in India. Political
and other considerations argued against the wholesale expropriation of
the landlords, who remained, indeed, part of the economic scheme
provided they were enterprising. In the colonial period it was the capitalist role which had priority, and proprietary peasants were favoured
because (and only so long as) they were believed to be able to perform
that role. Thus the underlying trends also mattered. They set the state's
rights and duties ultimately above those of all subjects. They pressured
the British to try to formulate measures which would re-design Indian
social relations. The Bengal Tenancy Act is shown to be one outcome
of this pressure because it not only tried to secure rights for occupancy
tenants, but also set out the characteristics which were supposed to
define the whole range of land-holding and land-using classes, from
landlords to under-tenants.

None of this would have happened without what began in the eighteenth century: the identification and reification of categories whereby
the officials and the laws could generalise. Classifications were supposed to be 'natural' because they were distinguished according to the
nature of each type, and hence they were thought to be organic. But in
fact they were peculiarly legalistic under the colonial system: they were
created and found their existence in rules, prescribed practices and
formal records. The proprietary peasant had to be categorised in order
to become an object of policy: hence the need for an Act which defined
his legal character. The law constructed categories which, in other
senses, were not natural (reflecting reality) but artificial. All classes
were described in terms of their properties, and all were expected to
express their character through the use of the properties which they thus
possessed—so that tenants were land-holders paying fair rents, able to
enjoy a definite and known proportion of the fruits of their labour. The
classes were supposedly fixed, which explained the importance of
pretended history to those who wanted to reform them. Categorisation
was *caused* by its defining incidents. Conversely possessions and rights
derived from categories. This rational categorisation was a particular

and not a necessary way of proceeding.

## IV

We will return to this subject, but first it will be useful briefly to introduce the second main element of this analysis, the consequences of tendencies in policy and ideas, and particularly that part of our inquiry concerned with the failings of concepts and aggregations. Classification, as applied in colonial India, was a culturally specific device for ordering knowledge. In British India the meanings of 'tenant', 'moneylender' and so on were artificially confined and distorted, almost by the language itself, in the face of a more complex reality, with serious implications for theory and practice. Our problem, however, is not merely the pathology of European colonialism, though that might seem sufficient; it is also the general unreality of categories and the fact that terms carry hidden norms and expectations. Beyond the commonplace of errors by nineteenth-century administrators, there is another, continuing difficulty of 'classing', which is inherent in the 'sciences' of law, government and anthropology which they advanced and we still pursue. How can we measure the 'errors' without also assuming that, according to production relations, property, culture and interests, there were significant similarities within different 'types' of household, in our case in the Bihari countryside? This too is a problem to which we will need to return.

The chief object of the Bengal Tenancy Act was the so-called peasant proprietor. He is also our main subject. Yet for much of India it is not true to say that his was a dominant mode of land control, that most land controllers were 'peasants'. The peasant was regarded as an original and necessary form, and we go on using the term in a loose sense. But we do not find everywhere, and certainly not in Bihar, the social homogeneity necessary to ownership by 'peasants', any more than (in a second volume) we will find a preponderance of family-farm production or a general lack of involvement in the market. On the contrary, if we examine the peasant landholder of Bihar, we discover that peasant holdings commonly did not represent autonomous units of ownership.[17] We find a variety of levels and kinds of land-holding,

[17] In volume two the same points will be made about production: how far there can be generalisation, and that commercialisation did not necessarily imply the replacement of old hierarchies of socio-economic relations, and that— partly because of various failures to maximise output, and the resilience of internal limits for agricultural production—the economic surplus continued to be extracted by unequal exchange, manipulated by existing social power.

especially roles for intermediaries. Social differentiation was a context for the employment of labour and the production of crops for sale.

Analysis along these lines helps produce a dynamic view of the way the society functioned. It was the existence of differentiation, and particularly of a strongly-placed middle sector, which meant that, when the British attempted to foster peasant proprietorship for all, they actually further skewed the distribution of opportunities and entitlements. They did not do away with existing rights and interests, because these were fragmented across many social levels. They did not simply create an engine for economic aggrandisement, not even for the rich and powerful. But they sharply increased tendencies which already existed.

It was not only the social structure which was misapprehended. The prospectus for change was also inappropriate. This brings us back to the overarching intellectual basis of policy, to the officials' ideas. The developmental beliefs of the British in India rested primarily upon an interpretation of how Britain had prospered. An agricultural revolution resulted, by this account, from secure property, technological change and labour replacement; nineteenth-century scientific investigations built on the work of earlier amateurs; international trade was the economic centrepiece, and industrialisation the consequence. In agriculture, 'Farmer George' was a symbol of the desired enterprise: improvements depended upon enclosure, management skills, specialisation, and improved crops, methods and implements—whether by direct labour (in India the model of the zamindari home-farm or *sir* land) or by substantial tenants assisted by capital and expertise (the model of the peasant proprietor).

When the grip of laissez-faire theory began to loosen and state intervention increased, the understanding of the means of economic change altered little. Nor did the Indian pro-peasant lobby dissent from a belief in the instrumentality of property, capital and trade. Yet the tenancy reformers were worried about the protection of past rights, and therefore did not try very hard to reproduce in India the conditions which had allowed enclosures, the dispossession of British smallholders, and the mobilisation of capital for agricultural improvement. Certainly, they endorsed the cause of the smallholder as an ideal proprietor. But the peasant of the Indian literature was somehow also to be an agricultural entrepreneur of the English type—as if no attention were paid to the size and character of the average holding in India. Drawing on the radical tradition of their mentors among political economists, consciously or unconsciously, members of the pro-peasant school also seem to have based their plans on the experience of Britain, whereby increased production supposedly resulted from extensions of cultivation and market-orientation, mainly on the part of landlords and large tenants who employed labour. Perhaps they supposed that eventually their policies might produce something like this in India; but they would have done so only had there been fewer problems of scale, less-entrenched interests, less inattention and a greater bureaucratic success at making policies work on the ground.

The official prospectus, whether or not it had merit in regard to Britain, and whatever its endorsement in the classics of political economy, does not after all constitute a universal nostrum.[18] Very early, social as well as physical scientists regarded India as special case. It still mounts a rather wide challenge to some modernist assumptions of development. Yet, while recognising this peculiarity, even depending upon it to justify their actions, the colonial officials proposed strategies which made sense only in universalist terms. The state's law and administration were trusted, in concert with inevitable economic instincts, to promote the desired revolution in production. Even in prevailing circumstances, such measures might have had a beneficial effect on output (if not necessarily general well-being) where a significant proportion of larger holdings could be created—for example in new canal-colonies or by schemes of consolidation and redistribution. They were much less appropriate to crowded regions densely layered by conflicting rights—in short, to Bihar. Arguably the varied fate of parts of India under colonial rule related in some measure to the differing degrees of compatibility between local institutions and policy initiatives.

In nineteenth-century India, the insistence upon property, in tenancy law and agricultural improvement, obscured the need to attend to actual units of production, and worries about fragmentation of holdings took a higher profile than attempts to improve the independence of farming households. Determined efforts were made to protect recognised tenants from unlimited demands and from insecurity of occupancy (the 1885 Tenancy Act and its clones), just as the Punjab Alienation of Land Act later tried to restrict landholdings to 'agricultural' castes. Much less concern was expressed about the known multiplicity, complexity and dependency of most actual land-holdings, or about providing the means

[18] See Keith Tribe, *Land, Labour and Economic Discourse* (London 1978). In the second volume I will show not only that nineteenth-century state intervention was largely restricted to the provision of law, better communications and freer trade, but also that attempts to define and spread the best agricultural methods and to introduce better machinery, even agricultural education, had the farm- if not the estate-manager in mind rather than the smallholder.

of achieving viable cultivating holdings and conditions for producers. On the contrary, British law and administration (in some contradiction of the tendency of developmental thinking) tended to generalise and then protect a confusion of local rights. In such conditions British efforts would constitute a pressure towards social and economic differentiation without offering the prospect of overall growth. In a similar fashion, the importance accorded to capital investments which would replace labour, defied the realities of agricultural employment—and credit—and hence the priorities of agrarian society in many parts of India. Parallel neglect of yet further elements may also have distorted or prevented change. No serious interest was shown in the wide transmission of information (for example through education) or the improvement of internal demand through the fairer distribution of wealth. There was limited understanding of rural social and land structures, just as of agricultural decision-making and the relations of production, in particular with regard to the intermediate levels.

## V

It has been explained that the subject of this book is an evolution in the state in relation to an agrarian economy. A premise is that study of the state may cast light on to social change and economic development. The immediate concern will be with land tenures. But it has also been suggested that we may see the state's involvement as a significant part of a far wider project, the creation of modern forms of national identity. In many recent studies this has been related to the establishment of boundaries, to representations and symbols, and to institutions.[19] The first draws attention not only to mapping, frontiers and territory but also to legal sovereignty, language, ethnicity and other standardised categories. Significant representations are found in histories, museums, ideologies, architecture, rituals and stereotypes, the symbols drawn from religion, myths, maps and metaphors (many complex and mutually reinforcing, in the way that the land as 'Mother' or 'Father' combines its nurture with its people's fictive sibling relationships). The institutions are of course those of the state, political parties, media, professional organisations, law and education, constructing a public space. These and other instruments of identity work by providing the sense of collective interests (in economics, international relations, and so on)

[19] See particularly Benedict Anderson, *Imagined Communities: Reflections on the Rise and Spread of Nationalism* (2nd ed., London 1991), and Partha Chatterjee, *The Nation and its Fragments. Colonial and Postcolonial Histories* (Delhi 1993).

and of common experience (language, education, propaganda, representative democracy, warfare, industrialisation, urbanisation). Less commonly noted is that these imply norms—that is, propriety in behaviour and in gender, family, social and economic roles, which in recent times have defined a broad collective identity notionally comprised of individuals rather than social groups. Contestations about the many changes in such relations—social, religious and political reforms —contributed to nationalism in India.

The process had many aspects, but changes in property law, agrarian relations and state interference also played their part. It was not entirely accidental that Indian political organisation and aspirations—as in the first meeting of the Indian National Congress—coincided in 1885 with the culmination of the great tenancy debate. For similar reasons, the familiar story of what was happening to the state, the people and the country in general offers a kind of metaphor for the evolution of agrarian policies and the agrarian system. Though this parallel has not hitherto been explicitly drawn, it exists—and particularly at the level of categorisations. The state was defining its subjects; it was also defining agriculturists. The state was exploring and changing roles; it was also interfering more in rural society.

To consider such developments at a general level is to attempt an overview of the contribution of British rule to the nature of the Indian state. Though much has been written about colonial government, this overview has yet to be provided—[20] and there has been surprisingly little attention to such questions in more general literature on the impact of imperialism. The recent synthesis by Cain and Hopkins provides some background, for example in its discussion of 'public virtues'

[20] Among existing works, and in addition to more specific studies, and to very numerous, more or less contemporary accounts by former officials, one should note Michael H. Fisher, *Indirect Rule in India. Residents and the Residency System 1764-1857* (Delhi 1991), Stokes, *Utilitarians*, Peter Penner, *The Patronage Bureaucracy in North India. The Robert M. Bird and James Thomason School 1820-1870* (Delhi 1986), B.B. Misra, *The Administrative History of India 1834-1947. General Administration* (Bombay 1970), Francis G. Hutchins, *The Illusion of Permanence. British Imperialism in India* (Princeton 1967), Bradford Spangenberg, *British Bureaucracy in India. Status, Policy and the ICS in the late 19th Century* (New Delhi 1984), D.A. Washbrook, *The Emergence of Provincial Politics. The Madras Presidency 1870-1920* (Cambridge 1976), ch.2, Dewey, *Anglo-Indian Attitudes*, R. Hunt and J. Harrison, eds., *The District Officer in India, 1930-1947* (London 1980), and David C. Potter, *India's Political Administrators 1919-1983* (Oxford 1986). There is also relevant material in several volumes of the *New Cambridge History of India,* notably those by Peter Marshall and C.A. Bayly.

emerging in place of 'private interests', and of the 'military fiscal state', the development of 'national interest' in economic policy, the extension of the 'gentlemanly order' to India, and the survival there of 'gentlemanly norms' after the first world war. But this work (of economic history) says relatively little about the role in British imperialism of modes of government: indeed, because it stresses the importance of a 'particular kind of economic development, centred upon finance and commercial services', and denies, on that ground, the policy and cultural separation some have seen between business and government (such as Robinson and Gallagher's 'official mind'), it seems bound to play down the development of the state as an independent actor.[21] In this regard it is typical of recent studies of imperialism, as of works from a non-metropolitan perspective.

What will be offered here is little more than a prospectus for further study, since only one aspect will receive full attention. But let us start from the obvious proposition that, as the East India Company's revenue policies confirm, there was a revolution in government in India in the nineteenth and twentieth centuries—not absolute change in all aspects, but major qualitative change in many.[22] C.A. Bayly uses the expression 'imperial revolution in government?', with reference to the late eighteenth century; he refers to the expansion and centralisation of British taxation under Shelburne and Pitt, coupled with necessary reforms in office procedure and personnel, but finds the active role of the state much more in evidence in other parts of the British empire, including India (especially the salaried, professional, accountable executive officers, with their language of 'civic virtue', introduced by Cornwallis). Bayly introduces the 'imperial' aspect briefly, in the need in

[21] See P.J. Cain and A.G. Hopkins, *British Imperialism:* [vol.1] *Innovation and Expansion, 1688-1914,* p.12 and chs.2, 4 and 10, and [vol.2] *Crisis and Deconstruction, 1914-1990* (London 1993), p.300 and ch.8.

[22] Parts of this chapter were originally prepared for a seminar in Osaka City University, during a visit to Osaka and the University of Tokyo in October 1993. I am grateful for comments and questions from those present on that occasion. In referring to a 'revolution', I adopt the usual terminology, to suggest something of the magnitude of the change rather than a sudden, complete or violent upheaval; the crucial aspects are administrative reform and broader socioeconomic goals. See Oliver MacDonagh, 'The nineteenth-century revolution in government: a reappraisal', *Historical Journal* I (1958) and *Early Victorian Government, 1830-1870* (London 1977); though Benthamite and reforming influences were important, MacDonagh stresses the practical rather than ideological impulses for administrative change. See also, agreeing with this, Hew Strachan, 'The early Victorian army and the nineteenth-century revolution in government', *English Historical Review* XCV, 377 (1980).

Ireland for the British state to take a more direct role for reasons of political exigency.[23] Government developed because it began to do different things. Three elements characterised the revolution: a new concept of territorial sovereignty, new bases for authority, and a new range of state responsibilities. Implied were the establishment of borders around and within the state, enlarged purposes and tax-base of government, and new machinery of administration, especially bureaucracy in local government.

In these respects, the Indian experience partook of an international one. By the nineteenth century many European nation-states were already defined through internal coercion (surveillance, policing, regulation), by ceremony, language, literature, and commerce (representing an internal consensus or coalescence), and by external rivalry— strategic, economic or military. Specific ideological features had developed. There was established a model of a state with histories and institutions expressive of borders, undivided authority, and national goals. The legitimacy of rule depended on actions and consent as well as myths, on the temporal more than the divine. The model had been exported. In India it was apparent even in the eighteenth century that English conquerors thought that everything must have place and boundaries, and that a single fount of authority, or sovereignty, was desirable or the norm. By the same token knowledge was assumed to be perfectible, and society capable of management and improvement. The past was seen as a continuum, producing the present, and thus the future could be changed through intervention. A similar binary and hermeneutic idea was applied to the state, which was distinguished not only from its subjects but from its personnel and institutions as individuals, just as the subjects, though collectively defined by the state, were also separated one from another in discrete groups. Specifically this evolving nation state depended on the labelling, the counting, the settled location and character, of national peoples. Parts of the process have been interestingly defined as narrative and enumeration.[24]

In producing such categorisation, under colonial rule, opinionated judgments and partisan calculations played their part; both propriety and property were considerations. The rulers thought it their task to decide and dispose; these duties belonged to the state. They expressed a British sense of *possession* within Indian borders. Its vehemence is per-

---

[23] See the sub-heading in C.A. Bayly, *Imperial Meridian. The British Empire and the World 1780-1830* (London 1989), p.116.

[24] Sudipta Kaviraj, 'The imaginary institution of India', in P. Chatterjee and G. Pandey, eds., *Subaltern Studies* VII (Delhi 1993).

haps surprising, and difficult to reconcile with some of the stereotypes of colonial rule.[25] From the first the British distinguished between 'their' territory and people and those of others. At the turn of the nineteenth century when terminology was still fluid, Europeans born in India could be called 'natives', so strong already was the sense of belonging to a locality.[26]

In large part, the idea of possession was obviously intended to promote control. This was reflected in the choice of allies and agents, and in attempts to break through intermediary power-structures and areas of ignorance so as to establish complete sovereignty or knowledge. In terms of indirect rule, the 1885 Act related land and classes in one of the swings of the pendulum, characteristic of agrarian policy in India, between favouring those assumed to be receivers or intermediaries and those regarded as producers. But because land revenue played such a large part in the income of states in India before the present century, there had been a long series of efforts by rulers— towards the end of which stood the 1885 Act—not only to co-opt local chiefs but to reach past them to the cultivators themselves. The Mughals and their successors, including the East India Company, attempted to create an agrarian system based upon key local managers, appointed, placated or incorporated at different levels. The system was monitored by a parallel apparatus of state officials, penetrating to greater or lesser levels of the society; the localities did contain generalised norms and some universal features. But in most political and fiscal spheres local autonomies vitiated the centralising efforts of the state, either to know or to manage their local affairs. The resistance is often seen as representing the force of community, but can also plausibly be regarded as focused by local controllers, whether hereditary or appointed. From at least the eighteenth century such managers had been increasingly locally-rooted, because appointees became hereditary and immoveable, or because old and emergent petty chieftains gained in relative strength and wealth, or because revenue-collecting rights were alienated to commercial men to whom higher levels of the state were in hock, or because newcomers, usually themselves locally strong, were

[25] The alternative is of detached officials engaged together in a process of exploitation; compare Spangenberg, *Bureaucracy*, for example on the rapid turn-over of appointments.

[26] Thus Colin Mackenzie (in his letter books of the Mysore survey, 1799-1810, in the Survey of India memoirs, NAI) would refer to his young sub-assistant surveyors as 'Native' or 'Native European', even though he also almost invariably used 'Native' to mean Indian, and though he knew the crucial importance of unquestioned European parentage, for example for military cadetships.

invited to bid for revenue posts (for example, as *ijaradars,* or revenue farmers) in order to bring in higher and higher quotas. These developments were replicated at different levels of society.[27]

In the late eighteenth century the East India Company had the same problems of distrusting its servants and lacking the means or the information to penetrate through all the layers of the society. It decided to make a virtue of the localisation of power, but also to codify and fix it by conferring distinct, permanent but alienable rights on identified persons. The Company tried to get back to the supposedly legitimate local controllers (where they did not constitute a military danger), as a reaction against the fluidity introduced by increasing localism, whether by newly detached state officers or by newcomers. But pragmatism, as ever, qualified this early introduction of theory and historical legitimacy into Indian policy. In the end the Company was content to settle with the best allies it could find. In Bengal it chose zamindars. Thinking that it was thus endorsing or creating a chain of being, a constitution of checks and balances, and a concert of interests, it began to dismantle the old dual systems of local management, most notably the state's village accountants who by this time (and perhaps always) were able to evade effective control. The new system had a twin advantage. It reduced the opportunities for obstructive Indian officials, whose knowledge was at once envied and mistrusted, and it reduced the temptations for Company men, merchant-adventurers whose self-interest was being newly defined as corruption in order to turn them into public servants. The Company's immediate goals were anyway limited at this stage to the maintenance of order and the protection of its trading monopolies, though already it professed long-term ambitions for the expansion of trade (mutually beneficial of course, according to theory) by means of the security of property and profit in the hands of individuals.

The Company claimed legitimacy through continuity or conquest, but it never fully commanded the old channels of communication or of loyalty. To enforce its will, it relied at first and ultimately on armed force. And it did not question its own concepts of sovereignty, of social and territorial integrity, of the state's monopoly of force and law. Hence, almost at once, from the 1770s, it began to construct a new law

---

[27] This subject might be pursued in, for example, Andre Wink, *Land and Sovereignty in India. Agrarian Society and Politics under the Eighteenth-Century Maratha Svarajya* (Cambridge 1986), esp. pp.67-85, J.R. McLane, *Land and Local Kingship in Eighteenth-century Bengal* (Cambridge 1993), esp. pp.3-24, and Bayly, *Imperial Meridian.*

and a bureaucracy to supplement the social intermediaries, just as in (if not in advance of) the parallel developments in England. This machinery, being impersonal and based on records and rules, was to prove more effective than any previous institutions at extracting fixed revenues and at standardising legal, economic and political structures throughout the Company's dominions. The process continued during the remainder of Company rule, assisted by the rapid and fairly comprehensive rejection of its initial counterpart, minimalist government and an aristocratic model of society and development for India.

We have already noted that state intervention was encouraged because India provided a challenge and an opportunity. The usual assumption, in the Indian case generally, is that changes were imposed from outside, by British rule; but there was a sense in which India and the conditions of colonialism also made demands upon the state. Colonial rule was imposed in the midst of incompatibilities and misunderstandings. The rulers had to invent when they could not adopt, or could not accept, what already existed, and often invented even when they thought they were conforming. They had to re-think. Thus the administrative reforms of, say, Pitt may be situated in a gradual acceptance of needs and the evolution of Britain; those of Warren Hastings or Cornwallis resulted from necessary improvisations as a new administration tried to gather in the reins of government. The result was always an amalgam of British pre-judgments with perceptions of Indian possibilities. One sees this again in the government's complicated search for allies and agents of economic progress in the later decades of the nineteenth century. In the end it seemed inevitable that the state's writ should extend below the initially-chosen collaborators, to seek the support and to promote the well-being of lower sections of the society.

As a result, however much officials identified with places in order to control them, they were bound also to personify places in terms of interests. A much later but typical example shows how officials were embued with the idea of *rights* deriving from *ownership*. H. Edward, the District Engineer of Shahabad in Bihar, was writing to the local Commissioner in 1896, having heard that the Maharaja of Benares proposed to build a masonry dam across the river Karmanasa (the boundary between two districts and provinces). Edward thought the scheme laudable and useful, but remarked that the Karmanasa rose in Shahabad, and that Shahabad had 'rights in the river which ought not be to be appropriated by others without protest'. The officiating Commissioner of Patna (J.A. Bourdillon) was if anything even more proprietorial, and pointed out to the Lieutenant-Governor of the North-

Western Provinces that 'the people of its [the Karmanasa's] right bank have claims not less than those possessed by those who reside on its left bank'. These rights were respected: the NWP government promised that nothing would be decided without consulting Bengal.[28]

Such attitudes and responses attest a perhaps unexpected colonial aspiration for pursuing an active socio-economic agenda. As advanced by the Tenancy Act and other agrarian investigations and reforms, this represented a late stage in the expansion of the state. Modern government had begun with an elite's concern for the external defence of a realm. It grew with the development of a public interest in internal order and protection. But it gained yet more functions when it devised a national interest in trade, beyond the rulers' own need for a surplus to tax, and thus in a national economy (itself an ideological construct). Then it assumed the task of knowing and mediating between all its subjects, embellishing social and political norms. Finally it assumed a responsibility for the welfare of its citizens both individually and collectively. Thus arose the claim of the nation to encompass and serve all its people.

In this sense there was no hiatus, in terms of public concern for national welfare, as opposed to methods and theories, when policies of administrative and legal standardisation and economic laissez faire intervened between the early establishment of East India Company rule and the interference and social engineering of the late nineteenth- and twentieth-century British raj. Though the officials of the time wished to restrict the growth of the state, and to free up trade and individual enterprise, yet they also endorsed the state's role as protector of the weak, as regulator of the powerful, and, if necessary, as mobiliser of social and economic improvement. Bentham wanted clarity and certainty in law. The reason was so that it could be understood by and accessible to *all*. James Mill despised India's past partly because he held it to be a tyranny of inherited and unchanging status.[29] Thus it was that respect for 'liberty' and 'individualism' paradoxically celebrated the broadening and standardising of the nation—as John Stuart Mill observed in his essay 'On Liberty' (1859)—and hence extended the tasks for the state. Thus it was too, and as part of the constitution of subjects as individuals existing in classes, that the supreme importance

[28] R&A Rev B 7-8 (January 1897). A theme of the subsequent volume will be the extent to which *departmental* bureaucracy and expertise, equally conceived in terms of possession, divided and even nullified this sense of general, regional responsibility.

[29] See Javed Majeed, *Ungoverned Imaginings. James Mill's* The History of British India *and Orientalism* (Oxford 1992).

of a contract supported by law came to be regarded as a universal measure of the level of civilisation in preference to the sanctions of religion or custom, the view proposed by Henry Maine in his *Ancient Law* or *Village Communities of East and West*. By the time late nineteenth-century officials were casting round for justifications to promote what they regarded as needful interventions for the public good, they had no shortage of authorities and European examples with which to combat the contrary reflexes of non-interference and laissez faire. The choice at one level was (as between Grandees and Levellers)[30] between the nation as oligarchy—this is unity by hegemony—and the nation as democracy, that is, unity by inclusion. It was no accident that the Utilitarians and radicals of the early to mid nineteenth century were opponents of oligarchy, and that they espoused the goal of the greatest benefit for the greatest number. Similarly some reactions against dislocations produced by industrialisation and urbanisation in Europe, or by law and commercialisation in India, gave rise to a new attachment to community, collective action, and a benevolent and protective state.

The administrative revolution was thus not only a question of improved methods. It was a matter of different goals: new methods were needed for a government required to take responsibility for the entire activities of its realm as part of a presumed (and eventually an electoral) compact with the people as a whole. On one hand were particular problems in India. On the other hand were ideas about the proper tasks of a 'modern' government, decided on a theoretical basis and in comparison with other countries. This was the context for the reassessments of agrarian policy in the last thirty years or so of the nineteenth century in India. Interference in agrarian relations was considered an acceptable and politically important function of the state (as in the Irish Land Acts). It required development of the administrative system.

## VI

The regulation of tenancy during the nineteenth century was, then, an aspect of a wholesale definition of India, its classes and peoples. It was a movement, as will be shown, away from informality towards formality, and away from local towards external mediation. It should not be regarded as an isolated quirk of colonialism. It occurred, and was so important, because it was merely one step in a modern project of defining everything. It was informed, as national identities were, by

[30] See J.P. Kenyon, ed., *The Stuart Constitution 1603-1688. Documents and Commentary* (Cambridge 1966), pp.291-324, and especially the Putney debates of 1647.

what might be called statistical imperatives—the idea that whatever could be measured and numbered had distinct existence and legitimacy. It was expressed also in law and in records, and thus was closely related to the concept of a bounded state which was reinforced or even introduced in India under colonial rule. To explore this context is to establish a fuller understanding of the debates on tenancy and landed property.

Nineteenth-century writers and rulers were quite explicit about the frontier, a specific form of bounded category, and what they saw reflected in it of the different stages in the evolution of states. In the most primitive, there might be personal allegiances but there was no impersonal citizenship within a particular territory. More recently social scientists have made similar distinctions.[31] The modern state, it was believed, has exact, known and permanent external borders, and within them there is an undivided sovereignty, and laws to which even the state itself is subject. (Here we come back again in effect to the notion that a nation embodies all the people—and thus to the *responsible* state.) In pre-modern states, by contrast, frontiers were zones of overlapping or intermixing sovereignty, and state jurisdiction was stronger at the centre, or in some matters, than on the periphery (geographically or in terms of function). There were fragmented states (in which jurisdiction and functions were divided, though often replicated in ever-smaller arenas); or military states dependent on booty and personal allegiance to a strong leader; or feudal states; and so on.

In just this way, Henry Maine saw the evolution of settled and ordered communities, 'held together by the land that they occupy' or which 'they till in common', as a kind of elaboration of single families,[32] but also as an historical process determined by the genius of the 'Aryan' people. In Baden-Powell's variorum this became a full-blown race doctrine that traced different types of village community, and the mapping of areas without them, to the ancient spread of Aryan peoples across South Asia. In the south, for example, the change was, with conquest and caste, 'effected by the individual, but repeated and cumulative, efforts of the Brahmans'; in the north by the influence of the Aryan Rajputs. The relevant distinction about land was also made by J.B. Lyall, in one of the many ethno-historical speculations of the great

[31] For example, Ainslie Embree wrote an influential article on India's transition; 'Frontiers into boundaries: from the traditional to the modern state' in R.G. Fox, ed., *Realm and Region in Traditional India* (Duke 1977).
[32] See H.S. Maine, *The Early History of Institutions* (London 1876), pp.77-82.

nineteenth-century settlement reports. The key difference, he held, was between landholding 'in the shape of an ancestral or customary share of the fields around the hamlet', and landholding 'rather in the shape of an arbitrary allotment from the arable land of the whole country': thus it was that settled villages and estates were rational as well as fixed in place.[33]

The British attempted to apply the 'modern' principles of boundaries to India. They investigated and surveyed endlessly. Above all they sought completeness, whereby there would be no gaps in the map, and certainty, so that each place was located according to standardised and objective measurements, and also in rank, time and culture. Then the British established laws and responsibilities which were universal within the realm as defined territorially. That is to say—just as in the nation-states of Western Europe in the nineteenth century, so in British India the boundaries were drawn precisely, both externally, mapping out the land, and internally, mapping categories, functions and rights. As a consequence, the British tried to insist upon settled populations (or at least regulated movements) within these limits, and on equally definite rights and responsibilities for all. These transformations went well beyond the comparable efforts of earlier states, and were turned into one of the major excuses for imperial expansion.

A telling instance is the way that, at the end of the eighteenth century, Mysore was known as Tipu's territory, or Hyderabad as the 'Nizam's Dominions', that is as a personal fief (in the fashion of the Belgian Congo later), rather than as an institutional state; the inhabitants too were usually the rulers' rather than the territory's people. Gradually, however, more impersonal nations and locational identities evolved. In the case of Mysore the emphasis changed quite suddenly at the partition of 1799.[34] The East India Company had its people, but in the sense of subjects, literally those subject to its law. Nothing in the British imagination equated this relationship with that which the kinsmen, followers, serfs and mercenaries were held to have to the Indian chiefs. This was surely so, unambiguously, not just from British constitutional ideas, but because the Company had begun its rule as a band of merchants and adventurers in an alien and largely unknown land. 'Tenant' and 'landlord' were descriptive and functional categories of this same kind—like citizens, subject to law, or in Hobbesian terms creatures of the sovereign's will. Commentators reminded their readers

---

[33] Baden Powell, *Village Community*, chs.III and IV, and passim; Lyall's Kangra Settlement Report of 1874 is quoted on p.133.

[34] See, for example, Colin Mackenzie's reports; note 26 above.

from time to time that the Arabic term *ra'iyat* meant, as Baden Powell put it, 'subject', 'protected', and 'hence any landholder subject to the Crown or a landlord'.[35] Of course earlier states had sought to regulate people, for example as they moved within their territory; but what in eighteenth-century India were called 'passports' or *dastaks* were really designed to secure security and assistance for the traveller from the host population and local officials, in conditions where there would otherwise have been few if any facilities available. In the late nineteenth century, by contrast, a passport made a statement about the holder's identity in an attempt to render his own state's protection extraterritorial.[36] The national subject was a necessary concomitant of the impulse to define tenants and other such narrower categories of people. The passport implied an intervention to delimit that identity in a manner parallel to the way a written record, lease or receipt established and fixed the incidents of landholding or tenancy.

In short, boundaries, like classes of people, were very serious matters for the colonial rulers. From the first, too, administrative doctrines were developed which dealt with the question of the state in terms of property and its disposal. The word 'public' is forever in the official minutes, not least in the eighteenth century, as a kind of disembodiment of the interests and rights of the state. The term puts the impersonal state, like the law, beyond time, away from individual caprice, and in a relationship of mutuality with its lands and inhabitants and their rights and interests. The impersonal definition in turn of the citizens (the distinction between the Nizam's *people* and the Company's *subjects*) was a necessary prerequisite for the admission of institutional state responsibilities towards all citizens, as distinct from

[35] B.H. Baden Powell, *The Indian Village Community* (London 1896), p.6.

[36] See for example Benjamin Heyne, 'Cursory remarks on a tour to Hyderabad in 1878', Survey of India Memoirs, M160 (vol.3), NAI; on one occasion Heyne was not permitted to cross a river without his passport from the Nizam. Such a passport, whereby a ruler secured safety and support *from* his people for an official, merchant or traveller, was the mirror image of later passports whereby states sought to secure support *for* its people abroad. In 1881, marking this transition, when the issuance of passports to *hajj* pilgrims was being discussed in the Indian Foreign Department, it was assumed that passports marked extraterritorial state responsibility (for example, to repatriate indigent holders) and hence could not be issued to all; on the other hand, it was still asked if passports could be issued to non-British subjects, such as Afghans, embarking at Indian ports; C. Grant concluded that such informal passports would be meaningless; see keep-withs to Foreign Department Proceedings, 1881, in Add. Mss.43575.

the personal favour or even religiously sanctioned duties previously expressed towards those with whom a ruler had relationships of various kinds and degree. And thereafter, whenever adjustments had to be made, whether in legislation or in administrative procedures, a language of rights and ownership immediately forced itself into the pragmatic and political calculations. For example, once quasi-permanent financial settlements were introduced between the provincial and central governments (later reformulated in the unpopular Meston award of 1919), the local administrations, always aware of themselves as legal entities, immediately responded to the consequences and opportunities in terms of their role as holders of property.[37]

In very many instances the officials appealed to concepts of value, expressed in legality, rationality and the public interest. As value is so often the stuff of debate, influencing outcomes, and thereby the nature of the regime, it is not enough to see it only as a convenient fiction covering economic or personal ambition.[38] The properties of the state (what characterised it) were expressed in its actions; it acted to protect, improve or augment its property (what it possessed). Thus, even in apparently trivial matters, a new state was being constructed in India. There was quite clearly a consensus on the separate responsibilities of the bounded state, and even an idea of state property being in trust for

[37] Financial administration was centralised in 1833, and devolved arrangements did not really begin until Sir Richard Temple's reforms in 1870. Quinquennial contracts began in 1882, under Sir Evelyn Baring, the terms revised in 1887, 1892 and 1897, mostly to improve the centre's position; in 1897 J.W. Westland thought the results bad and demoralising for the provinces, and proposed the quasi-permanent settlement (formalised in 1904); Meston's award was necessitated by the 1919 constitutional reforms. See Misra, *Administrative History*, pp.373-7.

[38] For example, in 1905, the Government of Bengal proposed to sell its old Board of Revenue building to the Government of India, and the Finance Department agreed terms. The Governor-General, Lord Curzon, intervened to dispute the local government's right to the building, which, he held, belonged in law to the Secretary of State, irrespective of any provincial settlement. Sir Andrew Fraser, the Lieutenant-Governor of Bengal, protested that Bengal should not be denied the value of the building, and Curzon agreed that the province might be compensated for the cost of putting its officers elsewhere. By 1907 it was agreed that, though technically ownership could not pass, it would be consistent with the principles of the quasi-permanent settlement for the Government of India to pay the full market price for the building, while calling it compensation. R&A Rev A 52 (June 1910); see notes by W.S. Meyer, 4 March, E.N. Baker, 4 March, D. Ibbetson, 8 March, Curzon, 22 March 1905, and E.D. Maclagan and G.F. Wilson, 23 May, and J.S. Meston, 28 December 1907, and various demi-official letters.

the people (or what the government construed to be their interests). The nationalist demand did not arise in isolation but in a context of thousands of unwitting concessions to its fundamental premises about the state. The same was true of the concept of tenants' rights. Like zamindari before it, tenancy became a bounded category, fiercely defended, and generative of common interests and institutions.

If we relate the concern for boundaries to the sense of state ownership and responsibility within territorial units, we see that there was an evolving process whereby public space was being defined and enlarged. In pre-colonial times the distinction between public and private can hardly be said to have existed. Where there were communal service arrangements, usually reflected in the possession of land, they extended naturally and indistinguishably to the performance of duties for and on behalf of the rulers. A headman and accountant would commonly have to see to the collection of revenue; local watchmen and others might be charged with providing for the provisioning of visiting emissaries of the *sirkar*. Moreover the linkages of society and government were expressed far more through regularities in the roles and relations of people than through territorial contiguities and exactitude, though these sometimes existed in theory. As a result everything seemed to be at once public and personal, not least matters of family and social practice.

But in the colonial period, for all the British efforts to conform with custom and not to disturb local arrangements, these interpersonal ties were increasingly substituted or supplemented by objective categories and borders of jurisdiction, and the effect was to begin to separate out (in theory) different kinds of relationship, the 'public' from the 'private'. Production, commerce, ownership, religion, custom and so on began to be regarded as private matters, while law, government, macroeconomics, professional standards, education, knowledge, even health, were public. The demarcation between the two spheres could be conceived differently, but the key fact was that they were distinct, and indeed antagonistic; alternatively the state's public responsibilities were considered to include the protection of private interests.[39] Partly because of that point of overlap, paradoxically the state took upon itself to define and regulate social categories more thoroughly and centrally than had been necessary within the public/private nexus of the past.

[39] New responsibilities and opportunities for the state provoked continual demarcation disputes. The introduction of the telephone for example caused the Indian Telegraph Department—guarding its fief and trying to optimise its productivity—to object to private lines; see the Council debate and Public Works Department memoranda, Add.Mss.43574, pp.531-5.

## VII

What emerged was a different concept of rights. Its basis was a central
feature of rational categorisation: emphasis on the integrity of forms.
Categorisation of the nation, for example, assumed a *whole* bounded
unit of territory, with a *pure* language and *norms* of behaviour, for a
*common* people and interest, expressed in a *single* history and set of
customs and characteristics; and all of these together, by their mutual
support, were reified as *one* identity or *race*. In recent centuries, for
example, standardised languages (subsuming spoken dialects and other
variants) have gained functions, particularly through printing, and
helped identify places and people.[40] Connection with and support of
such identities came to be necessary for 'modern'-ness and legitimacy.
Each was formed aggressively or defensively, on terms promoted by
rivalries of definition. Some of the identification was objective (resulting from broad forces of standardisation), and some subjective, depending on human agency through ideologies and organisation; both processes involved distinguishing and marginalising peripheral and heterogenous elements. And because of these categories' unifying origins and
goals, and their territorial base, it was inevitable that the growing state
should have a key role in their support, an instrumentality alongside
those of ideology, religion, warfare, print, travel, trade and so on.

'Landlord' and 'tenant' were categories of modern usage, because
they were supposedly classes of men of known character, derived from
a territorial right of a single type and origin, over a definite land-unit.
In nineteenth-century Bengal there were nationalist myths related to the
nurturing Mother of the land, and also to heroic Rajput legends (strug-
gles for land) which were popular because they allowed the 'marginal'
Bengali Hindus to partake of a shared Indo-Aryan heritage.[41] Similarly,
in myths of tenancy and landholding, as already mentioned, settled agriculture was regarded as the fount of civilisation, and as derived from an
Aryan past and peoples (despite their once pastoral and nomadic
character) and from the order which they had supposedly imposed on
the untamed land and on non-Aryan tribes.

[40] See Jürgen Habermas, *The Structural Transformation of the Public Sphere*
(1962; tr. Thomas Burger; Cambridge 1992), e.g. pp.159-75, on the role of
literary culture in the extension of the public sphere.
[41] Since this was written I have seen Norbert Peabody, 'Tod's *Rajast'han*
and the boundaries of imperial rule in nineteenth-century India', *Modern Asian
Studies* 30, 1 (1996); while referring only briefly to Tod's nationalist legacy,
this casts valuable light on it by locating and analysing his categorisations.

These colonial categorisations were instances of foreign imposition, but not that alone. They also often developed or gave new roles and definitions to existing institutions. We need to consider, therefore, whether the alien 'tenancy' was like the English language, imposed and shallow in impact, leaving existing evolution and structures relatively little changed, or whether it was more like a re-invented Hindi written in Nagri script—an indigenous form that was changed in character and function, standardised and differently distinguished from comparable forms, and supported by the British to the extent of seeing off many of its rivals. We cannot answer that question yet. In preparation, however, these discursions upon category have been intended to show that there was a common process involved in the deployment of theory, power, legislation and state interference in nineteenth-century India. A border was fixed, a binary type defined, a public sphere created, and a state responsibility admitted. That process explains the evolution of the tenancy law of Bengal, and without it the evolution would make little sense.

The admission of the state's socio-economic responsibility, and the terms on which it was applied, depended upon the establishment of borders. As the state grew it was bound to enunciate general laws and duties, and to draw on constituencies that would do the work it deemed important. Key 'interests' were identified—in India, the prince, the soldier and the cultivator would be reconstituted as 'subjects'. The result was a dialogue between two different views of social category, between past rights and future hopes, and between Brahmanical, Indo-Mughal and Anglo-Indian institutions. The great Bengal tenancy debate of the 1870s and 1880s established the alleged historic legitimacy of agrarian class, as a principle, potentially for all levels of society and production. Hitherto it had been applied on and off to the landlords, but had been effectively denied in the theory (though not the practice) of the alternative administrative and revenue systems based on all cultivators without distinction (raiyatwari) or on village units (mahalwari). Both of these eventually encouraged individual property, but neither of them sought to concentrate it in a particular class.

The first instalment of the new dispensation concentrated on a supposedly or would-be proprietary peasantry. As with the landlords in the past, this was a class, defined by law, and designed in hope of its economic dynamism. For some officials, landowning and religious or social status were twin components of success in a condition of equilibrium; but, as said, others argued that progress was needed and property had to be used for cash-cropping and market relations to produce useful citizens and hence civilisation. By the 1870s, the proprietary peasantry was the chosen vehicle of this dynamism, for one school of thought, in preference to an hereditary aristocracy (which also had its keen advocates). The stage was set for a major change not just in the object of colonial attention, but in the purpose of state policy.

The outcome, in the Bengal Tenancy Act of 1885, represented a shift from the protection of 'ancient rights' (which is what it pretended to be) in favour of the prosecution of 'future comfort'—that is, of economic and social development by social improvement, an attempt to succour what was thought to be the strategic level of an enterprising society, the upper peasantry. History provided a skin which covered the substance of reform. The surreptitious shift from an endorsement of existing interests towards the furtherance of supposed needs did not represent a new ambition; but it was one newly applied and extended. Also in the 1880s, there had been the so-called Ilbert Bill, proposing an extension in the powers of Indian magistrates, potentially over Europeans. It stood in the long tradition of legislation in India that was avowedly universal in application and principle. But it was extravagantly debated (mainly outside government) on the basis of the antagonistic interests of nationalities or races. A similar distinction had been made in the Vernacular Press and the Arms Acts, though, as in other measures, it had remained concealed there under a fiction of inclusivity. The Bengal Tenancy Act, sometimes called the second Ilbert Bill because of the violence of the feelings it aroused, also depended upon a division of the whole of the rural population into distinct classes and irreconcilable interests, which it was the law's job to regulate.

The Act was explained by three related elements: the definition of categories, the idea of public responsibility, and the growth of the state. These were to some degree substitutes for investigation or understanding of Indian conditions. Thus we will find, in the later chapters of this book, that the Act was based on false categorisation, particularly of landlords and tenants, zamindars and raiyats. It was applied to a society in which both were various and differentiated. The distorted standardisation was deliberate, because of the emphasis on property (hence on the transferability of land, the control of rents, and so on) and on capitalist farmers rather than cultivators, on the supposed controllers of production. On the other hand, the new law was made effective by courts, settlements and records, which, though faulty and partial, defined rights more directly, communicated concepts to the countryside, and helped frame and substantiate future claims. The changes benefited those able to secure regulated conditions on the land; that is, they did not benefit most dependant smallholders, sub-tenants, share-croppers or landless labourers. In addition, the policies, already political in their administrative and theoretical implications, further politicised land questions and thus helped perpetuate the privileges which the law had endorsed. The questions henceforth would not cease to be political, and thus the tenancy debates of the 1870s and 1880s marked one of the starting-points in India for class and even national demands —of, within, and against the state.

In Europe, according to Habermas:

Property rights became restricted not only by...interventionist economic policy but also by legal guarantees intended to restore materially the formal equality of the partners contracting.... Protective clauses in the interest of the tenant turned the lease into a relationship restricting the landlord almost as if it involved the use of public sphere.[42]

In India this same infraction of private law, this infiltration of private property by the state, also took place, under the pretence of preserving and protecting an ancient property in the tenancy. But it did so by external imposition and not out of an indigenous social and economic transformation; it did so where neither private property on the Western model nor bourgeois law already prevailed, in the sense that they were not yet fully internalised as Indian ideas in Indian culture. Habermas claims:

The concentration of power in the private sphere of commodity exchange on the one hand, and in the public sphere...on the other, strengthened the pro-pensity of the economically weaker parties to use political means against those who were stronger by reason of their position in the market.[43]

In India such changes *did* encourage the use of political (and judicial) means of redress, in the longer term even by the socially and econo-mically weak; but it did so slowly and imperfectly, for want of means and ideologies of cohesion among the weak, and because the inter-vention of the state disproportionately benefited the strong and the aware, the possessors of information. Politico-legal weapons were also readily adopted by the strong as another means of coercing the weak, and by the relatively strong to challenge those who were stronger still. This was surely the case in Europe too, but for a different reason—there the revolution was bourgeois in origin; in India it was colonial.

[42] Habermas, *Public Sphere*, p.149.
[43] Ibid. p. 145.

## Chapter Two

# *Official will and administrative capacity*

If the colonial state was gradually becoming a kind of pervasive, impersonal, sovereign, territorial state—developing in short into a new kind of state, defined by its borders and its self-knowledge of categories and classes—then, meanwhile, of course, the system of administration also was undoubtedly being transformed. This too is important to an understanding of the question of agrarian policy, because it has never been enough merely to make policy and to legislate. If there were real as opposed to rhetorical interventions in the Indian countryside, there must have been an administrative as well as a legal revolution. A later part of our consideration of the Bengal Tenancy Act will concern this question of the means of intervention, the changing capacity as well as ambitions of the state.

The issue is relevant because of the long-lived argument that the permanent settlement of the land revenues in 1793 transformed the agrarian structure of Bengal, whereby the zamindars gained an exclusive legal right of property as landlords, and the settled or *khudkashta* raiyats lost their privilege of occupancy and became tenants-at-will. In the celebrated words of the Fifth Report on the East India Company in 1812, the permanent settlement had effected a 'great transfer of landed property, by public sale and...dispossession', and also had denied rights of property of other kinds and sectors. The report claimed that 'much uncertainty still remained, in regard to the rights and usages of the different orders of people connected with the revenues', and yet that the government of Shore and Cornwallis had ignored this complexity and been, instead, wrongly 'impressed with a strong persuasion of the proprietary right in the soil possessed by the zemindars'.[1] We will be considering this question at length, because it is the core of the great nineteenth-century tenancy debate in India, and of the assessment of the impact of the Tenancy Act of 1885. Here we should merely note that it implies a capacity to effect fundamental change on the part of the East India Company and its laws. In the same way, any assessment of changes in agrarian structure brought about by the 1885 Act must depend on a measurement of the state's capacity and impact.

[1] Fifth Report from the Select Committee on the Affairs of the East India Company, 28 July 1812, I, pp.16-21 and 54-62.

36

The usual view is still that the permanent settlement was detrimental to the condition as well as the rights of the cultivators. Yet Eric Stokes reminded us, in a slightly different context, that 'undue attention to formal statements of policy aims...has grossly misled historians.... For all the paper planning at head-quarters...the British...had neither the financial means nor the technical instruments' to effect real change, in this case through a 'development programme'. There was no 'effective action' until the 1860s.[2] Stokes did not dwell on the point—his main interests lay elsewhere—but it seems worthwhile not to be satisfied with the simple negative but to explore it further. What would have been the available institutions and instruments? Were they capable of executing colonial policy? This issue of administrative capacity is the subject of this chapter. It asks what were the nature and results of this paucity of 'means' and 'instruments', in the case of Bihar after the permanent settlement. The answers lie in the circumstances of India and its government. We will then consider evidence that this capacity may have changed by the late nineteenth century, in line with the new concepts of the state just outlined. Without this discussion, we would be taking for granted the impact upon the peasantry of the Company's supposed neglect, and failing to establish the means whereby the 1885 Act could have had influence.

The question of will—priorities, and imported ideas—was undoubtedly important in assessing the impact of policy, but it was not a sufficient explanation. True, the East India Company understood its function to be (at least before 1790) to engage in commerce and collect revenue in order to 'yield a fund with which to trade'.[3] Later, it was greatly influenced by a need to raise money in support of the army, and thereby for the perpetuation of its rule.[4] Later still, its first priority, the prompt collection of revenue, was laid down in circular orders with brutal frankness: unlike in statements intended for higher authorities, and in the optimistic enthusiasms of individual officials, the orders did not bother with any secondary objectives such as justice and public welfare.[5] The contrast with the later protestations of goals of 'improve-

---

[2] E.T. Stokes, *The Peasant and the Raj* (Cambridge 1978), p.30.

[3] W.W. Hunter, *The Annals of Rural Bengal* (London 1897; 7th ed.), p.368.

[4] Alamgir Muhammad Serajuddin. *The Revenue Administration of the East India Company in Chittagong, 1761-1785* (Chittagong 1971), p.212.

[5] CO, 7 September 1835. The revenue system was set out in about ten major regulations in 1793. Tenant rights were avowedly protected by sections 7 and 8 of Regulation I, by the rent provisions of Regulation VII, and by restrictions in Regulation XVII (distraint powers). Rights in respect of rents were modified by Regulations IV of 1794 and V of 1812, of distraint by Regulation VII of 1794,

ment' seems rather stark, but perhaps it was exaggerated by the imperatives of the budget. More important may have been the fact that the
position, character and number of British administrators in India
restricted what could be done, and that even less was expected of Bengal officials than of those of other areas. For example, the establishments provided for Commissioners of Revenue, when they were
appointed in 1828, were significantly smaller in Bengal than in the
Western Provinces.[6] Collectorates in Bihar too were understaffed, and
repeatedly in the 1830s and 1840s had to be provided with special help,
even for the ordinary preparation of accounts.[7] Of course that very
disparity between these and other parts of British territory shows that,
at one level, the problem *was* one of will rather than opportunity; but
opportunity was also then curtailed. The level of staff and resources
was decided by financial shortages, by fears that sudden movements by
the state would disturb the populace, and by theories of minimal
government. Indeed, it is in this area of theory that the decisions of the
1790s were subsequently pilloried. The *zamindar* was supposed to have
taken on the roles of care and improvement, as the price for his
privileges. By that contract, the Bengal official remained primarily a
rent-receiver, isolated behind his permanent guard of soldiers, forbidden to lower his dignity (for example by wearing native dress),
forbidden to act without sanction, forbidden to employ the police for
revenue purposes. He was responsible directly even for minute concerns in his office (such as public works expenditure over Rs.500), yet
he was incapable in practice of coping with anything other than routine.
A more unlikely engine of change can hardly be imagined.[8]

Yet, as argued in chapter one, even without the influence of Utilitarian ideas the administration was bound to become enmeshed in

---

and by transfers of Regulation VIII of 1819. See below, chapter three, and G.H.
Huttman, *An Abstract of the Regulations enacted for the Assessment and Realization of the Land Revenues in Bengal, Bihar and Orissa from the year 1793 to
1824 inclusive* (Calcutta 1826).

[6] CO, 30 December 1828 and 17 February 1829. Here, and frequently in this
book, Bengal is used to mean the Presidency of Fort William—that is, including
Bihar.

[7] Bengal Revenue Letter, 12 September 1838, L/E/3/42, IOL. Except in quotations, in this book the term 'Bihar' refers to the modern region; the old
spelling 'Behar' is reserved for the district of that name, most of which later
became Gaya.

[8] CO, 7 February 1826, 20 November 1829, 21 September 1830 and 29
February 1832. The functions of Magistrate and Collector, separated in 1793,
could be held by one man after Regulation IV of 1821, and were formally
united in 1831.

India—far more deeply than was proposed in Cornwallis's ideal of a distant, limited revenue-collecting government. Administration took officials (not necessarily Englishmen) into the heart of rural society. It did so directly in sales and in estate-management (the latter in *khas* or government-held property). It did so indirectly as arbiters in partition, resumption and settlement proceedings. Why then did the Company long remain so peripheral to the major problems and developments of that society? The main reason was that the great preoccupations of the first eighty or ninety years of British rule in Bengal were not with the improvement of India but with the perfection of the administrative system. This attention was born of necessity not choice.

The system rested, as is well-known, upon rules and as far as possible previous sanction. But for four or five decades after the permanent settlement, even the collection of revenue (*tauzi*) posed problems, and nowhere more than in Bihar. In the north with a tradition of lawlessness and a multitude of small zamindars, a few farmers had been made responsible for the collection of revenue. In the 1780s the Collectors of Saran and Tirhut opposed a settlement with the zamindars as unworkable. It is true that when the area was ordered to conform with the rest of Bengal, collections actually improved, chiefly it seems through the use of tahsildars (local revenue officers or intermediary rent-collectors). Francis Buchanan, writing in about 1810, also reported this system to be in use for subdivided estates in Shahabad. But at the same time, in 1811, six tahsildari offices in Tirhut were responsible for 1,263 landholders, 646 of them paying less than Rs.100.[9] It goes too far, therefore, to say with W.W. Hunter that revenue collection, difficult in 1782 when the internal pacification of Bengal was incomplete, was a matter of routine by 1807.[10] Tahsildars in Bihar were often thwarted by zamindars and patwaris, or were themselves corrupt. Large zamindars, from whom collections were made directly, often had to be threatened or coerced before they would pay in full.[11]

In short, even though initially arrears were relatively low, the revenue system remained unperfected long after the permanent settlement. First, much effort was spent on the development of the sale laws to replace the old system of imprisoning defaulters, and the more the

---

[9] C.J. Stevenson-Moore, *Final Report on the Survey and Settlement Operations in the Muzaffarpur District 1892-1899* (Calcutta 1901), hereafter 'Muzaffarpur SR'; Francis Buchanan (Hamilton), *An Account of the District of Shahabad in 1812-1813* (Patna 1934), p.348.

[10] Sir William Wilson Hunter, *Bengal Ms. Records* (London 1894), vol.I.

[11] See, for example, on Hathwa raj, Anand Yang, *The Limited Raj. Agrarian Relations in Colonial India, Saran district, 1793-1920* (Berkeley 1989).

administration relied on sales the less punctual was the payment of revenue. Regulation XI of 1822 clarified the law, but it was still administered leniently (regardless of Bihari conditions), because the Board of Revenue believed that the sale law had caused the breakup of some of the big zamindaris in Bengal. The Board's control was relaxed by Regulation VII of 1830; but not until the 1840s did the postponement of a sale come to be a matter of comment. Secondly, just as the sale law was being refined, the position of the revenue authorities in Bihar was worsening in comparison with that of most other areas of Bengal, because of the high incidence there of the other major preoccupations of the day—the partition of estates (*batwara*) between cosharers, prevalent from about 1814, and the resumption of invalid revenue-free holdings, carried on between 1830 and 1850. The revenue roll increased enormously as a result, without a compensating increase in staff or efficiency. In Tirhut, for example, where there had been 1,351 estates in 1790, there were 3,018 in 1850. (There were to be 31,893 by 1895.)[12]

Not until the late 1830s is it possible to say with complete confidence that the revenue collection was a relatively stable and improving aspect of administration. It was helped in particular after 1839 by 'searching inquiries into every item of collection and balance' instituted through quarterly returns from Collectors to Commissioners. Even then it was not perfect, as occasional *tauzi* frauds and irregularities revealed. In 1838 the Board of Revenue asked for suggestions on how to check *tauzi* collections properly without placing a further crippling load on the Collectors; it had to urge rigorous and efficient realization of the revenue, reminding the Commissioners that they were responsible (promising support if subordinates were at fault); and to warn against consolidation of the various estates of one owner, and against omissions or removals of estates from the roll. In 1841 it still had to instruct Collectors not to transfer treasuries to the control of Deputy Collectors without sanction.[13]

One central problem which had had to be resolved was the problem of supervision. The picture, in this period, is of a government struggling against odds to establish a method of operation. The means of control, which were being elaborated and refined between 1790 and the 1840s, comprised three major elements: the fixing of responsibility, the use of financial penalties, and the institution of regular checks. Various

[12] Muzaffarpur SR; and see Huttman, *Abstract*.
[13] CO, 9 January, 29 May, 7 and 21 August 1838, 25 February 1840 and 24 November 1841.

measures contributed to the first of these. After 1813, partly to prevent Collectors leaving too much to their subordinates, the office of dewan was abolished in the Collectorates, which were then divided into departments—treasury, *tauzi, sherista, abkari* and so on—each with a separate head. Collectors were required to supervise the whole. In 1833 the sheristadar's general responsibilities (for example for authenticating documents and accounts) were also stressed. In 1836 it was pointed out that the sheristadar, in common with all officials, had a duty to report on malpractices—ignorance would be taken not as a defence but as proof of incompetence.[14]

Fixing responsibility was accompanied by attempts to mobilise self-interest. Later this took a positive form—in a short-lived scheme of six-monthly reports on covenanted officers (1834-6), and then by general exhortations and the extension of the principle of advancement by merit.[15] But initially the main sanction lay in the fear of punishment rather than the hope of reward. From 1788 Collectors were liable to be fined for failure to submit *tauzi* accounts. Throughout the period outstanding balances of revenue could be (and were) deducted from Collectors' salaries, though in justice this was suitable only for genuine short-falls, to punish inefficiency or corruption. (By the late 1830s the establishment of regular scrutiny of accounts had greatly reduced the number and amounts of such balances.)[16] Officials were required also to provide securities, either in cash or more usually in property, and in one of two forms—'malzaminee' (to cover the actual sums involved) or 'hazirnaminee' (to ensure the official's appearance to answer a charge of embezzlement). A *batwara amin*, for example, was paid a percentage according to the revenue of the estate to be partitioned—one third in advance, one third during the work, and one third on completion. In 1819, having observed that amins often pocketed the first payment with no intention of undertaking the work, the Board of Revenue ordered that they should be required to furnish security to cover the first two instalments of their fee.[17]

But such a security, which really covered the risk, was a luxury dependant on the availability of an uncomplicated bond and the involvement of relatively small sums, conditions which could not be guaranteed in all spheres of government, more especially as its func-

[14] CO, 17 December 1813, 19 April 1833, 27 January and 24 March 1836.
[15] See CO, 2 May 1834 (with Governor-General's minute, 15 January 1834) and 24 December 1836.
[16] CO, 4 June 1788 and 9 January 1837.
[17] CO, 16 April 1819.

tions grew. By the 1830s, the system seems to have been under strain even in the technical aspects. In 1835 Collectors were warned not to accept as security property within the jurisdiction of the Supreme Court at Calcutta, and the next year they were exhorted to make sure that titles were properly investigated. In 1837 they were reminded of their personal responsibility to reimburse the government if there were any deficiencies when their subordinates' securities had to be realised— they and not the government would then have to sue the individuals concerned.[18] The problem of covering the risk was more serious. In 1836, for example, treasurers were made subject to a scale of securities, starting at Rs.25,080 for collections of Rs.10,000, but ranging up to a maximum of only Rs.50,000 for collections of Rs.2,800,000 or more. In Wards estates, too, the sums involved were often well beyond the resources of any individual whom the government could afford to employ. Securities came to be 'bought and sold' so that officials who ostensibly provided them became in fact 'puppets in the hands of the wealthy individuals' who put up the bonds.[19] In the early 1830s for example over an estate worth nearly Rs.4 lakhs per annum, there arose a controversy between the Board and the government—the former worrying about the impossibility of demanding 'malzaminee' in such cases, the latter content with 'hazirnaminee'. The controversy showed that the system was rapidly becoming out of date for regular adminis- tration, though still useful where tasks were farmed out to non-officials (as in the case of stamps and excise).

A better answer was administrative reform. Bengal had the example before it of the Western Board. In 1833, with its own arrangements in mind, that Board assumed that the Wards question was academic. It imagined that actual cash was in the hands of treasury tahsildars who remitted all but small amounts to the *sadr* (central) treasury, with the result that embezzlement was unheard of in well-managed districts. In Bengal there was no effective tahsildari system and embezzlement was relatively easy through collusion between the Collector's subordinates. But, if the solution was less straight-forward, it could still be essentially similar: proper settlements and properly maintained records would pro- vide bureaucratic checks on the collections.[20] As time went on such checks became the most important of the government's three methods

---

[18] CO, 10 April 1835, 8 February 1836 and 6 February 1837.
[19] CO, 1 April 1834.
[20] Sudder Board to Bengal Government, 16 August 1833, and Western Board to Revenue Department, Government of India, 1 November 1833, CO, 1 April 1834.

of control. Increasingly at the heart of the system were records and periodic returns. Sanction before the event was important, but subsequent checks were vital.

The 1830s thus saw a flurry of activity as a chain of reports became established as the major weapon for controlling subordinates. The records had been notoriously unreliable. Even the Board of Revenue, though admittedly after moving office, admitted to confusion and corruption due to its 'ill-contrived system of conducting details'. It introduced a new system of regular and punctual entry and checking.[21] More particularly, the returns were thoroughly overhauled. There were a few additions—annual returns of resumed estates, monthly returns of unreported sales and so on—but most attention was paid to simplifying the process to make it more effective. As a result of a committee in 1836 (later made permanent), the channels of report were streamlined, uniformity of format was insisted upon, and the number of returns reduced. Thereafter most land revenue accounts went direct from Collectors to the Revenue Accountant. Lithographed forms were provided, with uniform dates according to the English calendar set out for each return. A total of 189 returns was reduced to 64.[22] This marked an important stage in the development of regular administration. In common with many reforms it was far from being a final answer—less than two years later the Board warned against changes being made in the periodic returns without reference to the statements committee—but it was a start on the basis of which further revision could be undertaken. In 1842, for example, a second effort was made to reduce the bulk of the returns and the labour of producing them, to ensure that they were ready on time, and to standardise the principles on which local and central reports were based.[23]

Various means were also suggested for simplifying accounts. In the cumbersome system before the late 1830s, perfectly regular but temporary or technically unsanctioned outgoings were included in the inefficient balances. They included advances in legal suits, the cost of food for imprisoned excise or revenue defaulters, *takkavi* loans, and various payments for salaries, contingencies, Wards establishments and settlement proceedings. In 1836 the Board spoke of the failure to achieve

[21] Bengal Revenue Letter, 9 May 1837, L/E/3/39, IOL.

[22] CO, 21 August 1832, 14 March, 27 July and 5 September 1836. With six returns omitted for deferred decision, totals retained (and dispensed with) were: from Collectors to Accountant 16 (19) and to Commissioners 21 (73), from Commissioners to Board 15 (19), and others 12 (15); or daily 1 (0), weekly 1 (2), monthly 11 (22), quarterly 8 (28), half-yearly 2 (24) and annual 41 (49).

[23] CO, 20 February 1838 and 11 May 1842.

regular adjustment of such balances under their proper heads as a 'growing evil'. Thus the rigid interpretation was relaxed, and at the same time irrecoverable balances of more than ten years' standing were written off.[24]

In the acute problem of control represented by corruption, direct sanctions similarly gave way to emphasis on administrative improvements. There were some new orders. Civil officers were forbidden to contract debts to zamindars (in 1827) and were required always to state that their nominees for appointments were not creditors (Regulation XXI of 1814 with a reminder in 1823). Remarkably late in the day, in 1833, it was provided that records should be kept of all amounts realised through fines, and of resumed and rent-free estates. (In the last case registers were to be kept under lock and key.) And in 1835, too, after embezzlement at Monghyr, treasurers were ordered to receive money only at the public office, and to employ certain stricter accounting methods.[25] The battle against corruption would never be won, but, having made substantial improvements in the higher (European) levels of the administration, the government now had the ability to minimise dishonesty among subordinate officials. In 1837 for example the Court of Directors questioned whether existing checks were sufficient, and argued that embezzlement had occurred partly for want of supervison by the Collectors. They had in mind a discovery in Murshidabad that there had been no receipts whatever by 1836 from an estate of 12,000 bighas declared liable for revenue in 1827, a fraud possible only by collusion among 'all the influential Omlah' and at best woeful ignorance on the part of the sheristadar. Further inquiry in the Collectorate revealed similar concealment of 56 *taidads* (registration documents) for lands over 100 bighas, totalling 17,478 bighas, as well as 1,649 *taidads* for smaller estates. In such cases record-keepers were prosecuted; but a greater likelihood of apprehension was the only real basis for improvement.[26] Again the 1830s saw attempts being made. For example in 1833 the Lower Provinces' Board simplified its settlement returns, avowedly to enable Collectors to check statements received from native subordinates, among other ways by comparing rent figures for neighbouring estates. It was borrowing the Western Board's system, and following a general reaction against over-complex surveys. The maxim even in an age of growing employment of Indians, was that 'nothing

[24] CO, 26 October 1836 and 9 January 1837.
[25] CO, 4 June 1822, 23 May 1823, 7 August 1832, 17 December 1833 and 20 February 1835.
[26] CO, 23 and 30 January 1837 (report by Murshidabad Collector).

can possibly be gained, whilst much risk and certain expense will be incurred, by allowing the Ameens or Tuhseeldars to proceed otherwise than under a complete conviction that their European superior is following closely upon their tracks'.[27]

More generally in 1833, Collectors were ordered to organise their offices efficiently and in particular to check on arrears of business in each department; in 1834 they were ordered to delegate matters of detail, so that they had time for proper supervision.[28] The encouragement of the use of English and the abandonment of Persian were also directed in part at making supervision easier. The vernacular (Urdu in Nagri script in the case of Bihar) was phased in over twelve months from February 1838, as the language of record in both judicial and revenue departments, and at the same time new rules were promulgated for the organisation of Collectorates. The two changes were intended so to improve and simplify matters as to allow a reduction in staff and the consequent improvement in the salary of the sheristadar as head of the native establishment. (At the same time, however, a team was set to work to investigate the accounting system, and consider whether in future the accounts should be kept in English.)[29] Similarly it was to help against abuses of power by subordinates that measures were taken in 1834 to clear and then to prevent the excessive accummulation of summary suits on Collectors' files—all but the most recent were to be transferred to the courts and thenceforth only those admitted which the office could manage.[30]

From the late 1830s moreover the machine was working well enough for efficiency to be sought through a new emphasis on the devolution of responsibility. In 1837, for example, the Government of India complained that Bengal reports on temporary settlements were being checked three times (by Collectors, Commissioners and the Board) and suggested that it would suffice if Commissioners had the final say whenever they were in agreement with the Collector. In fact, the reports were being revised by the Board alone, except for a sample retained by the Commissioners; but nonetheless the government's suggestion was adopted, subject to a right of appeal to the Board.[31] In 1840 the Board was empowered to remit all nominal balances, to allow

[27] CO, 12 November 1833.

[28] CO, 31 December 1833 and 21 November 1834.

[29] CO, 16 May 1837, 6 February 1838 and 26 February 1840; Bengal Revenue Letter, 4 August 1837, L/E/3/40, IOL.

[30] CO, 3 June 1834.

[31] CO, 27 October 1839 and 2 June 1840; India Revenue Letter, 9 October 1837, L/E/3/40, IOL.

refunds of less than Rs.500, and to sanction partition establishments subject to government orders half-yearly. Commissioners were allowed to remit nominal balances of estates purchased at auction, and interest where the principal had been paid, to make transfers in land revenue accounts (for example to correct errors), to refund sums collected from wrongly-resumed estates, and to make various other minor refunds or payments. By way of compensation, rules of 1840 provided that members of the Board of Revenue should make circuits of districts. In 1841 the moral was drawn: Commissioners were ordered to insist on Collectors taking full responsibility up to the limit of their legal competence. They were told to prefer personal discussions to lengthy correspondence, and to send up reports in minor matters, or in many other cases merely a Collector's letter with a covering note, and not to include masses of unimportant material as they had been wont to do.[32]

Devolution would increase efficiency and give time for proper supervision; but obviously these advantages had to be weighed against continuing doubts about the probity of government servants. In addition to the worries about Indian officials, even Collectors were dismissed for corruption or reprimanded for irregular conduct in this period—and it added to the seriousness that the British, steeped in ideas of legality, considered themselves bound by their own rules, so that dishonesty or carelessness of government servants could result in irrecoverable loss to the revenue.[33] Certainly reforms by the early 1830s had shifted the main worry about higher administration gradually from corruption to inefficiency. But a problem in some form remained, in the sense of putting a limit on devolution. Mismanagement, fraud or insubordination were reported in Monghyr in 1837, in Shahabad and Patna in 1838, and in Patna and Behar in 1839 and 1840/1—mainly involving Collectors or sheristadars. Indeed in Behar district, from which eight parganas had been transferred to Patna in 1837, conditions were so bad that after the censuring of H.V. Hathorn, the Collector, in 1840, it was not enough merely to replace him; proposals had to be put forward for a general

---

[32] CO, 6 May and 15 June 1840 and 13 January 1841; Bengal Revenue Letter, 22 January 1840, L/E/3/1, IOL. The origins of the devolution seem to have been the problems with resumptions (see below): in agreeing to extra staff at Patna the government told the Board that it was 'very desirable that the Rules of Practice should be immediately revised, with a view to increase the extent of discretionary authority entrusted to the Commissioners, and to relieve them from the burthensome duty of constant reference to the Board' (30 August 1836, with CO, 25 October 1836).

[33] See for example Bengal Revenue Letter, 3 August 1837, L/E/3/40, IOL.

overhaul of the revenue administration.[34] In such circumstances, if there were extensive devolution, what guarantee would there be that even essential work would be done—for example the operation of the sale law, regarded as the most 'uninteresting and harassing' aspect of the job? Even in 1861 when Sir Steuart Bayley was Collector of Shahabad, he is supposed to have told John Beames, on the occasion of the introduction of the new penal and criminal procedure codes: 'We shall all go on the old system as long as we can. Government will perhaps find out..., and will issue circulars..., but it will take six months or a year.'[35]

Moreover, the only sort of devolution which could have made a major difference to the capacity of the government would have been devolution from Europeans to Indians. There was some recognition of this. The question of educating government wards called forth an obeisance to the 'important objects of raising up a class of public servants of superior moral and intellectual qualifications to the present'. Indeed in 1838 while asking if Indian officials should be given some additional responsibilities, the Board wrote that the very extensive judicial and revenue powers with which they had already been entrusted was a sign of the government's confidence in their integrity. In fact, however, the British distrust of Indian officials was an insuperable hurdle. Official thinking concentrated on measures to restrict, not on how best to deploy the Indian employees. In 1837 the Board suggested formulating rules of procedure for Commissioners dealing with those accused of corruption. In 1838 a Deputy Collector of Murshidabad was convicted to four years' imprisonment for the theft of official funds, and Auckland urged the 'utmost caution' in making appointments. In 1841 the government called for reports on the numbers of Indians employed, and later that year set out rules to control the selection of uncovenanted Deputy Collectors. In 1842 the Court itself ordered that a register be kept of Indians dismissed for misconduct, to prevent their being subsequently re-employed. (One such case involving the sheristadar at Saran had come to light only after newspaper reports.)[36] And, even in this period, instances may be found of the familiar British plea

[34] Bengal Revenue Letters, 7 March 1837, L/E/3/39, and 9 May 1837, 2 January and 1 June 1838, 4 September, 13 November and 25 December 1839, 22 January, 16 April and 17 June 1840, L/E/3/1, IOL.

[35] Tirhut Coll to PC, 12 November 1839, Muzaffarpur SR; John Beames, *Memoirs of a Bengal Civilian* (London 1961), p.131.

[36] See Bengal Revenue Letters, 28 October 1841, L/E/3/1, and 11 August 1837, 2 January and 22 March 1838, 23 March and 25 May 1841, L/E/3/41, IOL.

that an Indian official of one religious community might prove un-
acceptable to members of another.[37]

Studies of the theory of Indian government see several discon-
tinuities in the early periods of British rule, and attribute some reforms
to Benthamite zeal for efficiency. This account does not deny the
importance of such ideologies, but supplements them with a different
rationale—competence and necessity—wrought in Indian conditions.
On both accounts, then, throughout the first fifty years of the permanent
settlement, it was necessary to tamper radically with the administrative
structure: it became centralised and regularised, but also had to devolve
powers in the interests of efficiency. It was a continual because a
largely unsuccessful process.[38] We find a similar picture in some of the
practical concerns of the government which were over and above
revenue collection, but themselves in effect continual adjustments made
in the interests of revenue.

II

In various practical aspects of administration, policy took the form of
expedients to meet the felt exigencies, in each case at once reflecting
incapacity or corruption, providing for intervention and regulation, and
creating further problems or damage. An obvious example is that of
government estates. By the 1820s a shift in opinion had ruled out the
disposal of such property in perpetuity; but direct or *khas* management
was equally distrusted because of its dubious efficiency. The Court of
Directors favoured leases for a term of years, especially to raiyats.[39]
Very soon, however, leases also came under suspicion: the government,
the Court complained, had not provided a single check on the abuses of
power by proprietors, *mukaddams* and farmers alike. The remedy could

[37] See for example Bengal Revenue Letters, 11 August 1837, L/E/3/40, IOL.

[38] The argument here, implying government weakness in the localities, is not
the same as that of (for example) Anand Yang in ch. 6 of P. Robb, ed., *Rural
India. Land, Power and Society under British Rule* (London 1983; Delhi 1992),
which alleges a *persistent* lack of influence, from the feebleness of local agency
(kanungos, patwaris and chaukidars) forcing British rulers to rely instead on the
blunt instrument of occasional military force. Yang's portrait of the local agency is accurate, but it underestimates the improvement and growth of administration even in Bengal, and the changing capacity of the colonial state to intervene by other means. In distinguishing different aspects and periods, this chapter assesses that development, as much as it recognises failures. See also P.G.
Robb, *The Evolution of British Policy towards Indian Politics* (New Delhi
1992), ch.2.

[39] CO, 15 June 1824.

not be a return to *khas* management, for that, unless there were a raiyatwari settlement, would leave land and people at the mercy of an official whose interest was 'to collect as much, and pay as little as he can', and who was unhampered by any definition of each individual's liability.[40] About the only method left was to give long leases to suitable contractors following a detailed settlement; but this was no solution either, in that it depended on the prior remedy of the very disabilities which had prejudiced the success of other methods. From the 1830s the improvement of *khas* management returned to favour. In 1832 there was a stricter insistence upon previous sanction for any farming leases on Wards estates, and this proved to be preparatory for a more considered reform ordered in 1833. But improvements proved elusive (as will be discussed in later chapters). In this, as in other matters, a large proportion of the problems facing the government was the creation not of external conditions but of administrative failures.

Proceedings for the resumption on to the revenue-roll of rent- and revenue-free land caused even greater strain and abuses in administration. They in particular demonstrated the wideness of the gap between the desirable and the possible. The enormous extent of such lands in North Bihar had been noticed at least as early as 1783, and indeed it was believed that as much as ninety per cent of assessed land had been thus alienated in 1658.[41] Such tenures were considered objectionable on practical as well as fiscal grounds (in Buchanan's view they encouraged 'neglect and sloth')[42] and eventually more concerted efforts were made to reduce their number. The work proved too arduous for the Bihar officers. In 1839 new and more lenient rules were introduced (in line with the North-Western Provinces). The government pointed to the great relaxation thus achieved, when responding to protests from the Bengal Landholders' Society. Lands automatically not liable for resumption included, for example, not only those held since 1765 or, if under ten bighas, since the decennial settlement (1789), but also those assigned for permanent purposes (whether or not in perpetuity), and those registered as rent-free where registers existed. (Non-registration would not itself justify resumption where there were no registers.) In addition, resumptions were somewhat discouraged where produce had been continuously applied to religious or charitable purposes or where there had been more than thirty years' rent-free occupancy—in any

---

[40] CO, 21 October 1831 (Court Despatch, 22 December 1830).
[41] Muzaffarpur SR.
[42] Buchanan, *Shahabad*, p.344, and *An Account of the Districts of Patna and Behar in 1811-12* (Patna n.d.), vol.I, p.269.

such case resumption had to be reported to government. Large and permanent additions to the revenue were still expected to be gained from the operations—Rs.519,669 were reported to have been added in 1840—but by 1842 the Board, calling for information about outstanding resumption cases so as to devise a means for accelerating the process, was apparently anxious to see an end to the business.[43]

By this time, it is true, the measures were drawing to a close in the Bihar districts, and had been reasonably successful: in Tirhut district, for example, 1,665 square miles of land (worth Rs.677,387 in revenue) had been resumed by 1850, leaving only 108 square miles as *lakhiraj*.[44] The local implications of the pressure of work, however, had been a failure to know, let alone properly to supervise, what was being done in the government's name. The Board, and even the Collectors, did not at first appreciate the vast extent of property which resumption threw temporarily into the hands of the mufassil authorities. When, in the early 1830s, the Board set about to compile a full report on the proceedings, they were 'entirely disappointed' because Collectors' reports were generally characterised by 'errors and incompleteness'. On investigating further, the Board decided that this confusion was a fair reflection of the real state of affairs, one of neglect and mismanagement. Resumption proceedings had been 'converted into an instrument of intimidation and extortion'. Officials had two main sources of profit. Firstly they could threaten to institute proceedings, or take bribes once proceedings had begun, with little fear of their manœuvres coming to the Collectors' notice, such was the camouflage available in the form of undecided cases—in 1832, for example, in Patna district 135 and in Behar district 661 suits were pending. Secondly native officers were often permitted to administer resumed lands (pending settlement) almost entirely without supervision, with a resultant loss both to government and to the proprietors, most of whom where entitled to a permanent settlement. In one case declared costs of administration actually exceeded receipts.[45]

Though the worst effects of this inefficiency, in terms of govern-

---

[43] India Revenue Letter, 3 February 1840, and Bengal Revenue Letters, 13 August and 7 December 1840 and 26 May 1841, L/E/3/1, and 5 September 1838, L/E/3/42, IOL; CO, 16 September 1842 (rules, 14 October 1839). See also Chittabrata Palit, *Tensions in Bengal Rural Society. Landlords, Planters and Colonial Rule 1830-1860* (Calcutta 1975), ch. 3.

[44] Muzaffarpur SR. See also Bengal District Gazetteers: L.S.S. O'Malley, *Darbhanga* (Calcutta 1907), claims 1,066,000 acres were resumed there between 1830 and 1850.

[45] CO, 20 August 1832 and 17 December 1833.

ment revenue, were painfully put right by the 1840s, the implications for the justice of the proceedings were not so easily disposed of. 'Errors' were found of such magnitude as to show that the government revenues had long suffered, but also almost certainly that revenue and resumption policies were affecting people unevenly, according to the success of efforts to corrupt the amins or to local power and prestige. The fact was that resumption work in the 1830s showed up the extreme administrative weakness of British government, in terms of accuracy and justice rather than collection of revenue, in a province where it had been established on its present system for forty years. The only permanent answer in this case was the end of the resumption work.

Revenue collection and a few related tasks manifestly exhausted the government's resources. The cause was partly and especially at higher levels the complexity and intractability of the problems in comparison with the government's capacity. The cause was also at the local level the fact that day-to-day jobs were disproportionately onerous. Communications were poor. In 1854, for example, there seem to have been a mere seven miles of *pakka* roads and thirty bridges in the whole of Patna Division, where in all only about 1,300 miles of road were even vaguely known to the Public Works Department. Most of those must have had little chance of being repaired at public expense.[46] Arrangements for transport and official provisions were accordingly primitive. They depended upon individual effort. Not only did they have to be organised, they had to be attended to in order to check corruption. John Beames provides a graphic description of the total dislocation of his work caused by the movement of troops through his district as late as 1865.[47] Even carts needed by government had to be requisitioned from private individuals, and we find subordinates 'seizing triple the number required, extorting handsome douceurs from the more respectable not to press their carts, and to a smaller amount from the less wealthy to release theirs after impressment'—'modes of proceeding' which, in this case in Kanpur in 1842 but, we may assume, elsewhere as well, were 'too well known to require any detail'. Such abuses were bound to result when so many official activities were *ad hoc* in character.[48]

Moreover, to the degree that it was dependent on a few individuals, the government was also peculiarly vulnerable to vagaries of personal

[46] *Statement Showing the Roads in the Province of Bengal under the Department of Public Works* (Calcutta 1854).

[47] Beames, *Memoirs*, ch. XII.

[48] CO, 20 June 1842. Taking a census of carts and rotating the requisitions, were recommended to Collectors to avoid abuses.

ability, health and knowledge. Auckland, touring in Rohilkhand in 1838, found that the trials following agricultural unrest had been seriously delayed, in part through sickness among the officers involved. 'The system of the Indian Government,' he noted, 'is exceedingly liable to derangements from causes such as these.' The Bihar districts were notorious for being unhealthy and for a consequently rapid turnover of staff.[49]

The conclusion must be that their circumstances played a large if not always conscious part in deciding the activities of the rulers. Auckland's despatch already quoted devoted close attention to details relevant to regulating the administration and preserving the revenues, but seized almost with an air of relief on occasions in which clear remedies might be proposed for perceived ills (in his case canal-building). Conversely, in an almost simultaneous despatch from Bengal, the government reported that chaudhuris in Assam were collecting from the raiyats the interest charged on arrears of revenue—indeed making a profit. But on this occasion the government gave no thought to preventing this abuse; they merely proposed dropping the demand for interest.[50] The contrast is instructive. We have seen that when extra tasks had to be done extra staff might be provided. But this was not only subject to the sanction of the Court of Directors, it also put a strain on the Company's finances, so that most extras had to be self-financing, at least in prospect. This was a government which could do little more than preserve the façade, and which could contemplate improving the lot of its subjects only through large-scale and apparently self-contained projects such as irrigation and railways—not so much a choice as the dictate of administrative failures. Much of this remained unchanged even as the administration improved under Bentinck and Dalhousie. Nothing was done to reduce the dependence on a tiny, imported, expensive elite, on a government designed for distant minimal rule. The greater use of Indians was a mere palliative which did not extend the range of the government's activities. These and other reforms, though important for the future, did little more than keep pace with the increasing complexity of routine business, and in some cases refinements of the system actually reduced the government's expectations and its involvement with the people. The moral is that the Company had the capacity neither to intervene directly nor to monitor the effects of its actions. If this had changed by the end of the century, the

---

[49] Auckland to Court of Directors (Judicial and Revenue Department), 13 February 1838, L/E/3/41; Bengal Revenue Letter, 9 May 1837, L/E/3/39, IOL.

[50] Bengal Revenue Letter, 23 January 1838, L/E/3/41, IOL.

rulers may have been moved not so much inclination as by possibilities.

This picture is reinforced by examination of the little the British did do about the condition of the people in Bihar and Bengal in this period. We shall return to the question of impact in more detail; here, considering official will, it will suffice to indicate that, despite all the measures introduced, the rulers did not seem to be trying very hard. Collectors were given few definite responsibilities and the peasants were left at best to the courts. Rules of practice set out in 1829 did not even mention the raiyats. Collectors were to investigate grievances and also to keep the peace, by force if necessary, under orders of 1788; in theory they could have intervened to enforce the regulations designed to protect tenants under the permanent settlement.[51] That was all. Yet the colonial dream of a 'progressive' India was quintessentially rural. Where there seemed 'any prospect of success', Collectors and Commissioners were expected to be in touch with agricultural societies for the encouragement of the growth of more valuable crops, such as cotton and tobacco. They were supposed also to see to the establishment in every district of 'good seminaries for giving instruction' in agricultural practice.[52] This policy had little impact, and, in so far as it did impinge, it introduced significant distortions, with consequences for the capacity of rural populations to resist crises of climate or extortion, because the official effort was directed towards items of trade rather than subsistence. It was noticeable that the East India Company largely retreated from the sponsorshop of grain production—formerly an important aspect of the *takkavi* offered by Indian states—while retaining a willingness to support crops such as cotton, sugar and opium, which directly or indirectly helped fill its coffers.

Calculations about the need to secure increasing revenue seem generally to have restricted interventions to redress rural grievances. These certainly were recognised readily enough. The government could set out the evils inherent in the indigo planters' system of giving advances to cultivators—who could be permanently trapped and, if they reneged, subject to illegal pressures, against which the courts were of little use. The government also knew the best solution: to abolish the advances. Yet it refused even to intervene in disputes, thinking its native officers unfitted to arbitrate between European planters and cultivators, and instead strengthened the planters' hands, and even told Collectors to help them further, in the vain hope that the planters' goodwill would prevail over their self-interest if they were given a free

[51] CO, 21 May 1788 and 17 February 1829; see Huttman, *Abstract*.
[52] CO, 2 March 1832 and 1 August 1837.

hand.[53] Why? Like the treatment of zamindars which it closely resembled, this policy was an admission of weakness, not an attitude born out of the permanent settlement. By this time disillusionment with the zamindars and subtle modifications of the settlement were common even in Bengal. In 1838, for example, the government refused a remission of revenue in Midnapur because relaxation would have a bad effect on the zamindars whom it considered 'very improvident' as a class. On the other hand the Board recommended leniency, contrary to the principles of 1793, in order to encourage agriculture in another case where problems were exceptional and long-term.[54] The strategy and preconceptions of the permanent settlement had been rejected. Action against zamindars and in favour of raiyats was inhibited by caution, political expediency and self-interest.

Even in this period, very many remedies were aired, much intervention on the behalf of the raiyats proposed.[55] Here we come back to the crucial point of administrative incapacity. In 1831, approaching the nub of tenant rights, the Court of Directors praised the example of a Collector who had given *pattas* (written leases) to individuals to prevent extortion by revenue farmers; in 1837 a fully-fledged scheme was launched to cover all government raiyats.[56] In 1832, a case in Behar district prompted the Board to endorse, in a limited form, the practice whereby, before the sale of a temporarily-settled estate, inquiries were made as to its circumstances and agricultural population and the situation of those liable for the revenue. In 1840 there were discussions about what to do on resumed estates about *shikmi* raiyats (those with hereditary rights to cultivate at fixed rents) and the suggestion was made to extend Regulation VIII of 1819 so as to give protection during transfers to all hereditary under-tenures, and even to make a register of all tenures. The Court of Directors too called for principles to be observed, as for example they did in 1840, by regretting the failure in the settlements in Patna and Tirhut to assess the raiyats' produce, labour and farming capital.[57] But all these schemes were still-born; there was no way they could be given general effect.

Similar shortcomings were revealed when concern was expressed

---

[53] Extracts from Governor General in Council, Judicial Proceedings, 9 June 1830, with CO, 29 June 1830.

[54] Bengal Revenue Letter, 22 March 1838, L/E/3/41, IOL.

[55] Some of the relevant regulations will be discussed in chapter three.

[56] Court Despatch, 9 March 1831, with CO, 10 July 1832; CO, 30 May 1837. The Collector was probably in Tirhut.

[57] CO, 4 August 1832; Bengal Revenue Letter, 17 June 1840, and India Revenue Letter, 6 April 1840, L/E/3/1.

about tenant rights which were at risk during land sales. Estates could be sold for their own arrears (not those of their proprietors' other estates, as the Board had to point out in 1834), and sales had taken place on two dates in the year, with considerable discretion for Collectors, under Regulation XI of 1822.

After Regulation VIII of 1830, all estates in arrears were put up for sale monthly, a change which made difficulties for individual zamindars, but which removed the ambiguity and delay which had been thought to encourage abuses in the past. But there was still a good deal of worry about irregularities and cases of corruption among officials in the mid-1830s, and equally the number of properties advertised but not sold, or sold and then relinquished to the defaulter, indicated that zamindars were using the system for their own ends, chiefly to injure tenant rights. The government knew this well enough. In 1838, for example, it declined to reinstate a sale which had been irregularly cancelled (at the request of the purchaser but without the owner's consent) on the grounds that it was thus saving the undertenants from 'vexation and loss' through the abrogation of their leases, without injuring the original owner, whose arrears had been met from money deposited by the purchaser. The government could do little, however, in the admittedly 'very common' instances in which the purchaser withdrew in collusion with the zamindar, or in which the sale went through but at a higher price than would have been gained privately, because the estate was unencumbered, having been sold for arrears. The general principles were refined further in 1841 (Act XII) but estates were still to be sold (on fifteen days' notice) free of encumbrances; not until 1859 was protection provided for all the parties involved, and even this was of little use as by then sales were rarely caused by inability to pay the revenue and almost always provoked for ulterior motives. At the end of the century villages were found where raiyats did not know their rights and rents had been increased at sale by as much as 168 per cent.[58]

That verdict means that large-scale administrative measures could not be undertaken to improve the lot of the mass of the rural population. It means that there were very limited chances to protect them from the results of policies, such as the legal changes of the permanent settlement, coupled with the expanding impact of the courts, which endorsed or extended the property rights of zamindars. A sense of helplessness even to prevent abuses arising out of their own actions seemed to grow rather than to diminish among the British as the century wore on.

[58] CO, 31 May 1833 and 19 June 1834; Bengal Revenue Letter, 2 January 1838, L/E/3/41, IOL; Muzaffarpur SR.

Revenue officials were closest to the problem. In 1833 the Collector in the Sunderbans was struck by the poor condition of the people and blamed it on the taluqdars (intermediate tenure-holders). They lent out what they had collected in rents, leaving the zamindars to borrow or rack-rent their own raiyats in order to meet the revenue demand. If the taluqdar were forced to pay up, he would merely levy an additional cess on his raiyats. The cultivators lost out whether directly under the zamindar or not. The government was not convinced that any solution to this problem could be found while the raiyats remained poor or improvident and were forced to borrow; the Board saw no hope of ending the system either, though it thought that powers might be taken to help the zamindars to collect in the first place, as existing regulations did not cover these estates.[59] This typifies the dilemma facing would-be reformers: either the problem was too large altogether, or (at best) it could be tackled only in specific cases or through agents whose goodwill could not be guaranteed. The particular situation was not found in Bihar, but similar points were often made there about thikadars, lease- or mortgage-holders who acted in the place of zamindars under a system of farming out the collection of rents.

The development of revenue theories meant that by the 1830s it had come to be accepted that the so-called hereditary raiyats were entitled to protection. Exhortations to record their lands at settlement (in the Persian though not the English record) were tempered only by the fear of 'creating' privileges.[60] The whole of this theoretical apparatus and debate, however, was circumscribed by the government's weakness. It was thought unwise to fritter away property 'among a multitude of needy cultivators' (as Bentinck would have it), and indeed prejudicial to the interests of government if those cultivators should be 'thrown entirely on their own resources and removed from all connection with their superiors'.[61] In the 1830s, in the aftermath of criticisms of the permanent settlement, this was no longer a simple assumption from physiocratic theory or aristocratic prejudice. Rather it was a recognition of the shortcomings of government in Bengal. The rulers could only govern, let alone bring about reform, through their relations with small numbers of people—zamindars or perhaps government raiyats. To seek to change the people at large would require vastly more sophisticated administrative machinery than was at hand. Thus, when the Bengal government referred to the interests of the 'higher classes of the agricul-

[59] CO, 31 May 1833.
[60] CO, 12 November 1833.
[61] Ibid., Governor General's minute, 29 February 1832.

tural community, and, *through them*, of their tenantry', the idea may seem primarily social or philosophical in origin; but it also had solid basis in the difficulties of Indian government.[62] The limitation was still more obvious for positive measures. Thus the arguments about differential rents for different crops were carried on at the highest levels of government in terms of economic theory, but in the Bengal resolution of 1838, advancing the view that no extra should be charged on lands producing more profitable crops, it was argued that the want of capital among the raiyats was the deciding factor, forcing the government to wait until agriculture had improved as a whole.[63] Doctrines probably convinced local men more readily in the negative sense, as when *takkavi* was branded as a 'practice which ought to be discouraged'. But even that was also troublesome, and the inconvenience to the Collector of having to report every advance he made was no doubt as powerful a disincentive as official disapproval.[64] The fact that later changes of attitude accompanied changes in priorities does not prove that either change was necessarily the product of the other. And what may be true of the North Western Provinces, where a system was being introduced, is not necessarily true of Bengal, where a system was being repaired. The conclusion is that a lack of capacity in the government reduced both the speed at which changes were felt, including any dispossession of the raiyats, and the chances of applying effective remedies as problems were discovered.

## III

Clearly the British were not constructing some kind of ideal bureaucracy in India; even romanticised accounts have admitted its imperfections and celebrated its rebels,[65] and there is now an alternative historiography which stresses the weakness of the system,[66] or the extent to which it was captured by local elites.[67] Turning to the late nineteenth century, a fair question is whether the bureaucratic reforms actually worked. The management of money was the most sensitive matter, and one in which we have already noted early short-comings. At the end of

[62] Bengal Revenue Letter, 11 March 1837, L/E/3/40, IOL (emphasis added).

[63] Resolution, 26 March 1838, CO, 17 April 1838; see E.T. Stokes, *The English Utilitarians and India* (Oxford 1959), pp.126-32.

[64] CO, 17 July 1829.

[65] See Philip Woodruff [Mason], *The Men Who Ruled India*, vol.1, *The Founders* and vol.2, *The Guardians* (London 1963), and Beames, *Memoirs* .

[66] Notably B. Spangenberg, *British Bureaucracy in India* (New Delhi 1984).

[67] For example, R.E. Frykenberg, *Guntur District, 1788-1848* (Oxford 1965).

the nineteenth century, the procedure for treasury returns, whether for land revenue or cesses, was that each clerk (on a salary of about Rs.20 per month in 1900) would enter payments in a ledger, and balance them in a separate register. The totals would be checked by a supervisor (on about Rs.30) who would prepare district returns. Clerks at this level were often not competent to work in English. The totals would be checked again by the head clerk, and passed by him, entered on a pre-scribed form, to the Treasury Officer, usually a member of the ICS. These procedures were frequently reconsidered, and from time to time new manuals were issued.[68] But still frauds occurred. In a case in Sha-habad district, Bihar, in 1896, entries were found crediting amounts not paid, repeatedly in favour of the same estates. Discovery followed investigation of a large discrepancy between the closing and opening balances at the change of financial year on 31 March 1895. Arguably this proves that the system did work. On the other hand, as was said at the time, the local accounts were shown by the incident, as in a similar case in Hooghly, to be 'extremely badly kept', often without regular balances, or with discrepancies between items and totals. It was thought that they had probably been 'entirely unreliable' for years.[69] The con-clusion might be, therefore, that the system did not work.

One problem was that security bonds were still used to ensure the honesty of some government employees and agents. Overwhelmingly they were based upon landed property, cash or bonds being practically unknown; and, as had been understood years before, this was liable to place the officials under an obligation to some landed backer.[70] Over fifty years earlier it had been recognised that this was unsatisfactory, partly because the sums at risk far outstripped the value of any security officials could provide, and partly because of the invitation to corrup-tion. Some officials in the 1890s thought the system should be finally

[68] For example the separate register for balances was introduced in 1891. See petition of Dhanukdhani Proshad, late road cess *tauzi navis* (treasury clerk), Darbhanga, R&A Rev B 17 (January 1902). Reforms by Charles Elliott had re-sulted in all ledgers being kept in English to facilitate checking; this inevitably caused problems with subordinate staff; see R&A Rev B 55-6 (June 1898).

[69] Shahabad Coll to PC, 11 April, and PC to Board of Revenue, 12 May 1896, PCR 366, 12/1 (1896/7).

[70] PC to Board of Revenue, 5 December 1891, PCR 354, 8/1 (1891/2). The advantage of land bonds came at the point of enforcing any forfeiture: attaching land was far easier administratively, raised fewer worries about the conduct of government agents acting without supervision, and required less local knowl-edge, than proceeding against moveable property. See Gaya Coll to PC, 15/16 May 1893, on the Public Demands Recovery Act, VII of 1880, PCR 358, 12/9 (1893/4).

abandoned, bringing all levels of the administration under the same sanction of bureaucratic checks rather than financial penalty. This was partly because even ICS officers remained liable for frauds perpetrated by their subordinates.[71] Obviously the imperfections of supervision still defined a limit to the revolution in government, in terms of ideals as well as procedures; they may suggest that it was still relatively shallow in its impact.

Fraud might subvert the intention of policy as well as weaken administration. For example, in the 1880s, it was decided (without devoting large resources to back up the policy) that loans should be provided for agricultural improvement.[72] A case in Saran district, Bihar, in the 1890s showed how an official in charge of dispersing loans was to able to abscond with payments which should have been made to persons against whom proceedings initially were taken for recovery of the debt, and who, receiving nothing, had renewed their application thinking it had been unsuccessful.[73] We might see this as an extreme example of how Indian enterprise could subvert the extended state introduced by the British. Secondly, vigilance against fraud in itself spawned measures which ran counter to the original purpose of particular policies. The Board of Revenue rules on loans policy required not only central *takkavi* registers which were supposed to be inspected daily (discouraging the officials), but also rigorous investigation of each application (discouraging the applicants).[74] Again, it may be said that bureaucratic conditions were restricting the extent of state intervention (a phenomenon not unknown in more recent times).

In some sense all state employees are engaged in the furtherance of their own careers, and this was most obvious, perhaps, for expensive,

[71] For a complaint about instances of such claims being enforced, see Officiating Coll of Saran (Pawsey) to PC, 27 September 1884, PCR 341, 14/1 (1884/5). The same file remarked that it was impossible for any office to function 'where the native staff is disloyal'. In this case, marking another self-imposed limit on the government's operation, but also its modernity, the Board of Revenue refused, on grounds of lack of evidence, to uphold the dismissal of a *peshkar* suspected, in a notoriously corrupt office, of having forged documents, even though dismissal had been recommended by successive Collectors and the Patna Commissioner. The *peshkar* was reinstated on full pay, including for the period of his suspension.

[72] See P.J. Cain and A.G. Hopkins' economic explanation of this, in *British Imperialism*, [vol. 1], *Innovation and Expansion, 1688-1914* (London 1993), pp.332-47.

[73] Saran Collector to Bengal Accountant-General, 18 April 1893, and reply, 17 August, PCR 358, 1/27 (1893/4).

[74] See Robb, *Rural India* (1992), pp.131-5.

imported civil servants in a situation of colonial rule. But, even in India, the benefits were usually indirect and systematic, and not incompatible with the ideals of service and duty espoused by the ICS.[75] By contrast, if officials were able to use their office corruptly for direct personal advantage, then the public character of the administration was being subverted. And, at the height of the imperial system in India, petty officials *were* able to execute frauds, as we have seen, and also to extort bribes for the favour of carrying out their normal duties. The sheristadar of the court in Behar district in the 1850s, Munshi Amir Ali, became the sole or part-proprietor of some 200 villages, during a period of not more than twelve years on a salary of Rs.50 to Rs.80 a month; he achieved this not by embezzling from the government, but merely by taking bribes and manipulating the deposit and court registers, in association with two accomplices, one a Muslim and one a 'shrewd' Hindu.[76] The implication was that some officials sought their chief rewards through but outside their office; and it would hardly be surprising if this had frequently been the case, given the relative paucity, for Indians, of rewards within the service. Similar lack of incentives or prospects of advancement had characterised pre-colonial bureaucracies as well; and this was the very problem addressed, especially by Cornwallis in the later eighteenth century, for English Company servants, through a ban on conflicting interests and the payment of more generous salaries.

Clearly too there were limits to what could be changed even in the large and growing areas which government controlled directly. For example, on government land, the rulers still had to choose whether to farm out the management, often to local people, or to administer it directly by paid officials. The same issue arose in regard to large private estates, with which the British intervened to ensure social stability and continuity in the face of threats posed by minority, insolvency or incompetence. (Something the same could be said too of princely states, especially in times of regency.) For estates, the instrument of

[75] See T.G.P. Spear, 'Stern daughter of the voice of God: ideas of duty among the British in India', in W. Doniger O'Flaherty and J.D.M. Derrett, eds., *The Concept of Duty in South Asia* (London 1978).

[76] Behar Coll to PC, 29 January 1857, Bengal Revenue Consultations 12 (March 1858). This may be the same Amir Ali whose fortunes later collapsed under a mountain of debt; see Robb, *Rural India* (1992), pp.135-6 and 150. However D. Washbrook, *The Emergence of Provincial Politics* (Cambridge 1976), argues that in Madras the claim that petty officials benefited from the state connection 'confuses potential powers...with the ability to fulfil them' (p.45).

policy remained the Court of Wards, providing for the secondment of officials (either full-time or from the district establishment) with a brief to establish more effective management. Here, and in the *khas mahal* (government estate), the tendency continued as before, in the 1830s: both to set up bureaucratic procedures and to enlist local agents. Commonly (though reluctantly) estates were farmed out to intermediaries, and village accountants (patwaris) and head raiyats were often paid a commission on the rents they collected:[77] this was contrary to the tendency for bureaucratic reform, but reproduced a pattern of estate management long established in India.

Even in the later nineteenth century, then, bureaucratic reforms did not mean establishing a wholly effective system, free of corruption or of various local influences. Neither the purposes nor the means of administration were wholly Westernised—though many areas, including the ICS, were jealously reserved for British personnel, methods and ideals.[78] Nonetheless the government significantly changed over the century, and an instrument of the changes was the development of the administration itself. The acquisition and ordering of knowledge and the framing of rules gradually coalesced into a set of bureaucratic principles and structures. Printing was vital, and the more extensive use of the English language assisted in easing supervision. But the key was a system in which tasks and responsibilities were precisely allocated and checking was simplified.[79] Information flowed into offices according to established routines, with actions logged at every stage. Secondly, definite spheres of delegated authority were established; and a sense of duty was inculcated deliberately in the services which carried out these tasks.[80] Career hierarchies were provided—promotion rather than

[77] See office note, 20 July 1892, PCR 356, 10/18 (1892/3). In Gaya district approximately 4 annas per *bigha* ($3/5$ acre) was paid to leading raiyats; in Shahabad a cess was recovered from tenants for the patwaris at a rate varying from $1/2$ or 1 anna per rupee to $1/33$ of the rental collected. As a step to more bureaucratic methods, however, some patwaris were paid a monthly wage rather than a commission.

[78] Queen Victoria's proclamation of 1858 promised equal opportunities in government service for all her subjects—a promise linked by some to the rapid pacification of India after the revolt of 1857 (see Lyall, *Dominion*, p.358) but very slow to be given effect in the ICS, usually on the excuse of a need to recruit suitable, gentlemanly officers.

[79] See above, and Robb, *Evolution*, ch. 2.

[80] One interpretation of this 'common view' is offered by Cain and Hopkins, *British Imperialism* (London 1993), vol.1, ch.1: 'The move to meritocratic recruitment was intended both as a device to maintain and advance gentlemenly status and as a method of rigging the market...once patronage had ceased to

punishment being the goad to efficiency. At least some rewards for
good service were of long standing—for example pensions and land
grants to Indians employed in civil, military or even advisory capacities
by the eighteenth-century East India Company, or by its Mughal and
other predecessors. But by the end of the nineteenth century, even in the
terms of service for subordinate officials, successive, more systematic
reforms had provided for advancement, even including promotion to
posts normally reserved for covenanted servants.[81] Proposals for district
administration by the Bengal government in 1906 were criticised for
having 'too many appointments in the lowest grade'. The Government
of India favoured grades on fixed pay, with incremental salaries for
those with no hope of future promotion; it had introduced reforms (in
1905) with the object of improving prospects for the clerks generally,
and thought this goal more important than minor economies.[82] Shortly
afterwards, though timidly, 'improved prospects' for Indians came to
include targets for the proportion of Indians in the higher services, and
in the officer cadre of the Indian army—reforms which were necessary,
as argued by the time of the Montagu-Chelmsford report, even at the
risk of some loss of efficiency.[83]

These bureaucratic reforms should not be taken to imply that office
work was highly regarded in the ICS, where a semi-mythical tradition
of horse-back rule undoubtedly had more glamour that the shifting of
endless paper. In a little noticed influence on the value placed on the
'man of the spot', the development of the empirical sciences meant that
observation and experience, and hence 'field work', were regarded as
superior or at least necessarily prior to theory, by colonial officials as
by their successor sociologists. Attitudes may be deduced from H.H.
Risley's remark about J. Bolton, onetime Commissioner of Patna Division, who was 'rather an authority on revenue work and office procedure generally', and so much so that 'Mischievous people were known
to describe him as a "first-rate Sheristadar"'.[84] On the other hand, we

---

be...socially acceptable' (p.27). Nowhere was this more true than in the ICS.

[81] See Robb, *Evolution*, pp.66-9.

[82] Office note, 9 July 1906, H Establishments A 113-17 (December 1906).

[83] See P. Robb, *The Government of India and Reform* (London 1976), p.56.
This did not mean that the supposed character of the service was not to be preserved: there was to be no 'rapid swamping' so as to reduce its 'qualities of
courage, leadership, decision, fixity of purpose, detached judgment, and integrity' (Report on Indian Constitutional Reforms 1918, para.314).

[84] Risley note, 11 March 1906, H Establishments A 113-17 (December
1906). Excessive innovation was also suspect: Sir D. Barbour complained the
union boards scheme 'sprang from the brain' of a Bengal secretary; though he
probably meant Sir C. Macaulay, and I suspect Sir A. Mackenzie, P.P. Hutchins

might think that the Indian sheristadar was a key player in colonial governance, and hence important to the impact of British rule.

A crucial point, perhaps, is that the bureaucratic revolution was carried out even by men who professed to have little taste for administration. It gained momentum from legal and institutional reforms, starting in the eighteenth century. Indian legal codes and procedures were standardised from the 1860s, the work of Macaulay and Maine, against some opposition from those who argued for the appropriateness to India of personal rule by district officers. Separate codes persisted for particular categories of people, including personal law on the basis of religion, and yet they too were codified, clarified, recorded and made subject to precedent, in just the same way, in principle at least, as were the administrative decisions.[85]

A consequence of this system was the separation of different government functions, and the professionalisation of those responsible for them. The revolution in government also reflected a revolution in attitudes to knowledge and to its practitioners. Perhaps especially in India, government came to be regarded as a science, with many separate disciplines. Departments grew, with particular tasks and know-how. Training came to be important—for recruitment, advancement, and also for carrying out the increasingly complex functions of the state. Inter-departmental feuds erupted; bureaucratic fiefdoms came to be defended. Change was inevitable, to match other revolutions, because the generalist government officer became unable to cope with the weight and complexity of business and information; there could no longer be the one fount of all state power and actions—even though something of that generalist tradition persists in India even to this day, in the district officers of the Indian Administrative Service, inheritors of the role of the Indian Civil Service.[86] From the mid-nineteenth century, the district officer's actual tasks were increasingly hemmed in by the jobs performed by other agencies—the police, the courts, the engineers, the medical officers, and so on—and they came to reflect the residual priorities of the government of the day. In the twentieth century they were strongly political in character.[87]

---

assumed he referred to the 'creative' MacDonnell. However, though that less than admiring epithet was often applied to him, MacDonnell rose very high. See H. Local Boards A 2-5 (February 1893).

[85] See D.A. Washbrook, 'Law, State and Agrarian Society in Colonial India', *MAS* 15, 3 (1981).

[86] See D. Potter, *India's Political Administrators* (Oxford 1986).

[87] This qualifies the common picture of the gentlemanly amateur surviving in the ICS, as recently summarised by Cain and Hopkins, *British Imperialism*,

The evidence of fraud or incompetence in the late nineteenth century has to be read rather differently from similar evidence earlier in British rule. The methodology, number of employees, range of activities, experience and precedent, in the normal functioning of the system, were quite different by 1900 from what they had been in 1830. This is not to say that the effort was commensurate with the needs—most of the 'modern' functions of government were notoriously underfunded. But it goes against common sense to conclude that there was no real difference between the bureaucracy of late nineteenth-century India and its predecessors. Some of the reports of advantage taken by Indian subordinates—and they are more frequent earlier in the century (as well as again after independence)—might be read as a transitional feature of a system that was markedly gaining in power. It is plain, though not readily quantifiable, that both the activity of the system and the extent to which it was monitored grew very noticeably as British rule continued: this is not merely an illusion of the archives created by the extensive printing and the systems of record-keeping which were part of the change. And in the final analysis, even had there been no qualitative difference in performance and efficiency, the mere enlargement of the bureaucracy would be sufficient to justify the term 'revolution'. This is to say that it provided effective means of implementing policy, but (as we shall see) without being efficient in response to Indian conditions or to emerging problems.

## IV

The shortcomings of government were not constant, and the early bureaucratic advances provided a base on which the state could expand. We may approach the issue in a different way, by considering the chief foundation of the expansion, which was undoubtedly the establishment and improvement of the system of taxation. In Bengal, as already mentioned, a permanent settlement with landlords was endorsed in Pitt's India Act of 1784; its permanence was debated especially after John Shore's decennial settlement of 1789 until the decision by Pitt and Dundas, under Cornwallis's urging, to which effect was given in March 1793; it provided titles of land-ownership to zamindars and indirectly to taluqdars (recognised subordinate or intermediary revenue-payers). The decision not to apply a permanent settlement to the annexed parts of

---

[vol.2], *Crisis and Deconstruction, 1914-1900*, pp.178-80. I will show in volume two of this study that this division of responsibility and change of emphasis had serious consequences for the ability of more interventionist government to effect improvements in the Indian countryside.

Mysore was taken around the turn of the nineteenth century, and this developed into the system of temporary settlements with the raiyats which was applied elsewhere in the Madras and Bombay presidencies, and finally formalised in 1855. For the ceded and conquered districts of north-west India the decision was taken in 1811. Holt Mackenzie's minute of 1819 formed the basis of the alternative periodic (usually thirty-year) settlements with villages or estates (*mahals*), provided under Regulation VII of 1822. Thus revenue settlement and hence land-property rights for 'landlords' as opposed to 'cultivators' or 'village communities' ceased to be the norm less than a decade after 1793, even though the final rejection of a permanent settlement came only in the 1880s and the issue was still being debated early in the twentieth century. The questions of who should own the land and what should be the term of revenue settlement were of course distinct, though associated in people's minds and in practice.

Considering for the moment only the more-or-less matching growth of state interventions and expenditure, there is much independent evidence of a gradual if uneven expansion in the tasks of government in India. We may ignore the early anomaly of the East India Company's involvement in trade, and legacies in the form of the opium trade, the salt monopoly and so on, and also the undoubted withdrawal of the British rulers from some expected functions, especially with regard to religion. These are large and possibly significant exceptions, of course; but without them the direction of the movement in revenue policy can be readily discerned. Centralising states seek when they can to achieve three things in this regard: to widen the fiscal base, to contact and control the real payers (the producers of wealth) and to relate demand to an objective standard such as income. But nowhere in the eighteenth century, not even in Britain, had the goal of a 'modern' system of state revenue been achieved.[88] The peripheries of the nation, geographically and socially, were barely taxed; collection was carried out largely through intermediaries; and the levels of taxation did not relate to many actual measurements. This implied limits on direct taxation, which was liable to meet with resistance—the notion of consent having been introduced—while indirect taxation (which had the measurement built in) represented a fairly small proportion of the total. In India too, in the situation which the East India Company inherited, the land tax, which constituted the great bulk of revenue, was not collected in the main from producers, and, for all the bureaucratic forms, central states'

[88] The following paragraphs are drawn from P. Robb, 'Ideas in agrarian history', *Journal of the Royal Asiatic Society* 1 (1990).

access to them had actually declined in many areas during the eighteenth century, with the growth of hereditary zamindaris, revenue-free land and revenue-farming. Outside Bengal, the amount and basis of the demand supposedly rested upon objective measurement in the past, for Todar Mal's surveys as for Domesday Book, and there were elaborate manuals relating to assessment, crop estimation and so on. But in practice the payments were decided mainly by negotiation and coercion. Thus they were uneven across territory and inequitable between payers. North Bihar, for example, was much more lightly taxed than South Bihar, partly because of its large proportion of revenue-free holdings; and everywhere high castes usually paid less than low.

The permanent settlement of the Bengal land revenue was thus to an extent just another quasi-feudal response by a weak state. The settlement deliberately refrained from seeking a relationship between the state and the cultivator; it effectively dismantled the local revenue administration; it had none of the eagerness of some later revenue surveys to base demand on the capacity rather than the output of soils, in order to discourage sloth. It was a system of revenue appropriate to a government which depended on inherited institutions and was still fearful of the competence and probity of its own direct employees, not least the Europeans—and which, for those reasons, intended to operate in the localities as its predecessors had done, mainly through quasi-independent intermediaries paid by means of rights over land.

Yet the permanent settlement also marked the beginnings of a transformation in the revenue-base of the state. First, it abandoned for ever the decentralised auctions of the farming system, and fixed the liability to pay upon the land itself, and hence upon its owners, known persons whose identity the state recorded and controlled. Second, though it deliberately refrained from relating payments to capacity, except in the broadest terms and at one moment, and indeed often set the amounts with regard to previous 'treaties', it nonetheless made them quite definite and permanent, thus removing almost all of the previous element of negotiation: there were arrears under the Bengal system but few remissions. Third, it allowed for some evening-out of the incidence of the demand, not at the outset, but through the subsequent resumption of a large proportion of revenue-free holdings on to the revenue rolls. In taxation therefore the British—in so far as they could give real effect to the system they instituted—had already in 1793 regulated the payers (meaning the zamindars) and fixed the demand, and they were soon to extend the revenue-base through resumptions. The boundaries of state control had thus been extended.

The pattern of linking taxation to property was continued across all aspects of revenue. The excise 'farm', the market-controllers' lease, the ferry-operator's tenure all produced contractors who, like zamindars, were state collectors having a property in their collection. Significantly the term for the *abkari* or excise right was the same as for a landed estate; it was *mahal.* Other rights, which were also offices, were named as if they were tenancies in land. This was the old decentralised mode of government, but it was also one whereby particular rights were defined and identified. Clearly that process was applied to the land itself. We have already noted some of the shortcomings of early surveys, but now we should also remark the significance of the order to which they subjected land and rights. British surveyors placed marking stones and prepared maps, and British laws defined categories of land and tenure. The definitions, however resisted or subverted in practice, acquired a special authority, and over time inevitably influenced behaviour. Designated forest lands were used differently; in a number of ways *khas* or state land was distinct from private, and a zamindari from a raiyati holding. These state-based categories were not the only ones or even the most important; nor were categories of this type peculiar to British rule. But their range and effectiveness were markedly extended throughout the nineteenth century. The same normative definitions were applied, with varying impact, to peoples, castes, customs, crops, resources, canals, taxes. Moreover the British were not neutral. They had preferences in regard to behaviour, expectations about acceptable occupations; especially they favoured the settled agriculturist, and at some points the peasant proprietor.

Of course it would be ridiculous to present the permanent settlement as a blueprint for an interventionist state. But it contained elements of this possibility, in substance, and also in form, considering that it was a body of regulations enforceable in courts, producing a corpus of rights and property permanently recorded in writing. It sowed the seeds also for later capacity, in that it was partly designed to educate and control the employees of the state. The British had recognised from the first the importance of information: a lack of it had inconvenienced Clive, but this began to be remedied under Warren Hastings, and the process continued more or less throughout the nineteenth century, reaching its apogee in the settlement reports, finally introduced to Bengal districts from the 1890s. The permanent settlement forestalled too, in Bengal, the probable initial revolt against increasing taxation, already felt in some senses during the eighteenth century, by establishing a countervailing interest in property. By contrast, later attempts to tax the landed interest further, for supposedly local purposes such as roads or police, were strongly resented in the countryside, and contributed to the undermining of the compact between zamindar and raj.

There seem to have been five distinct stages, in India as also in Britain, which marked a development towards a 'modern' fiscal structure. First, there was the institution of fixed property which provides security against the payment of tax—here the example was land in recorded ownership in place of personal liability, forced sales in place of imprisonment or torture. Secondly, there was a limited but definite demand, whether permanent as in Bengal or on a periodically-fixed scale as in so-called temporarily-settled areas. The intention was to free the income of both tax-payers and the state from the uncertainties of negotiation or force. Thirdly, there was an attempt at standardisation of payments between individuals or regions in comparable conditions: this was different both from the uncertain payments, and from the tendency for taxes to be higher in areas or from persons over which the ruler exercised closer sway. Indian states had repeatedly tried for this standardisation; the British succeeded for longer and more fully than their predecessors. Fourthly—and this really marks a second level of development—there was an expansion in the importance of alternative sources of revenue: more indirect taxes, taxes on consumption, taxes on income, user-payments for state services, and so on. In India the land revenue declined markedly in importance in favour of such alternatives from the late nineteenth century onwards.[89] Fifthly, there was a great widening in the range and number of tax-payers, necessarily accompanied by a certain shift towards graduated or progressive taxation. This consolidated standardisation by linking tax to the ability to pay. British officials tried to ensure this in much of India, outside Bengal, by calculating land revenue according to the qualities of different soils, and after careful economic assessments. In Bengal something of the same was attempted when setting the liability, of zamindars and raiyats, to local cesses. Other taxes, especially at first, were collected on the

[89] Land revenue increased markedly from the mid-nineteenth century onwards, but decreased as a proportion of the total, the main increases being in duties, excise and income tax; an illustration of the change may be seen in five-year averages of gross revenue received: in 1861-5 land revenue was Rs.19.7 crores, customs 2.4, income tax 1.4, salt 5.1, excise 1.8 and opium 7.4; the corresponding figures in 1891-5 were 25.2, 2.7, 1.7, 8.6, 5.4, and 7.4, with railways added at 20.4; in 1921-5 they were 35.3, 41.8, 18, 7.4, 18.9, 3.8 and (railways) 29.3. Excluding railways, where there was little net revenue, the percentages of the total in these periods from land revenue were thus 52, 49 and 28. (Calculated from Misra, *Administrative History*, pp.364-5.)

basis of estimated income, and pressed more on the poorer members of the commercial and professional classes. However, their avowed intention was to apply the tax-burden more equitably, as well as to raise necessary income. The same impulse led to the measures to spread taxes in the twentieth century, and the monitoring of the burden on particular areas and sections of the population. The variable incidence of taxation per head in different provinces was, indeed, one motive for the relative shift away from land revenue.[90] It follows from all this that, though formerly taxation may have been extremely high for some payers and though these excesses declined over time, yet the *total* income of the state vastly expanded as the system developed.

The revenue base did not remain unchanged, in the face of such late nineteenth-century expansions, quite apart from the increase in the numbers of payers through the partition of estates. In Bengal the new local taxes from the 1870s were claimed avowedly from tenants as well as from landlords, an extension of the net which was further augmented by the hesitant introduction of forms of income tax, initially on a far from objective basis, and then of course by the eventual shift towards indirect taxes: in that context the history and significance of Indian excise may not be as dull a subject as it sounds. Meanwhile, elsewhere in India, because of the rejection of the zamindari settlement at the time of the Fifth Report, a similar widening of the revenue-payers had occurred much earlier, within the land-revenue systems themselves, and there settlement work was precisely intended, at least from the 1840s, to relate demand to the capacity to pay.

The legal reforms of the 1850s and 1860s, and again in the 1880s, thus provided important scaffolding for an expanding state. New recognition of the complexity of Indian society added significant nuances and doubts. But perhaps a growing assumption of economic responsibility was the key: there was a move from building the infrastructure (public works intended to pay their way), to social responsibility

---

[90] The main example of progressive taxation was the shift in revenue described above; see ibid., pp.359-63. Licence and income taxes were a long time in coming—the first attempts were Act I of 1861 (repealed in 1862) and after 1867 a licence tax on trades, which became a certificate tax, and then in 1869, extended to the professions, an income tax at 2 per cent or more on incomes over Rs.500. Again dropped in 1873, licence tax was revived in 1877, and income tax became permanent in 1886. The figures for all taxation per head in 1881 were thought to be: Bengal 24.12 annas, NWP 30.84, Madras 40.85 and Bombay 56.01. Excluding land revenue they were, in the same order, 15.24, 11.24, 19.99 and 24.58. See ibid., p.372. There were also discrepancies in expenditure—military and irrigation spending greatly increasing the total, for example, in the Punjab and parts of NWP.

(famine relief and public works of a protective kind). There was a move
from support for external trade to internal socio-economic management.
More broadly, there was a move from purely military goals alongside
an acquiescence in the status quo of the society and economy, towards
social management and improvement—protective laws, social reform,
education, health, economic development. It is not suggested that these
programmes succeeded, and indeed there are many interesting questions to be answered about their relative failure. And yet they did
change what people, including the colonial rulers, expected the government to do.

There is good evidence for believing that in the earliest cases, as of
course during the twentieth century, resistance to British rule was
fueled by attempts to extend the amounts and scope of taxation. The
evolution in taxation, obviously, was merely the counterpart of the
revolution in the state's purposes and justification. It matched the
changes in the jurisdiction of government within borders, and the shift
from oligarchy towards democracy. In the case of India the greater
definition of the state and the nation, and the widening interference and
ambitions of the state, encouraged or reinforced the nationalist demand
for self-determination. It was not admitted by nationalists, but this
meant higher rather than lower taxation, with a view to the state's
mobilisation of 'national' resources; the colonial state's inability to do
this was one of the strong economic arguments against it.[91] If the
nation's management was the job of the state, it was said, it would be
done better by those who (supposedly) represented all the people. It
was sometimes uncertain whether the problem was one of colonialism
or merely an imperfection of Indian government generally; but British
rule came to be blamed for many failures and omissions. Such political
repercussions added to ideological ones, to make state expansion highly
controversial throughout the nineteenth century. The great rent law
debate, as will be shown, was a crucial working-out of this controversy.

## V

We began this discussion by noting that any will to improve India
needed to be matched by administrative capacity. It was evident that
capacity did indeed increase, a conclusion which will assume importance again when we consider the impact of the 1885 Tenancy Act
through survey, settlement and written records (as was clearly appre-

[91] It was made, for example, by H.N. Brailsford, *Subject India* (London
1943).

ciated even by the illiterate). It will be shown that, whereas land rights had once been lost for want of documentary proof, in resumption proceedings, later they were claimed and furthered, for some sections of the population having access and awareness, through copies of property registers or of formal leases. Many other, related aspects of this growing capacity of the state, and the use of its institutions by Indians, could also be adduced—most noticeably, perhaps, the large extensions of the court system and the huge aggregation of lawyers and legal disputes, focusing at this period upon rural property.

The process was not just mechanical. The expansion of the capacity of the state, as said at the outset, was in part also an expression of its will. Thus far the argument has related the expansion of the state to understandings of border and category, and ideas of possession and use. We have then asked how far the colonial state had the capacity to give effect to its impulses, and concluded that it had no great capacity, especially before the 1830s; to express this positively, it gradually became better able to intervene. Together these two sets of arguments start to explain the growth of the state in India. A major purpose of greater taxation, even in British times, was to enable the government to increase its activity, and the second means to this end was the reform of the bureaucracy. The different goals and procedures which undoubtedly *were* introduced, despite operational weakness, were important in themselves, and by no means shallow in their actual or potential impact. The colonial state had established itself by and for taxation but also for trade, and, as it largely ceased to be a trader itself, in order to promote the trade of others by general 'improvements'.

Latterly there came an erosion of confidence. India was after all unknowable. Its problems were all inter-related. There were renewed fears of social upheaval, which were often quite specific in the policies which they influenced, as, for example, when the uprisings of 1857 were traced to Christian missionaries' attempts at conversion or to government attacks on a existing rural order, or when property and contract law was held to promote indebtedness and the alienation of land. After more than a hundred years, British rule had to be regarded (by officials as well as economic nationalists) as part of the problem. Yet, though preventive and ameliorative measures were tried, in effect the past could not be reversed (as in the case of zamindari rights), and the core of colonial rule, including revenue policy and trade, could not be repudiated. The rhetoric, rationale and self-interest of British government demanded that they could not. Hence remedies took the form of renewed interference; they confirmed the direction and nature of the expansion of the state.

Bureaucratic changes should be associated with practical and technical possibilities, with the development of the state and the nation, and with political philosophy. There is no question but that they occurred in India because of British rule. This is one sense in which colonialism constituted a revolution in government. How far was what happened—even in terms of that revolution—a result of Indian conditions as well? It should not be supposed that radical elements come from outside, from the West, and conservative ones or continuities from India. This would be to accept one of the major imperialist denigrations of India. Of course sometimes that kind of argument *can* be made: as with regard to the way the frontier tribes (and incidentally topology) prevented the establishment of clear state borders and forced the strategy of the thick frontier, or the transitional zone, or of buffer peoples and territory, upon the British in India. But it is quite misleading to suggest that the Indian system was incapable of change, or of forcing the kind of response from the rulers which would extend the role of the state. Indeed it can be argued that the expectations in India, though for a different kind of state, were also often for a wider range of state roles than was the norm in Britain when British rule began in India. It would be a valuable project to investigate the extent to which these expectations and more broadly the needs of ruling India, changed the character of government.

At the very least it is plain that colonial government in India was affected by the fact that it had to take account of the need to recruit servants, to woo supporters, and to meet expectations among Indians. It is easy to find occasions when this large avowedly modernising government drew back from confronting Indian norms and beliefs—over caste for example—or when the new educated breed of British civil servant, who was busily engaged in what he regarded as scientific government (or for that matter technological innovation), expressed either his inability to change India or his amazement at how well India coped without him. In short the character of the state in India was decided partly because it was 'colonial'—importing solutions but also having to make special adjustments—and partly because it was anyway so largely Indian. This is to say two things. First, the reasons for the interventions discussed in this book, consequent upon the Tenancy Act, are too complex to be reduced to, say, a colonial search for collaborators, or a desire to help produce raw materials (and consumers) for English factories. Clearly they were also not, in any simple sense, merely a sop to keep oppressed and impoverished people quiet; the British seemed rather to envisage considerable if gradual changes in the society they professed to be preserving. Second, an *effective* intervention (both in form and execution) depended upon local agencies which were, in the end, beyond the reach of an alien government. The nineteenth-century extension of government went so far as to permit colonial interference, but not so far as to allow it wholly to mobilise or re-model the countryside.

Of course some aspects of the revolution in colonial government were brought about by the need to confront problems of alienation, adaptation and incorporation, and indeed to construct a new role and justification for rule in the midst of a range of conflicting interests, and to invent for Indians a reason why they should accept—even welcome —colonial rule (as some of them did). With some exceptions, such as James Fitzjames Stephen, the British claimed to be offering efficient and equitable government and economic policy, in order to gain Indian consent to their rule. This was true of those who held that British policy had to be responsive to Indian sentiment and practice, and also of the radical reformers who believed India had to be shaken out of a agelong sleep, with no sentimentality about its institutions. It was true of pro-peasant groups who had perforce to envisage widespread change, and also, though more narrowly, of those who argued that India had to be held by force and minimal interference rather than good government— for even they had to appeal to the self-interest of important groups, as in Lytton's appeals to the landlords and princes.[92] But Indians adopted what might be called a 'pick-and-mix' approach to British law; this implies that there was a need for the British to sell their rule and institutions to the Indians. It also follows from this that, although one school of thought attributed the empire to conquest, another (and an influential constituency of opinion in Britain or, this century, internationally) wanted it to be empire by consent—on 'trust' in the phrase later adopted by the United Nations. Certainly it needed at least as much consensus as force; and consent marked its successes and its limits.

Certain consequences had flowed from the colonial centralisations, in areas of rule which in India had formerly been fragmented, dispersed or localised. State responsibilities for general well-being had been recognised to exist, but were partly distributed among local magnates and intermediaries. In this respect Indian and eighteenth-century English expectations had shared some common ground. During the nineteenth century, objective forces disrupted such local arrangements. Local hierarchies were partly detached from the state, as it created distinct, generalised and centralised public spheres. Economic, military

[92] See Stokes, *Utilitarians*, pp.281-7.

and political change reduced the importance and resources of some of the landlords, village heads and moneylenders, or changed the basis of their operations and power. Once their capital had been particularly local and located—consisting of social prestige, followers, land, systems of exchange, often reinforced by the elites' cultures and religious beliefs. In the colonial period, external records and powers became more active in guaranteeing local rights and profits, and the imperative for local legitimacy was somewhat reduced. The locally powerful were also to some extent challenged by externally-based officials, traders, and moneylenders, and by less localised systems of wealth and power. Greater profits could be garnered at longer distances. Trade could be safely conducted, credit obtained, wealth stored and consumed, and labour reproduced, more readily beyond the immediate localities. For some there arose instead dangers in being too closely drawn into particular places; and many had less incentive than before to enter into interdependent systems of mutual support. Though (as said, in the introduction) it is not altogether helpful to call this the loss of a moral economy, because of what that implies about the basis of the old regime, yet it is at least apparent that some social tasks were no longer so necessary to local power as once they had been. Inevitably, then, out of specific changes within India, the state sought to re-enter the localities in the form of bureaucracy and generalised law, and to extend its sense of responsibility and its interpretation of its own interests.

What form did the social engineering take? Here we return to the importance of definition. The idea was that settled, hierarchical systems were both efficient and moral. Interruptions of the norm were dangerous: whether from disease, or crime, or famine (which disrupted the usual expectations of climate and subsistence). Mobility was worrying as contagion was. The rootless Pindaris supposedly had no 'proper' social and political structures, and hence no morality, because they plundered and did not work.[93] We may compare the ancient or post-Revolutionary fears of the mob as formless, irrational and amoral, or of the 'undeserving' poor as disorderly, feckless and dangerous. Agriculture (more than mining or manufacture) and trade were twin founts of civilisation. Hence improvement was sought through property, and the socio-economic reformers were far from endorsing change or fluidity.

[93] See for example Capt. Geo. Sydenham, Agent to the Governor General, Berar, 'Memorandum respecting the Pindaries towards the end of the year 1814', 5 October 1814, Survey of India Memoirs, M208A, vol.55, NAI: being (Sydenham explained) 'a heterogeneous Mass', 'accustomed to continual scenes of Blood and Rapine', and extremely mobile, the Pindaris 'naturally acquire the most evil Dispositions & the most licentious propensities'.

The intention was to give settled and substantial people a definable stake in production, law and the state. We now turn to the elaboration of such ideas which led to the great debate over land law, the Bengal Tenancy Act of 1885, and changes in agrarian structure.

## Chapter Three

## *A necessary reform*

In 1885, A.P. MacDonnell likened the fate of those condemned to a 'thorough study of the rent question' in Bihar and Bengal to that once faced by a criminal who was offered a choice between instant death and a perusal of Guicciardini's history: 'The criminal weakly chose the history, but repenting of his choice, after years of torture, craved immediate execution'.[1] MacDonnell spoke feelingly at the end of long years of controversy, in which heat was not proportionate to weight. And the rent question was not only tedious but also complex. At some risk therefore, this and the following chapters will examine the main ideas thrown up in the debate. The main purpose is not to explain the politics or even to describe the decision-making, but to identify analyses of rural society which continue to have influence to this day.

It has been claimed that the British were uninterested in recording who held land so long as they were able to collect the revenue, and became interested only when problems arose which seemed likely to threaten their collections.[2] We shall see later that there was resistance in Bengal to the institution of a fully public system of land transfer and a state-controlled register of mutations. But the history of revenue administration was central to nineteenth-century constructions of knowledge about agrarian India, to the operation of law, and hence to the rationale for the Bengal Tenancy Act of 1885. In particular the identification, regulation and encouragement of the landholder, not only as revenue-payer but also as producer, was the centrepiece of British land policy.[3]

[1] Government of India Legislative Council Proceeedings, 14 February 1885, Revenue Proceedings A 8, August 1885. The remark was attributed to Macaulay; the reference presumably to Francesco Guicciardini's *Storia d'Italia*, the celebrated history of Italy in his own times, 1494-1534.

[2] Dietmar Rothermund, *Government, Landlord and Peasant. Agrarian Relations under British Rule 1865-1932* (Wiesbaden 1978), p.41 and also chapter 7 which discusses the 1885 Act.

[3] A good overview and introduction, relevant to this and the following chapters, remains Thomas R. Metcalf, *The Aftermath of Revolt. India, 1857-1870* (Princeton 1964; 2nd ed. New Delhi 1990), especially chs. 4 and 5. Specifically on the background to the 1885 Act see M. Finucane and Syed Ameer Ali, *A Commentary on the Bengal Tenancy Act (Act VIII of 1885)* (second edition, edited by J. Byrne, former Assistant Settlement Officer, Bihar; Calcutta [1911]), introduction. See also M. Finucane and B.F. Rampini, *The Bengal Tenancy Act*

The 1885 Act extended this process of definition, once again involving policy-makers directly in assessments of Indian society. In these senses it continued work which began between 1765 and 1793, when the Bengal system evolved from attempts to determine rights and obligations sufficiently for a revenue settlement to be made.

The Company's assumption of responsibility for the *diwani* in 1772, the formation of a Board of Revenue, the inquiries known as the Amini Commission, the experiments with five-year and annual settlements, and with 'farming', supervisors and collectors, all may be regarded as part of an educative process preparing for the permanent settlement under Cornwallis. The lessons were in the possible forms of a system, rather than in the data for assessment. For example, in 1769 supervisors were instructed to investigate lands and revenue, but withdrawn in 1773 when such minute investigations were forbidden. Cornwallis's settlement was supposed to accord with the laws and customs of India.[4] The theory of landholding had by this time been much discussed, notably by Philip Francis in the 1770s. However, though Cornwallis was instructed in the Act of 1784 (24 Geo.III, cap.25) to institute further inquiry into land rights, and though the decennial settlements of 1789 and 1790 were expected to reflect and facilitate this process, the Court of Directors required the settlement to be made with landholders, and for any other rights merely to be maintained. The practice of the Bengal settlements was pragmatic. Landholders were found, in some cases by coercion. Only then, from their various roles, was there constructed a single legal form, a property right. It was conditional upon the payment of revenue at rates made permanent by the decision of 1793. This settlement applied to all land, other than some of that accruing to the state after 1793, and any still deemed to be exempt from revenue-payment after a new scrutiny of such entitlements (promised in the proclamation of 1793). As described elsewhere, much formally *lakhiraj* (revenue-free) land was gradually resumed on to the revenue rolls, and mostly within the terms of the permanent settlement. A centralisation of legal authority took place, focused both upon the regulations of the Com-

---

being *Act VIII of 1885* (Calcutta 1886). The *Commentary* also draws heavily for its introduction on a minute of MacDonnell, 20 September 1893 (in fact written by Finucane), and on works by Baden-Powell, Field and others noticed elsewhere in this chapter.

[4] See Finucane and Ali, *Commentary*. An illustration of the vagaries of the settlement (and of subsequent development) is C.D. Field's observation, in *A Digest of the Law of Landlord and Tenant in the Provinces subject to the Lieutenant-Governor of Bengal* (Calcutta 1879), that the ratio of rent to revenue varied between 2:1 and (on one Bhagalpur estate) 378:1.

pany, and in the person of recognised land-owners and revenue-payers, the zamindars. The initial destruction of local revenue and accounting offices and officers (patwari and kanungo) probably played a part in these concentrations of power.

The boundaries of estates, as of zamindari rights, were assessed rather than established in 1793. But thereafter the state proceeded to define borders more precisely. Though formal registers were not successfully introduced, other than in the revenue records, administration of various kinds (the sales, partition and resumption surveys and proceedings) did tend towards the measurement and definition of estates. Reflecting this development, it was eventually spelt out that the state owned any land which fell outside the recognised estates. This had apparently been assumed to be the case, since an original right of state ownership was often referred to in justification of the revenue demand; but it was not provided explicitly until Regulation III of 1828. By that time, therefore, all land had come to be subsumed (theoretically) under British law, either as public land or as private land governed by a permanent or temporary settlement. Private land was, in turn, defined according to the rights held over it. The most important distinction, taken up in 1885, was between zamindari private or home-farm land (*khamar*, *sir* or *zerat*) and raiyati land, that held by tenancies and on which occupancy rights could accrue.

The next standardisation and extension of power came through the definition of subordinate rights. These were slower in falling under comprehensive state purview, but they too were set out progressively in many regulations. Large numbers of different tenures were identified. The revenue-collecting right, or *malikana*, was also distinguished from other incidents of land-owning; and in some cases where persons were not or no longer recognised as zamindars or owners, residuary payments continued to be made to them and came, under Company law, to be regarded as a form of property. In 1885 the term 'tenure' was reserved for intermediary and quasi-proprietary holdings. Many of these had also been recognised in earlier regulations. The most important were the taluqdars. The origins of the term are obscure and its meanings various; it figured in the regulations of 1793. Taluqdars, as persons entitled to hold land, became in effect subordinate but quasi-independent landowners: their number included village headmen and holders of army jagirs (land-grants to pensioners and invalids). Some service tenures were also recognised. Other 'dependent' tenures were clearly not in any sense proprietary under the British law; the bulk of them derived from indirect management of estates. Mortgages, local agents and managers would be paid for, by zamindars, through the grant of such tenures. However some of the more permanent forms of such managing leases (*patni*) were recognised and protected by Regulation VIII of 1819; *patnidars* were larger leaseholders, intermediary between landlords and tenants, who were able to establish title predating the permanent settlement.[5]

The legal rights of subordinate landholders—that is, tenants—also evolved, and indeed the main development of the law was towards an ever-greater precision first in the kinds of title and then in their incidents and character. It became apparent, as also in the massive papers in the 1870s and 1880s, that there had been no clarity on these landrights in the 1790s. The Regulations of that date did not pay very particular attention to the situation of those they were making 'tenants'. It was noted that raiyats were already in possession of land; but the recognition was limited by a certain understanding of proprietorship. Cornwallis believed he was *creating* the landlords, and that henceforth they would more certainly possess their proper character and entitlements. Thus the landlord could make leases by contract, as he pleased, except in a few instances where other property rights intervened. The zamindar was being re-made, and the Regulations remarked, in passing, that there were some existing agreements which would need to be incorporated into the new legal regime. To confuse matters further, a few assumptions from British law, such as the presumption that property rights accrued after twelve years of occupancy, were added into the mixture at the same time.[6]

Much ambiguity thus surrounded tenants' holdings. However they were generally divided, according to colonial revenue officials, into

[5] See Sirajul Islam, *Bengal Land Tenure: the Origin and Growth of Intermediate Interests in the 19th Century* (CASP 13; Rotterdam 1985), which relates the growth of intermediate tenures not only to the land law but also to land reclamation and agricultural extension from about 1820 to 1880. For a valuable discussion of taluqdars and *patnidars*, see H.J.S. Cotton. 'Memorandun on land tenures in Bengal', prepared at Ilbert's request for the Select Committee on the Tenancy Bill, 31 January 1884, with Cotton to Primrose (PSV), 29 February 1884, Add.Mss.43584. Cotton regarded the registration of 1,221,417 *darpatnidars* (sub-tenure-holders) as a mark of relative prosperity, especially in Jessore, Bakarganj and Chittagong, and of the 'wide desemination of a permanent interest in landed property'.

[6] There were Sadr court judgments often cited: SDD 1846, p.358, and SDD 1849, p.413. See Keshub Chandra Acharya, 'Strike but hear: a treatise on the rent question in Bengal' (Bhowanipore, 1884). The debate in the courts was whether the twelve-year rule applied only to occupancy or to rents as well; it was settled as occupancy alone in 1856 and confirmed in the 1859 Act.

*khudkashta* (supposedly having residential status in the same village as
the holding) and *pahikashta* (supposedly belonging to a different village). In some senses the *khudkashta* raiyat is the precursor of the occupancy tenant of the 1885 Act. Many of the other terms for tenants also
persisted under the Company's law, and from time to time gained
formal definition. More generally, the incidents of tenancy came to
depend, in law, upon a series of rules. Of the more important examples,
the first was an entitlement to receive a formal lease or *patta*. The
second was a liability to pay rents on penalty of the distraint of
property, including standing crops and, in most cases, the means of
production; absconding raiyats were liable to arrest. This was the
infamous *haftam*, Regulation VII of 1799 (*qanun haftam*, the seventh
regulation).

Gradually the number and range of regulations multiplied. In the
early nineteenth century, amidst growing opposition to the zamindari
settlement from officials in other parts of the Company's Indian territories, attention came to be given to providing some protection for
tenants, particularly when estates were sold. But the general view of
this period was that the position of the tenants had been sacrificed to
the desire to protect the land revenue (enforced by sales for arrears) and
otherwise to please the landlords, especially by increasing the value of
land. H.T. Colebrooke's Regulation V of 1812 (*qanun panjam*) removed existing restrictions on the form and length of leases, modified the
law of distraint, and set out rules for enhancement. Ten years later,
Regulation XI of 1822 sought to protect certain anterior rights and
tenancies and existing rates of rent from the effect of land transfer,
while otherwise ensuring an unencumbered title to the purchaser. It was
later regarded as having put landlords in a position of 'abnormal superiority' over their tenants. But when it was repealed by Act XII of 1841
this arguably weakened the slight protection offered to tenants. The
new law still gave unencumbered title to land-purchasers, with liberty
to raise rents and eject tenants, except that it reserved the position of
certain named categories of tenants (*kadimi,* or *khudkashta*) holding at
fixed rents, of other fixed-rate tenures dating from before 1781, and of
registered tenancies at fair rents for specified areas and less than 20
years.[7] The purpose of all this was to push up land prices and to encourage purchasers, so as to help guarantee the revenue through the Sales

---

[7] These provisions were repeated in Act I of 1845, and again in Act XI of
1859, which ruled out ejectment for occupancy raiyats and restricted enhancement, amplifying the terms of Act X of 1859. See Finucane and Ali, *Commentary*, introduction.

Laws, a motive strengthened by the Company's war debts after Welles-ley. Later C.D. Field regarded these laws as meaning that land-sales disturbed all that tenants had thought stable, though his colleague J. O'Kinealy thought few raiyats had actually been affected, at least at revenue sales. The laws cannot themselves have been the sole instru-ments of change, but they appeared to coincide with marked increases in rates of rent for the majority of tenants, especially after 1822. Some official disquiet was expressed at the conditions of the cultivators in Bengal, and what was regarded as the growing enmity and litigiousness between classes in the countryside.

However it was primarily a desire for Benthamite consolidation which prompted the first of Bengal's major tenancy acts, Act X of 1859. Introducing the Bill, G. Currie said it would 're-enact in a concise and distinct form the provisions of the present law'; later C.P. Ilbert thought its most controversial sections had been introduced as an 'afterthought' and 'on a misconception of existing facts'.[8] It provided for the deposit of rent with the authorities in case of disputes, for the survey and measurement of land, for fixed rents and occupancy rights of tenants in some circumstances, and for rent enhancement on parti-cular grounds, restricted so as to give effect to the right of occupancy. Jurisdiction was transferred to revenue officers (acting as courts). Almost unnoticed at the time, the Act sought to define different types of land and of rights, for landowners and, especially, classes of tenants. Fixed-rate tenants had to have held at the same rents since 1793 and occupancy tenants to have held their land continuously for twelve years.[9] Thus, though there was overlap in actual cases and in terms of definitions, Act X was a modern Act in that it attributed rights to historical actions (available to all who qualified; open to proof in court of law), rather than to status, either granted or inherited. The right derived from the provisions of the legislation, as interpreted, and from the evidential record; and was not something inherent to a claimed social category, nor for that matter (in *theory*) dependent upon particu-lar balances of power. Act X was unlike *haftam* and *panjam*, and the various modifications of the Sales Law. It was trying to be compre-hensive and definitive, where they had merely presumed to clarify the position of existing rights and relations of classes of landholders under

[8] Finucane and Ali, *Commentary*, introduction. See also 'Note on the rights and status of the cultivating classes by Mr. Mackenzie', 6 January 1880, *Report of the Rent Law Commission* (2 vols; Calcutta 1880) [hereafter *RLC Report*], appendices.
[9] O'Kinealy's argument was that this was derived from an NWP order and not much discussed in Council; Finucane and Ali, *Commentary*, introduction.

certain new provisions of law.

The earlier measures had been held to have various deleterious effects, on landlords or tenants according to point of view. As said, they had probably helped a general rise in rents, though the details of this are obscure. Act X was bound to produce a far wider range of reactions. Soon landlords were complaining that it had made their position impossible, and supporters of the raiyats were arguing that it had reduced all of them, in effect, to the level of tenants-at-will. The difficulties derived from the new basis for claiming and contesting rights. Occupancy raiyats were now held to be as defined in the Act; this generalised a number of earlier privileges but based the occupancy right specifically on twelve-years' occupancy. It followed that anyone who did not fit this criterion was not an occupancy tenant. Much the same could be said for rents. The Act provided that rents were to be presumed fair, with a burden of proof to the contrary upon the landlord. But to provide such proof it was necessary to show only that higher rates were generally being paid by others of comparable status on adjacent, similar land. Another way of raising rents was to demonstrate that the tenant was actually holding more land than he was paying for. Another ground for enhancement was any increase in the holding's productivity (effectively in the value of output) which was not attributable to the efforts of the tenant.

In face of these regulations, landlords claimed that it was no longer possible to raise their rents; some of the technical rules of enhancement were found unworkable, and, despite attention in the two most famous rent cases of the 1860s, the provision relating to the increased productivity of the land was hardly used. Supporters of the tenants demonstrated that all the means of enhancement were open to abuse. It was doubtful that the rules limited rent increases for occupancy raiyats, but, even if they did, they then provided a strong incentive for the landlords to avoid the accrual of occupancy rights. The twelve-year rule allowed what a known (named) status did not, namely the manipulation of tenants as individuals so as to deny them rights.[10] Favourite devices, especially in Bihar, were moving them from one set of plots to another, or falsifying the zamindari records, so as to avoid providing proof of a sufficient period of continuous occupancy.

[10] This development parallels many; for example in Company treaties ceded territories were identified by name, and only subsequently would exact measured boundaries be established. See also the Bengal Administration Report for 1892-3, pp.92-3, which described the Act as having 'rather added to the difficulty than removed it' (in Finucane and Ali, *Commentary*, introduction).

II

By the 1870s these problems were being considered by government in a changing intellectual and political climate. The state was now attempting to penetrate and co-opt large sections of the population—which is also another way of interpreting the Bengal Tenancy Act of 1885. And at the same time as it involved more collaborators, the state's functions were increasingly specialised, and it felt the need to achieve measurable benefits, to change Indian behaviour, and to shape awareness in 'correct' ways. For example, merely because public health had been added to the list of state responsibilities, the administration was not suddenly competent and adequately-staffed to manage the health of the population. But it did become concerned about the provision and regulation of doctors, or the promulgation of appropriate medical knowledge; and these developments made the desired circles of involvement ever wider. When there was a cholera outbreak in Darbhanga gaol in 1896, volunteers were inoculated with a patent antidote, and a convict overseer was given a reward, contrary to standing orders, for helping with the work.[11] The case showed an aspect of the extension of the public sphere. It also played to the stereotype of the West as scientific, knowledgeable, and fostering modernisation and improvement in India.

Between 1880 and 1920, administrative reforms at the local level became a focus of attention, with attempts to improve reporting, policing, local courts, revenue administration, and to raise local taxes, as part of a powerful drive to locate British power and government more firmly in the countryside and with the involvement of rural people. Public health, as it happens, was an important part of this impulse. Politically, the bodies which were set up attempted to formalise some of the consultation which had long been sought with people regarded as having high status and influence. These efforts built on the Local Self-Government Act of 1885, and on earlier attempts to refine the machinery of very local administration. The need was to associate Indians in the new arenas of government, just as it had been in the initially favourable response of some of the British to the formation of the Indian National Congress, or in the attempts to widen the fiscal base by extending local taxation from the 1870s. Contributing also were conservative 'pro-peasant' policies evident in the Bengal Tenancy Act of 1885 and its counterpart in Awadh, and also in the Deccan Agriculturists Act of 1879, the Famine Commission reports of 1880 and

[11] H Jails B 75 (December 1896).

1901, and the Punjab Alienation of Land Act of 1900. Consolidations of these efforts included the Decentralisation Commission of 1909, the Public Services Commission of 1912, and the Montagu-Chelmsford report of 1918. Above all, the structures were intended to do what, in the 1880s, was generally agreed to be difficult, namely to interest Indians in matters of local public policy—famine relief, roads and education, for example. This need for allies was crucial to the shortcomings as well as to the advance of the colonial system.

If the enterprise was to create public space, then its borderlines on one view may delimit the change, while from another perspective they are margins at which its influence was spreading. The structures of the British state were enmeshed in the countryside and in local life. One possible conclusion is that the structures therefore were 'shaped' by Indian society at these moments of contact.[12] The mirror image of that argument is that the contacts marked points of entry for new concepts and practices of the state. Of course both these propositions may be true. The British extended the net of institutions somewhat against their own inclinations and assumptions. We find that they were more often reluctant than eager to widen the scope of the state, but that it grew nonetheless, under pressure from perceived need and also perhaps from Indian demands. The government attempted to reach out into the country at large by institutionalising some of the collaboration and local agency it commanded.

If the 1885 Tenancy Act sought to improve the position of settled tenants, we may conclude that it gave effect to an impulse that had not been necessary or feasible in any earlier period. The Tenancy Act of 1859, which had had similar elements, was widely held to have been either ineffective or counterproductive. The 1885 Act was launched when certain rural rights seemed to be threatened by British courts and administrators, and by socio-economic and demographic developments. Probably agrarian conditions had long been oppressive for large sections of the population—as in much of Bihar—and were in no sense simply a product of British laws. But by the 1870s and 1880s legal changes did seem slowly to be having practical impact, as in the land market.[13]

Circumstances were right for intervention not only from developments of the state, but also, it seems, in response to Indian conditions or demands. Certain rules were applied by the officials. They would not

---

[12] D. A. Washbrook, *The Emergence of Provincial Politics. The Madras Presidency, 1870-1920* (Cambridge 1976), p.45ff.

[13] See Jacques Pouchepadass's essay in Robb, *Rural India.*

support, say, religious endowments; they would not provide gratuitous relief in famines so as to interrupt trade; they would not permit dues to be collected in restraint of trade; and so on. The list is endless. But just as long is the story of exceptions to the rules in practice—and of Indian pressure on the rulers to break their own guidelines. Increasingly the breaches extended rather than reduced state involvement. Every market was permitted in practice to impose its own taxes and tariffs, and local officials also found ways of supporting new markets, just as they gave funds surreptitiously to religious endowments when it was politically expedient to do so. In famine relief, they provided money aid, forbad hoarding, and even imported grain (at least in the early nineteenth century) on occasions when such action was asked for by Indians who defined it as a normal function of the ruler: only later did the higher authorities enforce their doctrine of not interfering with merchants, or being neutral in religion, or forbidding local tariffs and taxes.[14] And in many of these instances—and notably on famine in the late nineteenth-century codes—policy gradually shifted nearer what might be called the original Indian expectation. The fixed distinction between what the state would do and what it would not proved to be moveable. Perhaps this helps explain why, for example, free trade and laissez faire were *espoused* more thoroughly than they were *applied* in India,[15] and why state intervention spread almost inadvertently from agricultural improvement to economic and social engineering—over land tenure, credit, regional economic planning—and on to price controls and eventually the mixed economy as devised by Nehru.[16] Even in the

[14] For instances of intervention with markets and endowments, see Robb, *Evolution*, pp.126-8 and 166-9; more generally for interference with religion see chs.4 and 9. On famine, see Sanjay Sharma, 'The 1837-38 famine in U.P.: some dimensions of popular action', *IESHR* 30, 3 (1993), pp.339-42. This is relevant also to the humanitarian as well as political and economic motives for intervention. Sharma's subsequent and so far unpublished work on yet earlier famines reveals debates among Company officials, under pressure from Indians, about the proper limits of state intervention.

[15] This was argued in a well-known but unpublished thesis by T.D. Rider, 'The Tariff Policy of the Government of India and its Development Strategy, 1894-1924' (PhD; Minnesota 1971). See also (and it is relevant more generally to this discussion) Clive Dewey, 'The end of the imperialism of free trade' in Dewey and A.G. Hopkins, *The Imperial Impact. Studies in the Economic History of Africa and India* (London 1978). For an account of a shift of attitudes at the other end of the century, from 1800 to 1820 when acceptance of laissez faire replaced conservatism with a willingness to innovate, see Neil Rabitoy, 'The control of fate and fortune: the origins of the market mentality in British administrative thought in South Asia', *MAS* 25, 4 (1991), pp.737-64.

[16] See P. Robb, 'Bihar, the colonial state and agricultural development in

colonial period, much of this might be shown to have been prompted by Indian demands—petitions, protests, campaigns—at all levels of society, from princes anxious to protect their privileges to beggars lobbying local officers for relief in times of scarcity.

A parallel argument can be made on the basis of more negative consequences of colonial rule. There were many instances of crises during British rule in India, some of them certainly attributed to the changes ushered in by the British. Collectively these too may be regarded as creating a pressure which forced different responses on government. Not only did Indian nationalists castigate British trading, investment and fiscal policies in India, but the influential officials of the Famine Commission of 1880 added pressure in much the same direction. They reported just as the Bengal Tenancy Act was being formulated, and helped focus the attention of the reformers particularly upon Bihar. But there was nothing new in such influence. Edmund Burke had made a connection between the avowedly exploitative character of early Company rule in Bengal and the great famine of 1769-70: he used the example to propose a doctrine of state responsibility, as indeed had Henry Verelst, from a perspective within India, as Governor of Bengal in the 1760s, when he urged the Company to take a long-term view.[17] Another great Company man, Charles Grant, saw the positive mission in evangelical terms, but also sought to expand Indian trade as a basis for justifying British rule and extending the means for ensuring improvements.[18] Early nineteenth-century experiments with cotton or tea, say, were interventions necessitated equally by Company dividends and Indian problems as perceived by Englishmen. The very diagnoses of India's failure commonly drew government into extending its role.

How much more potent then were experiences of the kind drawn upon by Burke: the commitment to public works which can perhaps be traced from Lord Auckland's confrontation with famine in the 1830s,[19] or the yet stronger interventions of the later famine codes which can be

India, 1880-1920', *IESHR* 25, 2 (1988), and Pramit Chaudhuri, 'The origins of modern India's economic development strategy' in M. Shepperdson and C. Simmons, eds, *The Indian National Congress and the Political Economy of India 1885-1985* (Aldershot 1988).

[17] Cf. P.J. Marshall, ed., *Problems of Empire: Britain and India 1757- 1813* (London 1968), pp.52-77 and 145-84, and H.V. Bowen, *Revenue and Reform. The Indian Problem in British Politics 1757-1773* (Cambridge 1991), pp.112-13 and *passim.*

[18] Ainslie Embree, *Charles Grant and British Rule in India* (London 1962) pp.88-113, 172-7 and 266-71.

[19] See Sharma, 'Famine', p.339.

attributed, in part, to the equally harrowing experiences of Antony MacDonnell when investigating conditions in Bihar. Famine policy, even in the 1870s, included notable qualifications of laissez faire. In 1873/4, a fairly interventionist local government in Bengal under Campbell wanted *inter alia* to prohibit grain exports, while the Government of India espoused the 'utmost freedom of trade as the best preservation against famine', and warned against artificial reductions of prices or any shaking of the confidence of the mercantile classes. Faced with this conflict, the Secretary of State for India (Argyll) expressed the belief that 'the operations of commerce and the ordinary processes of supply and demand could not be relied on', and that 'active intervention of Government was necessary'. Though the 'powerful agency' of commercial enterprise was not to be thwarted, yet, also, 'excessive reliance was not to be placed' upon it 'for the introduction of food, and still less for its transit to and distribution in stricken districts'.

This made it less than clear what the 'powerful agency' was good for. The Government of India too, though professedly opposed to intervention, was advocating vigorous public works, agricultural loans, advances for grain imports, special measures on the railways, relief committees, increased medical provision, and the encouragement of emigration. And, significantly for the argument of this chapter, in 1869 the NWP government had made it a formal duty of district officers to prevent deaths from starvation, even when private charity proved inadequate.[20] The importance of such a resolution lay not only in the aspiration, but in its status as a task imposed by regulation, in an administration governed by rules. The distinction is important, because it helped lay to rest the non-regulation system of government favoured by Dalhousie and most obviously associated with the Punjab system devised under John Lawrence. Here was a socially-conservative scheme of governance (to be discussed in more detail later) which saw the peasant as the engine of progress, under a personalised rule that was cheaper and supposedly more appropriate than one hemmed in by regulation (though of course there *were* very definite structures and rules in the Punjab system). It began the great interventions of the state, paradoxically, in terms of facilitating peasant agriculture, by irrigation and railway-building. But it had always been on a collision course with the parallel, Utilitarian enterprise to reform Indian government, law and society. What decided the outcome of this conflict was the growing size of the bureaucracy, the complexity of India, and the seriousness of the

---

[20] See abstract of correspondence between Government of India and Secretary of State, on the drought in Bengal, 1873/4, L/E/5/69, IOL.

problems which were increasingly confronted. The pro-peasant measures of the later nineteenth century had be legislative and regulatory in
form.

Clive Dewey has suggested that the 'paramount desire of sucessive
Secretaries of State' was 'to maintain the solidarity of the empire'
(meaning to ensure that the English people continued to value the connection with India), and that it was the first non-co-operation movement of 1920 which 'made "the happiness of Indian leaders" the great
knockdown argument in official circles'.[21] In a broader sense, however,
and looking beyond Secretaries of State (whose views were often
contested by British officials in India), it seems that Indian happiness
was a consideration far earlier, if only for the reason that Adam Smith
had suggested, that '...the revenue of the sovereign is drawn from that
of the people. The greater the revenue of the people, therefore, ...the
more they can afford to the sovereign. It is his interest, therefore, to
increase as much as possible that annual produce.' Smith argued,
against the East India Company's monopoly, that to do this required
'the most perfect freedom of commerce'.[22] But the converse of his
proposition was also true: that the sovereign was bound to intervene
when the people's income was being reduced. In such a case, most
sharply felt during a famine, which also increased state expenditure,
governments were obliged to interfere even with commerce. And what
is more, the records do not sustain the suggestion that the motivation
was purely economic, however much the balance sheet may have
mattered in the end. The fervour of, say, a Nicholson for co-operative
credit related both to intellectual conviction *à la* Raffeissen and also to
his surveying of conditions in agrarian Madras.[23] Concern about de-
forestation, and hence interventionist forest policies, grew first because
of arguments about the impact of vegetation on rainfall, and because of
actual experiences of drought.[24] The great device of nineteenth-century
policy-making was after all the inquiry, which produced 'expertise'

---

[21] Dewey, 'Imperialism of free trade', pp.63-7.

[22] Adam Smith, *Wealth of Nations*, ch.7, pt.3.

[23] Nicholson was appointed by the Government of India in 1892 to look into
the possibility of agricultural banks by surveying conditions in Madras; he reported in 1896. Duperneix was similarly deputed in NWP and reported in 1900.
See R&A Rev B 14 (June 1896), and Robb, 'Bihar', pp.210-16.

[24] See Surgeon-General Edward Balfour, 'The influence exercised by trees
on the climate and productiveness of the peninsular of India' (a matter first
raised by the Court of Directors of the Company in 1847); the conclusion was
that exposing soil to the sun did make droughts and floods more prevalent;
L/E/5/69, IOL.

and, very often, grand interconnected schemes of reform. Thus the great Settlement Reports and Famine Commissions reviewed land revenue, agriculture, irrigation, trade, prices, communications and information systems. Typical on famine was F.C. Danvers who drew on theories of political economy and the history of Britain, as well as experience of India, to argue that India needed not only capital investment in land but greater wealth which could 'only be introduced by the development of industrial enterprise and manufactures'.[25] Similarly, in order to meet the government's 'duty' (Ripon's word) to guard against famine, one strategy favoured by a railway enthusiast, pointing to the possible disadvantages of irrigation, envisaged improvements in transportation as the best means of 'storing' food: proceeds from the export of agricultural and non-agricultural goods would 'free the masses from their bondage to the local food production'.[26]

The implied agenda for the state stretched well beyond agrarian structure—further than many influential officials would countenance—but land law had to meet the same priorities. Attention to agriculture remained the key, even for those who would go no further than set up structures by law and communications. Mayo had suggested creating agricultural departments in 1869, taking up a suggestion by Colonel Dickens in 1867 after the Bihar and Orissa famine, and following the model of European governments. Early agricultural departments had mixed fortunes: there was opposition to them on grounds of expense, and on arguments about double government—against removing so vital a subject from the concern of district officers. But by the 1880s it was being generally agreed that nothing short of revived and separate departments would suffice to instigate agricultural reforms, 'rather to improve production than to avert famine or administer its relief'.[27] Direct attention and specialist expertise were now seen to be required; we shall return to this issue later.

We have remarked that some of the concerns clearly related to the impact of colonial rule and trade upon India. We might add the example of the economic dependence of North Bihar on indigo and opium, a situation directly attributable to British rule, which forced the government to try to assist the region in the early twentieth century—a

[25] F.C. Danvers, 'A century of famines', 27 December 1877, L/E/5/69, IOL. The case for industrialisation was heard more commonly later in the century.

[26] Note by Col. A. Fraser, 17 May 1881, keep-with to Public Works Department proceedings on railway construction, Add.Mss.43575.

[27] Notes by C.L. Tupper, 9 September (2 notes), C. Grant, 1 October, C.U. Aitchison, 2 October, F.P. Hutchins, 30 October, and J. Strachey, 22 November 1880, and others, Add.Mss.43575, pp.499-530.

policy that gave bureaucratic strength to the cause of the state's agricultural experts, already established in a specialist branch of government from the 1870s, and also led directly to the formation of India's
leading institute of agricultural science and technology.[28] But it does
not matter to this argument whether colonial policy directly created the
crises of the Indian economy, or whether they were problems exacerbated by the transitions and distortions inadvertently introduced under
British rule. The fact that India was changing and that challenges were
being thrown up, in itself obliged the government to try to do more,
either to facilitate 'progress', or to mitigate the worst of the problems
which arose—and this is true not only of famine but of social change,
urbanisation, the growth of trade, endemic disease, population growth,
religious upheaval, transport, and so on. In turn this state involvement
generated further demands from Indians that the state should intervene,
and also of course, as nationalist thinking developed, led to strong complaints that India's difficulties were actually caused by the failures of
the state. Similar debates today indicate that the Indian revolution in
government continues.

### III

The Bengal government began to consider amending Act X under
pressure from landlords. But the judgment of the Chief Justice, Barnes
Peacock, in *Hills* v. *Ishore Ghose*, a famous case in 1862, was that the
Act did not prevent enhancement up to the full market rate, which
meant in effect that (as Peacock believed) all tenancies were held by
virtue of a contract with the land-owner, whose ownership was
unfettered.[29] Though Peacock himself suggested amendment of the law
in 1863, his judgment delayed the introduction of a new law, especially
as it had been in favour of an indigo planter; relations between planters
and raiyats were already suspect. The government waited for further
legal judgments. One came when Peacock's ruling was reversed by a
full bench of fifteen judges in the Great Rent Case of 1865, *Thakurani
Dasi* v. *Bisheshur Mukherji*.[30] But this provided no answer to the problems of rent enhancement. It merely reaffirmed that enhancements
should be proportionate to the value of production, as was provided in
the Act, and already proven to be useless either to curb or to faciliate
increases in rents.

On the basis of his experience in the North-Western Provinces,

---

[28] See Robb, 'Bihar'. The example will be discussed in volume two.
[29] W.R. Special Number 1862-4, 156.
[30] BLR, supp. vol. (FB) 202; BLR, FB 326; 3 WR Act X, 29.

William Muir wrote in 1865 that everywhere in India there was 'a right of hereditary occupancy at the customary rates', but that it needed protection where there was also a proprietary interest.[31] As this became entrenched as the official orthodoxy, agrarian disturbances, especially in Pabna, and famine reports of terrible conditions, especially in Bihar, shifted the weight of opinion in Bengal. The government began to accept the need for a measure which would give some protection to tenants, by removing the loop-holes and ambiguities of Act X, and making a comprehensive provision for agrarian relations. The work was started by George Campbell when he became Lieutenant-Governor. He had a reputation as a reformer, and had written on the Irish land question. But his main contribution was the levying of new local cesses upon all holders of land. Some claimed that this violated the permanent settlement, but payment was due from tenants and landlords alike. The amounts payable were to be calculated from zamindari rent-rolls, which thus became, for this purpose, public documents. The new taxes added to zamindar's complaints, and to the numbers who argued for state intervention through a new rent Bill to regulate the exactions landlords were making upon their tenants.

A Bill was drafted in 1876 by Campbell's successor, Richard Temple, to make a definitive statement of agrarian rights as an answer to peasant protests, but, after various further inquiries, Ashley Eden (who took over in 1877) abandoned Temple's Bill, except for undisputed clauses restricted to facilitating the collection of rent arrears, passed as an Act in 1878. Instead Eden appointed the Rent Law Commission, which started work in 1879 and reported in 1880. Though given the limited task of amending Act X of 1859 to improve the procedures in regard to rent, this Commission was designed from the first to lead to broad reforms and as a device of public education rather than official enlightenment; its report was always intended for publication.[32] Meanwhile a Bihar Rent Committee, of officials, zamindars and planters, had

[31] Quoted by Rivers Thomson, 7 April 1882, Add.Mss.43584.
[32] Government of Bengal (Mackenzie) to G/I (R&A), 3 April 1879, in *RLC Report*, vol. 2. The members of the commission were H.L. Dampier (president; member of the Board of Revenue), H.L. Harrison (initially; Secretary to the Board of Revenue), C.D. Field (judge of Burdwan, on special duty to draft the bill), A. Mackenzie (Secretary to the Bengal Government), J. O'Kinealy (Legal Remembrancer), Brojendra Kumar Seal (Subordinate Judge, 24-Parganas), and a little later Mohini Mohun Roy and Peary Mohun Mookerjea, representing the zamindari view. See ibid., p.3. See also Bengal Supplementary Administration Report 1882-7 (Rivers Thompson), pp.94-9; also extensively quoted by Finucane and Ali, *Commentary*, introduction. See also Finucane and Rampini, *Tenancy Act*, introduction.

also called for a recasting of the law to prevent abuses.[33] The Rent Law Commission included a draft Bill, which then formed the basis of further discussions. In the Government of India, C.L. Tupper was set the task of summarising the background. C.U. Aitchison considered the proposed Bill raised all-India questions and was 'perfectly revolutionary and such that no Legislative Council...will pass'; A R. Thompson, then with the central government, also thought parts 'extreme', that raiyats could be protected by less radical means, and that opposition in Britain and 'almost every part of Bengal' would delay enactment. E.C. Buck, however, thought Tupper had demonstrated 'the necessity of a thorough reform', and Eden was determined to press on, not believing the Bill as unpopular, even among zamindars, as Thompson feared.[34]

Modifications and refinements were made after consultation in India and Britain. On the Secretary of State's Council, 'Much fear was expressed that... [Ripon's] Government would introduce the "three Fs" throughout India'.[35] Rivers Thompson, who succeeded Eden, was not only opposed to aspects of the revised Bill but also less effective in securing agreed proposals.[36] He was bypassed, and in March 1883

---

[33] The members were F.M. Halliday (Patna Commissioner), J.F. Browne (judge of Patna), C.F. Worsley (Muzaffarpur Collector), G.J. Hodgkinson (Saran Collector), G. Toynbee (Patna Collector), W.B. Hudson (Champaran indigo planter), D.N. Reid (Saran indigo planter), G. Anderson, (Darbhanga indigo planter), Bemola Churn Bhuttacharjeea (Gaya Deputy-Collector), Bhoop Sen Singh (Government pleader, Gaya), Joy Prakash Lall (manager, Dumraon raj, Shahabad), Harbuns Sahai (pleader, Arrah), and M. Finucane, secretary. See 'Report of the Behar Rent Committee', *RLC Report*, vol. 2 (hereafter BRC Report). The Committee met to discuss various submissions, proposals from the Bengal government, and rival draft bills, specially for Bihar, prepared by Finucane and Worsley, the latter following the 'more scientific and lucid arrangement' of NWP laws; the Rent Law Commission adopted the same approach. BRC Proceedings, loc.cit. (the quotation is from 9 November 1878).

[34] Notes, 10 August, 30 November 1880, 6 January and 31 October 1881, with R&A Rev A 16-46 (July 1883), in Add.Mss.43584; Eden to Ripon, 2 April [1882], Add.Mss.43592. Thompson was consistent in opposition; see his dissent from G/I despatch no.6, 21 March 1882; note, 7 April 1882, Add.Mss. 43584.

[35] Kimberley to Ripon, 21 March 1883, Add.Mss.43523. The reference was to Irish land law providing fair rents, fixity of tenure and free transfer.

[36] Eden was a 'little disappointed' that Bayley did not succeed him as Lieutenant Governor; to Ripon, 2 April [1882], Add.Mss.43592. Compare James Gibbs (from London and the Secretary of State's Council, reflecting a general view), to Ripon, 1 April 1882: 'Thompson's appointment was a matter of course as I understand it, and will be acceptable to the Baboos. I doubt his being so strong as Sir Ashley'; see also Gibbs to Ripon, 10 August 1883; Add. Mss. 43611. However Thompson's room for manœuvre was also vitiated by

Ilbert sought leave in the central legislature to introduce the Bill, now approved in almost all respects in London.[37] It was referred after two days' debate to a Select Committee, on the motion of Steuart Bayley. The Committee met between November 1883 and March 1884. Four members dissented from its report. The Government of India's conclusions were drafted in the Revenue and Agriculture Department by Bayley, a staunch supporter, subject to amendments by E.G. Patrick and T.W. Holderness. Bayley added a note at this stage to keep Ripon straight on the rights of resident raiyats.[38] A revised Bill was published and sent for comment to officials and others, including Divisional conferences. In September 1884 the Government of Bengal proposed various amendments. About this time there was concern over the fate of the Bill on Ripon's retirement, but, in November 1884, Dufferin was busy studying it so as to see it quickly through to enactment.[39] That month the Select Committee resumed, bringing its total number of meetings to 64, and accepted the main principles of the revised Bill, with some dissent. Bayley moved on the Select Committee report; after a two-day debate the government saw off a stalling demand for re-publication of the Bill. Clause-by-clause debates followed on five days between 2 and 11 March, when the Bill was passed. It became law on 14 March 1885. Most of it came into force in November.

The three main issues of contention had been the basis of the occupancy right, the transferability of raiyats' holdings, and the regulation of rents. On the first of these, the strong position was, as proposed by Eden's government, that the right should accrue to the land not the raiyat (in place of the existing twelve-year rule). In London, the Secretary of State, Kimberley, in order to sound out opinion on his Council after a long period in which the issue had 'happily slumbered', referred these rent-law proposals to a committee comprising F.B. Halliday, John Strachey, Eden, Maine and Muir, the last 'prepared to go to the stake' in opposing it. Halliday, having once been converted, also turned violently

vilification in the Indian 'native' press; the first meetings on the rent Bill occurred on 21 November 1883 in the midst of the Ilbert Bill controversy; S.C. Bayley to Primrose (PSV), 25 and 26 June, and to Ripon, 28 June and 20 November [1883], Add.Mss.43612.

[37] Kimberley to Ripon, 13 July 1883, Add.Mss.43523. In India a penultimate text was approved by the Viceroy, Bayley and Ilbert, and sent on to Bengal for comment, but not referred back to the Revenue and Agriculture Department in the usual way; notes by Buck and Bayley, 24 October 1883, with R&A file 46 of 1883, Add.Mss.43584.

[38] Bayley to Primrose, 18 April [1884], Add.Mss.43612.

[39] Kimberley to Ripon, 30 July, 18 September and 7 November 1884, Add. Mss.43525.

against the attachment of the occupancy right to all raiyati land, and accepted Eden's challenge to draft an alternative proposal adhering to the twelve-year rule. Eden fought what he called a 'hard battle', but on the point of attaching occupancy right to all land he admitted defeat, conceding that 'the public would [not] have accepted such a violent change in the present climate'. He was referring to a sense that things were going too fast in India, as they had in England and Ireland; and a fear of political excitement not only in India but in England influenced the members, the situation not helped when a negative paper from Rivers Thompson greatly disturbed the Council. Making the best of his defeat, Eden argued that his alternative, a right of occupancy for every raiyat who held any land in a village or estate for twelve years, 'really makes every settled ryot in Bengal an occupancy tenant'. He confided to Ripon his impression that, for his colleagues on the Secretary of State's Council, 'the mention of twelve years seems to make them quite happy'; they had not seen 'how nearly what they have done, comes to what you preferred'—because the landlords would not be able to exclude occupancy rights by moving tenants from one *village* to another as they had manipulated holdings under the 1859 Act.[40] The outcome was still that the simplest but most radical soluation was ruled out.[41]

Eden had leapfrogged the next possibility, espoused by the Bengal government in the final stages of legislation, that an occupancy right would be provided in his current holding to any raiyat who had held any tenancy for twelve years in the one district. A more restrictive possibility would have been for the qualifying tenancy to have had to be within the one estate (one zamindari as recognised in the revenue records).[42] Finally, in the Act as passed, the right was located as Eden suggested, within each village, a conclusion which (as we shall see) accorded with current notions of Indian social history.[43] There was a

[40] Eden to Ripon, 2 Apirl, 9 and 23 June, 7 July, 12 August, 13 November [1882], Add.Mss.43592; see also Kimberley to Ripon, 4 and 18 July and 14 and 18 August 1884, Add.Mss.43525.

[41] The Secretary of State refused it in September 1882; in October the Government of India re-argued the case. The Secretary still demurred but agreed not to veto the provision; and then the Government decided not to proceed against his objections.

[42] This was the Bihar Rent Committee recommendation; BRC Report. When the Legislative Council ruled out 'estate', discussion moved to definitions of village; but the Bengal government still objected to any limitation of occupancy rights by area; see Ilbert note, 20 October 1884, Add.Mss.43584.

[43] The 1885 Act provided that villages were to be defined from the revenue survey plans, which, however, were concerned to show the boundaries of *mauzas* (revenue estates); this will be discussedbelow.

presumption that all holdings were occupancy holdings until the contrary was proved; and, further to encourage investment, occupancy raiyats were entitled to register and to receive compensation for productive improvements.[44] On the other hand there was defeat for a provision espoused in the Bengal government under Rivers Thompson that even non-occupancy raiyats should have security of tenure for five or ten years on an initial lease, and be entitled to compensation at ejectment—instead they were allowed six-months' notice. Secondly, in the original Bill a occupancy raiyat was to be permitted to transfer his holding subject to a right of pre-emption for the landlord. Thompson's government proposed free transfer of occupancy holdings in Bengal and wherever it was 'customary' in Bihar. In the Act the right of pre-emption was struck out and transferability allowed everywhere subject to 'custom'. Finally, the reformers were anxious to construct a system whereby rents were set by rule, and therefore to resist demands that they might be established by private contract. If they could be made without reference to legal restrictions, it was assumed, they would be made after coercion of the tenants. Restriction was achieved in the Act by permitting an increase by contract of no more than two-sixteenths of the existing rent (the Bill had proposed a limit of six-sixteenths). The original linking of the ratio of rent to the value of produce (limited in the Bill to one-fifth of the gross produce for occupancy raiyats, and to five-sixteenths for others) was deleted, as were a rule that no suit for enhancement should increase rents by more than 100 per cent, and the proposed tables of locally-prevailing rent-rates, with classification of soils and so on, by which rents could have been fixed for 10 to 20 years.[45] Nonetheless the intention was to make enhancement more attractive by suit than by contract.[46] Field had argued that the 1859 Act already 'compelled zemindars to resort to the Courts for the exercise of their rights'; but, as the Muzaffarpur Collector, Worsley, explained, Bihar landlords preferred 'a cheap and high-handed mode of procedure to that presented by law'.[47] Later Finucane and Rampini, noting that proprietors were

---

[44] These provisions (sections 76 ff.) were adopted from the NWP Rent Act, but also borrowed from the Agricultural Holdings (England) Act 1883, 46 & 47 Vict., cap. 61; see Finucane and Ali, *Commentary*.

[45] Tables of rates were partly restored in Bengal Act III of 1898; this will be discussed further below.

[46] The main changes were identified in similar terms to these in the Bengal Administration Report for 1892-3, pp.92-3, and on that basis also in Finucane and Ali, *Commentary*, introduction.

[47] See Field, *Digest*, pp.228-9; and Worsley's marginal note on MacDonnell's 'Draft bill for Behar', disagreeing with MacDonnell over the unworka-

generally remiss in registering their interests, thought that in future failure to do so might jeopardise their success in law suits.[48]

Put briefly, then, the Act divided the land-holding society into landlords, tenure-holders, raiyats (fixed-rate, settled or occupancy, and nonoccupancy), and under-raiyats. It applied to all agrarian land, including government estates,[49] and was generally designed to encourage landlords and tenants to submit their relations to the scrutiny of the law. After much discussion of the principles of classification, by function, a tenure-holder was declared to be someone who held more than 100 bighas.[50] Fixed-rate raiyats held either at an unchanged rent, or at an unchanged rate of rent.[51] An occupancy raiyat was one who had a right of occupancy by custom or practice before 1885 (thus preserving all existing rights), but in addition (as noted) a settled raiyat was one who had held *any* land in a village continuously for twelve years. Rivers Thompson had entered a stout defence of the twelve-year rule when dissenting from the idea of attaching the occupancy right to all land, and his view prevailed.[52] On the other hand, not only was the legal presumption that all raiyats had held their land for twelve years until

bility of the law of distraint, *RLC Report*, appendices.

[48] Finucane and Rampini, *Tenancy Act*, on section 158, which allowed courts to ascertain the incidents of any tenancy on the application of either the landlords or the tenant; it replaced an earlier, seldom exercised right for tenants to sue for the issue of a *patta* and *kabuliyat*.

[49] Ibid. The conclusion was drawn from section 3, defining 'estate' so as to include *khas mahals*, and from the fact that the Act repealed Bengal Act VIII of 1879.

[50] This presumption was provided by section 5 (5), of the 1885 Act, on the recommendation of the Rent Law Commission and by analogy with sections 6 and 7 of Regulation XIX of 1793 which distinguished between revenue-free holdings of more or less than 100 bighas. A bigha was approximately 0.33 acres.

[51] Chapter IV of the Act did not explain how fixed-rate status was established, though this was contentious in the case law. *Guzashta* rights in Shahabad, for example, were specifically mentioned in eighteenth-century government papers, and frequently thereafter, as a form of fixed-rate tenure. This was confirmed in *Lal Sahoo* v. *Deo Narain Singh*, ILR, 3 Cal.781, 2 CLR 295, but not in *Juttoo Moar* v. *Mussamat Basmuttee Koer*, 15 WR 479, or *Missamat Tetra Kooer* v. *Bhunjun Roy*, 21 WR 268. See Finucane and Rampini, *Tenancy Act*; and also Harbans Sahai (22 February 1878) and Joy Prakash Lall (1 March 1879) to Patna Commissioner, for BRC, *RLC Report*, appendices.

[52] Note, 7 April 1882, Add.Mss.43584. Citing the authority of William Muir from 1865, he argued that the period had been carefully chosen in 1859 as according with Hindu and Muslim as well as British and Company law. E. Currie's draft of the 1859 Act had proposed three years, and was criticised as too narrow (being confined to resident raiyats) and too broad (based on too short a qualifying period).

the contrary was proved,[53] but also the occupancy right could not be waived by contractual agreement.

To make the right effective, such tenants were liable to pay only 'fair and equitable' rents, and could not be evicted for arrears of rent; instead their holdings were liable for sale in execution of a decree for the rent, a similar provision to the one, in the Sales Laws, for zamindari estates which defaulted on the revenue. Procedures were provided for the commutation of produce-sharing to money rents,[54] the idea being that produce sharing was oppressive and discouraging to enterprise. (The distinction was in terms of the way rents were calculated, and not of whether they were actually paid in kind or in cash.) Contrary to the recommendation of the Rent Law Commission, a power of distraint was retained to assist landlords in collecting their rents; it was not to be exercised summarily but only through the civil courts, with protection for the tenant.[55] Rules of enhancement were provided, whether by

[53] Settled status was presumed (section 20, 7) and heritable (section 20, 3), and also lasted so long as any land was held in the village (section 20, 5) and when land was recovered which was not voluntarily surrendered (section 20, 6). Under section 21 (1) of the 1885 Act, the land had to be held *as a raiyat*—that is not as an under-raiyat—and occupancy rights accrued only in respect of such land; but a similar presumption on other rights also applied in some cases to produce-sharing or even *utbandi* (year-by-year) tenants or to those with holdings on zamindari 'private lands'. The purpose was to avoid narrowing the range of those with occupancy, as was supposed to have been done by Act X of 1859, though Finucane and Rampini, *Tenancy Act*, argued that several cases in fact had favoured a custom of occupancy: *Hills* and *Thakurani Dasi* (see notes 29 and 30 above), and *Rajah Leellarund Singh Bahadoor* v. *Niroput Mahtoon*, 17 WR 306.

[54] Commutation (section 40) was based, according to Finucane and Ali, *Commentary*, on the English Tithe Acts. The procedure was not much used at first, but became more common after the settlement operations.

[55] The power of distraint had come from English law, and was first permitted to landlords by Regulations XVIII of 1793 and XLV of 1795; by Act X of 1859 the power was limited to crops on the rented land. In 1877 Eden singled it out (the Rent Law Commission agreed) as one of the abuses to be remedied; this will be discussed below. In 1885, under section 121, distraint could not be for recovery of rent in excess of that payable in the preceding year, unless a legal enhancement had been provided, or for parts of a holding sublet with the landlord's approval; by section 123, courts were empowered to institute further inquiries, and to depute an officer to carry out the distraint; by sections 124 and 126, tenants were permitted protect the value of crops which were subject to a distraint order, for example by harvesting them; by section 186, as the Bengal government had wanted, improper distraint, though also resistance to lawful distraint, were made criminal offences. See Finucane and Rampini, *Tenancy Act*; *RLC Report*; and G/I R&A despatch no.7, 21 March 1882, in Add.Mss. 43584. Distraint will be discussed further below.

registered agreement (a maximum of 12.5 per cent in 15 years) or by
the courts, chiefly after local inquiry into the rents paid by comparable
occupancy tenants, or in line with rises in the average prices of local
staple foods.[56] Non-occupancy raiyats too were offered some protection
in the way of enhancement and ejection, on the argument that no cultivator in India should be left entirely at the mercy of the market and of
contract. Section 61 of the Act allowed a raiyat to deposit his rent with
the authorities (for a fee) much more readily than the Bengal Acts, VI
of 1862 or VIII of 1869—for example when he had reason to believe
that a landlord (disputing the amount, say) would refuse it, or when
previously he had not been given a receipt. Similarly section 69
allowed the Collector to authorise the appraisal or division of the crop
for produce-sharing rents. Many of these measures, especially the registration of improvements and the deposit of rents, required direct and
close intervention by government officials or the courts. This was deliberate, reflecting in part an assessment that there were no adequate
alternative forms of protection. In Bihar, for example, where village
officers were creatures of the zamindars, attempts to revive the patwari
system had been abandoned as the Rent Law Commission deliberated.
By contrast the Commission proposed compulsory registration of intermediate holdings and mutations, superseding the inoperative voluntary
system of the 1859 Act. It will be argued later that the most significant
intervention of the 1885 Act was section X, which provided for survey
and settlement and a record of rights.

The purpose, spelt out in a special administration report, was to
create a 'system of fixity of tenure at judicial rents'. It was argued that
the 'ancient agricultural law of Bengal' had been founded on such fixity
'at customary rates'; that it had gradually proved unsuited to changing
circumstances; that attempts had been unsuccessful to substitute 'positive law' for 'customary usage'; and that consequently in some areas,
where land was scarce, landlords were all-powerful, while in other
areas, with lower populations, tenants refused to pay any rents except
on their own terms. The new Act therefore would give each raiyat 'the
same security in his holding as he enjoyed under the old customary
law' (hence the onus of proof on a landlord who denied occupancy
rights), would 'ensure to the landlord a fair share of the increased value
of the soil' (ascertained from price lists kept by government), and
would 'lay down rules by which all disputed questions between landlord and tenant' might be 'reduced to simple issues, and decided upon

---

[56] According to Finucane and Ali's *Commentary*, the price lists (section 39)
were little used. See below where the proposal is traced to Field.

equitable principles' (notably by applications 'to determine the incidents of a tenancy' and by rent settlement and a record of rights).[57] Thus would the tenant gain 'some share in the material progress of his country', while the landlord or auction-purchaser, aided by 'the executive agency of Government' in the 'reasonable enhancement' of rents, would have the means of realising the 'profit of capital invested in the land'.[58]

Legislation is bound to assume or seek to impose uniformity, a tendency extended when administration and courts are systems of record and precedent. In regard to landed property, the laws (including those from before British rule) represented progressive standardisations. The permanent settlement standardised the status of proprietors, especially when read with the enforcement of an initially high revenue demand and the analytical predilections of the courts. In Act X of 1859 the British believed they were resolving a conflict between proprietors and tenants, and codifying a wider range of relations in land. (At first the courts, on assumptions which they assumed to be universal, still opined that all rights in land derived from its exclusive owner, the landlord.) In 1885—although, following the Rent Law Commission, there was no attempt to impose a full system of written contracts on relations which were mediated informally or by custom—yet, in terms of agrarian structure, the attempt was no less than the regulation of an entire society into the four main categories which were defined (proprietors, intermediate rent-receivers, raiyats and under-raiyats), with their characteristics and privileges set out. This confirmed what H.J.S. Cotton had already proclaimed in 1884, in his memorandum on land tenures, that the old distinction between *khudkashta* and *pahikashta* was now 'obsolete'. On the other hand, he discussed as still existing many more distinctions of tenure than were confirmed by legislation in 1885—as well as many terms applied indiscriminately.[59]

Of course any standardisation appeared as a tendency, not an achievement. Confusions remained. For example, a 'holding' was land held by raiyats (not tenants); it could not be land held by proprietors, who had 'private lands', or by tenure-holders, who had 'tenures'. But the definitions of the Act provided that a landlord was not necessarily a zamindar but rather any person immediately under whom a tenant held

[57] *Bengal Supplementary Administration Report* 1882-7.

[58] *RLC Report*, vol.1, p.94.

[59] Cotton, 'Memorandum on Land Tenures in Bengal', prepared at Ilbert's behest for the Select Committee on the Tenancy Bill, 31 January 1884; also sent to Ripon at his request: Cotton to Primrose, 29 February 1884, Add.Mss. 43584.

land, and to whom he paid rent. In the view of Finucane and Rampini, by this definition the 'landlords' included rent-receiving raiyats, with their 'holdings'. Nor was the three-fold division of tenants, inspired by the Rent Law Commission, more consistently maintained. The 1885 Act sometimes conflated and sometimes appeared to distinguish between 'tenant' and 'raiyat', as in the Hindi and Bengali translations where the latter term was used but also *asami* or *praja*. As a result it was not always clear whether some general provisions on 'landlords' applied also to raiyats, and whether some on 'tenants' applied also to under-tenants.[60] Some implications of this curious and interesting confusion of languages and terminology will be considered later, in a discussion of custom and law.

---

[60] Finucane and Rampini, *Tenancy Act*; *RLC Report*, para.10. Bengal Act III of 1898 clarified some of these ambiguities.

Chapter Four

# The great rent law debate

From this overview we now move to more detailed consideration of particular positions on the tenancy reform, a series of comments on illustrative texts, the most important being the *Digest* of C.D. Field, an anonymously-published two-volume compendium called *The Zemindary Settlement of Bengal*, the Report of the Rent Law Commission of 1880, the two-volume report by the Government of Bengal from 1881, various government despatches (especially from Ripon's government in March 1882), and the later legal analyses by Finucane and Rampini, and by Finucane and Ali.[1] These sources reflect and typify the intense controversy that surrounded the introduction of the 1885 Tenancy Act.

Questions of revenue, property in land, and tenancy were continually discussed during British rule, but the argument over a rent Bill in the 1870s and '80s was perhaps the most sustained and wide-reaching of all the debates. The Ilbert Bill controversy has its place in the standard history of Indian nationalism, for what it showed both of the nature of British colonialism, and of the power of organisation. The land law, as the second great *affaire* of the 1880s, also produced mountains of documentation.[2] Thereby it enunciated theories of classes and of the state which were in some ways formative. Protagonists disagreed on history

[1] [R.H. Hollingbery], *The Zemindary Settlement of Bengal* (2 vols.; Calcutta 1879); Field, *Digest*; *RLC Report*; *Report of the Government of Bengal* (1881); Government of India to Secretary of State, 21 March 1882 [hereafter March despatch], and other papers, R&A Rev A 16-46 (July 1883); Finucane and Rampini, *Tenancy Act*, and Finucane and Ali, *Commentary*. For some of these records, including drafts and notes, see also Add.Mss.43584. For full citations of these and other frequent sources on the 1885 Act, see chapter three.

[2] The Bishop of Calcutta thought the extraordinary British reaction in Bengal was 'not really caused by the [Ilbert] Bill but...is the result of measures taken during the past few years against the Europeans in favour of the natives', a feeling that Ripon 'came out merely to put the native on the gadi'; offensive measures presumably included the pro-raiyat Tenancy Act, the Local Self-Government Act, the Arms Act, and the repeal of the Vernacular Press Act; Gibbs to Ripon, 23 March 1883, Add.Mss.43611. Conversely, the *Calcutta Review*, surveying the quarter, thought the Ilbert Bill furore had attracted attention to the tenancy debate in England; *Calcutta Review* LXXVII, CLV (1883), p.222. The comparable importance of the Tenancy Bill among Indians has been less noted, though see B.B. Misra, *The Indian Middle Classes* (Oxford 1961), pp.344-7.

and political economy. They read eighteenth-century conditions differently; were opposed in their impression of the present; and disagreed about the best policy to ensure general well-being. For convenience they may be divided into two camps, one which professed to favour the interests of raiyats, and another which made a case for the zamindars.

All statements of theory and principle in support of policy may be regarded, no doubt, more or less as rationalisations. In obvious or indirect ways, participants in the great rent law debate were using specific analyses to justify positions taken on more general, even subliminal grounds. The officials who supported the pro-raiyat position delved into regulations and memoranda of the 1790s and were not surprised to find justifications for a system of proprietary cultivators: they believed it essential for prosperity and economic progress. Arguments in favour of anterior property rights for the raiyats drew *inter alia* upon James Mill's criticisms of the permanent settlement.[3] The whole may seem to derive from the peculiar combination of *British* colonialism (with its passion for separation, categorisation and ranking, its preference for the particular over the general), with *Indian* rural society (with its layers of complex, ambiguous and collective interests, its rivalries and tensions).[4]

Rationalisations reveal underlying assumptions, and may be part of a process of forming and changing views. C.D. Field's *Digest* of rent law and the report of the Rent Law Commission were major events in this sense, informing opinions on the nature of agrarian relations over a quarter of a century and beyond. They fulfilled a role similar to that of the classics among north Indian settlement reports or the Famine Commissions of the same period. A new consensus grew. As noticed al-

---

[3] See, for example, Mill's *History* (Wilson ed., vol.1, p.205) on rents and the principle of the 'sovereign state'. See also 'The policy of the new rent law for Bengal and Behar by a district officer', *Calcutta Review* CXLIII (January 1881), and 'A memoir on the land tenure and principles of taxation in Bengal by a Civilian', discussed in Babu Ashutosh Mookerjea, 'The proposed new rent law for Bengal and Behar', *Calcutta Review*, April 1883 (pamphlet reprint, Calcutta 1883).

[4] Facile though they are, there may be something (at least as a topic for further research) in such comparisons, for example between on one hand French colonialists who, being passionate about universals, like French nationalism and intellectuals, subsumed everything in a potential Frenchness (leading to solidarity, save for acculturation, among each subject people, but violent metropolitan resistance to decolonisation), and on the other hand British imperialists who, like their class- or regionally-obsessed countrymen, became ever more acutely conscious of difference (producing nationalists and communalists, but a less contested relinquishment of power). Perhaps Indians fitted well with the British model because of their own obsessions with status and otherness of various kinds, for all that these were altered and hardened by colonial rule.

ready, the 1880 famine report in particular was obviously from the same stable as that of the Rent Law Commission, and with the report of 1901 may be said to have delineated a particular period in British rule. Ripon himself was important in securing the terms and passage of the Bill. His diaries just prior to his viceroyalty are filled with shooting and high mass, but they also evoke an interest in agrarian questions beyond that to be expected of an average English landlord. In July 1879, for example, Ripon met a representative of the Farmers' Alliance and then mused on the desirability of compulsory reimbursement for tenants' improvements. In the late spring of 1879 he had read Caird's 'English Agriculture in 1850 and 1851'; that winter he turned to Hume's 'Agricultural Reform in India' and Arnold's 'Free Land'.[5]

More important, a kind of personal and political alliance developed among those who advocated reforms to create or benefit tenant 'proprietors' and the constructive official interference with agriculture. It stretched from E.C. Buck, Secretary of the Government of India's Revenue and Agriculture Department, to Michael Finucane, secretary to the Rent Law Commission and Bengal's first Director of Land Records and Agriculture. A key figure was a personal friend of both Buck and Finucane, namely A.P. MacDonnell, whose own early hopes of advancement were encouraged at a time when he was writing a long memorandum on the Rent Bill in 1885, and who was to see himself in 1893 (when acting Lieutenant-Governor of Bengal) as defending the reformers' legacy against subservience to the landlords on the part of Charles Elliott. In 1906 Finucane was still appealing to the true path of protecting the raiyats.[6] Not all these people agreed on every aspect. As we shall see, there was an older liberal tradition represented by Eden and Bayley which believed in the efficacy of structural and legal reforms, and a parallel set of agrarian radicals, such as Buck and Finucane, who wanted the state, in addition, actively to promote improvements in cropping patterns, agricultural methods and credit, and so on. There *was* a consensus about the need for legal protection for tenants.

[5] Add.Mss.43642. The references are to James Caird, *English Agriculture in 1850-51* (London 1851), Allan Octavian Hume, *Agricultural Reform in India* (London 1879) and Robert Arthur Arnold, *Free Land* (London 1880).

[6] The MacDonnell Collection in the Bodleian Library, Oxford, gives some impression of the situation among officials; for this and the following paragraph, see his letters to his wife, 'Sunday evening' and 28 August 1885, Mss. Eng.hist.d.213; other correspondence, ibid., 235 passim, and Finucane's memorandum on the 1906 Amendment Act, ibid. c.368. See also above (ch. 3, note 3) that Macdonnell's minute of 20 September 1893 was published over his name to 'lend more authority to it' but actually written by Finucane.

This was a path originally set outside Bengal, specifically by the ideas of Henry Maine and the experience of the Punjab. And of course, though consensus was often reached, ideology might be a factor in isolating some officials from their fellows. The most notorious instance (to be discussed below) was a bitter public row in the 1880s between Bengal's Chief Secretary, Alexander MacKenzie, and the Bengal Chief Justice, Richard Garth. A little later Eden was contemptuous of his successor, Thompson. Elliott's relations with MacDonnell in 1893 were almost as hostile, while O'Kinealy was still reported at that time to be estranged from his colleagues on the High Court bench, on tenancy questions. On the other hand, even within Bengal, over a twenty-year period from the time of Ripon to that of Curzon, taking a pro-raiyat stance proved an aid to advancement in the service. Persistence in a more-or-less successful cause had its rewards. Of the members of the Rent Law Commission, Field and O'Kinealy were promoted to the High Court bench, Brojendra Kumar Seal became an additional Sessions judge, Harrison moved from the Board of Revenue to head the Calcutta Corporation, and Mackenzie was promoted from Bengal to the Government of India's secretariat. Ameer Ali, who contributed a pro-raiyat article to *Nineteenth Century* in 1883,[7] was alleged to have been promptly appointed on the strength of it, to the Governor-General's Legislative Council and the Select Committee. Later, during the twentieth century, political fortunes would again be made (and the Hindu-Muslim split worsened) on Bengal tenancy issues.[8]

Bihar was the proving ground for radicals within Bengal. Eden himself may have formed his attitudes in part during his experience as a Political officer in north Bengal, from where he wrote in 1864 of the 'scarcely credible' Bhutia oppression of Bengali raiyats;[9] but generally the officers who formulated the new tenancy policy had served in Bihar. Of those who served on the Rent Law Commission, Mackenzie began his service in Shahabad district in 1863, and also served briefly in Bihar a decade later on famine duty; apart from a stint of a few months as magistrate and collector in Murshidabad, Mackenzie was

---

[7] 'A note on the Rent Bill', P/T 1285, IOL.

[8] See Bayley to Ripon, enclosing O'Kinealy to Bayley, 30 January [1883], supporting Ali's Council appointment as 'the chief & most influential member of the National Muhammadan Association' who would also 'represent fairly and well the views of the ryots.... I can guarantee that he will identify himself, as he has done, with the just claims of the cultivators'; Add.Mss. 43612. See also P. Chatterjee, *Bengal, 1920-47. The Land Question* (Calcutta 1984).

[9] Government of India, Political Department, Political Branch Proceedings, October 1864, P/127/68, p.23, IOL. I owe this reference to Subhajyoti Ray.

pre-eminently a secretariat man, beginning early as an under-secretary and occupying various positions in the Board of Revenue and other provincial offices before becoming a departmental secretary in 1877—his three or four years in Bihar constituted almost the whole of his experience of the mufassil. O'Kinealy, his almost exact contemporary, began his judicial career, after transfer from the revenue branch, in 1874 in Bhagalpur district, a time when discussions were going on among Bihari officers about the condition of the poor and the oppressions of the zamindari system. Other officials too, who were influential in the policy-making, had served in Bihar in posts relating to famine or agrarian conditions—men such as Antony MacDonnell and Michael Finucane. In the mid and late 1870s, the time of Richard Temple and Ashley Eden, the Lieutenant-Governors' visits to Bihar also helped shift the emphasis towards questions of poverty and underproduction, and away from the problems of rent and rent-collection (as raised in the early 1870s under George Campbell). As we have noted, this produced the high-point of the government's reforming zeal, in 1880, just after the report of the Rent Law Commission, when Alexander Mackenzie set out the new aims of the long-proposed legislation.

Encapsulating this period and this school of thought, Field's *Digest* was a legal critique which justified the change in the law. Prepared under government orders, as the first part of the Rent Law Commission,[10] it was a summing up of nineteenth-century studies of tenancy, and the authoritative voice of the reform as eventually enacted. It followed in the tradition of such works as Phillips's Tagore law lectures of 1874/5,[11] but relied particularly on J.H. Harington's *Analysis* (1805-21), intended for the College of Fort William and for the use of junior officials before they entered the service. Modeled on Blackstone's Commentaries, then 'an essential part of every gentleman's library', the *Analysis* proposed to elucidate the 'elements and first principles upon which the rule of practice is founded', while admitting that the Company's laws, embodying as they did many rules of conduct for officials, could not be compared 'as a science' with those of England. Avowed policy-goals included the 'maintenance of the rights of proprietors and farmers of land, and of their under-tenants'. In 1866, as the work was out of print, and marking the new interest in tenurial questions, the

[10] Three preliminary meetings were held, and Field was deputed to prepare the *Digest*, which he completed by 19 August 1879; at the fourth meeting, the Commission began to consider a draft bill; *RLC Report*, vol.2, Minutes of Proceedings.

[11] Published as Arthur Phillips, *The Law relating to the Law of Tenures of Lower Bengal* (Calcutta 1876).

government reprinted those parts 'bearing on the revenue administration of the native Governments, and the rights in the soil of the various classes of proprietors and occupants in the Bengal Presidency'.[12] Harington had later prepared draft regulations, also closely followed by Field. Taking an overt view on policy (unlike the *Analysis*), these adopted the then orthodoxy that the 'insecurity and oppression' of the Bengal peasantry should be attributed to a long list of official errors: the 'omission of clear and definite Rules' in 1793 and afterwards, the prejudicial effect of some rules and the lack of enforcement of others, the misapprehensions of landlords' rights, and their abuses, the abolition of local agency, and the inadequacies of the courts. Harington admitted the difficulty of reconciling landlord and *khudkashta* raiyats' rights, thought a distinction had to be made between ancient tenures and those newly created by zamindars, and proposed to empower officials to mediate, on demand, between landlords and tenants. Holt Mackenzie had favoured an even more pro-active official role.[13]

Building on these precursors, Field's was a Benthamite project undertaken from a historicist perspective: intended to present 'the existing law exactly as it stands', but also to show that a consolidated law of landlord and tenant was attainable. Field described that as easier than supposed, requiring just two main amendments, making occupancy right transferable and providing a practicable law of rent; accordingly the *Digest* included two particular essays, a 'Note on the transferability of ryots' holdings' and a 'Note on the enhancement of rents'. The intention thus crystallised was to create a property in the 'right' of occupancy, to be recognised by provisions for transferability, and protected by a 'practicable law' of rent enhancement. We have already noted that Field regarded such a development in tenurial property as desirable, inevitable and 'natural'. His argument has at least five different elements which we need to consider: the state's right to legislate, the tenants' proper position with regard to rents and to alienation (together in effect the nature and extent of their property in land), the origin of land rights,

---

[12] *Analysis of the Bengal Regulations* (Calcutta 1866) would have been the volume used. *An Elementary Analysis of the Laws and Regulations Enacted by the Governor General in Council at Fort William, in Bengal, for the Civil Government of the British Territories under that Presidency,* in six parts, had been completed by Harington in two stages, the first in 1805-9 and the remainder in 1815, and then as a revised edition (3 vols.) in 1821. See especially the 1821 Introduction and the 1866 Preface.

[13] J.H. Harington, *Minute and Draft on Regulation of the Rights of Ryots in Bengal* (Calcutta 1827). See pp.1-2, 24 and draft regulation. An exception to its influence on Field was its warning against the pargana rate (p.39).

and finally the conditions justifying legislation in this instance. In all these, the relative weight of custom and legislation had to be decided. In particular, because historical legitimacy was a principal weapon of debate, what had or had not been done in the permanent settlement became a focus of contention. Field outlined a process whereby standardised property rights were provided for tenants. It began with the permanent settlement, and the first Regulation (VIII of 1793) whereby the British interfered to define legal rents as distinguished from illegal demands (*abwabs*). Field claimed that the principle of interference in tenancy by law was then repeatedly established, in a succession of enactments. In 1812 rights of 'free' contract were permitted, and leases were protected against any transfer of the proprietary right (Regulations V and XVIII). In 1819, as we have noted, Regulation VIII protected the property-rights of *patnidars*. In 1820 certain tenures were permitted to be sold (Regulation I) while Act VI of 1853 established official jurisdiction over such sales. In 1859 the first major tenancy Act (Act X) opened the way for a flurry of legislation: Field discussed nine Bengal Acts which affected tenant rights between 1865 and 1876. The point was not that this legislation was supportive of tenants; it was that it established definitions of tenancy as comprising the specific rights and obligations set out in the written law, which officials and the courts interpreted. This change was entirely deliberate.

In one sense in particular the intervention of law was regarded as new. The Mughals did attempt to standardise and categorise rural rights, and their influence may be gauged from the dispersal and longevity of their terminology. On the other hand, the evidence also shows their incomplete penetration, localised law, and variable or ambiguous agrarian structures. On that basis, the British could allege that Mughal government had dealt with raiyats 'at will'—that is, not according to law—and that such orders as it passed, to regulate its officials, were of varying effect (less powerful in more distant provinces, for example). This was contrasted with what, for these purposes, was taken to be the complete and uniform sovereignty of the British system.

The justification for intervention was that it was the arbitrary nature of Mughal power which had impeded progress: under the British, the raiyat was to benefit from the opportunities and the temptations of property, and to be provided with rental obligations that were both certain (or limited) and inescapable.[14] For this reason it was quite consistent to try to make it easier for zamindars to collect rents, and at the same time to render raiyats more secure in the occupancy of their holdings. Such

[14] Field, *Digest*, p.181.

changes represented a kind of economic plan. The interventions of law were regarded as conforming to a great, evolutionary logic which sometimes, in India, needed a helping hand. Thus it was that Field and those who followed his prospectus looked both forward and back. The historical precedents which were sought were intended to legitimate policies which allegedly restored or replicated earlier practices, and at the same time to provide evidence of the pre-existing 'natural' tendencies which legislation was merely assisting.

What was the starting-point of the evolution; alternatively the diagnosis of the problem? One view was that tenants had always had property, as will be discussed more fully below. Another was that, whatever the original position, tenancies did not now constitute real property, because their rental obligations and their transferability and heritability were doubtful. These matters had been settled, in the British law, for zamindari estates in 1793, and for tenure-holders (*patnidars*) in 1819. Therefore similar incidents of property would 'naturally' spread to tenancies as well; this had been ruled out by Regulation VII (*haftam*) of 1799, but was provided to some extent in Regulation XI of 1822. We have noted Field's view that the 'tendency of development' was towards alienability.[15] This was partly, he held, because it was in the zamindar's interest to sell holdings for arrears of rent, or to accept rent from whomever proffered it.[16] For such reasons, the basis of agrarian relations as a whole was bound to shift to one regulated in market terms. The development was partly just the extension of an idea of alienability as an 'incident of property', inevitable once that idea had been introduced.

Accordingly, in seeking to ensure raiyats' property, Field elaborated upon a long list of arguments for and against legislation to provide for the transferability of tenancies.[17] Their gist was fear of the exploitation of raiyats by moneylenders, and arguments about the diminution of the zamindars' property. The first, Field conceded, might justify special protective measures, but generally could be left to the countervailing benefit of property. The second he either denied or considered desirable: the property of the raiyat would prevent the extraction of illegal

[15] Ibid., p.165.

[16] Ibid., p.10. Receipts often showed rent received 'through' a third party, often an unregistered purchaser, and conversely zamindari records might retain an original holder's name even after he had left or died.

[17] In the 1885 Act, section 26 made holdings heritable (which had been in doubt after *Ajodhya Pershad* v. *Inam Bandi Begum*, 1 WR 528) but, as will be disucssed below, left transferability to custom. See Finucane and Rampini, *Tenancy Act.*

dues or the transfer of 'ryoti land' into direct '*khas* possession' (or *zerat*).[18] The creeping extension of *zerat*, he held, was contrary to the 'common law of the country'—a highly dubious claim, in that it was very unclear what that common law was, if indeed it existed at all in respect of such matters. In effect, Field was advocating an extension of the sway of state regulation and market forces in order to relate and fix rights in land at all levels. Progress had been hampered by the privileges and oppression of the zamindars, but change would follow once the raiyats were made 'independent and self-reliant', enabled to benefit from 'thrift and industry': thus would spread the 'magic of property', so that the great influence of peasant proprietors would be harnessed 'in stimulating industry, in training intelligence, in promoting forethought and self-control'. Here Field was quoting Émile de Laveleye on *Primitive Economy*, and referring also to J.S. Mill's *Political Economy*.[19] He argued that some progress in 'independence and self-reliance' was already evident under the 1859 Act, for example in the 'wonderful amount of industry and thrift' encouraged by 'the creation of a particular class of tenures' in East Bengal.[20]

The question of middlemen was not really addressed by supporters of the tenancy reform because it was inconvenient, intellectually and practically. The issue did provoke a number of inquiries into transfers of raiyati holdings, including one (made available to the Rent Law Commission) which analysed the purchasers at sales in execution of decrees for arrears of rent. The bulk of the land was acquired by zamindars or rent-receiving cultivators.[21] Field noted, in this connection, that it was argued that transferability of holdings would possibly bring undue benefits to occupancy raiyats, and/or throw the lands of tenants, many of whom were already indebted, into the clutches of mahajans who would reduce the raiyats to 'serfdom'. Field conceded this, and, in a not very distinguished response, suggested that special measures might help combat such 'known disadvantages'. We will find that a similar argument against transferability was put by Richard

[18] Such transfer could be a device either to improve direct zamindari control or to worsen the status of tenants; section 116 of the 1885 Act excluded occupancy rights on such lands, except on a perpetual lease.

[19] Field, *Digest*, pp.177-81. Émile de Laveleye was repeatedly quoted by Indian analysts, at least since Phillips' Tagore lectures Here the reference is to *De la propriété et de ses formes primitives*, translated as *Primitive Economy* by G.R.L. Marriott (London 1878).

[20] Field, *Digest*.

[21] See 'Statement of classes of purchasers of ryots' holdings and small undertenures under execution sales' [1878-9], *RLC Report*, vol.2, Appendices.

Garth, the Chief Justice, and similarly not really answered by the reformers, Mackenzie and O'Kinealy.

Field was aware of the different effects of peasant proprietorship in different conditions—he referred to the example of the Deccan raiyats as a warning (in view of the agrarian disturbances of 1875). But, in a novel conclusion from a familiar metaphor, he regarded institutions as being like plants, that 'may flourish in one climate as well as another, if only due attention be paid to guard against the particular unfavourable influences which each climate presents'.[22] In other words peasant proprietorship was universally beneficial, and no economic improvements could be anticipated without the possession of such property. However in Bengal and Bihar, a few adjustments would be needed to allow for peculiar local usages and other impediments to the expected development of landed property and enterprise—impediments supposed to include ecology, the malign influence on forethought and frugality of a climate which allowed several harvests in a year.

As another pre-requisite for the development of tenurial property, rents were supposed to be 'fair and equitable'.[23] Such provision was made for occupancy raiyats under the 1859 Act, but there were considerable ambiguities about what it meant. These were compounded when the Great Rent Case (*Thakurani Dasi* v. *Bisheshur Mukherjee*) permitted an increase with regard to the value of the produce (whether in general or on the land in question was unclear) and without allowance for any change in the costs to the raiyat. This uncertainty produced in some senses the motive power for the Tenancy Act of 1885. But it rested on a far older confusion which in itself may be said to have provided the core of the pro-raiyat case in the 1870s and 1880s. All tenants were entitled to leases, but these were on terms set at the landlord's discretion in the cases of those without occupancy rights. No rents were to be enhanced without notice, and yet the law did not establish very clearly an inalienable value in the holdings of any tenant, other than *patnidars*, such as would have clearly constituted legal property. In deciding what to do about this, the guiding principles were which 'rights' had existed in the past, and which would have most utility in the future. The result was that conditions of tenancy in the century before 1885 had to be examined.

Regulation VIII of 1793 had apparently envisaged four classes—

[22] Field, *Digest*, pp.178-9.
[23] In the 1885 Act this phrase was not defined. Finucane and Ali, *Commentary*, show that it derived from section 5 of Act X of 1859, so that there was case law upon it.

proprietors, independent taluqdars, dependent taluqdars, and raiyats. The last included *khudkashta* or permanent privileged raiyats, whose leases were not to be changed or cancelled, unless they were paying below the 'pargana rate', or too little through fraud or collusion, or unless there were a general measurement to equalise and correct the assessment. Field thought the last implied a wholesale revision by the proprietor; and in support cited the role expected of patwaris and kanungos, in Regulation IV of 1808, to assist in measurements of land on behalf of landholders or raiyats. Another possibility is that what was meant was a revision under government supervision—as also provided for in 1808. Either way, the result would be a new 'pargana rate'. *Abwabs* were therefore unauthorised (that is, unmeasured) increases, whether imposed by zamindars or the state, which occurred between these formal revisions. They had greatly multiplied during the eighteenth century; Sir John Shore thought they increased the demand by 83 per cent between 1658 and 1789. The implication generally was that the 'real' pargana rate was not fixed, but could be changed, in practice, either by additional demands from landlords, or after measurement and 'correction'. In the latter case, Field presumed the rise would be in line with the value of output, for there is an implication in the Regulations of 1793 and in subsequent discussion of Todar Mal's system that rents were to be set after an assessment of the productivity of the lands in question. That would have been taxation according to the ability to pay, and Field's notion of it may have been anachronistic.[24] He concluded that there was no decision in 1793 to fix raiyats' rents alongside the revenue demand. But he also argued that the *khudkashta* raiyats were not in the position of tenants-at-will. They were entitled to receive a lease, in order to set out the exact amount of rent payable. It was not in order to legitimise their landholding: they did not need that as they were already 'upon the land' at the time of the settlement.

Field assumed—it was rather a large assumption—that produce rents were taken in a fixed proportion, and thus would be reduced or enhanced in value according to the movement of prices. The Rent Law Commission proposed limiting the proportion of gross produce taken by the landlord, but disagreed about the limit.[25] Cash rents, for non-occupancy raiyats, were (Field thought) clearly a matter of agreement

[24] But see Field, *Digest*, pp.190-1, discussing section 51 of Regulation VIII of 1793, which limited any increase demandable, not from raiyats but from 'dependent taluqdars' (those not enjoying a direct revenue-paying relation with government), according to the conditions of tenure and to whether 'the lands are capable of affording it'.

[25] *RLC Report*, vol.1, p.16.

between the two contracting parties. It was the position of occupancy raiyats paying cash that was unclear. By a majority court decision in 1856, reached by analogy with the English law, it appeared that there was no limitation on any enhancement other than what was provided in legislation: the tendency of the courts was to drive out alternative jurisdictions.[26] But in practice it seems that, for whatever reason, occupancy raiyats paid less than other tenants in some areas, but more in others. What did legislation provide? Act X of 1859 allowed enhancement of individual rents up to the average, but no mechanism (other than a statistical one over time) of raising the average in each category. As we have noted, *Hills* v. *Ishore Ghose* ruled that the right of occupancy implied no privilege in respect of rents, which had to be paid at a 'fair and equitable rate', meaning (in the view of the Chief Justice, Peacock) a rate no lower than a non-occupancy tenant would pay, or in other words a 'market' rate.[27] It was unclear from this, taken in conjunction with the notion of 'fairness', whether or not the rent could be increased in real terms (that is, so as to take a higher proportion of the value of the output, in order to respond to the impact of population upon the demand and hence the price for land). If so, obviously the end-product, in a situation of land scarcity, would be the reduction of all tenants to the same level, and ultimately perhaps the removal of all distinctions between tenants and labourers.

However, few if any officials advocated the ruling in *Hills* as a possible or desirable solution.[28] Field, or even the judges, may well have had in mind a doctrine of rent which included a notion of 'prevailing profit'; the landlord could have extracted the whole of such a rent without reducing all cultivators to the same level. Field certainly applied his conception of political economy—and his reading of John Stuart Mill—to distinguish between an increase in value and an increase in price, that is the exchange value expressed in money.[29] The

---

[26] Sadr Dewani Decisions, 1856, p.617. The majority was four to one; the dissenting judge (Torrens) argued that it was false to equate English landlords and tenants with Bengali zamindars and raiyats. See Field, *Digest*, pp.228-34.

[27] W.R. Special Number 1862-4, pp.48, 131, 148.

[28] Field, *Digest*, p.241.

[29] See Field, *Digest*. Referring to Thomas De Quincey on 'exchange value' (*Minor Single Works and Essays. The Logic of Political Economy,* Edinburgh 1844), Field noted that, according to Mill, 'price' means value in money, and 'value' means command over purchasable commodities. This made it a mistake for the permanent settlement to have been fixed in money, and meant that 'price' should be used in regard to rents. Such gleanings from political economy probably indicate a practical man's search for authorities, rather than the adoption of new concepts which changed judgements as to what was needed.

same market price would give different net returns to different producers; prices could rise due to monetary or demand factors, and either generally or in commodity-specific ways. By this argument, the permanent revenue settlement should never have been fixed in money terms, and what was needed for rents was a means whereby 'fairness' could be calculated in relation to agricultural prices rather than as a fixed money rate. Many times the idea of fixing rates as a proportion of gross product had been advocated, for example by Sir Henry Ricketts in 1859, as deducible in principle from Indian 'custom'. The assumption was effectively that rent could be maintained in the same proportion to the value of the output, and not be affected directly by changes in the demand for land. *Thakurani Dasi* provided that enhanced rents should be proportionate in that sense, that is in a constant ratio to the value of the produce; but it applied only to 'customary' rents, that is in the absence of contrary contractual arrangements.

The conclusion to all this was that there was, at the time of Field's *Digest*, no satisfactory law of enhancement which could be consolidated. Therefore, though much of the effort in 1885 was to standardise what had always been heterogeneous in India, some of it was directed to sorting out the mess of contradictions imposed by the British legal system. The situation in Bengal was the more uncertain because, for all the apparent interference, government had not fixed rents—it had had no pecuniary interest in doing so, except on government estates, either generally or for individuals.[30] *Thakurani Dasi* also had not been used, and anyway relied on a test which was very difficult to apply. Experienced observers concluded that a prevailing or market rate too would be impossible to define, because actual rents were so extremely various. One explanation was that these rates always allowed the tenants something more than the wages of labour and the profits of capital (for example to cover risk and seasonal variation), and that rents (including this margin) were calculated according to the prices prevailing when the lease was agreed. One might say that rates would vary therefore either according to the date at which the agreement was made, or according to the level of the margin allowed.[31] In practice, conditions in villages meant that actual rents and rates varied without reference to leases, and in consequence of a great number of extra-economic consi-

[30] Field, *Digest*, pp.244 ff. He noted that Bengal Act VI of 1876 gave power for settlement officers to fix rents, but that it was never used. Arbitration on rents was also possible under the Civil Procedure Code, but again little used; Field wondered if it should be made compulsory.

[31] This was one of the elaborate attempts to find general rules. It was quoted by Field, *Digest*, pp.242-4.

derations. This conclusion is reinforced by the impression that they varied according to the ability of the raiyats to resist and of zamindars to insist—in other words according to political factors which must have been germane before 1793 as well as after—and with particular reference to the number of intermediaries between landlord and cultivator. Field decided that a new principle was needed, or at least an improved mechanism for applying principles that seemed dimly to exist: he envisaged the collection and publication of agricultural prices (as in the *London Gazette* as a result of Tithe Commutation Acts), and an enhancement of rents so as to maintain their value in terms of the price paid on average for the staple food crop.[32]

The object was a certain but bracing regime for the raiyat; a strong element of paternalism in Field wanted to improve the raiyat, not give him ease: the end was future comfort through individual effort. Just as he held that the responsibility of peasant proprietary rights would encourage 'thrift and industry', so too Field argued that 'one of the most important steps that can be taken in training is to fix the demand upon the ryot for rent, and to make him understand that this demand once fixed must be complied with faithfully and punctually'.[33] There is an undercurrent here of wishing to reform the 'feckless' raiyat, as well as of protecting the oppressed peasant.[34] Thus Field, and the reformers, balanced the apparently contradictory goals of assisting both rent-collection and peasant prosperity.

A related point will be worth foreshadowing at this stage. Field's thinking provided a model on which further refinements were considered. For example, E.C. Buck, when Secretary of the Revenue and Agriculture Department, produced an elaborate note refusing historical and economic legitimacy to any standard ratio of rent to gross produce. Holt Mackenzie, in Regulation VII of 1822, had argued, applying Ricardian principles, that the same fraction could be levied from all lands, regardless of quality, only at 'an early stage of society' and with a low population, when soils and outturn were uniform. Otherwise the rates, he held, must reflect the conditions of each village and field:

---

[32] Field, *Digest*, pp.250 ff. noted the lists of wheat, barley and oats prices recorded in seven-year tables as a basis for commuting tithes to cash.

[33] Field, *Digest*, p.181.

[34] John Beames, for example, who claimed sympathy with the raiyats, attributed their plight to wilfulness: 'Every one *will* marry, and *will* have heaps of children, no one *will* migrate, a vast majority *will* grow nothing but paddy and the poorest *will* spend in advance the earning of ten years on a marriage feast or a religious ceremony'; quoted in 'A note on the Rent Bill', 20 April 188[5?], P/T 1285, IOL.

Regulation VII required the ascertaining of 'the estimated produce per bigha, and the average value of the produce'. In Bengal proper, where money rents had long prevailed, Buck thought it equally impossible to find any merit in average rates of rent: the average would exist but could not decide any particular rent, either in a village or 'still less... individual fields'. He argued that Holt Mackenzie's principles were right, but the process he required 'too ambitious in detail and cumbrous in operation' to succeed. Bayley, the Member of the Government in charge of the Bill, agreed on the whole, adding that a gross produce rule was 'unscientific' because the outturn was less significant in assessing a fair rent than the costs of production. He suggested rules of rent enhancement which adduced the rise in agricultural prices, subject to a minimum return for the cultivator—his and his family's subsistence being 'the first charge on the produce'. The last requirement would mean that landlords must take a *smaller* proportion of the output as population rose. On the basis of such arguments, the various options for rent enhancement were debated and approved or rejected.[35] What should be noticed is the universal presumption of *individual* producers, and the use of measures drawn from a market rationale. The impulse, in terms of arguments about the 1885 Act, came essentially from classical economics and north Indian experience. Yet, at just this time, a special report on conditions in Awadh concluded from a sample of 28,477 tenancies that rents were generally first demanded *en bloc* and then allocated to component fields and holdings by the village accountant or proprietor.[36] Practice in Bihar and Bengal was not very different, in this respect. This apposition of individual enterprise with collective pro-

[35] Notes to R&A file 46 (1883), by Buck, 24 October and 2 and 27 November, and Bayley, 24 October and 28 November 1883, Add.Mss.43584. The options were to permit enhancement (1) up to rate paid on comparable land nearby, (2) with reference to potential output, (3) for changes in productivity of the land, and (4) for change in the area of the holding. Of these the Government of India disapproved of (1) and (2), from past experience and on principle, and as impractical in Bengal without expensive inquiries equivalent to regular revenue settlement (at a time when it was thought elaborate inquiries into land rights must cease). Draft rules for establishing average rates on the basis of at least 'five exemplar fields' were drawn up by Elliott and Buck; factors to be considered in assessing comparability included soil, manure, irrigation, proximity to markets, the skill of the cultivators. But Bayley insisted that even Settlement Officers' rates were suspect and inappropriate for setting individual rents, and Buck, noting the statistical tendency for rents to rise under any system of averages, suggested that an initial rent roll should be proven for each village, and subsequent rises permitted only for increases in prices or area.

[36] Quoted in J. Woodburn, Secretary, G/NWP, to Secretary, R&A, 21 December 1883, Add.Mss.43584.

cesses is important, and we shall return to it.

### III

An extreme but also typical formulation of the pro-tenant view was that
compiled in the *Zemindary Settlement*, presumably by the copyright
holder, R.H. Hollingbery, First Assistant-Secretary in the Financial
Department of Bengal from 1866 and 1879, and thereafter a government pensioner.[37] It allows us to focus on interpretations of the permanent settlement, and the concept of an original raiyats' property, which
lay behind the specific proposals which Field and others were making.
The fundamental point is that the zamindari settlement was intended to
apply to tenants as well as to landlords. Bengal raiyats had enjoyed
rights in land which Cornwallis had not intended to confiscate. It was
noted that the Court of Directors had desired that tenants should
continue to enjoy 'the same equity and certainty' as to rents, and the
'unmolested enjoyment of...long-established rights'. This was taken to
imply a property for raiyats analogous to the property of zamindars.
Real property rights were thus bifurcated, according to the *Zemindary
Settlement*. In support of this it argued that, as the permanent settlement
made no provision for the enhancement of rents, it had intended them to
be fixed at the same time as the revenue demand. The professed motive
of the *Zemindary Settlement* was to explain and remedy the parlous
state of the poor, identified rather casually with the body of the raiyats.
The book was too deferential to attribute blame for present conditions
upon more recent government policy, nor did it cite, as others have, the
excessive revenue demand of the early years. But the *Zemindary
Settlement* did criticise subsequent measures to assist the zamindars to
meet the revenue demand, by the use of coercion in the collection of
their rents. In this it took up a theme which had been a constant refrain
in north Indian condemnations of the Bengal system: it was based on
an image of a true and original Indian way.

These views may be compared not only with Field but with a later

---

[37] Hollingbery was not a member of the covenanted (ICS) but of the provincial service. A member of a Calcutta family, he is first recorded as working in
the Military Auditor General's office in 1844; he moved to the Financial Department in 1863. His other activities included being secretary and treasurer of
the Parental Academic Institution, a Christian school founded in 1823 to provide instruction in English away from the 'bad influence of native servants'.
The following paragraphs discuss this work and the large amounts of documentation it provides. The latter will be identified in the text, but, for reasons of
space, separate references within the *Zemindary Settlement* or to the originals it
quotes will not be included.

summary, itself much influenced by the arguments of the rent law debate, that of W.W. Hunter, in his 'Dissertation on Landed Property and Land Rights in Bengal'.[38] In an account which is still useful, Hunter seems at first sight to confirm the interpretation of Hollingbery. Hunter also stressed the varied nature of the forms of land-holding rights in Bengal, and the incomplete penetration of the Mughal system. What was remarkable in 1793, by this account, was the creation (in law) of a single form of proprietary right. Hunter believed that the rights of Bengal raiyats had not been derived from the zamindar, as a tenant's supposedly are from a landlord. The raiyats, he thought, had owned the cultivation (and were obliged to cultivate), just as the zamindar owned the rent (which he was obliged to collect). It followed that rents were fixed by custom in each area, according to a so-called 'pargana rate', and not by agreement between the parties concerned.

It could not be denied that the Act of 1784 (24 Geo.II, cap.25) had provided for an inquiry into land rights, a settlement with existing holders, and the preservation of other existing rights. It was equally undeniable that Cornwallis's final codification gave a proprietary right to the zamindars, subject to prompt payment of the land revenue, at rates fixed unconditionally in perpetuity: this made the rate inherent in the land and not its owner, and reduced all zamindari property to one type. Also certain was that this landlord-right was qualified only by the requirement to pay revenue and not by any subordinate rights. Landlords were *required* to issue leases (*patta*) to their tenants and to receive acknowledging counterparts (*kabuliyat*); it may or may not have been imagined that rents would remain unchanged, or be kept at standard rates; it was probably desired that some protection should be provided (Shore said as much). It was expected that it would be in the zamindars' interest to treat their tenants moderately (they would become to the landlords, in Thomas Law's words, 'a part of their necessary property').[39] But land ownership was not conditional upon the fulfilment of such expectations. On the contrary, Shore's desideratum was ignored, of determining and simplifying the rules of rent enhancement, and, as Field pointed out, Cornwallis believed tenures existed by *agreement* with the zamindars. Moreover, during the ensuing decades, to ensure

---

[38] In W. W. Hunter, *Bengal MS. Records. A Selected List of 14,136 Letters in the Board of Revenue, Calcutta, 1782-1807...* , vol.1 (London 1894).

[39] The quotation came from Thomas Law, Collector of Behar District (Gaya) in the 1780s, responsible for the terms of the settlement there and influential more generally; see his *Letters to the Board submitting by their Requisition a Revenue Plan for Perpetuity* (Calcutta 1789). See also Ranajit Guha, *A Rule of Property for Bengal* (2nd ed.; New Delhi 1982), pp.173-86.

their allegiance and the uninterrupted receipt of revenue payments, the zamindars' legal position was strengthened *vis à vis* that of most of the tenants. Cornwallis wrote in 1789 (and is quoted by the *Zemindary Settlement*) that a landlord with 'a permanent property in the soil' would find it 'worth his while to encourage his tenants, who hold his farm in lease, to improve that property'; he would forego small temporary gain for 'future permanent profits'. Though implying some safeguard for tenants, this must also mean that zamindars would gain income through increased rents. It does not show that rents were to be guided by some general principle, or controlled by government, and otherwise not expected to rise.

The *Zemindary Settlement* claimed that the zamindars' dues were limited to a set 'percentage of the rents of their lands'; but, if this *malikana* was fixed, it was as a proportion of the state's rent (or revenue) rather than of the raiyats' payment. Both varied in practice according to relative power before and to an extent after 1793. The *Zemindary Settlement* also cites Cornwallis's arguments about the disadvantages of fluctuating dues—disincentives resulting from the liability of a tenant to dispossession for refusing to pay a rent increase, or of a landlord to imprisonment or loss of property for non-payment of revenue. But the permanent settlement with the landlords made sense only if it produced an increase in prosperity (from which a still-trading and taxing Company would also benefit). This did not mean a licence for the landlord to exact more from the land without any increase in output: such was the objection of Shore to new cesses which 'subverted the fundamental rules of collection', exactions as were measured merely 'by the abilities of the ryots to pay'. For this reason, he thought, the zamindar's settlement with the raiyats should become 'a matter of record'. Cornwallis agreed: he distinguished two distinct demands, the state's revenue and the landlord's rent—the fixing of the first would help simplify the latter—but, in considering how rents would be determined, he supposed it would be equitably 'by both parties' and in accordance with the 'value of the produce'. The government's role, by this dispensation, was to record agreements, and not to prevent zamindars from raising rents, or reaching 'agreements'.

With all the late nineteenth-century arguments from the past, we face the fallacy of reading back terms and conditions, a problem that Shore recognised when he explained that rights could not be the same under different systems of government and law: he expected it would take much time before a consistent system could be produced to 'reduce the compound relation of a Zamindar to Government, and of a raiyat to a Zamindar'—each of them part proprietor and part vassal—'to simple principles of landlord and tenant'.[40] In the case of the permanent settlement the difficulties were increased by the lack of attention paid to the tenants at the time: one of the chief advantages perceived in the permanent settlement was that it would relieve the government of any need to intervene at this level of society. Lord Grenville claimed in speeches in 1813 that the late eighteenth-century Board of Control had thought no tax more 'detestable' than one on husbandmen; if so, they expressed this by agreeing to Cornwallis's plan to make the zamindari settlement permanent. Insofar as he thought about the matter, Cornwallis too was generally limited in his imagination by his European experience and concepts. The more one considers the authors of the permanent settlement to have been imposing a particular vision, the less credible it seems that they were intent to safeguard the interests of the raiyats. Certainly Cornwallis claimed to want to 'secure happiness to the body of the inhabitants', and to protect tenants against capricious eviction. Of course it would be 'a wanton act of oppression' to dispossess a cultivator 'with the sole purpose of giving land to another'. But Cornwallis thought land had to be cultivated 'under an expressed or implied agreement' as to payment, and (though this was a period in which the talk was more of re-capturing absconding raiyats than of dispossessing others) that rents were 'on most cases fully equal to what the cultivator can afford to pay'. Cornwallis knew that rents had been enhanced; but when he asked 'how could it be expected, whilst the Government were increasing their demands upon the zemindars, that they, in turn, would not oppress the ryots', he meant to be understood as advocating the removal of one motive for *oppression*, not as proposing a permanent settlement of rents.[41]

This interpretation of the permanent settlement is not only obvious; it was also an orthodoxy of the period between the Fifth Report and the Mutiny. In trying to rehabilitate Cornwallis as a defender of the raiyats, the *Zemindary Settlement* was thus advancing a radical argument, and playing to a particular audience in changed circumstances. One major change was the new cogency of appeals to history and to property. The latter included the attempt to advance the cause of landlords and of permanent settlement; obviously this implied that claims for raiyats would

---

[40] Minutes of 18 June (also in the Fifth Report) and December 1789, quoted by B.H. Baden-Powell, *Land-Systems of British India*, vol.1 (Oxford 1892), p.520.

[41] Field, *Digest*, pp.194-5, noted that the fixing of rents was considered in the 1790s, but presumably abandoned as it did not appear in the Regulations.

be couched in parallel terms. The former appeal, reflected in H.H. Wilson's qualifications of James Mill's critique of India,[42] and in questionings of classical political economy, married the legalism of Bengal administrative traditions with the priority long given elsewhere to 'appropriateness' to Indian conditions. In pursuing this new strategy, the *Zemindary Settlement* was at its most extreme, but also at one with certain explanations of India's evolution, when it insisted that the raiyats were the original proprietors of the soil. It was concerned to acquit Cornwallis of James Mill's charge that he had confiscated peasant rights through aristocratic prejudice. It considered the legal proprietorship awarded to the zamindars to have been a convenient fiction which did not remove existing raiyati property. This partly reconciled zamindari and peasant-proprietary models. It did not mean that the raiyats paid no rent to intermediaries; according to a dictum of James Mill, rent-paying was compatible with proprietary rights when rates could not be raised at the will of the collector or for improvements made by the rent-payer. In this we appreciate the importance of the supposed prevailing or pargana rate, which removed discretion from landlords, and also of the various safeguards provided to tenants in the 1885 Act.

But history could be made to tell many different stories. Rivers Thompson had made use of the *Zemindary Settlement* when reluctantly challenging the Government of India's letter of 21 March 1882 to the Secretary of State. Expressing his dissent from the granting of occupancy rights in respect of all raiyati land, and defending the twelve-year rule, Thompson had argued that distinctions had always been recognised between Bengal's cultivators on the basis of residence. He quoted Shore's famous minute of 1789:

> Those who cultivate the land in the village to which they belong (resident ryots), either from length of occupancy or other cause, have a stronger right than others, and may in some measure be considered as hereditary tenants, and they generally pay the higher rents. The other class (the *paikasht*) cultivate lands belonging to a village where they do not reside; they are considered tenants-at-will; and, having only a temporary accidental interest in the soil which they cultivate, will not submit to the payment of so large a rent as the preceding class; and when oppressed, easily abandon the land to which they have no attachment.[43]

This formulation, clearly riven through with terminology and assump-

---

[42] James Mill, *The History of British India*, 10 vols. (1817; 5th ed. by H.H. Wilson, London 1858). For a valuable discussion see Javed Majeed, *Ungoverned Imaginings. James Mill's* The History of British India *and Orientalism* (Cambridge 1992), pp.129-30, 133-5 and passim.

[43] A.R. T[hompson] note, 7 April 1882, Add.Mss.43584.

tions drawn from English law, could be taken to mean that there were two classes of raiyat (or types of tenant). But it could also be read as saying that there were two types of right (or modes of tenancy) so that all raiyats could have occupancy rights in land which they held in their hereditary village. The one was the version according to Thompson; the other the view of the *Zemindary Settlement*. The reformers generally took Shore to mean at least that all tenants who resided where they cultivated should have entrenched rights in the land—they earned the privilege either from time or some 'other cause' but in essence from residential status.

The second stage in this argument went much further because it insisted that the resident cultivator had a status and rights that were *superior to all others*. Lord Moira's Revenue Despatch of 21 September 1815, for example, already referred to 'indigenous proprietors or cultivating zamindars' (in opposition to the revenue-collecting *malguzars* who had 'no special privileges or exclusive rights') as having the 'only hereditary possession' of land and being the 'only persons fundamentally connected to the soil'. In Bengal terms, the *khudkastha* raiyat was the 'indigenous proprietor' and most of the zamindars merely *malguzars*. The Select Committee of 1812 had found the landholders in the Raja of Banaras's territories to be village zamindars who paid the revenue jointly with one or more partners or *pattidars*, descended from the same common stock: such taluqdars were merely members of a lineage who organised the collection from their kinsmen, but it was just such men (it was concluded) who had been made into exclusive landholders in Bengal proper. The original system, and therefore the better one, was the one still extant in Upper India. In 1819, inheriting this new orthodoxy, the Court of Directors took it as a certainty that a wrong had been done to the Bengal raiyats because their payments had been treated as rents and not revenue. The *Zemindary Settlement* went further still and conflated these revenue-paying raiyats with the body of tenants and cultivators present in the permanently-settled areas almost a century later. They were identified too with the village communities to be found elsewhere.

The critical questions for the *Zemindary Settlement* and for one aspect of the legal reform were, then, first original property rights and second a consistent narrative. It was on this superstructure that Field built his proposed remedies for the condition of the raiyats of Bihar and Bengal. In the late 1870s the Bengal government decided that modest reforms had the best chance of success. As the reformers' ambitions became more comprehensive, they nonetheless preserved the façade of changing little. Finucane and Rampini acknowledged that the 1885 Act materially altered the law, but reflected the pretence of conservatism when they also accepted that it was 'restoring rights' and consolidating existing enactments (as stated in the preamble to the Act).[44] In the tenancy debates, the legal history itself was extensively homogenised and made to appear internally consistent, partly through cross-referencing and cross-fertilisation. The Bengal Government under Ashley Eden, the high point for pro-raiyati influence, was persuaded that official experience, from the days of George Campbell at least, represented a connected and consistent movement towards the opinions of the pro-raiyat school. Alexander Mackenzie, while Chief Secretary to the Government, wrote a long and not very memorable minute to illustrate the continuous gestation of the 1885 Act.[45]

Such rationalisations were largely disingenuous or deluded. The central example was the dictum of the Rent Law Commission of 1880, as in the *Zemindary Settlement*, that the permanent settlement had intended to endorse the raiyats' 'property' in land as it had supposedly existed in the eighteenth century.[46] This amounted to the creation of categories by legislation, under the pretence of recognising what already existed. Later there was a rearguard action against this process, in a case on fixed-rates raiyats, when two judges (Trevelyan and Beverley) found that the 20-year rule did not turn an occupancy raiyat into a fixed-rate raiyat, and merely provided for his rent to be fixed. But the verdict was overturned by the Full Bench in 1898; and, according to Finucane and Rampini, Privy Council rulings, from 1873 to 1907, were 'strongly in favour of accepting custom...as giving rise to a presumption that tenancies are permanent'.[47]

Such a teleological, instrumentalist history obviously raised as many questions as it settled. First could land-ownership be subdivided? Theory and the Indian past had to decide. According to Philip Francis, the revenue farming system of the 1770s had been wrong in ignoring proprietary rights. Warren Hastings, too, had conceived of 'rights of property...vested in the Zamindar'. While apparently acknowledging some rights of possession for raiyats, he had denied that these could be 'positive or exclusive' or contradictory of zamindari rights. Shore had

---

[44] Finucane and Rampini, *Tenancy Act,* on the preamble.

[45] A. M[ackenzie], 'Memorandum on the history of the rent question in Bengal since the passing of Act X of 1859', in *Report of the Government of Bengal on the Proposed Amendment of the Law of Landlord and Tenant in the Province with the revised Bill and Appendices,* vol.1 (Calcutta 1881).

[46] See evidence and report volumes of *RLC Report.*

[47] Ibid.; *Bansi Das* v. *Jugdip Narain Chowdury,* 1896, ILR, 254 Cal.152.

made a similar theoretical point in a minute of 18 June 1789, that, if they were to 'admit the property of the soil to be solely vested in the zamindars' then they could not acknowledge any rights for the raiyats other than those granted by zamindars. Even to the *Zemindary Settlement*, determined upon a primary right for the raiyats, any division of rights had to be explained in terms of *dominium* and *servitas*, of lordship and service, whereby the former was a fundamental right in the soil, and the latter a portion 'broken off' and provided to the state. Whether *dominium* belonged ultimately to the crown or the lord, this implied a single form of ownership, though one which could be shared. Harington's *Analysis* and Phillips' Tagore lectures too were cited as showing that zamindars, descendants of 'ancient rajas, native leader[s] and robber chiefs', had traditionally 'owned' the land in India, while only the rents belonged to the sovereign; Phillips explained how, since British rule, the official aspect of zamindari had tended to decline while the proprietary was strengthened.[48]

Other commentators sought to solve the problems of categorisation by separating out the different attributes.[49] Resolution I of 1820 implied that a greater variety of distinct rights had once existed, by recognising that the regulations of 1793 had had a generalising effect which tended to abrogate any unregulated rights. The Resolution identified a full, hereditary and transferable right over the 'whole of the land' for the *malguzar* or malik, but also the permanent, heritable and sometimes saleable right of the settled or *maurasi* raiyat. This still standardised the categories of right, but implied a range that overlapped or co-existed— that is, cultivating or intermediate rights. Similarly, in 1819 the Board of Revenue's evidence on Banaras wrote of the village zamindars explicitly as an intermediate class between the Raja and the cultivators. The pro-tenant case built upon such analyses to favour the raiyats. The consequences of this ambiguity will be discussed later.

Characteristically, in his *panjam* Regulation, Colebrooke had wanted to 'reduce to writing a clear declaration and distinct record of the usages and rates according to which the ryots of each pergunnah or district will be entitled to demand the renewal of their pottahs'. In short, he wanted to marry a customary framework with 'modern' precision and contract, so as to maintain 'a right of occupancy', supporting the raiyat (in parallel with the zamindar) 'in his ancient and undoubted privilege of retaining the ground occupied by him, so long as he pays

---

[48] See above notes 11 and 12.

[49] The following examples are taken from 'A note on the Rent Bill', 20 April (1884?), IOL P/T 1285.

the rent justly demandable'. The 1885 Tenancy Act continued this effort. Field too had considered the now-familar case, put by the advocates of the raiyats' rights and crucial to the question of rent, that the repeated references to custom and local usages in Regulations from 1793 onwards, implied a pre-existing, independent right of property analogous to that provided for the zamindars.[50] Field remarked that Regulation XLIV of 1793 had limited the rates (not the total rents in cash terms) for new leases, and also that, when there was concern at the ability of zamindars to meet the revenue demand, the law on tenancy was quickly altered to permit the abrogation of most leases at the sale of an estate. An occupancy right was not, he concluded, a necessary provision for all who qualified under the twelve-year rule—that would be to spread the net more widely than the 'customary' right of *khud-kashta* status—but on the other hand after 1793 the landlord had not had the right to eject any tenant who paid his rent. In deciding on the currently legitimate rights in land, Field was combining the force of both custom and of law in order to create single, consistent categories.

But he was not doing so, despite his claims, because the law was clear. Nor could the history lesson be simply applied to the occupancy tenant. Some genuinely set up alternative legal schema based upon the incidents of indigenous categories. H. Bell, the Legal Remembrancer, for example, argued that 'There is no magic in the number twelve; and it is submitted that a "khood-khast" ryot, who settles and builds his house upon the land, possesses from the commencement of his tenancy a right of occupancy in it'.[51] But most of the debate kept within the terms of English jurisprudence. The effect on the Rent Law Commission was that arguments led on to continual refinements of more advanced positions, after last-ditch defending. Mackenzie and O'Kinealy, as we would expect, had started with an extreme interpretation of the *khudkashta* raiyat—as anyone admitted to a village with the intention of settling. Field argued that, whatever the original situation, a period of residence was now needed for the right to accrue. Mackenzie accepted this, and wrote in 1880 that it was 'acknowledged that the effect [of Act X of 1859] ...has been to inflict serious injury on resident ryots', but that, contrary to Bell's view, 'time' was now essential to status, and it was imposssible to go back simply to 'residence'.[52] What

---

[50] For example in Regulations VIII of 1793, s.57, ch.1; XLIV of 1793; VII of 1799, s.15, ch.7; XI of 1822, s.33, and so on.

[51] He quoted his edition of *The Law of Landlord and Tenant*, p.16; see 'Draft Bill for Behar', *RLC Report*, appendices.

[52] See note 8 above.

period would suffice? Dampier and Field favoured retaining the twelve-year rule of 1859.[53] Having given up their first point, however, Mackenzie and O'Kinealy then voted, with the support of Seal, to reduce the qualifying period to three years on their original argument that occupancy right was intended for all resident raiyats. Dampier, Field, Harrison and Roy opposed this.

As a compromise, special provisions were then proposed for raiyats holding for between three and twelve years, and thus a legacy of the strong position on occupancy found its way into the Report (supported by Dampier, Harrison, O'Kinealy, Mackenzie and Seal against Field, Mookerjea and Roy). On the other hand, in deciding whether occupancy rights could be sold without the landlord's consent, Dampier, Harrison, O'Kinealy, Field, Mookerjea and Seal thought not, but Mackenzie, Roy and Harrison were in favour.

The questions behind these manœuvres were: who is this propertied raiyat? By what rights might one identify him? These questions came up repeatedly, and overlapped with the issue of how to best to protect raiyati interests in future. One proxy for the debate concerned the distinction between tenure-holders and raiyats, on which the case law had been inconsistent. Particularly difficult was the legality of sub-letting by raiyats: did this make them tenure-holders, or was it evidence of their property rights? One answer was to consider the purpose for which interests were granted; one judgment proposed as the 'only test' whether the rights were granted on empty land (hence raiyati, an interest created for cultivation) or on land where raiyats were already in possession (hence tenure-holding, an interest created for rent-collecting).[54] The same questions could be put with regard to all sorts of transferability: one judgment claimed that any raiyat with a transferable holding was a tenure-holder.[55] The Full Bench ruling in *Ajodhya Pershad* was that occupancy right was not transferable except by custom. But later cases quite often found that the custom existed. The Bengal government in its 1883 report on the Tenancy Bill argued that free transferability existed in almost all Bengal and Bihar districts (citing 32,633 transfers recorded in 1881-2). To the riposte that this was always subject to the landlord's consent, the reply came in the government's report on the Bill in 1884, to the effect that sales occurred 'throughout these provinces' without such consent. Any such right was

[53] Mackenzie note, 20 January 1880, *RLC Report*, vol. 1.
[54] *Durga Prosanno Ghose* v. *Das Dutt*, 9 CLR 449.
[55] *Krishtendra Roy* v. *Aena Bewa*, ILR, 8 Cal.675, 10 CLR 399 (discussed in Finucane and Rampini, *Tenancy Act*).

preserved in section 178 of the 1885 Act.[56]

The Bihar Rent Committee had debated transferability, coming down against it for occupancy holdings, after weighing the dangers of throwing raiyats into the hands of mahajans against the assertion that a right of transfer already existed widely.[57] The Rent Law Commission too wanted to treat tenure-holders as intermediate landlords, and therefore to distinguish them from raiyats. But they considered different criteria—rent-receiving, heritability, transferability, quantity of rent—and decided that none was reliable.[58] The Commission thus sought to meet the situation by 'an authoritative enunciation of what is accepted in customary law', namely that occupancy holdings were freely saleable (though their division, for example at inheritance, required the landlord's consent). To keep away the mahajan, they proposed secondly that occupancy holdings should not be mortgageable. Dampier, Harrison, Field and Mookerjea also wanted to restrict the raiyats' use of the land to agricultural purposes; unsuccessfully opposing them had been Mackenzie who, with the support of O'Kinealy and Seal, had wanted to place no restrictions.[59] The Commission also proposed (paragraph 22) that all tenures of 15 years or more should be deemed permanent, and that all such tenures should be registered; but this plan was dropped, after opposition led by the Maharaja of Darbhanga and the British Indian Association, and given the difficulty of deciding on transferability. The further signifance of this issue will be considered shortly.

## IV

Among the vignettes that may serve to delineate the great rent law debate, the campaigns of opposition must play their part.[60] The landlord

---

[56] See Finucane and Rampini, *Tenancy Act.*

[57] BRC Report, pp.270-1.

[58] *RLC Report*, vol. 1, pp.12-13.

[59] See *RLC Report*, vol.1, p.16, and vol.2, Minutes of Proceedings, 17 February 1879.

[60] There are dozens of such pamphlets preserved in the India Office Library, London, several of them being reprints from newspapers, others reports of the proceedings of public meetings, for example of the East India Association or of the London Committee formed to oppose the Bengal Tenancy Bill, and yet others studies commissioned by interested parties such as the Central Committee of Landholders. References to pamphlets in this chapter are drawn from this collection. Leading pamphleteers included Ashutosh Mookerjea, Henry Bell, Roper Lethbridge and W.S. Seton-Kerr. To counter this campaign, extremely full government papers were also published, in reports or as supplements to the *Calcutta Gazette.*

interest was the best orchestrated. We have noted some of its arguments already, and will consider just three advocates in detail. The first, Ashutosh Mookerjea, who represented the major voice of the Indian zamindars, contended in refutation of the *Zemindary Settlement* that the permanent settlement had deliberately made proprietors of the landlords.

He cited Cornwallis's minute of 3 February 1790 in which he suggested that, whatever the theory of zamindari rights, in practice they had been nugatory not least because of the state's unlimited claim to revenue: the permanent settlement decided to 'stamp a value on them hitherto unknown'. The impulse came, as Mookerjea recalled, quoting Philip Francis in 1776, from the desire to preserve an intermediate level of profit: for the 'scheme of every regular Government requires that the mass of the people should labour, and that the few should be supported by the many, who receive their retribution in the peace, protection and security which accompany just authority and regular subordination'.[61] The decision in favour of landlords, Mookerjea suggested, constituted a contract between government and the zamindars. A similar contract would govern zamindars' relations with raiyats. The contracts had to be interpreted from texts, to discover the law-as-it-is, and not with reference to other information or deductions about the intentions of the lawmakers. The theory here was obviously derived, in a general way, from eighteenth-century English constitutional ideas; Mookerjea was internalising Western thought in defence of colonially-defined privileges. A novel feature, however, was the assertion that the permanent settlement transferred to the zamindars the state's 'duty...to protect all classes of people'. This new contract the state itself was bound to respect, treating it as 'unalterable like the physical bounds and divisions of the country' (an interesting comparison in view of the colonial fixing of such boundaries, for property as for states).[62]

Thus far the argument depended upon rights given by the state. But in addition the zamindari supporters wanted to prevent the state from giving rights to anyone else. One suggestion was that to do so it must also take away rights given to zamindars, thus breaking the contract. But, as we have seen, the zamindars also had to counter a much stronger, primordial view of rights which was advanced by the pro-raiyat faction—their idea of the primacy of the cultivators' right in the

---

[61] Ashutosh Mookerjea, 'The annals of British land-revenue administration in Bengal from 1688 to 1793' (Calcutta 1883). Mookerjea was then a vakil of the Calcutta High Court; later he was Vice-Chancellor of Calcutta University.

[62] Ashutosh Mookerjea, 'The proposed new rent law for Bengal and Behar' (*Calcutta Review*, October 1880; reprinted Calcutta 1880).

soil, from first Lockean principles and from their reading of Indian traditions and history. Mookerjea tried to turn such arguments against themselves. For example, he appealed to a passage in Harington's *Analysis* which appeared to support the cultivators' rights. Harington argued that the variety of rent rates in Bengal resulted from a discretion allowed to the zamindars to add to the rates approved by the state; *abwabs* were an innovation subsequently sanctioned by custom. The government could and did intervene to prevent oppression, and some raiyats had the privilege of fixed rates. On the other hand no raiyat should be given a right to which he was not already entitled. Presumably the principles evoked were that custom and the state were somehow co-equal, for change might be legitimised as practice but was also subject to state regulation; and that rights were otherwise fixed and inviolate. By contrast Mookerjea's argument depended not only on a primordial right of the state but also on rights of the zamindars acquired by an act of the state. He faced a slight awkwardness in regard to the salience of custom.

He introduced a second element which rather contradicted the legalism of the first. Presenting himself as a practical man facing high-handed theorists,[63] Mookerjea now played up the special needs of India. He appealed to Émile de Laveleye's Cobden Club essays,[64] and asked whether legal changes could 'extinguish the influence of instincts or tendencies whether inherent in the race or the historical product of centuries'. This doubt perhaps had been implied in Harington's position also. But Mookerjea's gloss on this was to regard the raiyat as 'no better than his landlord' in his instincts, and never known 'to postpone the requirements of his family to the requirements of political economy': hence the prominence in Bengal of the problems of over-population, subletting and subdivision. Now, in what was at root a racial doctrine, endorsed by Mookerjea, custom became supreme, if only because ignoring it would not overcome the impediments it presented to economic rationality, as the reformers hoped. Taking Field's argument about transferability, Mookerjea asserted that that too

---

[63] Ibid, p.53: 'Theory was very powerfully represented in the [Rent Law] Commission, and swayed with a high hand all its deliberations; but practical acquaintance with the realities of peasant life in Bengal, and, above all, practical common-sense views of what was just in the actual circumstances, were much too inadequately represented.'

[64] Ibid. De Laveleye published Cobden Club essays, 'On the causes of war' (1872) and 'The provincial and communal institutions of Belgium and Holland' (1875), but Mookerjea's page reference (242-4) is to an unidentified compilation.

should only come about where it was 'suited to the locality'. To provide for it by rule in other places 'cannot but prove mischievous'. This view originated partly in Jones's critique which, Mookerjea thought, showed Ricardo's theory of rent, and its supposed mobility of capital, to be applicable only in England. Mookerjea professed to be well aware of the distinctions of Jones, as adapted by J.S. Mill in *Principles of Political Economy*, and by Whewell, between different kinds of rent—labour, *metayer*, raiyati and cottier. Jones's theory had the merit, in Indian conditions, of showing that rent might increase according to political factors beyond what economic calculations supposed possible—an awkward argument for the zamindari camp.[65] On the other hand Jones's 'raiyati' rent also implied, of course, a different view of the state as sole landed proprietor: the rent was the monarch's share of the produce collected by his agents for a percentage, the amount depending on his (and their) power or forebearance, and not upon economic factors such as soil quality or returns on capital. The state's role, one may suppose, was to secure the cultivator on its own land, in return for the share of the produce. What the permanent settlement had done—and here was the beauty of the two theories together—was to transfer this state ownership to the zamindars in perpetuity. The cultivator was entitled, under the state or the zamindar, only to such a share as would enable him to cultivate, live in reasonable comfort, and participate in the progress of the country. Thus Mookerjea interpreted Philip Francis's version of the social hierarchy.

It is difficult to assess the importance of ideas when two opposite tendencies are thus marshalled in support of the one point of view. These modes of argument seem to be the means but not the cause of the positions taken. On the other hand the arguments were won or lost often on the basis of some previous 'authority', by virtue of what he had *said*—usually a reflection of the intellectual currents of *his* day—without any real sense or concern about demonstrating that it was true, empirically. The cleverness of Mookerjea's argument was that it used almost the same premises as his opponents—the terms which most people accepted—in order to reach an opposite and equally extreme conclusion. One may compare it with that which the Rent Law Commissioners espoused when they suggested that the legislature had the

---

[65] On Richard Jones' importance to tenancy debates in India, see Eric Stokes, *The Peasant and the Raj. Studies in Agrarian Society and Peasant Rebellion in Colonial India* (Cambridge 1978), pp.90-119, referring to Jones, *Essay on the Distribution of Wealth* (1831). The reference to William Whewell, presumably his 'Elements of morality', has not been traced.

power and duty to 're-distribute property in land...in the interests of the entire community'. If this duty of care existed, then, according to Mookerjea, it now belonged to the zamindars. If it were taken on fully by the state it became, in Mookerjea's term, 'socialistic'.

In a further pamphlet in 1884 Mookerjea was tempted by an even more bold argument, of appearing to concede that the raiyats had rights in 1793, but arguing that if so these had been lost by legislation passed then, and subsequently, in favour of the zamindars. This was a somewhat exposed position for one who railed against the government's imminent 'confiscation' of zamindari rights. By this time Mookerjea and the landowners were contending with the pro-raiyat case as set out in draft legislation, and therefore had to attack the acceptance of arguments about raiyats' property. Mookerjea rested his case on Lord Hastings' resolution of 1 August 1822 to the effect that the Bengal revenue code was founded on the recognition of private property in land. But he also had to reply to S. C. Bayley, who, supporting the pro-raiyat case, quoted the Court of Directors' letters of 19 September 1792 and 7 October 1815. Mookerjea countered that even the latter—which referred unequivocally to the resident raiyats' 'established permanent hereditary right in the soil'—had implied a residuary right for the landlord in remarking also that these tenurial and proprietary rights had to be reconciled. Another account suggested that the privileges derived from those provided when land was originally settled (implying a pre-existing zamindari right as a kind of first cause), and that they were thus properly restricted to those who could trace their inheritance to the first settlers. More generally, so the argument went, the zamindars were like the petty rajas of ancient India. The implication was that most peasant rights were an import from other parts of India—this writer cited Holt Mackenzie's Act and the record of rights in the NWP—and that the peasant proprietary interest had never existed or had been lost in Bengal; no less an authority than Harington stated that the region had 'no such little republics or village communities'.[66]

C.P. Ilbert, in his speech to the legislature on the tenancy Bill, had pinpointed the difficulty once it was conceded that there were two rights; it was that a contract between two parties (government and zamindars) could hardly affect the rights of a third party, the raiyats. Yet Halhed, in his 'Memoir of the Land Tenure and Principles of Taxation in Bengal', declared firmly that Cornwallis had abrogated the 'allodial rights' of the cultivators; on 12 July 1820 Colebrooke referred to the merging of all village rights into the zamindars' property. If the

---

[66] K. C. Acharya, 'Strike but hear'. Acharya was a Mymensingh zamindar.

government were sovereign, and the zamindars held the superior, residuary rights, why not accept that the raiyats had simply had their rights 'confiscated' in 1793? The question would then be again one of the position of the state: was it truly subject to law, that is bound by its previous decisions? Could a lawful government go back on its promise to the landlords? The question was repeatedly asked. It was significant that the pro-reform party seldom suggested that it should, only that the promise was not what it was purported to be. For them the zamindar was an owner subject to restrictions.

Mookerjea's new line was perhaps only slightly less perilous than one which allowed for a sovereign legislature, though it neatly accomplished the trick of suggesting that reality was as the Regulations described it to be. The rights, Mookerjea proposed, departing at this point from Ilbert, were not after all created *de novo* in 1793. The zamindars were not revenue collectors who became owners. Unlike the revenue farmers, they were already owners whose ownership gained effect and value by the limiting of the government's revenue demand. In the turns of this casuistry, Mookerjea had lost sight of, or rather suppressed, as it is still hidden here, his 1880 version in which the state was the original proprietor making a gift of proprietorship to the zamindars; and perhaps this confusion was a fair reflection of the avowed intention in 1793 *either* to preserve *or* to create landlords. Mookerjea concluded in short that zamindars had *and* were given absolute and unlimited rights in the soil, both in the permanent settlement and by ancient custom. Other rights—of a particular class to hold at fixed rents, of another class to occupancy—also existed, in so far as they were recorded in the Regulations. This was consistent with a principle that (he conceded) still applied, the right to legislate for the general good. But Mookerjea also alleged that legislation should not be passed in order to benefit one class at the expense of another. Ilbert had not really tackled this argument. His speech took the limited view that zamindars gained only such rights as the government of the day had been able to share, that the Regulations reserved a right of future legislation, and that other rights, including those not mentioned at the time, also existed and could now be supported by new laws. It was a peculiar kind of reasoning, subordinating state to private or social rights, and less satisfactory, in its historical legalisms, than other more pragmatic, public-policy justifications for the Bill. In common with much of the rest of the legislative debate, it operated in effect on Mookerjea's ground, and gave so many hostages to fortune—or to such a subtle advocate as Mookerjea—that it became a focus of the pro-zamindari attack during 1884. It may perhaps have contributed to the weakening of the tenancy Bill in its final stages.[67]

Our second opponent of the Bill, representative of a large group, was Roper Lethbridge, former Press Commissioner of India. His attack was straightforward. He quoted opinions that the Tenancy Bill was an 'ungodly measure of wholesale robbery' (*Hindoo Patriot*), an 'abuse of plenary power' (the *Englishman*), depriving zamindars of proprietary rights (Behar Landholders), revolutionary indeed to the 'horror and dismay' of the Chief Justice of Bengal, and an attack on the rights, social position, and the 'very means of living' of the landlords (Maharaja Sir Jatindranath Tagore). But Lethbridge concentrated not on these issues of justice and principle, but on the consequences of the measure. If a 'hitherto absolutely unknown' transferability of raiyati holdings were allowed, then, he claimed, control of the estates would pass from zamindars to occupancy-raiyat middlemen of whom the actual cultivators would become serfs; it would make these raiyats unthrifty and give 'a most unwholesome stimulus to over-population, already the great difficulty' being faced in Bengal. The chief thrust of this was, first, that raiyats were not already miserable, not even in Bihar (those who claimed so were sadly mistaken, including Florence Nightingale in the *Contemporary Review*)[68] and, secondly, that they would be made miserable by the errors of this reform.[69]

Lethbridge and his fellows brought to the fore two other elements as well—personal attacks and comparisons with Ireland. The latter were important especially in London where opposition was led by former India hands in alliance with Irish landlord interests: the Indian Constitutional Association (with Lethbridge to the fore) and the Liberty and Property Defence League chaired by Lord Wemyss and March. Some supporters were moved by fear of a general attack on property—Sir Herbert Maxwell, MP, spoke in such terms to a meeting in 1885—[70] and by the support of Bright and others for the Rent Bill.[71] Though

---

[67] Ashutosh Mookerjea, 'An examination of the principles and policy of the Bengal Tenancy Bill, written at the request of the Central Committee of Landholders' (Calcutta, 1884).

[68] Lethbridge quoted Raja Shiva Prasad, who claimed in the Governor-General's Council in March 1883, that he had nowhere found a 'stronger set of ryots, happier or better off' than in Bettiah.

[69] Roper Lethbridge, 'The mischief threatened by the Bengal Tenancy Bill', paper read to the East India Association, 31 October 1883 (London, 1883).

[70] '"The Bengal Tenancy Bill". Report of proceedings of a meeting held at Willis's Rooms, King Street, St. James's, on Wednesday, February 25th, 1885' (London, 1885).

[71] J. Dacosta, 'The Bengal Tenancy Bill' (London 1884). Eden had predicted

their alliance was not formalised until the middle of 1884, their pressure, and the involvement of a number of MPs, as well as Indian civil servants and Calcutta merchants, probably played a part (alongside the objections of the Secretary of State's Council) in ensuring that further consideration was asked for in Hartington's despatch of 17 August 1883, and that Kimberley rejected, on 15 December, the occupancy right attaching to the land and not the tenant. This group in particular also made personal attacks on Ripon, described by Lord Fortescue as 'the present rash and reckless Viceroy, a benevolent man, but a man of some socialistic theories'—a delicate insult combining hints of personal acquaintance and Ripon's temporary tenure, with allegations of his weakness and poor judgment, and a surely intentional echo of Hamlet's lament for the 'wretched, rash', *interfering* Polonius. It was also suggested repeatedly in these circles, as by Garth and others, that support for the tenancy Bill could be traced to 'certain officials' and to the strong views of Ashley Eden backed by the Viceroy. C.T. Buckland, a Bengal civil servant and formerly senior member of the Bengal Board of Revenue, complained that the requests to divisional Commissioners for advice had instructed them to take a vote among their subordinates; he was sure that every official would have responded predictably, quite able to 'see which way the wind blows if he wishes to please the Lieutenant-Governor'.[72] A.P. MacDonnell, then Revenue Secretary, was a particular *bête noire*.[73] When Ashley Eden fell ill in November 1883, MacDonnell stood in for him on the Select Committee and 'urged, in threatening words' (according to Buckland) that the Tenancy Bill should be passed at once.[74]

---

an organised opposition in Britain, on hearing that money was being sent from India; he considered British opinion 'pretty sound', with the important proviso, he told Ripon, that 'you do not go too far'; to Ripon, 1 June 1883, Add.Mss. 43592. Kimberley too reported to Ripon a growing feeling, not only among Tories, that he was 'introducing too many internal changes'; to Ripon, 16 February 1883, Add.Mss.43523.

[72] Mackenzie to Primrose, 26 January 1883, Add.Mss.43615.

[73] London Committee formed to oppose the Bengal Tenancy Bill, pamphlets 1-6: 'The Bengal Tenancy Bill' (*Morning Post*, 1 February 1885), 'Indian opinion on the London Committee' (K.D. Paul, member of the Imperial Legislative Council), 'The Indian tea industry endangered by the Bengal Tenancy Bill' (*Morning Post*, 28 February), 'Mr. Seton-Karr's lecture on the Bengal Tenancy Bill' (C.T. Buckland), 'Mr. Seton-Karr's letter [to *The Times*] on the Bengal Tenancy Bill' (Buckland), and 'The Government of India on the Report of the Select Committee on the Tenancy Bill' (Buckland).

[74] C.T. Buckland, 'The Bengal Tenancy Bill as amended in the Select Committee of the Legislative Council of India' (London, 16 June 1884). Buckland was part of the London group opposing the tenancy Bill.

The London Committee to oppose the Bill, its activities well publicised in the *Morning Post*, produced a barrage of pamphlets, claiming that the Government of Bengal had an animus against the zamindars (presented by Charles Campbell, brother of Sir George, as out-squiring the English squire) and that it ignored the principles of political economy (meaning the market laws of supply and demand). The group even suggested that tea-planters would be unable to settle their labourers on land, and that English shareholders would suffer. Eden claimed to Mackenzie that he had prevented publication of a 'tremendous onslaught on Ripon's revolutionary policy' made by 'fearfully ignorant' people who believed Ripon intended every raiyat to have the right to hold in perpetuity on a fixed rent and not to be liable for eviction even for non-payment. The bitterness of the exchanges which we will see shortly, between Garth and Mackenzie, were repeated in the pamphlet war. They were fierce because they occurred within a close community (one wonders if the animosities ever spilt over on, say, the committee of the Bethune School committee in Calcutta on which both served);[75] but also because of issues of principle to which people were intellectually committed.

Lethbridge had argued that tenancy reform, originally undertaken to help and compensate zamindars after the Cess Acts which he thought breached the permanent settlement, and to redress the balance after the 1859 Act, had been taken over by a school of reformers deluded by 'absurd descriptions' of the raiyats' poverty, and 'dazzled by the splendid achievements of slap-dash land-reform in Ireland'.[76] This brings us, secondly, to Lord Wemyss who reported that in Ireland the 'fair' rents rule had set the landlord's rent below the market rate, allowing the tenant to sell land on the market. The result was to divorce the labourer on the land from the ownership of tenancies, which he could not afford. Largely on the basis of this supposedly conclusive comparison—by those who after all mostly argued that landlords and tenants were everywhere alike—Buckland similarly feared the creation of middlemen in India.[77] Lethbridge, in 1885, declared that to create them was the main purpose of the Bill; and J. Dacosta, a former Calcutta merchant, derided the attempt to present the Bill as supportive of actual cultivators by those who had no sympathy for the middlemen who, he claimed, would

---

[75] Thacker's Directory for 1880.

[76] Lethbridge, 'Mischief'.

[77] Buckland, '"The Bengal Tenancy Bill". Report of a meeting held at St. James' Hall, on Wednesday, June 25th, 1880' (London, 1884).

be the real beneficiaries.[78]

In its pure form the doctrine of this group was as laid down by a final representative critic, Fleetwood Pellow, the Commissioner of Dhaka Division. It went like this: eighteenth-century Bengal had been one-third waste land, savaged by dacoits, its government (the Company) in financial difficulty. The zamindars had had hereditary and residuary title—hence the institution of *nijjote* and *khamar* (or *zerat*)—and raiyats were entitled to a fixed proportion of the produce, ensured by pargana-rate tables revised periodically with reference to custom, land use and prevailing prices. The zamindars had been sorely tested by eighteenth-century revenue demands, and were losing out to 'men of capital' on smaller properties, men who made improvements but were 'hard in their dealings'. The permanent settlement stopped this process, and improved prosperity, the only problem being sub-infeudation. Act X of 1859 created a new right of occupancy for some (a broader category than the *khudkashta* raiyats). Pellow observed, in addition, that in Eastern Bengal these 'old' raiyats had become proverbially wealthy, and frequently were giving up actual cultivation. They were becoming middlemen who benefited at the expense of both the zamindar and the cultivator. These under-raiyats and field labourers (*kurfa*) were the true poor identified by the Famine Commission.

The historical aspects of this are not all convincing, but there is some interest in the observations, in view of the more egalitarian picture of the region, and the sudden appearance of a Muslim rich and middle peasantry, as described in recent literature.[79] In the great rent debate, the attention on the past directed attention away from such present observations and predictions. But Pellow's was not an impressive piece, and (despite Buckland's certainty of official self-interest) he mixed in a great number of points which, whatever their validity, could have been calculated not to persuade his superiors, convinced as they then were by the proprietary peasant above all—points about the proposed definition of *khamar* discouraging zamindari improvements, or the value of zamindar's loyalty, or the disadvantages of perpetuating the occupancy right. Pellow also remarked, more pertinently, that the Bill was 'framed on the basis of refusing protection to those who are of necessity cultivators, and affording it to those who are only accidentally

[78] Dacosta, 'Tenancy Bill'.

[79] See Sugata Bose, *Agrarian Bengal. Econony, Social Structure and Politics, 1919-1947* (Cambridge 1986); Partha Chatterjee, *Bengal 1920-1947. The Land Question* (Calcutta 1984); and, for an argument tracing this stratification to the later nineteenth century, Nariaki Nakazato, *Agrarian System in Eastern Bengal c.1870-1910* (Calcutta 1994).

and occasionally such...'.[80] There were very many other occasions on which similar points were made, since, on the Rent Law Commission, H.L. Harrison had regarded the prohibition of sub-letting as the key-stone of the necessary legislation. Surely it was an ideological fixation upon the 'magic of property'—on both sides of the argument, and by all the cleverest and most vociferous advocates—which prevented decisive weight being given to this serious and realistic point about how Indian agrarian society worked. In practice sharp differences of opinion remained on this issue throughout the debate. Interestingly, in the exchange of views in London in 1884, when W.S. Seton-Karr lectured on the subject to the Society of Arts, Sir George Campbell advocated the welfare of labourers, while the lecturer (who was critical of aspects of the Bill) wanted to benefit raiyats but not under-raiyats.[81] It was all too easy for Pellow's point to be dismissed as just another facile objection from the mediocrity, or just another piece of special pleading by the zamindars. Successful, articulate and influential men were certain about the raiyats' property as a device for future prosperity, and perhaps also of their loyalty and manly virtues (as already was the perception of the Punjab).

V

The outline to be discerned in the *Zemindary Settlement*, with its echoes in Hunter and Baden-Powell, was worthy of attention because it exemplified many of the arguments employed by the tenancy reformers before 1885. The main lines taken by the opponents could be discerned in the writings of Mookerjea and Lethbridge in particular. But the most dramatic contest between these views was the public row between two of the highest officers in Bengal—the Chief Secretary, Alexander Mackenzie, and the Chief Justice, Richard Garth—over the 1885 Act. Also involved as a judge with experience on the revenue side was J. O'Kinealy.[82] Where the other debates vied in their interpretations of the permanent settlement and their prediction of future agrarian relations, this dispute was also crucially about the proper role of the state and of law.[83] One of the instructive features was the extent that the

---

[80] Fleetwood H. Pellow, 'The rent question in Bengal' (London, 1883).

[81] [Buckland)], 'Mr. Seton-Karr's Lecture'.

[82] The memoranda discussed below may be found with R&A Rev A 16-46 (July 1883). See also Add.Mss.43584. An earlier version of this account was published as part of 'Ideas in agrarian history'; see the Acknowledgments.

[83] There may have been personal as well as policy issues. Garth also clashed with Ripon over a proposed reduction in High Court judges' salaries, and over

protagonists considered the tenancy issue a matter of public concern, in Britain as well as India; it was important, to their minds, both in politics and theoretically, at a time when the obscure details of Indian agrarian history were thought to raise significant intellectual issues.

For several years, during all the discussions, Bengal's Chief Justice had held aloof. He was on leave abroad, or he was ill, or (as he said, when he broke his silence in 1882) he was unwilling to oppose the strong pro-raiyat views of Eden until they had taken definite shape. But, finally, after the Rent Law Commission's report had been turned into a draft bill, and that draft had been amended by the local government and further changed by the Government of India, and yet another version had been prepared to meet the objections of the Secretary of State, Sir Richard Garth did put pen to paper. His previous silence did not prevent him from complaining that the High Court had not been properly consulted. But he saved his venom for those whom he called the extremists of the Rent Law Commission, two of the younger members who were responsible, as he saw it, for 'revolutionary provisions' which, 'unjustly and unnecessarily', would dispossess the landlords of rights they had enjoyed for nearly a century, and relegate them to a position 'far inferior to that which they occupied before the Permanent Settlement'—that is, before the foundation in 1793 of the Bengal system of revenue, land law and administration.[84] Garth objected above all to the extension of the occupancy right and to limits on rent enhancement. The young men in question were Mackenzie and O'Kinealy, both of whom at that time had had some twenty years' service in India. The interference they proposed was justified by them, Garth complained, on a ground '(if it is worth to be called by that name)' which was as 'transparent a pretext as ever was presented'. Their

---

the appointment of Mitter, J., to act as Chief Justice while he was on leave. Earlier he had similarly objected to the appointment of an Indian barrister such as W.C. Bonnerjee (whose ability, power in court and legal knowledge he admitted were 'second to none') or Manmohan Ghose, as Standing Counsel for the Bengal government, as 'however good he might be' an Indian appointee would 'generally be distasteful to the Bar', and awkward in some political prosecutions, and because of the expectation of promotion from Standing Counsel to Advocate General; Garth to Ripon, 20 September 1880 and 10 July 1882, Add.Mss.43610. Ripon later objected that Mitter was to be passed over for the substantive appontment as Chief Justice; to Kimberley, 8 February 1886, Add. Mss.43526.

[84] This was a conventional viewpoint for the judges; it was endorsed on the Rent Law Commission by P.M. Mookerjea in a note dissenting to measures which would 'assail the very foundation of private property'. *RLC Report*, vol. 1, p.96.

extreme views, he wrote, were supported by no one, and by nothing save their own 'constructions' of previous legislation, and indeed were contradicted by all the eminent men who had expounded the law since the permanent settlement—men who were, it was true, 'unfortunate enough to have differed in opinion with Mr Mackenzie'. Loftily, the Chief Justice trusted that 'even Mr O'Kinealy' would learn 'some little respect for authority and precedent' when he became 'a permanent member of the High Court'; Garth hoped he would before long.[85] Garth then published his memorandum in the newspapers; it was seized upon eagerly by the well-organised opponents of the Tenancy Act, and was also translated into Bengali and Hindi and circulated widely in the province.[86] There followed various correspondence, including letters to *The Times* in London. Some of the readers must have been glad of Garth's assurance that, as he was 'happy to say', O'Kinealy and Mackenzie were two gentlemen who were 'both very good friends' of his.

At one level this was just another round in the long rivalry between Court and executive in Bengal. That, in turn, was a special variant of the rivalry between regulated and arbitrary methods of government. As Henry Cotton wrote to Ripon in September 1893:

The point is this: our present form of administration organised 100 years ago is still adequate and well suited to the requirements of the masses of the population with whom the *hakim ka hookum* is still an article of belief. To the Oriental mind the concentration of authority in one responsible head is the only conceivable system of Government. But the spread of English education during the past two generations has created among the educated classes a demand for a revised method of administration based upon the English model. It is impossible not to admit the justice and reasonableness of this demand but the difficulty is to accede to it in a manner which shall not in any way impair efficiency.[87]

---

[85] O'Kinealy was officiating on the High Court bench; in December 1882 Garth had recommended him for the full appointment, as having 'by far the highest claim'; to Primrose, 8 December 1882, Add.Mss. 63610.

[86] The publication of the material infringed the sensitivity shown towards the security of internal notes; see S.C. Bayley to Ripon, 1 August [1882], Add. Mss.43612, tracing copies of Rivers Thompson's confidential memorandum. Kimberley considered whether to take official notice of Garth's note; his instinct was to ignore it, as 'the public has a notion that the independent position of a judge warrants him in speaking his mind, however foolish that mind may be'; to Ripon, 24 January 1883 and also 24 October 1884, Add.Mss.43523. Garth later remarked that he had intended his minute to be an official communication and not a private letter, as the government were regarding it; if private, he agreed, it would have been improper to have had it published as an official document; to Primrose, 19 December 1882, Add.Mss.43610.

[87] Cotton to Ripon, 10 September 1893, Add.Mss.43618.

Oddly, Garth, who was quite hostile to any such advance, nonetheless represented another strand of pressure for it, as in judicial review, or insistence upon proper form and precedent, designed to moderate executive discretion. He clearly envisaged general codes within which the state should operate, codes of consistency and good purpose in face of competing rights. These were doctrines to limit state power, while presenting the courts as the defenders of higher and (by Cotton's conventional stereotype) non-Oriental principles.

Garth complained that measures passed by one Lieutenant-Governor and confirmed by another, should not be lightly set aside; otherwise the public would have no security that in another ten years another Lieutenant-Governor might not arise who would take another view and cause another general revolution. According to Garth, legislation, if it interfered with rights, was justifiable only in a real emergency; and rights, though they might derive from legislation, rested ultimately upon the common law. Thus, any occupancy right for the tenants must have depended, before 1793, upon prescription; that is, it was a common law presumption of legal title on the basis of possession from time immemorial, a provision recognised in Roman law and given legislative form in England (with a thirty-year limit) in 1832. Boldly, Garth accommodated this precedent to Indian experience by supposing that 'prescription' was really the same as what Indians meant by 'custom': these 'poor people', the raiyats, he explained sadly, knew no difference between the two, and in fact probably had no word in their language to signify 'prescription'. In short, in opposition to theories of an Asiatic way, he supposed that the underlying principles of law were universal. Fundamentally he was convinced that property was a natural state of man, that it was regulated by contract, and that, though either might evolve, neither should be overturned by governments. Nor should the courts be required to intervene in transforming or denying them: Garth was concerned that the rent law would create a 'frightful amount of ill-feeling and litigation'. On the other hand he recognised also that practice differed, and that enactments could alter things: he imagined that the period of prescription required for tenant rights had varied from place to place before 1793, and that afterwards the zamindars 'took advantage of the liberty of contract which they acquired' in order to 'break in upon existing customs' by requiring written agreements from their tenants, setting out rents and the duration of tenancies.[88] But he

[88] See Garth's 'Proposed new rent law', minute no.1, 8 January 1880, *RLC Report*, Appendices, arguing that zamindars had 'almost as much freedom' as English landlords, and that Act X of 1859 was 'an invasion of the landlord's

argued both that such changes had produced new rights which could not now be overturned, and that the consequences of extending similar rights to tenants would be to create in the occupancy right a valuable property, a prize for land speculators: the more valuable it was, the less likely the cultivating classes would be to acquire it; indeed the condition of the actual cultivator would probably decline.

This last was a shrewd thrust at the advocates of tenant-rights, but generally Garth was a man of narrow imagination: the law had a concrete reality for him to an extent with which the revenue officers had little patience. It was far from the case that agrarian relations were being regulated by law-courts to the degree that Garth believed, though the laws of property had undoubtedly made an impact on the situation of zamindars; on the matter of contract for example it was known that very few formal leases were issued between landlords and tenants.[89] It was not until somewhat later that the courts did intervene to an increasing extent—the ten-year averages of rent suits almost doubled between 1890 and 1903—and the increase was in large part attributable to the Bengal Tenancy Act (as Garth had predicted), and to the greater access provided by Small Cause Courts (with jurisdiction in cases worth up to Rs.500 for subordinate judges) and by an expansion in the number of munsiff's courts (competent in civil cases worth up to Rs.1,000).

The replies to Garth concentrated upon the legal arguments. It was pointed out that proprietary rights in Bengal were very concentrated and very lightly taxed, and that rental incomes had increased vastly since the permanent settlement; but the reformers were convinced that there was no need to justify change on such arguments of public policy. What was now proposed—the words come from H.S. Cunningham, another High Court judge—was not a subversion but a re-establishment of the law, exercising a right reserved in 1793 for the state to intervene to prevent the 'raiyats being improperly disturbed in their possessions'. According to this view (as we have seen) the great mass of resident raiyats had commonly possessed occupancy rights throughout India. It will be plain from our earlier discussion that there was an interesting confusion or conflation here. Mackenzie and his fellows believed the usual cultivator was a resident; they thought that 'resident cultivator' was a fair translation of *khudkashta* raiyat, and that the privileges of

rights'. He himself admitted: 'I may have been induced to look at the matter rather too much from an English point of view'.

[89] Garth had argued that the registration of all leases would put a stop to a vast amount of litigation; as raiyats were mostly illiterate, he proposed official registry offices where records would be explained to both parties; 'Note by Sir Richard Garth on Mr Field's Digest', *RLC Report*, Appendices.

such raiyats were well-established. Therefore, the usual cultivator had (or should have) the same rights, which only the previous errors of government and the courts had obscured. It now seems clear that not all residents, not even all resident cultivators, were *khudkashta* raiyats; and indeed that not all *khudkashta* raiyats were true cultivators or even necessarily resident. Rather there were categories of privileged proprietary tenants; there were village residents who inherited tenancies and other obligations or benefits, but without such privileged status; there were resident cultivators who had little or no land directly from a zamindar, or who were otherwise not regarded as full members of the community; there were *khudkashta* raiyats in one village who occupied fields in another, as *pahikashta* (non-privileged) tenants; and so on: the picture, as will already be plain enough, is of a very great complexity. There was no pair of categories neatly covering all the possibilities, and available for Western legislators.

O'Kinealy wrote along similar lines to his colleague, Cunningham, and with rather less circumspection than might have been expected from one yet to receive his permanent appointment to the High Court. He had been a reluctant recruit to the Rent Law Commission, he explained, and returned to the subject only to meet Garth's 'rather personal attack'—one written, moreover, calmly in England (in fact during the sea-passage) and not in India or in the heat of discussion; one then published in the Indian newspapers. Reluctant or not, O'Kinealy was unable to refrain from citing what he regarded as factual and legal errors in Garth's submission. There was rather a long list of these, for some of which O'Kinealy drew on his twelve years of experience as a revenue officer. This gave him a different view of the intellectual capacities of the average raiyat—as for their not understanding 'prescription', for example, he could only say that since becoming Government Legal Remembrancer, supervising the drafting of government pleadings, he had seen hundreds of documents making just that plea. But, as a former revenue officer, the main difference was in his approach to the legal record. Garth interpreted the current state of the law mainly from the perspective of universal legal principles. O'Kinealy scanned the many authorities from Cornwallis onwards to reveal general support for the idea that, in India, 'no tenant could be ejected except for non-payment of rent, nor could his rent be enhanced beyond the customary rate'. Thus armed he suggested that it was the Chief Justice and not he who should learn to respect authorities, and that 'It is not by mere general statements in regard to us or our motives that our arguments can be set aside'.

As will be already apparent, however, this was to take a rather sanguine view of the history of enactments, legal statements and judgments by the British in Eastern India over the preceding hundred years. Indeed had O'Kinealy been correct, the need for a new tenancy law would not have seemed as obvious as he otherwise claimed it to be. What O'Kinealy was doing was interpreting a diverse series of statements of principle which purported to describe what the existing situation in India was in regard to tenant rights. In other words, just as Garth's ultimate authorities were the analytical principles of the law, those of O'Kinealy were the customs of India: each of them supposed that their authorities had a unique validity. In detail, however, O'Kinealy derived his understanding of custom from the statements of British administrators, whom he therefore had to assume had an accurate knowledge of Indian realities. He declared that the permanent settlement and subsequent regulations did not give the zamindars freedom of contract; therefore he assumed they had previously been bound by custom. He argued that rents were not, as Garth thought, customarily a share of produce, but expressed as a money rate; he believed therefore in the reality of a district or pargana rate, moderated by the state, and which zamindars were bound to apply. He found that *khudkashta* raiyats were not regarded as 'settled' in the meaning of English law, and that regulations in 1793 specified periods of prescription; he concluded that such rules reflected actual rights generally held in eighteenth-century Bengal.

Mackenzie's reply was similar. 'The situation is no doubt serious', he commented, 'when the Chief Justice of the Province thinks it his duty to use language like this of any Government measure, and when he not only makes these charges in general terms, but, in the face of the public, he impeaches two officers of Government by name as the authors and instigators of all the mischief'. Mackenzie denied the last point vehemently, giving details of the votes on the Rent Law Commission: the views he and O'Kinealy put forward were not original to them and mostly were not opposed on material grounds, and indeed were supported by the Indian judicial member (now the first Bengali district judge), a man 'deeply read in Indian law and well acquainted with Indian custom'.[90] If there had been a radical among them, on

[90] Seal did indeed largely vote with Mackenzie and O'Kinealy. On the other hand, though Field largely drafted the Commission's report, Mackenzie, at his most eloquent, had led the attack on the Commission's dissenting minority, Mookerjea and Roy, who, he claimed, reflected 'Every prejudice arising out of Western notions of property'. *RLC Report*, vol.1, pp.96 ff.

tenant rights, it had been H.L. Harrison, the Secretary to the Board of Revenue, cited by Garth as if he supported his views; Harrison had wanted to 'protect the actual cultivator whoever he might be'. This Board-of-Revenue view (for it received some support from the Commission's chairman, H.L. Dampier, a member of the Board) represented the pure voice of pragmatism, interpreted in the way then current: that is, the revenue officer's appreciation that the real problem was to find some way of protecting the agricultural producer from those whose rights in land (or for that matter over capital) enabled them to batten on his output. It was this thinking—the conclusions drawn from the evidence of starvation and agrarian riots—which Mackenzie described as the 'stern logic of facts' which had forced reform upon a reluctant government. He represented this as helping the landlords: the Act would be their 'salvation', for the alternative to a settling of the rent question would 'lead them into narrower straits than they have ever dreamt of'.

In this defence, Mackenzie was marshalling authorities, including himself: being in his forties, he had (he wrote) rather liked being called 'young', but he pointedly contrasted his decades in India with the brief experience of the London-trained barrister who had been parading his seniority. From the authorities, as already remarked, he could find an initial premise that the 'old law and custom of Bengal made no practical distinction between resident and non-resident ryots, and that all ryots without distinction of class (not being mere casuals or nomads) were entitled to hold their lands without disturbance, so long as they paid rents not less than the established rates'. Moreover the British laws had not turned these raiyats into 'mere contract tenants'. This was the basis of the local government's reply to some objections from the Secretary of State; but it was a remarkable claim, considerably beyond anything contained explicitly in the much-vaunted authorities. Mackenzie subverted customary divisions of ancestry, caste or kind in favour of a generalised right apparently derived from (or at least expressed in) the action of paying a standard rent. Elsewhere he referred to the 'unfriended peasants', supported only by 'much dry study of old records, old laws and old books', on the basis of which he, the peasants' champion, had 'been led to hold that there is, both in law and fact, a living tenant-right in Bengal—a right, that is to say, belonging to the cultivator, limiting and restricting the proprietary rights of the zemindar, and which, though seriously damaged by ill-advised legislation, has not yet been altogether destroyed'.[91]

[91] *RLC Report*, vol.1, p.110.

But the true origin of the idea was theoretical; we can recognise in it, as in the *Zemindary Settlement*, the living presence of the notion of the Indian village community. India was divided, as Baden Powell put it, into groups of holdings called villages, in which a collective owner- ship derived from the bond of union among the original tribe or settlers. This was the primary form of landholding in India. By contrast, the zamindar was an intermediary who owed his position to his having swallowed up some of these communal rights in land.[92] Mackenzie did not conclude from this that it was possible to return to the pristine con- dition of the village in Bengal, but he did conclude that the govern- ment's goal was to secure an occupancy right for settled cultivators, so as to exclude 'land jobbers and mahajans' and to create 'a well-to-do peasant class, able to resist the vicissitudes of seasons and to pay a fair rent'. He was concerned at any further decay in the primary rights of the village land-holders at the hands of outside speculators or money- lenders—his view of the village community was that it was a sealed unit, distinct from the world surrounding it—but he did not take Garth's point that their depredations would be increased as a consequence of vesting valuable property in the tenants. On the contrary, he believed that property would enable the raiyat to defend himself. In short, his priority was not to protect the vulnerable cultivators but (while saving the landlords!) to help support a 'class'—his word—of proprietary pea- sants. He agreed, as all did, 'about keeping moneylenders out' but added, significantly, 'if we can'. In his book on *The Indian Economy*, Pramit Chaudhuri refers to the idea of a 'kulak state', seeking economic growth rather than redistribution.[93] Clearly, if it existed, it was not an invention of independent India.

At the time of the tenancy debate, concern was expressed for the 'actual cultivator', his subjection and vulnerability to famine. Obvious- ly, in the aftermath of the Deccan riots and the 1879 Agriculturists Relief Act, this could translate into worries about transfers of land to moneylenders and other non-cultivators. Some who advised on the leg- islation, as we have seen, opposed transferability because they feared for social cohesion and political stability. Mortgages and land transfers to and from different categories of people were regularly monitored after 1885, as part of the reports on the working of the Act. But defects in the categorisation meant that agricultural moneylenders, sub-letting

[92] See B.H. Baden-Powell, *The Indian Village Community* (London 1896), ch. 1.

[93] Pramit Chaudhuri, *The Indian Economy. Poverty and Development* (Lon- don 1978), ch. 9.

and terms for the employment of labour were largely unremarked and unregulated—and intentionally so. For all the emphasis on original rights, the predominant theme of the debate was change not continuity, and transferability was seen as a means of economic progress. By sleight of hand the 'actual cultivators' were identified with agricultural entrepreneurs. In that calculation, consolidations of holdings, a capacity to invest and security of individual ownership became the crucial goals. The next chapter will go back and consider in more detail how this important decision emerged out of the competing social and economic prospectuses on offer, and how (in short) custom gave way to law.

## Chapter Five

# *Custom and the law*

We may conclude from chapter four, unsurprisingly, that the 1885 Act originated in colonial perceptions. Noteworthy in the debate was the paucity of direct justification for the favourable prognosis—the future comfort—which was promised as a result of the reforms. Instead, alongside the cases made for historical legitimacy and present poverty and oppression, an adverse trajectory was presented: the fate of tenants since the permanent settlement. This appeared as a professedly factual account, but contained an implied counterfactual (what would have happened if tenant rights had been preserved by law), which reduced the need to verify either the past ruin and its causes, or the future promise and its means. At issue, instead, was the subject of this chapter, the role of law and custom—as explanations or as remedies for present conditions, and in relation to a goal of improvement. Considering these questions, which appeared in several guises, this chapter will further trace the impulse to *legislate*, as the outcome of colonial perceptions.

The reality of past or future conditions did not matter deeply to the tenancy debate; what was vital was that tenants were perceived to be poor and oppressed, and their fate linked to legal rights and structures. Though (as discussed in chapter two) it was unlikely that conditions were changed solely or directly by government policy, there were indications that the tenants' position was worsening. These were seized upon by the reformers, who concentrated on the damage to subordinate rights over the nineteenth century. An empirical gap was left for the landlords to allege that the material prosperity of the peasantry of Bengal was increasing and that zamindars treated them well. Characteristically the method was again to present the 'evidence' of official reports —of price rises in rice ahead of rent increases in Presidency Division (1876), of improvements in houses and consumption in Dhaka and Patna divisions (1877 and 1882), on the liberality and public spirit of zamindars (in the famine of 1873-4), and the growing knowledge of their rights amongst raiyats (1878). Ashutosh Mookerjea quoted the *Calcutta Review* of 1853 on the favourable condition of the Bengal raiyat in comparison with the Scottish and Irish peasantry, and referred to the evidence of expansion of cultivation and then of population, the second following from the first (in accordance with Thorold Rogers'

*Political Economy*) and thus not forcing people on to inferior land.[1]

But the better of the argument was had by those who stressed that the law was a dead letter (Bihar, 1870s), that raiyats had widespread debt (Nadia, 1876) and that the majority of landlords were grasping and oppressive (Tirhut, 1873). It was perhaps significant that in Dhaka the condition of 'raiyats' was 'excellent' in 1873/4 but that they paid 'low wages'.[2] About the same time, C.H.T. Crosthwaite was writing of Awadh that the cultivators 'as a body [had] suffered from our Government more poverty and oppression than fell to their lot under the Nawabi'. The British had 'changed or destroyed the conditions which protected them, without supplying any other safeguards in their place'; this was not 'a mere question of the just treatment of one class by another', he added: 'It concerns the welfare of the Empire.'[3] For Bengal the reformers also asserted that tenants had been in a more advantageous position in the eighteenth-century. A story of the decline of the tenantry derived from or shadowed the narrative of raiyats' rights.

Whether or not the decline was new depended on the situation before 1793. What was the administrative or socio-economic mechanism whereby the 'rights' of the raiyats would have been protected? What capacity had the laws of the East India Company to create changes in practice? Instead of considering such questions, Field argued that the lack of evidence of enhancement in locally-established rent-rates, by contract, showed that enhancement was illegal in the eighteenth century. His was a circular argument derived from the definition of *abwabs*; it should be set against the certainty that actual demands did increase, and that measures of coercion were taken to keep cultivators on the land. On the other hand, economic strategies were sometimes used to attract tenants, especially short-term favourable rent-rates and even grants or loans for productive purposes. Some of these and many other practices seem to have persisted through the later nine-

[1] A. Mookerjea, *The Annals of British Land-Revenue Administration in Bengal from 1698 to 1793* (Calcutta, 1883). The reference was to J.E.T. Rogers, *A Manual of Political Economy for Schools and Colleges* (Oxford 1868). Rogers, formerly and later professor of political economy at Oxford, was at this time Radical MP for Southwark, notable for his editions of Bright and Cobden, and for works on agricultural prices and on wages.

[2] Tarini Das Bannerji, *The Zemindar and the Ryot in Bengal* (Calcutta, 1883).

[3] Crosthwaite note, 15 June 1882, Add.Mss.43584. Interestingly for the discussions elsewhere in this book, Crosthwaite argued that the near-starvation of large numbers of tenants-at-will was 'a matter of grave *national* importance' (emphasis added), and that the answer was not direct state intervention but laws to ensure rights so that people could protect themselves.

teenth century—including 'proper' shares of the harvest for landlords and village officers and servants, and differences in rent-rates for different castes. It is interesting that, even well into the twentieth century, land tenanted by 'industrious' castes was sold at a premium, even though generally, by then, population pressure had shifted the advantage to the landlords. The result was multiple not standard rent-rates, and no guarantee that rents would be stable.

Though, over time, there were of course real changes in agrarian conditions, there is an element of farce in trying to decipher them from descriptions by eighteenth-century East India Company servants filtered through the partisanship of late nineteenth-century polemicists. But perhaps we may assume that parts of the terminology and hence of the concepts of British agrarian analysis, for the 1790s and beyond, *were* derived from Indian practice. There must have been some indigenous notions of appropriate rates of rent and revenue, and of inappropriate demands. There were possibly even fixed principles of rent-rates, for example entitlements to a proportion of the product, say one-sixth for the landlord as in the code of Manu, though such rates were probably always controversial, or if not always, then by the later nineteenth century. In Dhaka district, landlords contested the idea that they should take only one-fifth, and inquiries concluded that in practice they were extracting anything from one fortieth to one half.[4] Similar disputes continued well into the twentieth century. Conversely, the exceptional persistence of known rates, or indeed rights and status, *but not necessarily of actual payments*, or practices, generally bedeviled assessments of rents, wages and social conditions in India.

Given a variety of conditions, the existence of ideas of proper or prevailing rates need never have implied that actual payments conformed over whole districts; no doubt, in practice *abwabs* greatly enlarged the amounts of rent actually paid even before 1793. Yet it was Field's contention that customary rates had *become* shadowy and that they declined in importance during the nineteenth century. He might have made (though, like the *Zemindary Settlement*, he did not) the point suggested by Nuffer Chandra Bhatta, a sub-judge of the 24-Parganas, that the very heavy revenue assessment (one of the motives for giving ownership to the zamindars in 1793) had forced rent increases which

---

[4] Field's *Digest*, pp.245-50, discusses this in the context of suggestions that rents ought to be related by law to gross produce, as proposed by Ricketts in 1859. This plan was also ruled out, in his view, by the variety of crops, and by the variety of the rates (influenced, Field thought, by the number of rent-receiving intermediaries). See chapters three and four for the full references for such sources.

had 'obliterated' the pargana rate before 1812, in favour of competition and contract rents.[5] Field did note that, as early as 1812, Colebrooke was calling for written declarations and records of the rates at which leases might be renewed, and suggesting (as provided in Regulation I of that year) that the rent-rates on new leases, replacing those abrogated at a revenue sale, should relate to what was paid on similar or adjacent land (or to previous rents paid on the land in question). Field took the view that this alternative was the origin of the 'prevailing rate' which recurred, much refined, in the Act of 1859 (whereupon it vanished for impracticality and disuse). The need for it in 1812 implied that it was then already difficult, at least in some cases, to identify a pargana rate and that rents were under upward pressure.

It seemed to the reformers that, for the majority of tenant land-holders, obstacles to rent-enhancement existed before 1793 in so far as extra-legal conditions and notions of proper rates restricted the demand for *abwabs*, and that they had been eroded since 1793 by legal changes and court decisions. This was the basis of the usual assumption, mentioned earlier, that colonial laws caused rents to rise. The Regulations probably *assisted* in the perpetuation of some privileges which had existed in the eighteenth century, and which were formally recognised; but in all other cases the law was gradually tending to encourage the enhancement of rents (and eviction). In 1822 (Regulation XI) rights of occupancy were protected, but the courts took this to mean rights established prior to 1793; in 1841 (Act VII) enhancement and hence 'competition' rents were generally permitted in all cases, except for 'fixed-rates' raiyats and those where 'fair rents...for specified areas' had been prescribed in written leases. Field concluded from the court records that all, except those with agreements dating from before 1793, had become effectively tenants-at-will, as indeed the Court of Directors had claimed in a despatch of 15 January 1819. The process was exaggerated when Bengal Act VIII of 1869 transferred rent suits from the revenue to the civil courts (from Collectors to judges).

The assumption was that there were norms and trends influenced by the state. At least some of the differentiation visible in nineteenth-century Bengal, whatever its origin, had to be attributed to the settlement made by the British—the amount of land revenue payable, and the person or body made liable to pay it. Similarly one argument for protecting the tenants was that the outpouring of legislation and the expansion of the judicial system after 1859 in itself forced the regulation of agra-

[5] N.C. Bhatta, *The Principle of the Bengal Tenancy Bill Legally Examined* (Calcutta, 1883).

rian relations into the courts, and that therefore the legal system must be adapted to meet needs which formerly would have been met by extra-judicial means. Field made this argument about the legal enhancement of rents, which he held had effectively been prevented by the inade-quacies of the existing law. Referring to the occupancy right, he con-cluded also that it had had no rapid impact both because the raiyats knew little of it, and because the landlord anyway probably did not have the right to eject a tenant who paid his rent. Others argued that the tenants were left at the mercy of the landlords, not just from illegal oppression, but because of the excessive discretion which the law allowed. An analogous point was that the collapse of village-level administration had removed one line of defence for tenant rights.[6] A pragmatic approach was ranged against the 'freedom of contract' touted by supporters of the zamindars. Whereas one side of the case argued that the courts had never protected the long-standing customary rights of the tenants (that is, supposedly, to equitable rents and security of tenure), this other faction argued that the Rent Bill of 1883 would 'deprive a large class of people of the protection they now receive'— that is, the judicial enforcement of tenancy 'agreements'.[7] At the least there was considerable ambiguity about the legal position.

Another crucial question about land-rights was raised by Hunter. He considered that there were different categories of raiyat, with tradi-tionally different privileges and rates of rent. He did not ask if a resi-dent raiyat in practice could exercise independent rights against a pro-prietary raja, or even a Mughal jagirdar, any more than against a British-style landlord. But he did introduce the idea of economic and demographic influences upon agrarian relations. He believed the famine of 1769-70 reduced the advantages enjoyed by resident raiyats because of terms offered to attract new cultivators; a parallel point might be made about any incentive to extensions of cultivation through revenue increases or commercial expansion. Shore too was reported to have thought that *khudkashta* raiyats did pay at known rates, so much per *bigha*, and on unlimited 'leases'; his authority was also deployed by

---

[6] In addition to discussion elsewhere in this book, see, for example, E. Stir-ling, Collector of Aligarh, 8 November 1831, claiming that in Akbar's system the kanungo was 'the protector of the husbandmen', and that amils were still in-formed about district conditions in the 1830s. The effective abolition of such officers by the 1830s, especially in Bengal, obviously reduced any such protec-tion; E.C. Buck note, 30 May 1882, Add.Mss.43584.

[7] J. Dacosta, 'Report of a meeting on 29 December 1883', in Dacosta, *Re-marks and Extracts from Official Reports on the Bengal Tenancy Bill* (London, 1884).

zamindari supporters to suggest that there was, at that time, 'no uniformity whatever...in the demands upon the ryots', the conclusion being that the diversity was due to decisions by zamindars, and that any permanence or inheritance of tenancies was attributable to the shortage of raiyats at a time of low population. Moreover, as will be discussed later, the failure of the *patta-kabuliyat* system was attributed to a general unwillingness of tenants as well as landlords to have the areas and rent-rates of their holdings measured and recorded. This implied that real rates varied according to concealment as well as power and status, or other conditions, and that both sides found advantages in flexible and ambiguous arrangements. In a sense we have to assume as much for the eighteenth century, on the grounds that, given what is known of conditions in the late nineteenth century, to think otherwise would be to accept the paradox that a once centralised and standardised system decayed as it came under an ever more strongly generalising influence. It then follows generally, as Hunter and Baden-Powell explained, that agrarian relations varied according to political, economic and demographic conditions. For example, the Sale Law of 1841 permitted purchasers of estates to eject tenants even though they had paid their rents (the first time, in Field's view that they had had this weapon), but very few of them made use of the provision, because 'the competition used to be between zemindars for ryots, not between ryots for land': only when there were more raiyats than available land would it be a useful device.[8] A further (or alternative) argument of those who advocated a new tenancy law was thus that economic conditions were altering the balance of power in the countryside. Holderness believed the 1859 Act to be providing 'a very powerful engine of enhancement in the hands of the landlords' just at the moment when canals, railways and higher prices made them anxious to make use of it.[9] He saw that pressure for a broader, remedial state intervention derived in part from the pressure and increasing speed of change.

One effect of these extra-legal forces, and more important than them in shaping the reform, was that they brought a questioning of the role to be attributed to custom to the heart of the debate about economic prospects and historical rights. Custom sometimes seemed decisive. Secretary of State Hartington ruled out extending occupancy rights to all raiyati lands, on the ground that to do so would violate the 'deeply rooted' distinction between *khudkashta* and *pahikashta* status.[10] But, though

---

[8] Field, *Digest*, p.228.

[9] T.W. H[olderness] note, 21 July 1884, Add.Mss.43584.

[10] He wanted too the twelve-year rule established in 1859; Revenue despatch

custom became a more prominent issue in official British thinking by the later nineteenth century, this fact is ironic. Aspects of custom, especially the supposed autonomy and collectivity of the 'village community', were being endorsed by a government which proposed to interfere as never before and which espoused commercial agriculture and individual rights before law. This very counterposition, of ancient and therefore appropriate indigenous institutions, against disruptive, modernising, *colonial* innovations, was made explicitly in the tenancy debates as in others, by officials for whom it might have seemed a poignant and two-edged weapon.[11] Here the question had three contentious aspects: what was the custom in particular matters, the extent to which custom could be permitted to determine proper practice, and how far it would provide for change unaided.

It was inevitable firstly, given the importance accorded to historical legitimacy, that one aspect of the tenancy debate would be sparring between rival versions of custom. The kinds of argument are indicated on one hand by the assertion of Mr. Justice Cunningham in 1883 that distraint formed no part of Indian law but was an innovation of Regulation XVII of 1790,[12] and on the other hand by the dubious riposte on behalf of the zamindars of Ashutosh Mookerjea, citing Henry Maine's *Early History of Institutions*, that on the contrary the law's remedy was 'a bequest of the Aryan Hindus to the communities of the West'.[13] It may be noted here that 'custom' was equated not with current practice but with historical precedent. The Maharaja of Dumraon, for example, in a speech delivered at a meeting in the Calcutta Town Hall in December 1883 (chaired by the Maharaja of Darbhanga), claimed that the Dumraon zamindari rights predated the Mughal conquest—thus offering up a sort of battle-challenge on historical precedence to the advocates of raiyats' property. In practice too, some aspects of custom were emphasised by zamindars, but not considered by the tenancy

---

no. 54, 17 August 1882, Add.Mss.43584. See above, chapter three.

[11] The ironies did not end in the nineteenth century. Similar points might be made about zamindari abolition and panchayati raj under Congress hegemony in newly-independent India, reforms billed as remedying colonial evils.

[12] 'Minute on the Bengal Rent Bill' (reprint), *Englishman*, 24 January 1883.

[13] A. Mookerjea, 'The proposed new rent law' (1883). Allegedly distraint of cattle to compel debt repayment was approved in *Vyavahara Mayukha*, presumably meaning *acharitam* or confinement ('tying of…son, wife, and cattle'); V.N. Mandlik, *The Vyavahara Mayukha...* (Byculla 1880), p.109, or Borradaile's translation (Standard Hindu Law Books, Madras 1879). Mookerjea thus echoed contemporary critiques (Mandlik, pp.xliv & ff.) of the narrow range of legal authorities then used; but Bhatta Nilakantha's text, not itself very ancient, envisaged debt-recovery mainly by sanctions against the person.

reformers (and *vice versa*). Dumraon, while protesting that Bihari rent rates were generally lower than those in Bengal, and that his fellow zamindars were not tyrannical, drew attention to the fact that many of the landlords were of the same caste (Brahman, Bhumihar, Rajput, Kayastha and so on) as their tenants, and that they could not 'disregard the voice of the community among whom they live'. It is curious that appeals to custom took no account of this possible alternative, zamindari tradition, or of the impact of differentiated social norms and allegiances which cut across the categories of landholding and revenue-paying. The failure is indicative of the sway of the peasant proprietary model in the current accounts of India's history, and its supposed 'civilisational' pedigree.

How far things could be left to custom, and how it would evolve, were questions even nearer to the core of the debates for and against government intervention. Doubts over the acceptable degree of meddling with custom had always diverted colonial laws from the path laid down by theory. The result was incoherence. In addition, then, the desire to define tenant rights arose partly because the formal provisions on Indian tenancy were so ambiguous: they seemed to offer no internal, coherent explanation—this was not just the inevitable complexity of the real world, but the imposed confusions of contradictory representations and interpretations by the colonial legislators. In Regulation VIII of 1793, for example, there were provisions which seem spectacularly vague, relating to dependent taluqdars' tenurial terms and to rent increases. The taluqdars were entitled to pay revenue through the 'actual proprietors' and for the same period of time as the latter's agreement with government. Taluqdars had to agree to the rent and its terms, which also had to be such as the proprietor was entitled to demand from them. The conditions of the tenure could be settled either by custom or contract; and the rent could be increased if the contract or 'special custom of the district' permitted, or if the taluqdar had rendered himself liable to an increase by having received an earlier abatement—and provided the lands were capable of affording the increase (section 51). The 'remaining lands' (not held by dependent taluqdars or certain specified categories of fixed-rent leaseholders) could be let 'under the prescribed conditions in whatever manner [the proprietor] may think fit' (section 52). The prescribed conditions laid down entitlements to leases and receipts, and forbad *abwabs* (additional cesses levied after and outside the 'rental' agreement). A debate between Field and Alexander Mackenzie on the meaning of 'remaining lands' in Regulation VIII was popularised as the 'matter of the colon'—that is, whether or not (in section 53) the right to let lands at will applied to all raiyati land, as Field suspected, and as zamindari supporters believed to be plain in the vernacular translation of the Regulation.[14] On the Rent Law Commission, Mackenzie and O'Kinealy argued that the word 'let' was used loosely in Regulation VIII, because the relationship between zamindar and resident raiyat was not one of landlord and tenant and not intended to become so. Opponents retorted that 'let' meant what it usually means; this supported their contention that zamindars had or had acquired proprietary rights of an exclusive kind.[15] This confusion of 1793 with its scholastical echo in 1880 so closely foreshadows that which the 1885 Act provided in regard to the alienation of tenancies as to suggest that some general influence was at work—presumably the balancing of Indian custom and Western theory, pragmatism and principle, fear and hope.

Some matters were left to 'custom' in 1885, the most notable being whether or not a landlord could refuse alienation of a tenancy or demand a fee (*salami*) upon transfer. In important ways these provisions were designed to legitimise the *status quo*, as when it was to be presumed (under section 27) that an occupancy raiyat's rent was fair—replacing the alternative notions that fair rents ought to be divined from competition or as a proportion of the net value of the produce. Such presumptions, as on occupancy itself, were intended to protect incumbents from arbitrary demands. On one occasion Garth found, in favour of a man who occupied waste land and cultivated it, that he was assumed by 'established usage' to have the landowner's consent and to be his tenant, even though there was no formal contract between them.[16] This kind of argument, a mirror image of the raiyats' contracting out of rights (which was forbidden),[17] allowed a partial accommodation between Western and Indian systems. Thus custom supposedly allowed landlords to transfer land from one tenant to another, but the law added that they could only do so by decree. The law permitted the

---

[14] See ibid. Punctuation—the colon—allegedly affected interpretation. In Field's view (*Digest*, pp.194-5) 'the term "let" was not a very appropriate expression' for *khudkashta* raiyats. See also ibid., pp.190-1, on sections 48 to 54 of Regulation VIII.

[15] Mookerjea, 'The proposed new rent law' (1880).

[16] *Rani Surnomoyee* v. *Deno Nath Gir Sunnyasee*, 1883 ILR, 9 Cal.908. The 1885 Act referred to express or impled contracts which would establish the landlord-tenant relation.

[17] Notably by section 178 which superseded section 7 of Act X of 1859, and section 7 of Bengal Act VIII of 1869. Several cases later tried to water down this provision.

abrogation of occupancy rights at the sale of an estate, but only where custom did not maintain them; conversely the law forbad raiyats to transfer their interest in parts, but, when custom permitted the transfer of tenancies, any new part-holder's title would be good, once rent had been received from him, even if it was not recorded in the landlord's accounts.[18] Again, under the 1885 Act, three years' practice was held to confirm a rent, in the absence of a contract; but when landlords tried to use this loophole to increase rents in defiance of the provisions of the Act on enhancement, the gap was filled by further legislation.[19] By such accounts, law did not only bring change; it also reflected it.

A notion also existed whereby an *evolutionary* custom would remedy the defects of legislation, or render it irrelevant, or change in its image. Maine had defined custom as 'habitual practice', and we may recall how Field and the reformers concluded that it *must* evolve (towards contract), in the same way as law, though by a different process. Thus custom, as the term was used in the tenancy legislation, was not necessarily a fixed point. Before 1885, as when upholding landlords' objections to the sale of tenants' holdings, the law had distinguished between custom and usage.[20] Afterwards it did not, and courts came to decide that practices were legitimate if 'well-known and acquiesced in' rather than necessarily ancient or uniform.[21] One judgment found that a custom could not apply to a given tenure unless it had existed when the tenure originated, but it was apparent in several other cases that a right to transfer occupancy holdings could be recognised on the evidence of previous purchases, even against the will of the landlord.[22] By this means the law started a process which indigenous

[18] *Kripanath Chaki* v. *Dyal Chand Pal*, 1874, 22 WR 169.

[19] See Finucane and Ali, *Commentary*, on section 29. Landlords would set higher rents by 'compromise' with their tenants, and after three years claim they were lawful by custom. The strategy received some encouragement from *Sheo Sahay Panday* v. *Ram Rachia Ray*, 1891, ILR 18 Cal.33, but the gap was filled in Bengal Act I of 1907 as confirmed in the High Court in 1908.

[20] This was established in many cases between 1864 and 1874, notably *Hurro Mohan Mukherjee* v. *Lalan Moni Dassi*, 1864, 1 WR 5. For this and other notes on this paragraph see also Finucane and Ali, *Commentary*, on section 26.

[21] *Shakarpatti Thakurani* v. *Saifullah Khan*, 1872, 18 WR 507, and *Kripamoyi Debia* v. *Durga Gobind Sircar*, 1887, ILR, 15 Cal.89. Finucane and Rampini, *Tenancy Act*, concluded, on English precedents, that custom meant a reasonable and certain practice which was generally recognised and acted upon in a particular area.

[22] This is discussed by Finucane and Ali, *Commentary*, on section 183. One High Court judgment, on *Dalgleish* v. *Guzaffer Hossein*, 1898, 3 CWN 21, found that the landlords' consent as well as previous transfers had to be proved, but other judgments at this time tended to extend the right of transfer.

practice could develop. Act X of 1859 had been interpreted to mean that occupancy right was not transferable, though a holding might be. After 1885, though one case suggested that this rule still applied at the execution of a decree for rent arrears,[23] others held that occupancy right could be transferred to a third party, where usage allowed, even if the landlord objected.[24]

However, in such processes of change, at any one time or place custom was still assumed to be definite in nature and extent. It needed to be, if it was to be susceptible to findings of fact. The complications of custom were thus readily regarded as proving their inadequacy, and justifying interference. Moreover, it was plain that in the end custom was subordinate to law and to order. Section 183 of the 1885 Act, for example, purported to reserve to custom, or at least recent or current usage, anything not specified in the Act—a degree of residuary authority. But such custom also had to be general, definite, peaceable, agreed, and not contrary to public policy, which meant a norm of individual property-rights and capitalist relations. By contrast, Indian custom might have been supposed to represent a body of norms and beliefs which defined or made sense of practices in terms of collectivities. When the colonial laws proposed other meanings and possibilities, the different forms thus did not merely co-exist; they competed.[25] This was apparent, for example, when the 1885 Act confirmed the existing law to the effect that a registered co-sharer could not abrogate the rights of other co-sharers.[26] Individual rights were protected between joint land-holders, who in turn were treated as one corporate entity for purposes of ownership—for example, in section 93 which required co-proprietors to act as one or through a manager, in order that individual tenants might not be disadvantaged.

The regulation of rent enhancements is also relevant here. On one hand it was typical that the Rent Law Commission should have pro-

[23] *Ram Lal Sukul* v. *Bhela Ghazi*, 1910, 14 CWN 614.

[24] *Palakdhani Roy* v. *Manners*, 1895 ILR, 23 Cal.179. The argument was based on sections 22 (transfer of an occupancy right) and section 26 (devolution of the right from an intestate holder).

[25] The sense intended here is that to which attention has been drawn by the philosopher Charles Taylor, among others—namely that the meanings and possibilities of an individual's social actions are influenced or determined by the meanings and possibilities prevailing in society. See also the discussion of language and agriculture in P. Robb, 'Peasants' choices? Indian agriculture and the limits of commercialization in nineteenth-century Bihar', *Economic History Review* XLV, 1 (1992), pp.97-119.

[26] *Boikonto Nath Das* v. *Bissonath Majhee*, 1868, 9 WR 268; and see Finucane and Ali, *Commentary*, on section 86.

posed substituting a 'customary rate' for the elusive pargana rate. In part this reflected Field's attitude when he satirised the 'scientific' approach to Indian tenancy: 'Some people talk of pergunnah rates as if they remained fixed for ever, and were some quantity determinant in the nature of things, which could be discovered by swinging a pendulum *in vacuo*'.[27] But then official enquiries confirmed that no 'customary' rate existed either. This meant that indigenous rent-rates conformed either to no objective, general principles, or to ones which were unrecognised by a European government and its political economy: 'Not only was the multiplicity of rates found to be almost inexhaustible, but little relation could be traced between the existing rates and the quality of the soil'.[28] Repeatedly therefore (as said) the concept of a rational norm proved useless for enhancing rents under a British legal system. Before 1885 the prevailing rate had been held to be that paid by a majority of the same class of raiyats in the same neighbourhood;[29] in the absence of other information, local classifications and terms were followed as reflecting the status and productive capacity of different lands. Some judges argued that an average could be said to be 'prevailing',[30] but most disagreed. One judgment accepting an average was balanced by another which held that the lowest rate should be counted. All were seeking categories based upon *similar* conditions. But in India the very concept of 'rates' of rent might not operate, in that rents were not set uniformly in units, appropriately to land or tenure, but separately in lump sums for unmeasured areas.

In desperation, an amendment in the Bengal Act III of 1898 (section 2) allowed comparisons with neighbouring villages. But the officials were also anxious to avoid progressive increases through manipulation of prevailing rates, and therefore added a proviso that the rent had to be deemed fair, in terms of price rises—which, incidentally, came to be

[27] Field, *Digest*, p.193.

[28] See *Selections from Papers relating to the Bengal Tenancy Act, 1885* (Calcutta 1885), p.417, and Finucane and Ali, *Commentary*, on section 7 (enhancement of tenure-holders' rents).

[29] This was provided in *Shadoo Sing v. Ramanugraha Lal*, 9 WR 83. In the 1885 Act, however, section 31 set out how the rate was to be calculated. See Finucane and Rampini, *Tenancy Act*. Similar provisions applied also to non-occupancy raiyats under Chapter VI of the 1885 Act (section 46). For under-raiyats rents were limited to 125 per cent of the landlord's (rent-receiving raiyat's) rent, or to 150 per cent by registered agreement (section 48); this proved largely inoperative as most sub-tenancies were on part-holdings only. See Finucane and Ali, *Commentary*.

[30] This was provided in the NWP Rent Act, XVII of 1873, and was said to be 'disastrous to the raiyats'; see Finucane and Rampini, *Tenancy Act*.

assessed for the staple food crops, rather than all produce, so as not to discourage the growing of higher-value (frequently export) crops.[31] As in earlier rules allowing enhancement for the increased value of output (and thus assuming that it would be marketed), assessments of proper rent were moved towards market economics. Further, when the Bengal government proposed abandoning the whole charade of prevailing rates as 'illogical, unnecessary and mischievous', it argued that it was wrong to regulate a raiyat's liabilities with reference not to his own rights and position but to others' rights which 'it was not his business to maintain'. A rule of 'prevailing rates' left individuals at the mercy of 'the feeblest, stupidest and most venal' of their class. This resounding denial of community was endorsed on all sides. Even Elliott, in considering amendments which were to become law in 1898, argued that it was just that a tenant should have his rent raised if he paid less than others without sufficient reason. As the approved reasons were mainly economic, this was a competition rent by another name, and the rump of the prevailing rate became (as indeed the reformers had intended in 1885) merely a device to ascertain what a fair rent might look like, in a situation in which a market test could not be applied because of occupancy rights.[32]

Another part of this process was that all payments by tenants to landlords were held to constitute rent. This followed Regulation VIII of 1793 (section 54 consolidating old *abwabs* and section 55 prohibiting new ones), which had been repeated in Regulation V of 1812 (section 3) and reinforced by punitive damages allowed to the tenant in Act X of 1859 (section 10) and Bengal Act VIII of 1869 (section 11). The principle was announced by the Full Bench after the 1869 Act that 'Nothing

---

[31] This was of course an alternative basis for enhancement. In an elaboration of *Thakurani Dasi*, courts were empowered under section 32 of the 1885 Act to approve rent increases which were proportionate to the excess of prices in the ten years before the application (and during the currency of the rent) over those of any other appropriate ten-year period (not necessarily the time when the rent was first fixed). Such enhanced rents were then fixed for 15 years (section 37). Section 39 provided for government monthly price lists.

[32] See Finucane and Ali, *Commentary*, on section 30. Bengal Act III of 1898, section 31A, provided that, in notified areas, the pargana rate need not be what anyone actually paid (it might be what was paid for a single, large field if need be) but rather the rate at or above which a majority of the land was held. Elsewhere (section 31) it had to be 'generally paid', that is by the majority of tenants, and a competent officer (of rank not below a Sub-Deputy Collector) was permitted to declare a rate. Caste was not normally to be taken into account, but it could be if proved relevant by custom. For all this the measure remained unused. The question of the amendments will be taken up again in later chapters.

could be recovered for the occupation of land except one sum'. But the courts interpreted these provisions unevenly, because their effect could be either to consolidate all demands (including state cesses) into a lawful rent, or to rule out new demands.[33] Ultimately the attempt was to reduce all agrarian relations to tenurial ones.

Among those payments ruled out or consolidated by judicial decisions was a tax on *gur* (molasses) production (1867), a cess to make up for the death or disappearance of neighbours (*nagai*, possibly implying co-operative cultivation of such abandoned lands; 1866), festival dues (1869 and 1875), sums collected for *naprasan* (the first eating of rice after the birth of a son to the zamindar; 1870), patwari and other village dues (1875), and forced labour (*begar*; 1894). Such demands did not suddenly disappear. But clearly the intention of the British law was that they be replaced. Often what they represented were continuing communal forms, whereby a zamindar might be involved in production or in maintaining his raiyats' subservience, whereby villages might collectively support its officers, festivals, cultivation and payments of revenue. In place of such forms the British imagined individual rights, where known rents would express a purely tenurial relationship, on fixed holdings of land. Either of these conflicting sets of social norms might be oppressive or liberal, and each might have overlapping features in practice; but clearly they are substantially different in their nature.

The British often appreciated the complexities of Indian praxis and deployed them in argument; but they could not entertain them in policy overall, lest they preclude the making of laws. Indian conditions of landholding were diverse and complex. In the 1880s, for example, the Commissioner of Patna Division complained of draft proposals for setting out fair rents and in particular to the drawing up of tables of rates. 'These sections...', he complained, 'contain a Procrustian scheme of enforcing uniformity in matters in which, from the nature of things, no uniformity exists. The rates in a village are about as numerous as the fields of the ryots, and cannot be classified without an arbitrary disregard of actual facts.' The same Commissioner, however, supported the legal categorisation of occupancy raiyats, and most of the incidents of that status which the legislation proposed.[34] In short, where the

---

[33] *Radha Prosad Singh* v. *Bal Kowar Koeri*, 1890 ILR, 17 Cal.726 (FB). These points are discussed by Finucane and Ali, *Commentary*, on section 74.

[34] The Commissioner, F.W. Halliday, was reporting views of Collectors after a conference in July 1883. The remarks were later taken up by pro-landlord interests; see Dacosta, *Remarks and Extracts*. See also H.J. Reynolds, 'Memorandum on the Rent Bill', 18 May 1881, in *Report of the Government of Bengal* (1881).

British admitted diversity, they tried to manage it, and present it as comprising definite sets of categories. Even when professing their sensitivity to Indian realities, they assumed that custom itself was a generalising force. In the debate about the tenants, this tendency implied that all were poor and oppressed, or that none was.

In justification of the reform was a multitude of reports, especially from Bihar, stressing that the problem was a want or misuse of law. This implied external, inappropriate forces with malign effects. But the second step was that custom, though it should be respected, was also inadequate and needed to change. The papers relating to the part played by the law of distraint provide good examples. So urgent was the matter that, in 1882, Eden was proposing a brief Act to check abuses, in advance of the main legislation. Many reports, including MacDonnell's on north Bihar in 1876, had claimed distraint was used oppressively against tenants, even a whole village, to enforce enhanced rents: tenants might be forbidden to harvest, for example, and thus stand to lose all. Finucane referred also to the depredations, often using distraint, of the many thikadars in Alapur in Darbhanga raj in 1875/6, the worse because they were 'petty rent-jobbers not residents'. Often the result was that raiyats were forced to borrow from beparis (travelling merchants) on unfavourable terms. But was the problem the law of distraint? Could the abuse of rights not be old practice, masquerading under a new legal guise, or equated with it by observers?

In Shahabad, peons would be stationed to prevent the harvest, with no attempt at legal distraint. In Gaya, too, as soon as crops began to ripen 'dikdars' would be sent to prevent their being cut, and sowars quartered on refractory villages, until all dues were paid. None of these devices employed the British law. Again, a local barrister reported that when the law of distraint *was* formally used, it was often merely as a device to secure a victory in some unrelated dispute. The Gaya government pleader claimed that tenants *generally* did not receive their legal entitlements, for example to written leases, set rents without *abwabs*, freedom from eviction or enhancement, and so on; instead 'our gomashtas and barahils go and sit at the door of his house, preventing egress and ingress, and depriving him of the use of the village wells until he pays off our rent'. Or he might be imprisoned in the zamindar's *kachchari*. He dared not protest to the authorities, but rather was intimidated by the power of the written word: the 'terrifying influence exercised over him by the *bosta* [*basta*, bundle of documents] of the putwaree or gomashta'.

On the other hand the written word might be a solution: 'At the root of the present evil', wrote R.C. Money, 'is that ryots, not being given pottahs, do not know what their rights and positions are. Abwabs, kurchas and salamis have become so numerous that no ryot knows...how much he may be called on to pay.... He may have a general idea...but experience has taught him that he will most probably have to pay that sum twice over ere he has satisfied everyone's demands, and hence a natural reluctance to pay at all'. Dhanesh Chunder Roy, personal assistant to the Patna Commissioner, agreed: 'in 99 cases out of 100 the ryot has no pottah; he does not know what amount of land he holds, or what rent he has to pay'. If the problem were want of law and uncertainty of information, then this might propose a remedy.

In Champaran, by contrast, J. Ware Edgar, the Collector, reported on the Madhubani lands of Bishen Pergash Narayan Singh:

The ryots have of late taken their stand on the rates shown in the settlement papers [of 1850], and some of them declare that they have never paid any more. There was a very strong attempt to make me believe this when I went among the villagers; but when I got the older and more respectable ryots singly, they frankly acknowledged that they have for many year[s] paid rates far higher than the settlement rates. But they object to the increase now claimed, and still more to the constant enhancement and to cesses exacted on various occasions, and from time to time consolidated with the rent to form a starting point for fresh cesses to lead again to a fresh enhancement. They also complain of not getting receipts, and some of them of not getting pottas.

These raiyats appealed to a new order; alternative ways echoed *Vyava-* · *hara Manukha*.[35] Edgar had been an author of the plan to make occupancy right 'inherent in the cultivation of ryoti land'; he advocated this repeatedly to Tupper, to Reynolds, to Finucane and at the Bankipur conference, on the argument that the real evil was not formal enhance-

[35] G/I despatch R&A no.7, 21 March 1883; demi-official by D.W.M. Testro, Gaya Coll, 3 October 1877; R.C. Money, 13 September 1877; D.C. Roy, 1 October 1877; J. Ware Edgar, 15 January 1881, from G/Be Rev (March 1881); P. Nolan, Offg. Coll. Shahabad, W. Kemble, Gaya Coll, and Edgar, 18 January 1881, from Behar Rent Papers, vol.III: Add.Mss.43584. There were a few dissenting voices: Beames thought the power of distraint was not much used (or abused) in Burdwan, Midnapur and Bankura; the East Bengal Landholders Asociation claimed the same for their region, and said that the interposing of court action (proposed by G/I, 5 May, and in a G/Be circular, 24 May 1884, and in chapter XIII of the Act) would so delay the process as to render it useless— similar points were made at conferences in Patna, Bhagalpur, Rajshahi and Presidency divisions. Against this were such as Field, Dampier, R.C. Dutt, and B.M. Mitter who thought the power used only by bad landlords; loc.cit. The so-called Madhubani Babus' estate mentioned here was a former jagir of some 37,000 acres near the Nepal border in Champaran, granted in 1763/4, resumed in 1819, and reconfirmed to the family in 1850. See also above, note 13.

ment but illegal cesses backed up by wrongful distraint. He admitted: the 'weak point in my proposal is that it undoubtedly does to a certain extent fail to recognise the customs, feelings and ideas of the people'.[36]

A desire to make the crooked straight—the Biblical overtones are quite appropriate—both justified the reforms and helped fix their terms. Rights regulated in law, or in contract (as in the *patta-kabuliyat* system), are different from those derived from a set of social relations and historical norms. Much of British practice may be seen as an attempt to reconcile the two. The problem concerned, as much as anything, whether or not Western unitary categories could be made to fit the complexity of Indian conditions. The crux of the matter was that it was mediated by legal process in the English manner: that which facilitated it was to be encouraged, on abstract principles. Once again, behind the readiness to provide tenants' property was the urge to instil responsibility and enterprise—and behind that lay a preference for legal sanctions to be levied against property rather than the person (the positive side of distraint of crops), because 'imprisonment for debt is...a relic of barbarism' as Mackenzie, Eden and Bengal's Advocate-General all agreed.[37]

The case was made by 1880 that the law now needed to help protect tenants; it contains some elements which help explain features of the 1885 Act, and also (as will be discussed later) its impact. We have established that the motive was either to re-establish or to create (the same ambivalence as was applied to the proprietors of estates in 1793) a property of the tenants, as peasant proprietors. It was assumed that this must mean unfettered transferability, as a defining incident of private property. Occupancy right was chosen as the means of securing this property. Legally, it derived from continuous tenancy over twelve years. In his *Digest*, Field had suggested that if the right were to apply to any land of equivalent area and quality, within an estate, this would cope with cases when raiyats' holdings were regularly changed, as in Bihar, to avoid the acquisition of occupancy rights.[38] Raiyati land meant agricultural land (as many court cases had established)—that is, excluding *zerat*, whatever land was in direct possession of the zamindar. The implication of the proposals in 1885 was, therefore, that, alongside any gain for occupancy raiyats, there would be a reduction in the varieties of status of permanent holders of land, and potentially between different legal categories of agricultural land. Many objected

---

[36] Edgar to Tupper, 11 December 1881 (2 letters), Add.Mss.43584.

[37] Mackenzie note, 28 October 1881, Add.Mss.43575.

[38] Field, *Digest*, p.38.

precisely to this uniformity;[39] it reinforced the consequences already noted in respect of agrarian dues. Contrasting with the 1885 Act's simplifications and inflexibility, a sample list of tenures in Bihar (themselves already subject to judicial interference and regulation) gives a image of a complex and subtle agrarian society attuned to particular needs and processes.[40] By defining occupancy right in 1859, the law had in some ways restricted it (to those who could prove twelve years' occupancy of the same holding). Field in effect suggested that the same procedure be adopted for all agricultural land. Under the permanent settlement it was already likely to be regarded as *zerat* unless held by a raiyat; but the new law implied that it could be *zerat* even if held by a raiyat, provided it could be shown to have once been in the landlord's immediate possession as defined by law. After all, then, the expected contribution of evolution and of law was to generalise custom and direct it into a single track. It was standardisation too that made crucial the decision on how to apportion the benefit, whether by policy or precedent.

When the colonial officials considered these questions, they projected two opposing narratives. According to the first, the inherent defects of Indian custom had necessitated intervention through law, which would produce improvements. According to the second, arbitrary pre-colonial or misguided colonial laws had created defects; once the law was reformed, custom would suffice to induce social and economic development. These two versions, though mirror images, combined to produce the Bengal Tenancy Act. But then law effectively eclipsed

[39] See Peary Mohun Mookerjea, *Opinions of Mofussil Landholders on the Bengal Tenancy Bill compiled from communications received by the Central Committee of the Landholders of Bengal and Behar* (Calcutta, 1883).

[40] Those noticed by Finucane and Ali, *Commentary*, included the following: *assamiwar* (created by indigo farmers), *ayma* (by royal charitable donation, *inam*), *bhatottur* and *bhoguttur* (for Brahmans), *chakran* (for service) including *chaukidari chakran* and *ghatwali* (for military or police), jagirs dating from Shah Alam, *kartauli*, *zarpeshgi* or *sadna patna* (part or whole sub-leases for usufructuary mortgages), *mukarrari* or *istamrari* (perpetual fixed-rate), *thika* (rent-farming), *malikana* or *arazi* (retained rent and revenue-free by proprietor when selling estate—supposed by Shore to have originated in compensation to the zamindar-middlemen when the Mughals wanted to deal directly with the raiyats; not found in Bengal proper), *khoris* (temporary to support a relative), *inamat* (rent-free for Muslims), *birt* (rent-free for Hindus for religion), *nakdi* (cash), *shikam* or *shikmi* (fixed-rate cash), *chakath* (temporarily cash, often for reclamation; or cash commuted from produce-sharing), *paran* (cash for sugarcane and poppy, and produce-sharing for rice, on rotation), *agorbatai* (produce-sharing, on the threshing-floor), and *danabandi* (produce-sharing by appraisal of the standing-crop, often paid in cash).

custom. Both the combination and the displacement were possible because the elements in the story were not all equal. Custom was constituted as autochthonous practice in the first version, but in the second as the universal or natural tendency (as Field would have it). Therefore, though the village community or the peasant proprietor were lauded as indigenous forms, as zamindari too had been once, they were chiefly favoured because thought efficient for progress, which could only be achieved by means of property, capital and trade. Law too had to conform with this universal prospectus, as was seen when zamindars' property and rights were qualified in the interests of tenants, the better to produce economic improvement. Similarly, whether Indian custom or Western law was at fault in producing the crisis of the later nineteenth century, they were agreed to be incompatible. Unsuitable conditions of late nineteenth-century law and economy endangered Indian practices, but protecting the indigenous could only be part of the remedy, because it was impossible to escape the universal trends of politics, economics and demography, and the universal pre-eminence of property and commercial production. This chapter explores several more instances of these anomalies. It shows that by them the state was inspired to act, but that because of them it sought not social or individual protection, to redress oppression or provide for equity, but rather to ensure an economic hierarchy which would mobilise resources and harness economic rationality. The 'actual cultivator' was the rhetorical but not the effective focus of care.

There was a certain intellectual muddle behind the tenancy reforms: it both added to and helps explain the complexity of the question. It was as if ideas developed by accretion rather than selection, and perhaps this was appropriate for Bengal where the landlord model of the permanent settlement had been maintained since the early nineteenth century on the basis of an official (though not judicial) commitment to the quite contrary principles of revenue settlement and property rights for 'actual cultivators'. The conclusion must be that the decision to enact the 1885 Act was produced from a recognition of the ambiguities of the law, added to an illusion of certainty about the malignant tendency of landlord-tenant relations (due to legal, economic and demographic conditions). The course of change in Bengal was considered inauspicious, while the general principles of social evolution were reaffirmed. According to such arguments historical justifications and future prospects were equally salient, in both law and custom; and in both there was expected, at the same time, inevitable evolution according to universal laws, and the persistence of pecularities of locality and civilisation (which had therefore to be seen as different stages in the one process). The implication was that Indians needed special remedies and could not be left to their own devices.The basis of rights was historical, and particular circumstances were recognised as requiring special measures. This section began not by searching for indications of some real changes which explained the decision to legislate in 1885, but with a suggestion that it was the perception of need which mattered. Henry Cotton warned at the time and later: 'The experimental introduction of agrarian theories', substituting contract for personal relations between zamindar and raiyat, was 'calculated to produce nothing but disorder'; he railed against interfering in the great variety of 'old customs', and against the 'most dangerous doctrine' that the government should *avoid* placing landlords over tenants.[41] Indeed the great rent law debate concerned matters which perhaps could not be understood, and on which nothing would have been done, without 'theorizing'. The keys hidden among the contested concepts of ancient rights were the power of personal conviction and the hopes for the future. The last was apparent in the despatch which Kimberley endorsed on 11 January 1883. It trusted that the land law would be settled on a 'firmer, juster, and more satisfactory basis; to keep the cultivation of the soil in the hands of a substantial peasantry...'.[42] For all its quibbles of detail, it represented a consensus in favour of 'improvement', a commitment to legislation. The element of personal conviction was also perhaps over-abundant.

## II

The Bengal Tenancy Act was passed in 1885, after more than a decade of deliberations, for reasons which included criticism of the existing state of the law, mainly as consolidated in the Tenancy Act of 1859, and worries about landlord-tenant conflict in Bengal. The conflict was instanced in rural violence which played an important part in persuading the government to take the tenancy question seriously. We now turn to these specific antecedents, which also helped shape the Act, particularly in terms of establishing the state's right or duty to intervene, and the reformers' understanding of the roles of custom and law in securing change. In 1864 the landholders had objected to a proposal to determine, 'once and for all, what is a fair and equitable rate of rent payable by every ryot having a right of occupancy at such rates, and to fix it in

---

[41] Henry Cotton, *New India or India in Transition* (1885; revised edn. 1907), ch.4; see also Add.Mss.43618, passim.
[42] See Add.Mss.43523.

perpetuity'.[43] In 1881 Mackenzie did not go so far. As had earlier compromises on similar issues, he stopped short of fixing all rents and thus truly creating a property for the raiyats. Eden wanted, wrote Mackenzie, modestly enough, 'to define and strengthen the position of the great mass of cultivators, while giving landlords a reasonably cheap and effective procedure for regulating and revising rents'. But, in addition, as noted at the start of this book, the intention was that the raiyats 'as a class' were once again to enjoy 'those rights which the ancient land law and customs of the country intended them to have', namely protection against arbitrary eviction and 'a reasonable proportion of the profits of cultivation'. The hope was that they would thereby attain 'substantial comfort' and capacity to resist 'the occasional pressure of bad times'.[44] In short, the diagnosis was that the province's agrarian problems derived from the insufficient margin left to the actual cultivator by the zamindar; and the remedy was for the state, under the guise of providing 'effective procedure', to regulate rents and agrarian relations. In many ways, this would involve even greater or more frequent interference than the more radical alternative of fixing rents in perpetuity.

Paramount in establishing the wider agenda, as already explained, was concern at the plight of the Indian poor and a belief in the need for government intervention. These were also expressed by John and Richard Strachey on partly fiscal grounds, and in the Famine Commission Report of 1881. In addition, freedom from oppression was regarded as an absolute good, and a boon which a British government had to provide.[45] In eastern India, the suggestions referred particularly to conditions in Bihar, as they had been revealed in various studies and reports during the 1870s. However, the issue originally inspiring the Act of 1885 had been the conditions of indigo cultivation, initially in Bengal proper. Above all, it sparked off a debate on the proper limits of state power, and helped establish, in principle, an acceptance of further interference. In this it continued a protracted process whereby discussions of the proper roles of the state led to new policy initiatives. Already there was a clear opposition of custom with law. The discussions sometimes invited interference, in the interests of colonial power, revenue or trade, or on arguments about the special inadequacies of India (including Indian expectations of despotism), but very often they also revolved

---

[43] Mookerjea, *Opinions*. The quotation is from Cockerell.
[44] See above, p.1.
[45] This was the rhetoric shared by Dadabhai Naoroji in his check-list of the pros and cons of British rule in 1871; see W.T. de Bary, ed., *Sources of Indian Tradition*, vol.II (New York 1958), p.113-17.

around issues of law, rights, precedent, political economy, conservation, or expediency, which might restrict the state's intervention. The range of government expanded in the nineteenth century, but there was less change in the kinds of argument conducted about proper policy.[46]

One extended departmental debate in 1864 will illustrate a process whereby concern at conditions of production was translated into action to change the tenancy law.[47] Spurred on by the so-called 'blue mutiny' of indigo cultivators in 1859-60,[48] and inspired to some extent by the findings of the Indigo Commission of 1860, officials became alarmed by many aspects of the relations between indigo planters and their raiyats. Frequently, in mid-century, officials concluded, as did the Governor General, John Lawrence, in 1864, that the planters were implicated in harsh and injudicious proceedings. The European indigo planters, though certainly assisted on the whole by ready access to their official compatriots, were also often regarded by them with suspicion or disdain. Particular objection was taken to the planters' informal and irregular methods of control, or to formal contracts which were regarded as abnormal or inequitable in character. It was thought that the planters and their agents were possibly keeping within the law, but that the double duress of debt and rent, under which they held the raiyats, was not 'wise, or just, or politic'.[49] Official concern at the abuses of the indigo system and at protest movements then generated attention to tenancy and land-rights. In response—foreshadowing later arguments— Bengal landholders protested that the government were proposing to reward tenants for their having combined to commit 'murderous assault[s]': what now would be the condition of Ireland, they asked, if concessions had been made whenever there was an agrarian outrage?[50] The landholders interpreted proposals made in 1864 as implying a transfer of beneficial interests in land from the landowner to the tenants.

In short, the debate began with indigo, an issue which slid inexora-

---

[46] Apart from examples elsewhere in this book, and in the literature generally, this question may be pursued for the earlier period in a forthcoming London PhD thesis on NWP famine policy, by Sanjay Sharma.

[47] The file on which this is based is H Judicial A 26-46 (18 June 1864), hereafter 'Indigo files'.

[48] The best introduction to this well-known saga remains B.B. Kling, *The Blue Mutiny* (Philadelphia 1966; Calcutta 1977).

[49] J[ohn] L[awrence], note, 16 May 1864, 'Indigo files'.

[50] J. Beckwith, Secretary, Landholders and Commercial Association, to F.R. Cockerell, Officiating Secretary, Government of Bengal, 3 May 1864, H Judicial A 20-1 (13 September 1864).

bly into a discussion of agrarian relations more broadly. Indigo was not enough by itself: in the Home Department in 1864, E.C. Bayley remarked that, if general legislation were envisaged in order to curb the excesses of the indigo system, then it would have to be 'determined on far broader grounds'.[51] Just such arguments would be provided by famine, Bihari poverty, and new doctrines. But indigo was an important trigger. In 1877, when Eden became Lieutenant-Governor, he had also decided that the Bihar indigo system was intolerable. He gave the planters an ultimatum through S.C. Bayley, then Commissioner of Patna—six months to co-operate. To an extent they complied and formed their Association, with a secretary on £1,800 a year, to inquire into and remedy abuses; MacDonnell acknowledged that improvements had been made under Bayley's influence.[52] Bihar indigo had become controversial also through publicity—notably representations by an Irishman, C.J. O'Donnell, the sub-divisional officer in Gaya (where there was little indigo production) from 1877 to 1879. O'Donnell was author of 'The ruin of an Indian province' (19 July 1880); his brother was a British MP.[53]

Accordingly by the 1880s the draft legislation was designed not to aid landlords but to redress the balance of power in favour of the tenants, in order to reduce oppression, ameliorate poverty, and unlock economic progress. Indigo helped establish and sharpen this response because the debate of the 1860s had already rehearsed all the positions we have just established as existing in the great tenancy debate. E.C. Bayley noted that 'the power which has been declared by the High Court to reside in the landlord, has been used, and effectually, to compel the tenants to what is manifestly injustice with the result of smothered hatred and ultimate guilty violence'.[54] At the core of the official reactions was British credibility. Charles Trevelyan asserted that conditions were such in some Bengal districts as to injure the

---

[51] E.C. B[ayley] office note, 11 May 1864, 'Indigo files'.

[52] Eden to Ripon, 14 January [1881], enclosing Eden to Northbrook, 19 November [1881], MacDonnell to Judicial Department Secretary, G/Be, 7 September [1880], Add.Mss.43592

[53] Ibid. See also notes by C. Grant, 28 July 1880, C.L. Tupper, 10 April, and A.R. Thompson, 23 September 1880, Add.Mss.43575. Than O'Donnell, however, there was not, in Eden's view, 'a worse, or more useless, officer in the Bengal Civil Service'. According to F.C. Daukes, 25 August 1881, O'Donnell had also proposed to the Maharajas of Hathwa, Bettiah, Dumraon and Darbhanga that they fund an association in London, with himself as paid secretary, to combat the 'despotic' Government of India and the loss of their rights, as by the landholders in Ireland.

[54] Beckwith to Cockerell; see above, note 50.

'strength and credit of our Government'.[55] The response of the Bengal authorities was to propose that the tenants should be assisted by the fixing of their rents, thus securing them in their property and giving them the resources to resist the exactions of the indigo planter. In the Home Department the case of indigo helped draw attention to the fact that the law currently equated fair rents with market rates (whatever could be obtained from a new tenant). Lawrence thought it would be 'most desirable if the proprietors of land could be induced to come to a compromise with the hereditary ryots of their land to receive a largely enhanced rent, to be fixed for ever', and where this could not be achieved it would be expedient to provide 'a summary and simple' means of rent enhancement by law such as would 'preserve the just interest of both landlord and tenant'. As the papers passed around the government, even Major-General Sir R. Napier thought it impossible for the rent law to be left as it was without 'determining the limits of a fair demand on the ryot'; G.N. Taylor echoed Lawrence in favouring rents 'fixed in perpetuity as a full and sufficient equivalent to the landlord's present and prospective claims'; and Maine was prepared to countenance a 'permanent sub-settlement' by which (as he ruled out legislation for 'fair and equitable' rents, or any rates set by government) he seemed to mean fixity of tenure and an entitlement for settled raiyats to rents at a percentage below the market rate.[56]

There were arguments from existing rights—as ever, because the British professed to run a government subject to the rule of law. On the one side, G. N. Taylor advanced what would become the familiar argument that the permanent settlement had transferred only such rights as belonged to the government, had guarded under-tenures and had preserved a right of future state regulation; that was the basis on which he thought the state should now establish the 'precise nature of the tenure of the occupancy ryot' and fix a permanent rent. On the other side, in the Home Department, the evils of the indigo system did not at once overcome objections that perpetual rents would be inconsistent with the permanent settlement (which had prohibited rental agreements of longer than ten years), that it would not be proper to deprive the land-

[55] Sir Charles Trevelyan, minute, 27 May 1864, and note to Bayley, 17 June 1864, 'Indigo files'. On later papers from Bengal, Trevelyan remarked that they threw 'a stronger light on a lamentable and disgraceful state of society—disgraceful I mean to the Government which fails to apply a suitable remedy without unnecessary delay' (note, 25 July 1864, loc.cit.).

[56] Notes by B[ayley], 11 May, Grey, 13 May, Lawrence, 16 May, Napier, 6 June, Taylor, 13 June, and H.S. Maine, n.d., 'Indigo files'. These notes are also drawn on for the following paragraphs.

lord of discretion and any 'fruits of his own good management', and that it would be difficult either to decide what rates were fair or to find means of making them permanent. The Home Member, W. Grey, endorsing such views, thought the Bengal government's radicalism must have been prompted by a sense of danger, but that it still should not have been aired before soundings were taken from the Government of India. The restraint of law by law was an argument regularly raised to government by Bengalis for at least half a century, and was the one advanced by the pro-zamindar camp when it alleged a violation of the permanent settlement.

Even Maine feared that if legislation were required—as he agreed it was, to check the infinite enhancement of rents—then Europeans might seek compensation for a loss in the value, as defined hitherto by the highest courts, of any property which had been purchased after 1859. But Maine also thought the permanent settlement itself would be no obstacle. He declared that, unless the landlords could be held to have promised future prosperity (which they had not delivered), then the settlement had not been a contract but a treaty without consideration (*pactum sine causa*). It could be modified at the will of the government, the 'party which gave everything and received nothing', in order to remedy a 'formidable political and social evil' which had resulted 'to any class of the population'. He implied that state interference was justified for a public good—that is, for the benefit of a class in the community, as opposed to an individual or private purpose. In addition, when it came to theoretical principles, Maine conceded that all 'the ordinary economical maxims are adverse to interference between landlord and tenant', but he suggested that the 'peculiar and exceptional constitution of Indian society' (though that alone) would support regulation.

Such limits on the task of law were somewhat arbitrarily set. Trevelyan argued that the law could do damage, as it had when the British ignorantly interfered with the landed tenures 'moulded according to the common law and custom of India', and created four classes on the land: so-called zamindars with a conditional title; hereditary peasant proprietors; tenants entitled to occupancy on payment of a customary rent; and tenants-at-will. Then (he went on, in what we have seen became an orthodox view), Act X of 1859 had inadvertently facilitated rent increases while trying to enhance security, by setting general conditions for rent enhancement and bringing the issue before the courts. Because they had interpreted fair rents as the highest obtainable competitively, and because indigo planters were taking advantage of this to force their will on all cultivators indiscriminately (the threat being to enhance rents if the raiyats did not agree to provide indigo), effectually the judiciary had been enabled to 'settle the rents of a whole Province', which would be 'an ever re-commencing, never-ending task'. Trevelyan insisted that it was the state's (and the courts') job only to define and protect property, and not to decide rents, which were a matter for individuals and private agreement.[57]

Here we may see how the relationship later established between law and custom represented a further advance of British intervention and standarisation; but also how this advance was inherent in the ideas of earlier officials. Trevelyan's claim was that, unlike property and for reasons unspecified, rents were determined by particular cases, and not according to general principles or so as to set precedents. They were not, in Maine's sense, public matters. Yet Trevelyan was not averse to all interference. He cited the Commonwealth's abolition of hereditary feudal privileges in seventeenth-century England, and regretted its failure to achieve the same trick in Ireland. He welcomed the replacement of hundreds of thousands of uncertain inherited *inam* (assigned) rights in Madras by a regulated system of revenue-paying 'freehold' tenancies. He favoured a commission to go from district to district in Bengal, as the Inam Commission had, to 'investigate and adjudicate the landed tenures...according to fixed rules'. He then wanted the state to protect such private property, and expected capital to take on the task of social and economic improvement. On the other hand:

I altogether repudiate the idea of importing into this question the consideration, whether it is most conducive to the progress and improvement that land should be held by peasant proprietors, as in Belgium, Switzerland and India, or by large proprietors, as in England and some other countries. My belief is that in an early stage of society, when capital is scarce and agriculture is rude, peasant proprietorship is best; and that, as society advances, scientific agriculture requires concentration of capital and division of labor, and the evil works its own remedy, as is taking place in Ireland. But, however this may be, we ought to protect persons who have a permanent interest in the soil in their rights, whether their interest be large or small, and whether the right be founded on the custom or common law of the country, on long possession, or on any other ground. We may rest assured that the protection of actual rights, whatever they may be, is a necessary foundation for every other improvement. If we succeed ...in establishing certainty and security of landed property, estates will be rapidly re-cast in the form which the circumstances of society demand. Capital is as powerful in Bengal as in England; and, when it is that the hereditary and occupying Ryots have to sell, the process of absorption and concentration by mutual consent, for mutual benefit, will make rapid progress.

[57] Trevelyan, Minute, 27 May 1864, 'Indigo files'.

The history of the tenancy law, as of the state itself, shows that the line set by Trevelyan could not be held. His was a curious and inconsistent mixture of protection and laissez-faire, of principle and pragmatism. Far from endorsing 'actual rights, whatever they may be', Trevelyan clearly believed, like some latter-day physiocrat, in the superiority of the 'English way' of large landowners, and in the duty of the state to promote it indirectly. Yet he did not think it the task of the state otherwise to take a view about the most efficacious form of landholding, or even about land-rights of different origin; he wanted the state to preserve 'rights' in land, but not to protect them artificially against capital. Earlier political economists and nineteenth-century novelists alike had noted the necessity of poverty, meaning a lack of independent means, as an effective spur to labour. Trevelyan seemed to imagine that this incentive of economic disparity could be achieved by consent and the market—by evolving custom—provided only that there was a guarantee of one kind of property, possession of land. Apparently a parallel right of property in one's labour (that is, surety that it would not be coerced or exploited) did not need to exist, except indirectly in the different degrees of landed property, whereby hereditary raiyats at fixed rents, occupancy tenants at fair rents (fixed in perpetuity), and tenants-at-will, and so on, would all be recorded by field survey, title-deeds and registration.

As Trevelyan denied the state's right to legislate for a desired form of landholding, and implied that law had to be socially appropriate, manifestly he believed that some invisible hand would re-create among the raiyats of Bengal the capitalist landlords he preferred. But if the state was not to make them by law, it had to find some way of identifying which 'rights' to protect (so that the invisible hand could do its work). Trevelyan fell back on history, on 'permanent' interests. His recipe was to recognise these so that they might the more rapidly give way to ones devised by the market! Many of the tenancy reformers no longer shared Trevelyan's reluctance to legislate, but they followed parallel contortions in their search for remedies. They found it impossible to avoid taking a view of the optimum form of society, in framing the laws, but they clothed it in historical legitimacy so as to conceal the extent of their engineering. In assessing the state's right to intervene, they appealed to the public interest, as Maine had, as a limit. It was also a licence.

The colonial administrators had long sought reassurance from what they conceived of as holders of inherited privilege in India, whether Brahman informants, Mughal overlords, princes, landed magnates or village headmen. The British were therefore disposed to legitimise land rights historically, from grants, conquest or settlement. Equally (as was the case with *lakhiraj* resumptions in Bengal, with the *inam* rights to which Trevelyan referred, or with the community or caste-based land-ownership later provided in the Punjab Alienation of Land Act), they tended to confiscate possessions which could not be justified from the imagined or recorded past. In part this was derived from a European legal and rationalist tradition; in part from what was or was thought to be (which of these is not our present concern) a peculiarity of India. Rudyard Kipling reflected the stereotype in his story, 'Tods' Amendment', in which Tods, a child brought up in India, reveals the flaw in a Bill which proposed to restrict leases to five-year terms on the ground that:

if the landlord had a tenant bound down for, say, twenty years, he would squeeze the very life out of him. The notion [explains the story] was to keep up a stream of independent cultivators...; and ethnologically and politically the notion was correct. The only drawback was that it was altogether wrong. A native's life in India implies the life of his son. Wherefore, you cannot legislate for one generation at a time.[58]

On this matter, the 1885 Tenancy Act, with its ancient rights and future promises, was of the same opinion as Tods. Act X of 1859, as noted, also had been framed on such principles. The addition of the missing element in Trevelyan's prospectus, a beneficial proprietary peasantry, will be considered shortly.

A British view of historical legitimacy, as in caste for example, may well have refined several Indian institutions, in terms of their benefici-aries and their origin or basis. The practical result was not necessarily to homogenise classes—say, 'peasants' as tenants or settled cultivators —but rather to differentiate society along new, more standardised lines. But, in doing this, the law was also recognising civil and private properties or arenas which the state itself had to respect, and which were partly the creation of state actions or forebearance: this was true of religion (curiously enhanced by colonial neutrality), of land-rights, and even, to an extent, of political opinion and organisation. Hence the project in 1885 involved not only a paternalist re-structuring in the colonial interest, but also an extension and guarding of individual ownership.

Similarly, in 1864, the problem which the indigo production system presented was of an 'abuse of rights' according to universal principles. One European planter, for example, explained that the terms he offered

[58] R. Kipling, *Plain Tales from the Hills* (1888; Aylesbury 1986), p.133.

to the indigo cultivators were less onerous than they appeared—this was a common excuse—because they did not specify the lower rents and the remission of debt which he also allowed.[59] What this showed, however, was that significant elements of the planter's relations with his raiyats were hidden, and personal or discretionary; the implication was that violent coercion and injustice could be a part of the planters' operations. The colonial state was tempted, by contrast, to make all relations regular, formal and visible to law and government. The conditions for tenure and rent-enhancement provided in the tenancy acts were examples of that process, and they were designed to attack just the kind of informality which was apparent in the conduct of indigo planters, whether or not it was actually oppressive. As H.L. Dampier wrote: if the planters' obligations were specified in the contracts, 'much of the opposition now offered would disappear'.[60] Eric Stokes offers a succinct summary of the underlying doctrine here, according to Bentham and as adopted by James Mill: 'Government was an artefact, a creation and expression of will. Sovereignty was single and indivisible; its instrument was law speaking the language of command. Rights had no meaning except as they were a creation of law; liberty was but the absence of restraint, and found a place only where the law was silent.'[61]

The debate in the 1860s was firmly couched in Western law and related to categories or classes defined by rights. The issues of disagreement concerned the proper nature of those rights, and the extent to which government would be justified in legislating them into a more secure existence. According to Maine and others, the problem had arisen because indigo planting had grown up outside confines of regular law, with the connivance of government; Maine was confident that proper policing and properly organised courts would provide a remedy for this want of law.[62] Charles Trevelyan agreed that the situation had

---

[59] The planter was Hills of the celebrated rent case.

[60] Dampier to Officiating Secretary, Bengal, 6 May 1864, and see J.L. Oliphant, joint magistrate, Nadia, to Nadia Magistrate, 14 April 1864, 'Indigo files'.

[61] Stokes, *Utilitarians*, p.72.

[62] His confidence was not borne out by events. Much remained invisible or problematic to the law and other regulated systems, even after the 1885 Act. The Bengal Settlement Manual of 1908 (p.114), for example, following up section 52 which was designed to ensure that any excess area was real and material to the rent, required Settlement Officers to inquire into the extent to which differences between old and new measurements were genuine, taking account of false records and distortions such as the inclusion or exclusion of the *ail* (the partitions between plots, included in official surveys). Another problem, to be discussed below, was the variable length of measuring poles. Similarly sections

been anarchic and mediæval, and that 'the antagonistic classes' could now do battle in the courts. But he doubted that such a 'silent revolution' would suffice in this case; the rights of property existed 'only in a very imperfect form': hence his expectation that capital would do its work once property was secure. The power to make laws, in the minds of these officials, was limited by law itself; the principles of intervention were also universal, and law the remedy if properly conducted; but the need depended upon specific, Indian conditions.[63]

The consequence of this reasoning was that the law would seek to ensure evolution, and to move the 'ancient rights' in the direction of 'future comfort'. Field, and those who followed him, were proposing (once again) an extended role for the state and law. The elements in their analysis of forces of progress were, in effect, economic rationality, legislation and practice. Different analysts saw the balance differently. All imagined a line of development over time. Some believed, according to laissez faire doctrines, that it should not be interrupted by state interference. Some argued that it needed special help in India. Some believed that custom was one of the impediments to be overcome; others that it must be respected if meaningful progress was ever to occur. Field, like Trevelyan, was saying both that natural economic forces existed, and that law had to free a way for them to operate.

How was one to achieve the goal of improved conditions for the cultivators? As was readily admitted in this debate, one way was by 'natural forces'—in the case of indigo contracts it might be by the

---

55-8 of the Act provided for rent receipts with the intention *inter alia* of checking the Bihari practice whereby they did not specify what they were for; but the Patna Commissioner wrote in 1893 that this rule was still universally ignored and that civil courts continued to recognise irregular receipts. See Finucane and Ali, *Commentary*.

[63] Maine, undated note, 'Indigo files' Also see his comment following the verdict of Grey (note, 20 July 1864) that the 'whole cause of this mischief is indigo'. Bengal had censured one officer (destined for high office), J. Westland, for 'confident and off-hand' opinions on 'a very difficult question which has long engaged...the attention of officers more able and far more experienced than himself'. But Maine wrote: 'Despite his youth and inexperience, Mr Westland ['one of the most distinguished of the competitive Civilians', though bitterly criticised by the Bengal government—possibly in part because of his mode of entry to the service] is the only contributor to this correspondence [among Bengal officers] who has noticed a fact which my own inquiries (which have been exclusively among officials) have brought to my attention, the fact that a great part of the pressure (in some districts the whole) is put on the ryot by unexpected decrees for damages, in other words, by a perversion of the purposes of Civil justice' (note, 22 July 1864; and J. Geoghegan, Under-Secretary, G/Be, to Nadia Commissioner, 14 April 1864).

'commercial self-interest' of planters or from pressure from raiyats, who tended to desert the more oppressive indigo factories.[64] But already there had emerged the main argument which we saw in the 1880s, and which, incidentally, had been reinforced in the intervening years by such measures as the 1879 Deccan Agriculturists' Relief Act. It was not only that Indian society impeded progress, but also that British rule had profoundly altered the balance of advantage between the parties in social and economic relationships. Demographic and ecological pressures reduced the alternatives available to many exploited workers. Economic changes and opportunities—growing with the revolution in transport and exports—often enhanced the relative strength of landowners, moneylenders, processors, transporters, wholesalers and merchants. The colonial state provided legal, administrative and punitive support for employers and landlords, helping them to collect rents, and put down violent resistance: these public measures more than compensated for the restrictions placed by the state upon the private exercise of force. The British also privileged written records. Generally they increased the power in the hands of elites and intermediaries. Inevitably, the state would try to use the same weapons to remove abuses. It was agreed, quite readily, and partly because of the recognition of social difficulties, that the government should intervene if 'natural' forces did not provide a remedy. However, an important motive, increasing in the later nineteenth century, was also to try to retard the rapid social change that was inherent in the forces then being unleashed: hence the 'abuses' to be addressed could be either impediments to social and economic progress, or upheavals in the existing order.

In a recent study, Javed Majeed has made a special point of pinpointing the distinctions between various approaches to India, divided into two main camps. In the first, Majeed places William Jones as an orientalist radical, important because his work was empirical and comparative, both attributes intended as a means of acquiring an empowering knowledge, so that Jones learnt Persian and Sanskrit, for example, partly so as to study India's history and Hindu laws independently of the distortions of informants. But also (in his own words) Jones wanted to 'unlock the stores of native genius', a metaphor implying an original, recorded essence, albeit one that he knew to be imperfectly recoverable. For Jones, the legitimate form, for India, remained 'authentic' Hindu laws and an Oriental idiom as revealed in accurate history. (At one stage Majeed compares this with Coleridge's idealist view of institutions, defined in terms of the original and ultimate aim which they

[64] Office note by E.C. B[ayley], 11 May 1864, 'Indigo files'.

embody.) For all the offence Jones gave to some orthodox opinion, his was therefore a conservative position, similar to that which generally was revitalised and made more assertive among aristocratic sympathisers in England in defiance of the revolution in France. For Robert Southey too the Orient was a fount for religious, political and aesthetic fantasies, though he professed them to be accurate reflections of local mythologies and history, again as part of a conservative definition of national culture. The Irishman Thomas Moore took this further, by arguing in effect in favour of national self-determination. All these we might call advocates of 'ancient rights'. The second camp, in Majeed's analysis, is one which sought 'future comfort' for India by subordinating it to universal but British-made laws of political economy. James Mill was a philosophic radical who, like Bentham, attacked the predominance of common law as a refuge of privilege, and the confusions of law as an instrument of oppression. Applying such ideas to India meant treating its 'native genius' as merely the 'ungoverned imagination' popularised by Southey and Moore. For Mill, progress was linked to discipline and uniformity, to the utilitarians' universal rationalist prescriptions—universal because defined by abstract and scientific principles. Such principles constituted impediments to any self-government on the part of 'irrational' and 'uncivilised' peoples. They encouraged the kinds of legal intervention which we have seen in the 1885 Tenancy Act.

Majeed's other key point is that Indian images and examples were important to *British* intellectual arguments, a kind of mirror image of Stokes' famous conclusions about the impact of utilitarianism upon Indian policy. Mill's *History of British India* was written to confront conservative tendencies, as part of a British political and social agenda. H.H. Wilson, in his edition of the *History*, entered the same argument by reasserting the value of observation and practices 'on the spot'. For our purposes all this suggests that the value attributed to 'ancient rights' and the preferred means for producing 'future comfort' in India (whether as a rationalisation of imperialism, a cover for exploitation, or any other reason) were radically different by the mid-nineteenth century in comparison with the late eighteenth. The two principles, and their interpretation, by the late nineteenth century, thus represent a combination, if not a resolution, of the former divergent approaches. This is true in many senses, particularly in terms of political stance, but there was also some common ground. Majeed suggests, for example, that a revitalised conservatism in England was related to the agrarian patriotism discussed by C.A. Bayly: that is, the desire to harness a national commu-

nity in order to improve agriculture. Mill and Bentham objected to the
patriotism as a derogation from universal principles; they also objected
(as in Mill's endorsement of the raiyatwari system) to the aristocratic
party's equation of property and virtue. But of course they did not
object to the agrarian improvement. In the Indian rent law debate, we
have—co-existing—concepts of property, claims about the legitimacy
of past forms, and goals of progress. Officials feared social upheaval,
and frequently appealed for the preservation of a supposed Indian
society; but to them Indian norms had instrumental use but little intrinsic value: not least, evangelical Christians encouraged contempt for
Indian thought and traditions, and racist doctrines had now been constructed to explain societal difference and European conquest. Indian
norms were expected to conform to 'rational'—that is, Western—principles. Thus was 'custom' massaged and devalued. To Mill, as Majeed
tells us, India was poor economically as well as spiritually and historically. It needed uplift, through a functional government and law
which would facilitate and harmonise individual efforts.[65]

The 1885 Tenancy Act represented an important example of the
fertile mix of apparently opposed goals and ideas. The 'ancient rights'
were not *wholly* redefined as Western precepts; nor was the goal of
progress ever unqualified. Strong elements remained, even in this utilitarian thinking, of arguments about the 'special' character of India,
including what it contained of the role of imagination rather than
rationality, and the importance it accorded to collectivities rather than
individuals. The protection of what was perceived to be Indian culture
and society did still imply some recognition of the value of 'native
genius', comparable to the adjustments utilitarians had had to make to
Indian realities all along. Nevertheless, in the end, such 'custom' had to
a large extent to give way, because law provided a better protection for
individuals and for property. The measure of custom's inadequacy was
the man of substance already met in earlier chapters. We now turn to
his economic role as embodied in the 1885 Act.

He mattered because, above all, in regard to tenancy, 'rationality'
meant recognising the necessity of individual property to economic
progress. Of course this idea had its aristocratic versions (which the
next chapter will consider), but it also continued to be potent through
all the utilitarian influence on policy in India—in the raiyatwari
settlements, the would-be Ricardian revenue demands, the reforms of
the laws relating to landed property or tenancy or debt, the efforts to

---

[65] Majeed, *Ungoverned Imaginings*. See also Stokes, *Utilitarians*, and Bayly,
*Imperial Meridian*.

change cropping patterns and to promote improvement in agricultural methods, and indeed the very idea of an empire justified by 'good government'. The result was that official worries were repeatedly translated into a concern for ancient rights in *property* (though also in social status, religious belief and custom), as well as for future comfort through *improvement*. In short there were also continuities in British thinking about India, from Jones, through James and John Stuart Mill, to Maine, Mackenzie and MacDonnell. To these continuities and their consequences we will now turn.

## Chapter Six

## *The magic of property*

It is evident that not only the perceptions of the tenancy debates but also the impulses for reform were essentially ideological. Both provided for law to triumph over custom, intervention over 'natural' progress, standardisation over variety. At the core of the triumph were the diagnosis and the remedy proposed—that is, property. Indigo abuses helped focus the willingness to legislate, as did famine and Bihari poverty, and (paradoxically) a host of other dissatisfactions with the nature and impact of British law and administration. But, as ever, as in Trevelyan quoted in the last chapter, property was the programme— whether to promote economic improvement, or to protect the subjects against an overweening state and from one another. The Tenancy Act was also, therefore, a marker of particular decisions about the nature and advantages of unequal possession, for classes and individuals.

In the definition of property rights the Irish example has been recognised as having been important.[1] Several officials—MacDonnell for example—were personally interested in the Irish land question; all were aware of it, and many referred to it, as one of the great political questions of the day. Officials were familiar with the three 'F's, of fixity of tenure, fair rents and free transfer, as the embodiment of the conditions of a protected tenancy. Several of these features were translated into the Indian setting, or introduced into arguments in support of particular solutions to Indian problems. The existence of an intellectual tradition in which free transfer was regarded as an essential incident of property doubtless reinforced the reformers' insistence that tenancies should be transferable—in practice if not unequivocally in law, as we have seen—and their unwillingness to entertain the arguments, put forward by their opponents, to the effect that the ability to sell and mortgage holdings would place the raiyats in thrall to the moneylenders, the true cultivators at the mercy of intermediaries. Nonetheless, too much can be made of this Irish influence, which in any case was mainly that

[1] Dietmar Rothermund, *Government, Landlord and Peasant in India. Agrarian Relations under British Rule, 1865-1935* (Wiesbaden 1978), provides a full account, especially from p.90, which presents the Irish legislation as experiments made by what is there (though not always in his book) the monolithic 'British', and as having 'taught them some lessons'.

of general European ideas about property rather than anything more specific. Ireland's particular importance was greater at the polemical than at the ideological level: it was a fraught party issue. As such, Mackenzie questioned Garth's 'good taste', in the course of their debate, when he referred to the 'terrible fruit' of the 'confiscation' of property in Ireland. Responding nonetheless in kind, Mackenzie retorted that 'Ordinary people' had been under the impression that agrarian outrages in Ireland had resulted from 'the confiscation or non-recognition of the rights of the *cultivating* classes'. Holding up the spectre of agrarian outrages in India was a favourite ploy of tenancy reformers.

Such party divides apart, however, much that occurred in India was related to experience and debates within the country, and was reinforced rather than modified by the exigencies of Irish politics. The preferred remedies arose in contexts which favoured particular strategies and assumptions. The usual accounts of the opposing social propensities of colonial policy have assumed them to be opposed and consecutive: the permanent settlement gave way to the raiyatwari, and peasant proprietary policies succeeded zamindari ones. It should be noticed that these changes suggest three different, even contradictory trajectories: in the officials' willingness to approximate to 'Indian' conditions, in the development of ideas of political economy, and in related assumptions about the best means of securing economic and social progress. Our purpose, however, is to explore something of what they shared.

Here it has been argued that, for all the inventive readings in the records, the idea of co-extensive peasant-proprietary property would have been unintelligible to the officials' eighteenth-century predecessors. At that time, although the elements for the construction of such a theory were present, the possibility of a re-definition of real property was not considered. The British then believed in two models, in one of which indivisible ownership was derived from sovereignty, and in the other of which indivisible sovereignty was derived from ownership. In India, as the British were unable to find individual ownership, they had concluded that the state owned the land and granted subordinate rights in it. This seemed to them a primitive state of affairs, inimical to the kinds of economic and social progress achieved in Britain. They resolved therefore to do away with it in Bengal. They offered absolute rights in landed property, subject only to payment of the revenue, and sought to strengthen or create an aristocracy on what they thought the model of a well-regulated society. It is true that they intended an autocratic government for Bengal, and therefore held on to the state's claim to original ownership and rights over surplus which justified the land-revenue demands. They also proposed that land law should be universal and that administration, though minimal, should be general and bureaucratic. Hence landlords could not be admitted to be ruling over little fiefdoms. But it did not occur to them to reserve some original property to the raiyats; they merely asked that the terms of voluntary alienations—contracts and leases—should be equitable and certain, by agreement between the parties, so as not to disturb the peace or jeopardise the revenue. The state's renunciation of its own land rights was to set an example for moderate behaviour by the landlords.

By contrast, as we have seen, the radicals in the 1880s, while conceding that the rights of zamindars could not be confiscated, argued that it was the duty of the state to intervene to restore some of the position of the resident cultivators. In the past the state's power had regulated rents through fixing a 'pargana rate'; the inadvertent abandonment of this practice had impoverished the tenants and enriched the rentier class. The outcome included famine, subinfeudation and political unrest. The role of the state had therefore to be reasserted. Here was a view of public policy whereby the government was required to arbitrate between the naturally selfish interests of its subjects. The outcome was not unqualified intervention;[2] but it violated expectations that the state should merely provide conditions in which the beneficial influence of social and economic processes could flow.

Yet we must incorporate the mid-century trend, lasting almost until 1885, which favoured an extension of the permanent settlement of the land revenue, and which may be contrasted with the influence of the Punjab and its model of the peasant proprietor, to be considered in more detail in a later chapter. The two tendencies were not as incompatible as they appear at first sight, and both underwrote the remedies proposed for Bengal in the Tenancy Act. The British created a regime concerned that 'rights' (or property), as guaranteed by government and the courts, should be an instrument of social and economic progress. It was a well-established truism by the 1860s that in India effective

---

[2] A cameo to sum up the distinction is provided by proposals in the 1880s for legislation for the protection of birds. F.C. Daukes, backing the Pune Sarvajanik Sabha, claimed that such a law would involve 'the most objectionable features of all legislation, viz., interference with the social economy of the people' with no corresponding benefit. Ripon's response was that he did not object to such legislation provided it was 'in accordance with the habits and feelings of the population affected' or, *where it did conflict with feelings and interests, if it met an object of sufficient importance.* Notes of 15 April and 20 June 1881, Add.Mss.43575.

landed property originated from British revenue settlements. The permanent settlement had been an attempt to protect land rights, and further measures had extended the principle to other levels of landholding, even before Act X of 1859. By the 1870s the efficacy of property was again strongly being advocated: possession was a bulwark against oppression and a measure of prosperity; if secure, it would be a long-term remedy for famine. This justification had applied to the permanent settlement, the extension of which was then being discussed, and to fixed terms for temporary settlements. For example, Canning's government considered that settlements for terms of years 'would be free from many of the objections to which at present temporary settlements are open, and would greatly improve the tenure of land'. But the argument applied also to protected tenancies, and more widely still, as when Baird Smith, reporting on the famine in the North-Western Provinces, advocated established 'water rights' by means of a record of rights and fixed rates.[3]

One paragraph of Baird Smith's report led to inquiries about the desirability of instituting a permanent settlement 'as a general measure, applicable sooner or later to the country at large'.[4] Thus the tenancy debate overlapped with an argument about opposing types of revenue settlement, representing also different administrative styles. By the time of Crown government, after the great rebellion of 1857, the emphasis was once again on a new formalisation of government and law. In this context, old debates about a permanent settlement took on a different complexion. The development of the state was furthered by the introduction of civil-service entry examinations and promotion on merit, the growth of specialist departments of government to complement and sometimes to rival the main executive cadre, the spread of the courts structure, and the establishment of legal codes and of Acts to regulate an increasing range of public and private activities. Why then should a permanent settlement have appealed once again, as government grew? Three main reasons may be suggested: the search for cheaper means of extending the state's activities, the fear of social dislocation as a supposed modernisation proceeded, and the desire for bulwarks against excesses of authority. To all of these property was the key.

[3] The Home Department's covering letter sending Colonel Smith's famine report to the NWP Government quoted the Governor-General in Council on temporary settlements. H Public A 20-6 (7 October 1861).
[4] Ibid.; see paragraph 62 of Smith's report. See also A. Colvin, *Memorandum on the Revision of Land Revenue in the North-Western Provines* (Calcutta 1872), and B.H. Baden-Powell, *Land-Systems of British India*, vol.1 (Oxford 1892), vol.1, pp.341-9.

The advent of government on scientific principles—meaning on the basis of an allegedly exact knowledge of the country and its people (hence the greater interference)—was accompanied by the running post-Mutiny financial crisis, and subsequently by a loss of confidence in the likelihood that India would be transformed under the supposedly civilising influence of European rule. The conflicting influences were the fear of Indian revolt, the incessant worry over government revenue and commitments, and the embracing of European intellectual currents, including renewed denigrations of Indian society or an appreciation of the complexity and difficulty of all kinds of reform. In the midst of their revolution in government itself, the British became both suspicious of and anxious for change. In this context, there was pressure for a return to a minimal, indirect revenue structure. As an aspect of the changing administrative circumstances there was a renewed enthusiasm in some quarters for a permanent settlement, and for the aristocratic model of society which it implied. In the 1860s and 1870s the fashion was strong in the secretariats though it remained fairly impotent in practice. It was related to the restoration of the so-called natural, taluqdari order in Awadh; it promoted some protective legislation for encumbered estates; it engendered numerous but ultimately irrelevant myths about the relationship between Indian princes and magnates and their British overlords. Accordingly the idea launched in the North-Western Provinces in the aftermath of Baird Smith's report was for either a one-off payment to redeem future land revenue dues (this was vetoed by the Secretary of State), or alternatively a permanent settlement, which it was agreed could be considered in districts where existing rates had been revised, where 80 per cent of the culturable land was in cultivation, and where no increase in land values was to be contemplated other than by the investment of the owner. A permanent settlement, it was supposed, once again, would create a loyal and prosperous landed class, preserving social harmony, acting in the public interest, and reducing recurrent administrative costs.

The permanent settlement was finally buried, as a matter for prosyletising, in 1883. The Secretary of State, prompted from India, issued the final warrant in a despatch in February 1885. The state was henceforth to claim not just a residual right to its share in the produce of the soil, as original owner, but the right to enhance that share as required. The share was taken, or so theory proposed, from the 'unearned increment' obtainable on better soils; but—with the usual contradiction between styles and ideas—the government would claim its enhancement on the basis of general trends rather than a minute inquisition, field-by-field.[5] A resolution of August 1879 had required local governments to consider likely cost benefits when planning revision settlements.[6] The returns from the great works of survey and settlement were apparently insufficient, in financial terms, whatever their alleged merits as producers of 'better government'. At one level this may seem a victory for the school of personal government, allegedly appropriate to a people who had experienced and understood only despotism. At another level it was a tribute to believers in impersonal forces of history, and in minimal government within certain general rules.

The plan for permanency was squeezed out in part by administrative ambition. Intellectual considerations which (as said) played a special part in policy-making favoured the construction of the reasoned minute and report, which became the mark of the successful official, even where the avowed tradition was of open-air paternalism. By these means, from the 1870s the temporary settlement system and the concomitant trust in close, personal administration, came once again to the fore. The advocates of 'peasant rights' endorsed the potency of the semi-independent revenue officer, perennially touring his district, as the true representative of an Indian government and the surest transmitter of the 'civilising' message. But they spread their influence upon policy by effective deployment of secretariat skills. The extended permanent settlement was defeated also by the prospect of price inflation, and by the observation that permanently-settled areas were not more dynamic or prosperous than temporarily settled ones. It was defeated by economic necessity—famine expenditure compounding military debt—as well as intellectual and administrative priorities. Even in Bengal, official efforts from the 1870s onwards were designed to increase the revenue-take from rural areas, partly in order to facilitate an increase in government activity. The call for permanence was related, peripherally, to the perennial disagreement between finance departments which sought to maximise income and to take account of price inflation when setting revenue demands over a thirty-year period, and the settlement

[5] One suggestion was to record classes of land according to productivity and security from scarcity, and then to apply revenue increases in relation to staple prices; C.H.T. Crosthwaite and E.C. Buck, memorandum, printed 2 June 1882, Add.Mss.43584. Here the influence on discussions about how to regulate tenants' rents is particularly obvious. For scepticism about the proposal, see S.C. Bayley to Ripon, 22 August [1882], Add.Mss.43612.

[6] This did not rule out re-settlement—revenue increases in Bombay, for example, had easily justified the cost of re-survey—but the tendency was to reduce the scope of the settlements; E. Stack, Officiating Under-Secretary, H R&A, 4 October 1881, extract from proceedings, Add.Mss.43584.

officers who argued that over-assessment would stem the prosperity or exacerbate the impoverishment of districts which they had so minutely examined.

The Secretary of State took his decision in the 1880s in the context of his desire to ensure the enhancement of revenue without the need for regular settlement: a system was proposed whereby the officials, after inquiry into the economic state of a particular tract, would fix a general rate of enhancement in accordance with prices, actual rentals, the sale price of land, and even its letting value, subject to a maximum increase of fifty per cent. Regular re-assessment would be reserved for 'backward' areas—that is, of course, those in which there was most to hope for from an increase in economic activity. It sounded very much as if the Secretary was eager to maximise revenue, by ensuring that government took its cut of the profits of commercial agriculture and market rentals, and indeed encouraged the landowners to seek the greatest possible returns. As a strategy it seems ill-calculated to promote economic expansion (if the government were set to swallow a large proportion of increased income) or the well-being of the tenants.[7] But it reminds us of the importance given at this time to the improving of agrarian production and profitability: the Bengal Tenancy Act may be included among the measures directed to that end.

Despite the formal set-back, arguments for permanent and secure property remained influential in the favour shown to long and fixed settlement periods. They lingered too in the minds of outsiders to the original dispute, for whom the Bengal settlement took on a different meaning or purpose—Indians who interpreted it as a route to economic advance. Expressing sectional rather than general interest, they saw it as a means of transferring wealth and influence out of foreign and into indigenous hands (and indeed the Bengal settlement had produced some notable patrons of commerce and of political, intellectual and religious life). The famous debate by pamphlet on this subject between Rameshchandra Datta (R.C. Dutt) and Curzon's government was a strange echo of an issue which had long since ceased to have any official relevance, but which was nevertheless of public significance.[8] In the 1880s E.C. Buck too had been ready to cite the evils of temporary assessment—the need for and heavy cost of settlement and revi-

---

[7] R&A Rev A 36 (February 1886).

[8] See 'Land revenue policy of the Indian government', Resolution of the Governor-General in Council, 16 January 1902 (Calcutta 1902). Dutt had written a series of letters to Curzon's government in 1900, prompting an extensive investigation and this reply; they also were later published. It was interesting that Dutt endorsed the British diagnosis: secure landed property was needed.

sions, the depressing effect on investment from uncertainty and consequent revenue increases, and discontent from errors and harassment— but he also insisted that general re-assessments were never desirable because of the variability of soil and conditions. The only possibility was to maintain complete and accurate local records, and then to increase the revenue demand in individual cases in line with increased area, increased prices, and increased output where it was attributable to improvements at government expense. If this were done, it would limit government demands in respect of improvements made by the revenue-payer—a step towards a permanent settlement—and then it would also be necessary to impose some limit on the demands which could be made from tenants. Perhaps they too should be fixed for the settlement period; otherwise the sufferings of the Bengal cultivators would be reproduced in the temporarily-settled areas. Why a lower government demand should increase the pressure on tenants is not entirely plain; nor was the factual basis of the analysis secure: G.E. Erskine, reporting on Awadh, thought that rents there had been raised so as to 'press severely on the tenants'. The parallels are obvious between Buck's reasoning and the justification and shape of reform in Bengal, but also (as we shall see) in the shortfall in policy-execution, the lack of local records that were sensitive to variations.[9]

Most important, by this time, and (as said) alongside the discussions of permanent settlement, *a common concern for occupancy right* was to be found in many provinces. This too promoted standardisation. A lasting legacy of the debate about permanency may be found in the certainty that security and interrupted enjoyment of property were necessary for social stability and progress. Behind the advocacy of a permanent settlement lay a feudal dream—a line of thinking about India as a precursor of Europe, and of maxims about social forms which were conducive to progress, stretching from Philip Francis, through Tod, to Maine and Harcourt Butler. This dream did not disappear when a permanent settlement was ruled out. It dissolved into new forms, one of which was the 1885 Tenancy Act. The rent law debate both expressed and gave a boost to pro-peasant strategies unprecedented since the Fifth Report. But, as then, they were expressed in terms of property.

[9] Buck to Secretary G/NWP, 9 May 1883, and Erskine to J. Woodburn, 1 June 1883, with Add.Mss.43584. The difficulties did not go away in the 1880s. William Muir had declined to apply a permanent settlement in NWP, but later attempts to devise principles for reassessment on a statistical basis, rather than by inspection or survey, also led to the conclusion there that a purely mechanical system was impractical; see J.R. Reid, Secretary G/NWP, to R&A, 17 May 1884, loc.cit.

There was a real divide of opinion, as in the Bengal tenancy debate, between those who favoured great landlords and the advocates of tenant proprietors. The latter often slid, as among the Utilitarians and Radicals, into a denigration of landlords as consumers of unearned surplus and a glorification of cultivators as producers of wealth. Yet a consensus about property confused the battle-lines.

In Madras, for example, J.B. Penington, the Collector of Tanjavur, writing in 1885, felt safe to assume that it would generally be admitted that agricultural produce was originally shared between government and cultivator in India, and that zamindars were persons to whom the government made over the management of its share on condition that they behaved well to their 'tenants'. The problem in Madras, therefore, as he saw it, was that the government had continued to settle with the cultivators directly without noticing that they had become great landlords who controlled tenants-at-will rather than mere labourers. When finally observing this phenomenon, the government had declined to interfere for fear of destroying or injuring property rights. Penington argued that, on the contrary, the government should try to create a 'prosperous, contented tenantry' with secure rights which were as good as those of the landlords. He wanted, in particular, to fix the share of the produce which could be taken from the 'actual cultivator', and for government thereby to intervene actively on the side of the 'poor and needy'.[10] Earlier Penington had joined those who advocated instituting a permanent settlement throughout India; he wanted to do so in order to secure the rights of landlords at a time when a tenants' charter was being introduced.

The Government of Madras refuted Penington's analysis by re-asserting their own categories and assumptions about agrarian life: the mirasdars of Tanjavur, in their view, were small-holders, and those whom Penington called tenants were merely labourers. By this account, the government should encourage the application of capital to agricul-

---

[10] But obviously in other respects as well, his ideas were influenced, in substance and justification, by those current in Bengal. The advocates of tenancy reform had marshalled their arguments in Field's *Digest* and in the report of the Rent Law Commission. Penington was in receipt of these, intellectually-speaking; he quoted from both sources. An understanding of historical process was crucial to his argument; perhaps his respect for current authorities allowed him to escape from thinking his arguments through. How, for example, had the cultivator become transformed into a landlord? It might be said that this change was an unexpected bi-product of British rule, but even so it implies a mechanism whereby agrarian relations were not arbitrated solely by the state—and in that case there is little reason to suppose that they had in fact remained in the pristine condition which Penington described even at the start of British rule.

ture and endorse 'customary rights' in land by means of the law; but they should not presume to 'regulate the wages payable to the farm servant'. This verdict was then, in turn, challenged from above, when the Government of India insisted on a clear statement from Madras on the status of sub-tenants, labourers and others in the expected settlement report on Tanjavur district.[11] In such ways did changes of ideological fashion impinge on policy. Obviously, this dispute over tenant rights rested once again upon two main props: interpretations of the past, and definitions of agrarian classes. Different demarcations of the state's role, and different ideal forms of society, were promoted. But the past and classification were consistently employed to define property—whether for small-holding mirasdars with labourers, or for 'actual tenant-cultivators'; for zamindars or for raiyats—and it was property which was to be protected and also to be the instrument of change.

Similarly, in the North-Western Provinces before 1880, the question of occupancy right had been endless debated but largely ignored. Perhaps the fact that a fashion for tenant-right could co-exist with advocacy of summary settlements reflected the relative unimportance of the former issue in the supposedly raiyatwari areas, or perhaps (since Awadh was central to the issue in the NWP) it was a luxury to be afforded by government only where there was no prospect of enhancing its own income at the tenants' expense. Moreover, economic or administrative considerations were not generally cited as showing that the tenants required protection. R.M. Bird had proposed that government should fix the rent rates for tenants-at-will, but, starting with Bentinck's government, this had consistently been rejected, for example in the NWP tenancy debate of 1865-7. The Awadh Rent Act of 1869 abandoned previous attempts to protect tenants from rack-renting, and maintained privileges only for a small group of ex-proprietors. In 1872 William Muir concluded that, for 'those whose traditions fail to connect them with an original interest in the soil, the process may be left to work itself to an equilibrium, and the proprietors to push their claims to the utmost'. Thus where there was interference, it was to maintain 'classes whose customary rights...are liable to be injured or ignored by our land laws, and by the changes inseparable from our system of government'; for Muir this meant ex-proprietors who were being ousted by low-caste cultivators. Generally, then 'custom' was supreme.

This attitude was still confirmed when, from the 1860s to the 1880s,

---

[11] The Madras case was quoted by Cunningham. J., in the *Gazette of India*, 24 January 1885, R&A Rev A 7 (December 1885).

several NWP investigations were prompted by inquiries from Bengal. The investigators concluded tautologically that all long-term tenants had occupancy rights subject to paying a 'fair'—that is, a market—rent; no particular term of occupancy guaranteed this right, such as it was, and no right existed to hold land against the will of the landlord. Only 'original proprietary title' guaranteed a higher claim. Though settlement showed haphazard variations in rent-rates, these were generally raised in line with the capacity of the land, and frequently for whole villages at one time. Supposedly (from settlement reports), the rates of effective occupancy rights ranged nonetheless from 33 per cent of tenancies in Banda to 71 per cent in Allahabad. Despite these variations, only very wealthy or powerful landlords could eject their tenants every twelve years, and some areas showed a marked rise in the number of secure and independent tenants. A.C. Lyall, reflecting on this history in 1882, concluded that the growth of occupancy-tenant rights had not worked well in the province as a whole, probably could not be fitted in to 'modern relations between landlord and tenant', and should not be extended to Awadh.

But he went on to show how views were changing. He accepted that there was a problem of insecure tenancies, that all tenants should be allowed a certain fixity of tenure at fair rents, and that the state should help secure this. He was ready to offer protection to the 'whole body of cultivators', and to 'equalise the position of the two contracting parties', though not to provide the tenant with 'an anomalous and imperfect title'. He proposed an official rent-roll, or special courts to adjust rents, or (as planned for the Central Provinces) a right of compensation for evicted tenants. As a first stage, the NWP government proposed recording all *de facto* twelve-year occupancy by tenants in the province. The first survey under this regime was due in Banaras and Ghazipur in 1885. In 1882, in accordance with the Secretary of State's instructions, it was proposed to reduce 'field inquisitions' as far as possible, but also to give occupancy rights to almost all tenants, and to approve limited rent enhancements on a uniform basis mainly in relation to price increases. The Secretary of State baulked at the second and third of these measures, but they show how far, and how suddenly, the NWP had been converted to the principle of occupancy rights. The local government had been moved also by a perception that rents were rising and evictions rapidly increasing in NWP as population increased—the previous policy had allegedly been influenced by the advantageous position of many tenants in lightly populated regions. Now interference (as the Government of India put it in 1884) was 'justified on the broad ground that it is imperatively necessary, in the interests of the general community, that the complete efficiency of the agricultural industry be maintained'. In short, at the time of the rent law debates in Bengal, the NWP government was also considering giving an occupancy right to almost all tenants, on the model proposed for Bengal, with rents to be raised only in line with prices. Their suggestion, considered too radical by the Secretary of State in 1882, harked back to the 1830s, when Bird had proposed fixing rents in relation to the revenue demand. As we have seen, some of the would-be reformers in Bengal propounded the theory that such rent-fixing had been intended, or that, in law, it should have been unavoidable, in the permanent settlement as well. In the NWP the proprietary right had grown, as in Bengal, in the absence of such control, though the cultivators' rights defined in the Act of 1872 fell far short of a permanent interest in the soil. In NWP, there was not to be a *property* for the raiyats. Occupancy right would lapse where there was sub-letting. It would not be heritable, Lyall fearing opposition and litigation from the landlords, and incessant subdivision and over-crowding on tenanted land as population increased. Nonetheless the effect of Lyall's scheme, as he recognised, would be to give what amounted to an occupancy right, after all, to most tenants, in line with what was being proposed in the Central Provinces and Bengal.[12]

Evidently there were some fundamental differences between the possible approaches to reforming the land law; they imply the influence of local circumstances, and thus relate to our earlier consideration of the balance between custom and statute. The particular expedient, first proposed in the Central Provinces and adopted for Awadh, whereby

[12] For the preceding see minute by A.C. Lyall, 28 December 1882, R&A Rev A 16-21 (April 1884), quoting *inter alia* W. Muir minute, 4 July 1872, notes by Yule and Wingfield, December 1862. See also J. Woodburn note, 26 July 1882, recording ejectment notices served on tenants in Awadh:- 1869, 25,744; 1870, 52,151; 1880, 56,686; 1882, 91,000. Of those served notices in 1880, 30 per cent remained at increased rent, and 29 per cent at the same rent, 12 per cent were evicted from part-holdings, and 29 per cent were evicted from all culti-vation in the village (including 6 per cent who took up land in another village, 10 per cent who later acquired land in the village, and 2 per cent who aban-doned agriculture—all these remaining in the village—plus 5 per cent who were *pahikashta* raiyats from elsewhere and left the village). See also G/I to S/S, 30 September, G/NWP to G/I, 6 September, and NWP Director of Agricul-ture to Board of Revenue, 31 March 1884, R&A Rev A 21 (September 1884); also B 77 (December 1884); R&A Rev A 19 and 36 (February 1885), including NWP letter of 17 October 1882, and S/S despatch of 22 March 1883; and G/NWP to G/I, 12 May 1884, and G/I to S/S, 7 June 1884, R&A Rev A 1 (June 1884).

tenants had to be compensated for eviction, was an elaboration of a provision of the Irish Land Act of 1870. It was thought not to have worked in Ireland, and opinion in the NWP government in the 1880s was that nothing short of fixed statutory periods of tenancy would really make the tenants secure. However, the Central Provinces suggested matching the compensation to the scale of rent-enhancement, severely punishing large increases, which might, it was thought, have the desired effect of encouraging the landlords to settle with their raiyats *at rates below those which would be obtainable by outside competition.* It was not certain the NWP government would go so far; at one point they welcomed an occasional 'opening for the market rate' of rent (once in seven years), and the Government of India retorted that 'under the present circumstances of the province', including having 409 people per square mile, 'the market-rate is synonymous with the highest rack-rent that the landlord chooses to ask'.[13] But clearly the NWP government too was prepared to move some way towards a non-competitive system. The present situation in Awadh, explained NWP Secretary Woodburn, was that the law had ascertained and defined 'prescriptive rights and customary privileges of certain classes', and thus allowed a kind of proprietary tenancy to grow. This was the position reached in Bengal in 1885. The question was now, Woodburn went on, in a contemporary recognition of the contest between custom and law, 'in what way the law should intervene so as to regulate beneficially the non-privileged cultivating tenures...and farming contracts' (sharecroppers). In Bengal, he claimed, 'the rent law proceeded by way of...maintaining, reviving and declaring rights, ...working upon material familiar to jurisprudence'. The appeal was to 'principles which took their rise in remote antiquity' and which therefore were 'within the hearts of the people'. The avowedly more radical stance in the NWP, necessarily tentative, implied securing rights to all manner of cultivators, and altogether excluding from such rights those who had very large holdings or who sub-let land to others. Otherwise: 'It is open to doubt whether the absorption of small farms, on which at least the tenants manage to make a living, and the consequent relegation of their occupants to the rank of labourers with a most precarious subsistence, would not be attended by much suffering'. By such policy, government regulation stood out (with no certainty of success) against the ravages of competition.[14]

---

[13] G/I to S/S, 7 June 1884, R&A Rev A 1-2 (June 1884).
[14] J. Woodburn, Secretary to G/NWP, to Secretary, R&A, 21 December 1883, Add.Mss.43584, commenting on Erskine's report (1883).

Two points may be noted. First the appeal to history and custom, in Bengal, was still a device for extending state interference, for having laws which overrode and shaped practice by 'declaring rights'. So Mac-Donnell, noting abuses connected with distraint under the Darbhanga raj, had hoped that the proposed Tenancy Act, 'if *honestly enforced*', would 'assure a kind of millennium to rural Behar': 'the spread of education and awakening of intelligence may be trusted to secure a more prosperous future to the people of this province; but for the present it is the duty of local officers...to effectuate the intention of Government'.[15] Secondly, however, 'principles of remote antiquity', 'in the hearts of the people', also avowedly influenced the form which these legal definitions took, leaving further improvements to other forces of evolution. To MacDonnell, as just seen, the outcome of the rights promised in the legislation would be intellectual and political regeneration; and the state's job was to act as a stopgap to enforce the rights until they had wrought their effect. Custom and 'natural evolution' were not wholly unseated. It followed that the Bengal efforts were less pitted against the market or against tradition, but also less firmly in favour of actual cultivators, than were the measures Lyall and Woodburn contemplated for NWP.

These local variations do not refute that fact that rights of occupancy became a general remedy. There was a shift of focus, from landlord to peasant proprietor, which gave new life to some ideas of political economy that might have been thought to have been tested and found wanting. In addition, in the particular case of Bengal, the main idea thus advantaged was the 'magic of property'. Supposedly, it had not overcome the Indian environment in the case of the zamindars. Like the NWP government, Field had a ready answer: sub-letting, that undesirable diversion from the path of economic rectitude, had appeared spontaneously in nineteenth-century Bengal because 'alienability, not to be suppressed, ...[had] asserted itself'. Thus it was that legislation was needed not only to hurry up the inevitable evolution of custom, but to channel it into productive forms. Sub-letting 'grinds the cultivator down', but transferability of peasant holdings would encourage thrift.[16] To Field's political economy was added the special stamp of James Mill's Utilitarianism, or even of Samuel Smiles: particularly hateful was any form of unproductive rent-receiving (such as the thikadars of Bihar); if it was important to keep estates in the hands of managing

[15] MacDonnell to Bengal Secretary, 7 September 1880, Add.Mss.43592 (his emphasis).
[16] Field, *Digest,* p.183.

zamindars, it was even more desirable for holdings to remain in the possession of 'actual cultivators'.

But always possession was clearly superior to labour. Repeatedly, in the land-revenue debates of the previous half century, paternalists had wanted to preserve the supposed property rights of cultivators, by fixing their rents and securing their tenure; pro-zamindar elements had argued that such privileges should not be introduced by the state as they were incompatible with the landlords' rights in the soil; and radicals had envisaged the free operation of market forces, which would simplify agrarian relations and turn the mass of tenants into agricultural labourers. The compromise which emerged outside Bengal in the 1830s provided that tenants had security through a record of rights—which retained some of the complexity—but, especially after the 1860s, also that rents were not to be fixed in perpetuity. Utilitarians succeeded, as Stokes explained, in restricting both absolute landed property rights and laissez-faire economic ideals; they provided precedents for the state's right and duty to intervene, over rents and tenancy as in other aspects of social and economic life. On the other hand they did not abandon property in practice; rather they intended to extend it, for example to superior 'cultivators'. In this respect the main thrust of north Indian policy contrasted with the more egalitarian system introduced in Bombay under the influence of Wingate and Goldsmid, where intermediaries were removed and rents were supposedly related to the different potential of different holdings.[17] The 1885 Tenancy Act reflected these north Indian or Punjabi propensities.

## II

Social conservatism, like that of Trevelyan or of Maine, did not preclude either state responsibilities or Indian progress. The salience given to both of these indicates the continuing importance of universal and evolutionary elements in colonial attitudes to India. It was theories of a universal character, owing much to philological and ethno-historical researches, which traced coparcenary rights on settled and conquered land to supposedly tribal and pastoralist Aryan origins. In the modern world, as Maine proposed, such communistic rights were or should be replaced by private property. The presence of such elements in the debate implied that the tenancy reform would be based upon essentialisms of categorisation or about India, and in dogma about social and economic progress. The particular consequence was a search for the

[17] For the preceding see Stokes, *Utilitarians*, especially pp.117-39.

propertied and maximising peasant, a prospect long ago held up by
Richard Jones, and presented here both as truly Indian and as potentially progressive. But the underlying principle was the positive impact
of prooperty and ownership.
    It was camouflaged by a supposed faithfulness to Indian history and
custom. As MacDonnell put it, quoting Maine (in another context,
while advocating the gradual extension of the elective principle in
India), it was not until the 'warlike people' of the north-west had been
subjugated that the true proprietary unit of India was discovered; he
meant the 'village republic', made up of proprietary cultivators. This
idea underpinned the radical core of the pro-raiyat stance, which as we
have seen was the idea of co-extensive rights of property—that is, the
interest in land divided into different aspects between landlord and
cultivator. It was argued, as the Bengal government put it, that raiyats
had and should have 'substantial rights of a proprietary character',
expressed in security of occupation, and rents which took account of
their 'beneficial interest' in the soil.[18] Rent-receiving rights, it was said,
ought to be qualified by this property in the cultivation. The idea has its
roots in theories of Asiatic or Indian social formation, polity and
production, and has become familiar not just to readers of Henry
Maine, but to those of Karl Marx and more recent historiography. But
the idea itself (though not all its Hegelian echoes) was novel in official
and public circles in Bengal in the 1870s and 1880s.[19] It was introduced
by officials of the reformist persuasion. They had been alerted by
agrarian conditions in Bihar, and proposed North Indian remedies.
    Clearly the state's expanding role had had to be accommodated to a
theory of Indian rights:

[18] Government of Bengal to Government of India (R&A), 27 July 1881, in
*Report of the Government of Bengal* (1881). The notion may be traced back to
the early nineteenth century, for example, Holt Mackenzie's minute of 1819,
repeatedly quoted in the 1870s and 1880s.
    [19] As is well-known, Hegel wrote of India as a 'phenomenon antique as well
as modern; one which has remained stationary and fixed, and has received a
most perfect home-sprung development'; he also added: 'When they [the Eng-
lish] conquered Bengal, it was of great importance to them, to determine the
mode in which taxes were to be raised on property, and they had to ascertain
whether these should be imposed on the tenant cultivators or the lord of the
soil. They imposed the tribute on the latter; but the result was that the proprietors acted in the most arbitrary manner: drove away the tenant cultivators, and
...gained an abatement of tribute. They then took back the expelled cultivators
as day-labourers, at a low rate of wages, and had the land cultivated on their
own behalf.' Georg Friedrich Hegel, *A Philosophy of History* (tr. J. Sibree;
New York 1956), pp.139 and 154.

My own view [wrote Mackenzie in 1880] is that, under the law and custom of Bengal, no zemindar is entitled to rack-rent *any* cultivator admitted to settlement on the village lands. On his demesne lands (his khamar, nij-jote, or seer lands) he can ask what he likes, but on the village lands the rates should be uniform, customary, and fair, and such as to *divide*[20] equitably between the zemindar and the cultivator, *in accordance with the custom that may have established itself in the village*, the *net* profits of cultivation, after defraying all outgoings and the actual cultivator's wage. This is what I conceive to be the constitutional theory of ryots' rents in Bengal, even at the present day.[21]

We have had reason to notice the free-for-all (or free-for-a-few) revealingly proposed for demesne lands. In regard to raiyati holdings, Mackenzie was here presenting himself as a realist, making concessions on the principle (pre-British raiyati rights) in order to reflect the present situation (division of profits according to custom). He was being disingenuous, in view of the current arguments about unqualified zamindari property, but he thus indicated the consensus among the reformers and within which the Rent Law Commission conducted its arguments, even those members who disagreed with Mackenzie. In the spirit of his manifesto, when the Commission rejected free competition without legislative interference as a means of regulating rents, they did so by urging that classical (Ricardian) theory was appropriate only to capitalist farming, and by noting that more 'modern' political economists anyway defined rent as 'surplus profit' without Ricardo's reference to the minimum set by the worst lands. They added that in India, where government had ever taken a proportion determined by itself, the cultivators sought subsistence and not profit.

But then, rather giving away this argument, the reformers recommended government-regulated enhancement *on the basis of existing rents*, which were to be presumed 'fair' as the case law had decided.[22] In the 1885 Act the expression 'fair and equitable' was used, but was not defined. Finucane and Ali show that it derived from section 5 of Act X of 1859, so that there was case law upon it. Finucane and Rampini suggest that it was a charter for raising rents, in that all rents were

---

[20] A marginal notes adds: 'It is almost certain that in 1793 it was intended that the cultivator should get the whole net profits, after paying the rent as *then* fixed, or at any rate after it had once been raised to full pergunnah rates; but this privilege has been lost to him, and now the two parties having proprietary interests in the land must *divide* the surplus accruing from the increase in the value of produce since then; and the one who has the most risk should get the larger share.'

[21] Mackenzie, 'Note on the rights and status', *RLC Report*, vol.2, p.403 (emphasis in original).

[22] Following Trevor, J. in *Thakurani Dasi*, 3 WR Act X, 41.

assumed to be fair until the contrary was proved (section 27), meaning that rents which were out of line were susceptible to reduction (section 38) or more probably enhancement (sections 30-34), though that increase also had in itself to be fair (section 35). As will be discussed below, a different view is that, as the *Commentary* concluded, the outcome was that existing rents, the result of custom, haggling, or oppression, could be changed, in law, only on proven and specific grounds: 'The effect...is to give occupancy-tenants practical certainty as to the amount of the rent which they may legally be called upon to pay at any particular time.'[23] Why should this have been thought such an obvious advantage, if not to promote investment and increase property values?

On rent, the reformers supposedly rejected an untrammeled role for the market and for competition on better soils, and argued for political intervention to fix levels which would secure a sufficiency of income to the tenants. For their theory, they preferred Jones to Malthus or Ricardo. Rent was regarded not as the necessary expression of economic factors creating a 'net product', but as a variable traced originally to power. They criticised the landlords' present oppression. Yet the grounds they favoured for allowing rent-increases (prevailing rate, excess area, increased productive capacity, increased value of produce) were all, as said, to be worked against the yardstick of *existing rents*. The reformers (and the grounds for enhancement) also assumed production for profit. By ruling out differential rents for different crops the Rent Law Commission endorsed earlier criticisms of this practice as discouraging the growth of higher-value crops: they mentioned the disapproval expressed of special sugarcane rents in the revenue despatch of 12 December 1792, and that implied in 1837 when the Court of Directors argued that the 'productive power of the land' and not the crop should guide assessment.[24]

The reformers adhered, in short, to general theories, many of which are still influential. They clung still to the capitalist model of production and the 'magic of property', the belief that ownership was a necessary engine of economic advance. They clung to it, while arguing that the landlords of Bengal had failed to create prosperity; they insisted that the ideal was for the owner and the producer to be combined. The

---

[23] See Finucane and Ali, *Commentary*, on the sections cited, and Finucane and Rampini, *Tenancy Act*. This would be beneficial only if the rents were not raised at the same time. Finucane's earlier view had been that raiyats preferred illegal cesses to increased rents, as they knew the former could not be recovered through the courts (!); Darbhanga estate, Alapur Settlement Report, with G/I R&A despatch no.7, 21 March 1882, Add.Mss.43584.

[24] See *RLC Report*, vol.1, pp.31-2.

landlord was a parasite, neither placed nor concerned to increase production. How unlike the peasant proprietor! He was the indigenous
figure in the Indian landscape, and his selfishness could be harnessed to
the development of the economy, thus combining social harmony with
prosperity. If he in turn should grow rapacious, as the reformers suggested at one awkward moment in their proposals (to a chorus of
derision from their critics), then the government could intervene again
and redress the balance. By such nimble footwork, a path was struck for
an interventionist policy through the prevailing thicket of laissez-faire.

Pro-zamindari advocates objected to interference with the supposed
contract of 1793. We have considered some of their views. The pro-
tenant reformers argued that the settlement had not intended, or had not
been competent, to deprive raiyats of rights in land. They interpreted
the zamindari settlement, in ways fundamentally opposed to its principles, with an eye to supposed economic and political benefits; they
wished to remove obstacles to progress and justice which they identified in the existing rule of property in Bengal. At the same time the
reformers professed to advance the interests of the 'actual cultivators of
the soil'. Because of the historical arguments, however, the beneficiaries of the tenancy legislation were identified with holders of traditional privileges rather than with persons currently engaged in cultivation.
They sought to advantage 'men of substance'. The Rent Law Commission 'seriously considered' limiting the occupancy right to actual cultivators, but shied away from this step into the unknown.[25] At one stage,
the newly-retired Permanent Under Secretary at the India Office, Louis
Mallett, prompted by an article in Allen's *Indian Mail*, became most
alarmed at the possible consequences of transferability. Kimberley saw
'there is a danger' but not 'the way out of the difficulty'.[26] In consequence, many of the occupancy raiyats, as defined in 1885, were not
'peasant' proprietors; nor indeed, in a market-oriented economy, could
the self-sufficient smallholder be preferred over the capitalist farmer.

In the 1885 Act, it was provided, as said, that all permanent tenures
were transferable, in whole or in part.[27] It also was stated that sub-lets
of less than nine years might be registered, though otherwise they
remained subject to the landlord's consent. These provisions rather
recognised subletting than restricted it, by confirming that occupancy

---

[25] *RLC Report*, vol.1, p.13.

[26] Kimberley to Ripon, 3 October 1883, Add.Mss.43524. For some reason
Kimberley suspected that an occupancy raiyat could be just as much in the
moneylender's power even if transfer were prohibited.

[27] See Finucane and Ali, *Commentary*, on sections 3 (8) and 11, defining tenures as permanent if they were heritable and not held for a term.

raiyats could enter into such agreements, and sub-let all or part of their holdings, without changing their status. The previous law had permitted an occupancy raiyat (whose right was already established) to sublet only provided he did not thereby alter the nature of his tenancy,[28] or become a middleman.[29] It was later held that such agreements (even if for longer than nine years) were void only in regard to a dissenting landlord of the principal raiyat, and not between the contracting parties (so as not to confiscate the putative rights of the under-raiyat).[30]

The 1885 Act defined a raiyat primarily as a person who had acquired land for purposes of cultivation—which followed the existing law—but it did not make this definition exhaustive, so that persons who had the right to cultivate but did not do so could still be considered 'raiyats' within the meaning of the statute. In addition, even the weak restriction thus implied (on raiyats being rent-receivers) referred to each holder only in respect of each holding or tenure; the same individual could have a different status in regard to another interest in land.[31] Given the legal sanctions against the splitting of holdings, it seemed thus that aspects of the Act unintentionally encouraged subleases or share-cropping. By case law, confirmed in 1885, raiyats were not permitted to split their holdings without consent, and part-holders could be evicted as trespassers; similarly landlords were prohibited from dividing up raiyati holdings and redistributing them.[32] This encouraged subletting in preference to partition. Moreover, though the 1885 Act was unclear on whether or not occupancy rights could be gained by subtenants, this had been ruled out for land let for a term or year-by-year in Act X of 1859 and Bengal Act VIII of 1869, and even more broadly in the courts. An amendment in 1907 protected the rents of 'occupancy' under-raiyats, possibly meaning those who existed by custom, as the 1885 Act allowed.[33]

Harrison put in a note to the Rent Law Commission suggesting that

[28] *Ram Mungal Ghose* v. *Lukhi Narain Saha*, 1 WR 71, which held that sub-letters became tenure-holders.

[29] *Durga Prosanna Ghosh* v. *Kali Das Datta*, 1881, 9 CLR 499.

[30] *Gopal Mondal* v. *Eshan Chunder Banerji*, 1901, ILR, 29 Cal.148. On the other hand, in chapter IVA, section 18 (a) & (b), of Bengal Act I of 1907, it was provided that a transfer without the landlord's consent was not evidence of any incident of tenure, including transferability.

[31] See Finucane and Rampini, *Tenancy Act*, on section 5 (5), and, for the existing law, *Ram Mungal Ghose* v. *Lukhee Narain Saha*, 1 WR 579, and *Kalee Churn Singh* v. *Ameerooddeen*, 9 WR 579.

[32] Following *Ruheemuddy Akun* v. *Poormo Chunder Roy Chowdhry*, 1874, 22 WR 336. See Finucane and Ali, *Commentary*, on section 88.

[33] See Finucane and Rampini, *Tenancy Act*.

actual cultivators and not middlemen should be secured in the right of occupancy. Field and Mackenzie countered with their own notes, Mackenzie arguing that Harrison's idea was impractical: substantial raiyats, he explained, generally did sublet, and their subtenants (*korfas*), being of low status, would be unable to maintain any privileges awarded to them. The only way to stop sub-infeudation, he held, was by limits upon rents. After three more meetings, at which O'Kinealy backed Mackenzie, this position was substantially accepted. Mackenzie was absent from the dozen or so ensuing meetings at which rent-enhancement was discussed, but this had been a telling point: it implied that Mackenzie and the Commission accepted that occupancy rights, to be effective and useful, had to be secured for men of substance.[34] Mackenzie admitted as much in 1884 by giving up some of the provisions he had sought in the Bill to protect non-occupancy raiyats: 'It is a distinct object in the policy of the Govt.,' he began, 'to *foster* the growth of the "residuum" [of tenants] into occupancy ryots'; but, after seeing MacDonnell, he agreed that '*if the occupancy ryot is carefully safeguarded*, it would solve many difficulties to leave the "residuum" to the existing law or nearly so'.[35] Even in 1882, in apparent qualification of his insistence on securing occupancy rights for all cultivators, he had conceded that no one thought *pahikashta* raiyats had any 'ancient status';[36] if this mattered in the 1880s, then it was an easy elision, from resident, to established or privileged raiyats, as the beneficiaries of policy. The reformers found themselves in the ambivalent position of proposing rights based on history (inherited customs and status) and not upon agreement (acts of creation), while at the same time trying to construct new rules which would after all create such rights—rights which might have been supposed to be fixed were discussed in the form of laws which were yet to be made. The reformers were able, therefore, to take decisions, in the guise of respecting what existed, which were in fact determined by the outcome they wished to achieve—in this case a society of independent peasant-proprietors. We noted earlier a different conclusion for Awadh.

The supposed justification for all this potential for change was agricultural improvement. To the raiyat as rentier was to be added the raiyat as capitalist—the possibility which Richard Jones had identified. The

---

[34] *RLC Report*, vol.2, Minutes of Proceedings, 20 January, 2, 16 and 29 March, and 30 March to 4 June 1880.

[35] Mackenzie to Primrose, 26 February, and to Ripon, 28 February 1884, Add.Mss.43615 (emphases in originals).

[36] Mackenzie to Primrose, n.d. (logged 10 August 1882), Add.Mss.43615.

1885 Act allowed tenants to benefit from and to register their improvements in the productive capacity of their holdings. They were also permitted to do anything on their holdings, without consent, including house-building, which did not permanently damage the land for agriculture. This provision (section 23) in conjunction with sections 24 on fair rents, 30(b) ruling out enhancement for the growing of more valuable crops, and 82 and 83 on compensation, constituted a definite strategy to create 'improving' raiyats. For similar reasons, and in order to promote certainty, the Act displayed an animus against produce-sharing rents. Considerable inquiry had been made into these tenures in Bihar, concluding that they needed to be regulated. Though not objectionable as such, it was said—even useful if providing for irrigation, at times 'very popular' and 'perfectly satisfactory'—yet, given the relative power of Bihar landlords, they tended to keep tenants 'in a depressed condition and incapable of maintaining' their legal rights.[37] The Bihar Rent Committee suggested requiring landlords to file their accounts, which the Rent Law Commission thought impractical. Other controls considered were a ceiling on the proportion of the output taken as rent, and powers to the Collectors to appraise or apportion the crop.[38] The existing case law was that produce-sharing (*bhaoli*) rents could be enhanced and, even if fixed as a proportion of the output, could not be 'fixed rents' under section 4 of the 1859 Act.[39] From prejudice against produce-sharing rents, this was confirmed by section 28 of the 1885 Act, which restricted the enhancement of *money* rents to the grounds provided in the Act. The intention was to encourage raiyats to seek commutation to cash rents. On the other hand, to discourage landlords from extending produce-sharing tenancies, section 71 gave possession of disputed crops to the raiyat, for harvesting and storage, pending adjudication. Again commutation to cash rents was the intended outcome.

In the end, the 1885 Act, far from providing safeguards and means of improvement for all raiyats, tended to increase any dangers they faced.[40] Not least, the reason was that it permitted the occupancy right

---

[37] Patna Commissioner to Board of Revenue, 21 August 1858, and BRC Report.

[38] See *RLC Report*, vol.1, pp.73-4.

[39] *Thakoor Pershad* v. *Nawab Syed Mohammed Bakir*, 1884, 8 WR 170.

[40] This is deliberately expressed as a trend and not a universal rule. As will be shown in chapter ten, the trend was that some raiyats, who tended not to be 'pure cultivators' and to have relatively high status, gained some benefits against their landlords. Note, however, the advantage taken by some 'agricultural' castes of middling status, or the instances of Namasudras in Bakarganj seeking commutation of rents and standing up to their landlords in 1908, coin-

and all its advantages to be enjoyed by non-cultivators. As at least one commentator remarked, echoing J.P. Grant, the district judge of Hoogh-ly, such a 'misnamed occupancy ryot' was likely to become enriched as a 'new middleman', at the expense of zamindars and cultivators alike. Such 'petty middlemen', the Collector of Murshidabad argued, were the most oppressive; *they* would be the rack-renters instead of the zam-indars, claimed E.V. Westmacott, the Collector of Dhaka. But the tenancy reformers *intended* to create a class of agricultural entrepre-neurs amidst the smallholders of Bengal and Bihar, and they did not see how they could do so without providing them with a property in their tenancies. That property, being necessarily heritable and transferable, obviously could be lost through mortgage, or acquired, in a highly stratified society, by those who would employ labour and lend capital. In mitigation, case law (according to Finucane and Ali) implied when interpreting the 1885 Act that a raiyat should not be a mere rent-receiver, entirely divorced from cultivation. However, an occupancy raiyat could buy and sell rights, and did not have to be resident (unlike a settled raiyat) provided he continued to hold land (under section 20 his rights would lapse if not exercised, after one year). No measures against external or professional moneylenders could have prevented this; nor could a ban on sub-letting on occupancy holdings (suggested by, among others, J. Monro, Commissioner of Presidency Division).[41]

By the same token, if the Act did not discourage those raiyats who were landlords, equally it did not necessarily curb the proprietors in their control over land. In addition to sharing in many of the weapons already discussed, the zamindars also had the chance to benefit from the Act's indecision over demesne land. The draft rent bill for Bihar had tried to re-define *zerat* because it differed in Bihar from what was envisaged in Regulation VIII of 1793, and because it was so easily extended in many estates. It was partly for this reason that the presump-tion of occupancy right (section 120 in the Act) was strongly supported by Bayley and Mackenzie;[42] and some other safeguards were also included in 1885: Bihari lands cultivated directly by indigo planters and called *zerat* were not recognised as such in the 1885 Act because of the rule excluding tenure-holders. More generally, there was little use of

---

cidentally with settlement operations, as described in Sekhar Bandyopadhyay, *Caste, Protest and Identity in Colonial India. The Namasudras of Bengal, 1872-1947* (Richmond, England, forthcoming, 1997), ch.3.

[41] Dacosta, *Remarks and Extracts*. The references above to official comments are taken from this source also.

[42] See chapter II, clause 9, of the draft bill, and section 39 of Regulation VIII of 1793, 'Draft bill for Behar', *RLC Report*, Appendices.

the survey procedure to establish such lands, and Finucane and Ali reported: 'Every year that passes makes it more difficult for proprietors to prove that lands held by them directly are true legal "private lands".'[43] On the other hand, claims were encouraged by, and such lands recorded in, the main survey and settlement operations. Moreover, whereas sections 37 to 39 of Regulation VIII of 1793 had recognised as *khamar* those lands already recorded as such on 12 August 1765, sections 117 to 120 of the 1885 Act admitted as *khamar* whatever land was shown currently to fall within the definitions provided.[44] The zamindars quickly understood how to manipulate these aspects of the law.

The pro-raiyat school in Bengal was selective in its radicalism. It was inventive when it came to re-interpreting agrarian relations in the eighteenth century, but not when defining the nature of the property which was to be provided for the tenants. The intention, of course, was to give rights of occupancy to the vast majority of raiyats. But this property was not to be any inalienable good, or a right inherent in the cultivation of land: such proposals foundered on the twin rocks of practical politics and incomplete theory. This property was to be an exclusive personal possession in precisely the sense in which the courts had hitherto usually supposed the landlord's estate to be. It was to be bought and sold, because property, it was assumed, had to have value and marketability.

Consideration of the arguments for and against legislation makes it plain that conditions only 'made sense' if reviewed in terms of a strong external hypothesis. The ideological certainties contrast with the real difficulties of the record. In particular, judgments remained firmly located within assumptions about exclusive ownership which were characteristic of British ideas of property. Those who regarded tenancy legislation as a confiscation of zamindari rights quickly discovered early and apparently supportive texts which fitted in with the historicist flavour of the current discourse. But *a priori* assumptions were not confined to the zamindars' advocates. The Rent Law Commission did not even collect its own evidence or have public hearings from interested witnesses, as one critic pointed out.[45] The reformers made no real attempt to derive their proposals from, or even to reconcile them with, Indian conditions. They knew that sub-letting and labour-exploitation would be a problem,

[43] *Commentary*, p.539.

[44] Namely, that cultivated by the proprietor directly, or by his servants or hired labour, for twelve years, or recognised as such 'by village usage', or let out as such before 2 March 1883. See Finucane and Rampini, *Tenancy Act.*

[45] J. Dacosta, 'The Bengal Tenancy Bill. Remarks on a paper read by W.S. Seton-Karr at a Meeting of the Society of Arts' (London, 1884).

but they preferred to ignore it, because of an intellectual conviction that transferability was essential to 'true' and useful property, and also that property would transform its peasant possessor into a capitalist who would need no special help to remain true to his economic interests and to enterprise. However, given the emergence of a consensus in the Punjab about the problem of indebtedness in the 1890s, it may be that a decade later officials would have been convinced, on the contrary, that because of his property the peasant-proprietor needed to be protected from outsiders who would exploit him—that is, protected from himself. After all the features of the 1885 Tenancy Act were derived from a particular conjunction of the events and attitudes of its time.

We have seen that the Tenancy Act redefined three major aspects of agrarian relations: types of land, different classes of land-holders, and the kinds and limits of rights, especially as regards transferability and rent. In attempting to fix and secure such definitions, the Act also provided for settlement and record-of-rights proceedings, though their outcome was probably quite different from what had been intended. In all these aspects the Act was chiefly concerned with categories of property, abhorring any gap or ambiguity either of land or of status, even though it retained some poorly defined distinctions—for example, one that was important but as yet unmeasured, between zamindari and tenants' land. The point, already made, that zamindars could benefit by extending *zerat*, rested on the principle that all land (including the state's) had to be either zamindari or raiyati, at any one time, and that the incidents of each were quite different. For example, by section 6 of Bengal Act VIII of 1869, reinforced by section 116 of the 1885 Act, no occupancy rights accrued in respect of the so-called home-farms of the landlords (not tenure-holders), which were called *nijjot, khas, sir, khamar* or *zerat*, and recognised in effect as any land thus specified, supposedly by custom, even if held by tenants, plus any land that was untenanted. This *zerat* included land not held by tenants in 1793, or which had since come into the 'immediate possession' of the landlord, for example by the relinquishment or annulment of a tenancy.[46] In the Bill introduced in 1884, the statement of objects and reasons had included the need to see that *khamar* land was not further extended; Ilbert reiterated this in his speech. But the relevant clauses were dropped, and the determination of such land was left to the revenue officers, by survey, as requested by government or individuals. A result of the Act was therefore (as said) to encourage the already-extensive claims to

---

[46] Field, *Digest*, p.22. Regulation VIII of 1793, section 52, referred to the 'remaining lands' of the estate.

*zerat* land, identified as a special problem in Bihar. By contrast, tenant lands were defined according to the status of their holder: we have seen how the reformers abandoned their earlier attempts to associate occupancy rights with all raiyati land and not with the occupant. The reformers held in their minds a picture of a stable Indian village made up of largely undifferentiated tenant-cultivators, so that it seemed to them not to matter if rights were vested in occupants rather than land. But this left open several possibilities: transfers of land from weaker to stronger occupancy raiyats, the further creation of under-tenancies, and the loss of presumed tenant rights by legal or other manoeuvres. We shall consider these consequences in a later chapter.

Legislation thus occurred under the influence of ideas whose limitations it reproduced. Particular distortions can be traced to social theories and views of India which made up the mentality of the officials, whether large ideas with a wide currency or specific interpretations with a restricted appeal. Two intellectual reflexes were apparent: one historicist and the other essentialising. First, the reformers insisted on a necessary evolution from the past to the present. Thus, in his *Digest*, Field accepted that 'alienability was not an ordinary incident of landed property in its early stage', but, as noted earlier, he also argued that the tendency of development in any society was towards that end.[47] Accordingly the government, in supporting early drafts of the 1885 Act, set about investigations which purported to prove that raiyats' holdings were in practice readily transferred throughout the presidency, if only at the behest of landlords who sought to oust a defaulting tenant. It was held to be wrong to restrict transfer; it had already appeared in the natural course and in advance of any legislative interference. Opponents retorted that transfer was mostly very uncommon, and certainly did not take place without the landlord's consent. To introduce it by legislation would thus be 'mischievous'. A little later, the desire to restrict land transfer would seem to be a fixture of the pro-peasant school of thought, part of an inheritance taken up chiefly by Denzil Ibbetson and to be found in published treatises on Indian law from at least that of Raymond West in 1873. But in fact it was not essential. Both sides of the argument on transfer paid at least lip-service to the ideal of appropriate rather than universal legislation, and both also adhered to the evolutionary ideas which Maine had expressed.

Eden's government, in 1881, aimed not only to 'encourage the growth of a substantial cultivating class', but also to 'discourage the

---

[47] Field, *Digest*, p.165. Once the idea was established, he argued, extending it to raiyats' holdings 'was only natural progress'.

conversion of men originally cultivators into mere middlemen, or speculators of rent'.[48] But evolutionary theory stood in the way. On one hand the government admitted the impossibility of 'changing the face of the country by statute', and thought it would continue to change by natural processes, as it had already, from a community of subsistence peasants, to a society marked by various classes and occupations. Social differentiation, like markets, resulted from change over time; it was the product of innovation and not part of the original fabric. On the other hand, Eden's government also shared the view of the majority of such interpretations, that most of the change was comparatively recent, and the result of Western government and influence. Some distortions had been introduced, either from indigenous failings or sometimes by errors of British government; but the process of change was thought inevitable and (often enough) 'civilising'. Hence, though sub-letting would be objectionable, it was impossible to avoid entirely, and transfer of land between occupancy raiyats would be welcomed as a sign of progress—it would create a class of well-to-do cultivators with larger than average holdings. Such reasoning remains common in analyses of colonial impact and of development strategies.

The first implicit essentialism of the tenancy reform thus concerned the alleged immobility and lack of social differentiation in rural India in pre-British times, and the subsequent evolution towards dynamism and stratification. More importantly, in the rent law debates these same ideas clearly contributed to the essentialist notion of a uniform peasantry; the term used was resident raiyat. There was a recognised eighteenth-century category of villagers with security of tenure, or rather an obligation to remain in the village. One assumption was that this single category was eroded during the nineteenth century, to be replaced by an unprecedented free-for-all which reduced all tenants to another singularity: the tenant-at-will. Such categories were not, as is sometimes assumed, mere reflections of reality. They resulted from theory and discrimination. We can now see that the notion of a resident raiyat and a successor tenant-at-will was defective: it tried to describe conditions on the basis of speculation about the origins of property rights.

Against all such standardisation we must place the multiplicity of relations on the land. Indigenous categories existed; and they were legion, local and subject to change. On the one hand the permanent resident remained a powerful idea. In the 1880s one of the arguments against expecting competitive rents was that on the whole men did not go about looking for holdings, and rents reflected very local demand for

[48] *Report of the Government of Bengal* (1881).

land.[49] On the other hand landed interests had been complex long before the British appeared. They were influenced not only by customary expectations but also by ideological inputs and commercial and political forces. There is abundant evidence that in the eighteenth century some people moved in order to sell their labour and to take up holdings as non-residents: the very concept of a non-resident cultivator implies this.[50] Clearly raiyats could compete, and even residence was an advantage of shifting import. If there were changes in these respects during the nineteenth century, they were a matter of degree not of kind. By British accounts, someone who employed labour was an anomaly; this was admitted but not faced. Also anomalous was someone who sublet part of his holding and cultivated another part. After 1885, officials uncovered hundreds of such different types of relation and right which they had to squeeze into the categories provided in the Tenancy Act. Not only were there rights which did not fit in; there were individuals who performed in several roles at the same time.

The assumption that there was single category of peasant, and that its natural state was one of stable evolution, helps explain the failure of the reformers in the 1880s to inquire more fully into the identity of the 'bonâ fide cultivator' who was to be protected. Implicitly the reformers relied on an ideal definition whereby those who collected rent could be wholly distinguished from those who cultivated using their own labour. We have noticed that the 1885 Act contained two kinds of distinction, partly contradicting each other: a binary one between rent-payers of all kinds and rent-receivers (called 'landlords' in the Act whatever their legal status), and another beween the four major headings, from landlord to under-tenant. In its confusions, this terminology effectively assumed that the 'raiyat' was not a rent-receiver, whatever he might be in reality. If we compare this result with the writings of the pro-raiyat group as a whole, we find how the chosen terminology of the Act obscured the original concern with the 'actual cultivator'—code in this context for the peasant proprietor as opposed to non-cultivating owners or landless cultivators.

## III

The ambivalence of the radicals' ideas contributed to some of what are now regarded as failures in the 1885 Act. It has been suggested that the

[49] This view was put forward by Phear, J., in the Great Rent Case, and adopted in the *Report of the Government of Bengal* (1881).

[50] See Aditee Nag Chowdhury-Zilly, *The Vagrant Peasant. Agrarian distress and desertion in Bengal 1770 to 1830* (Wiesbaden 1980).

consequence of allowing occupancy holdings to be bought and sold was to sever ownership from production once more, creating petty landlords who oppressed an ever-more impoverished labouring class.[51] Just such an outcome was predicted by opponents of the 1885 Act, and admitted by some of its defenders as early as the 1890s. Obviously one effect of the prevalent assumptions was to suppress the implications of evidence that was known to all. This included information that had helped provided the impulse for the 1885 Act. In 1878, the Collector of Patna wrote of visiting the houses of petty traders and cultivators—Telis, Banias, Gowallas (Ahirs) and Halwais—and seeing the manner in which they lived. He would not have believed their abject poverty, he said, if he had not witnessed it for himself. In Bihar, he argued, the specific problem was low wages; the general one was that the region was too poor to buy up its own harvests. Many of the cultivators farmed only two or three bighas—an acre or less—and ten to fifteen per cent of the population were landless labourers who were barely kept alive by those who held ten or more bighas and wanted their labour.[52] About the same time Antony MacDonnell attributed famine, more succinctly, to the 'inequitable distribution of the produce of the soil'.[53] Yet these conclusions were lost sight of in more generalised assertions about oppressed raiyats and rapacious landlords. It was assumed, in effect, even by MacDonnell, that zamindars were taking too much from tenants generally, rather than that various groups towards the bottom of the society had too little on which to live or were vulnerable to downturns in economic conditions. Explanations were sought in effects which might be supposed to impinge broadly (and which also relied on general theories): such factors as a rising population or the rapaciousness of the mahajans.

But law did affect agrarian relations as a generalising tendency. It has increasingly been recognised, but not yet much reflected in interpretations of revenue and tenancy law, that differentiation was the

---

[51] For a statement of this view see Asok Sen, Partha Chatterjee and Saugata Mukherji, *Perspectives in Social Sciences 2. Three Studies on the agrarian structure in Bengal, 1850-1947* (Calcutta 1982). See also B.B. Chaudhuri, 'The process of depeasantisation in Bengal and Bihar 1885-1947', *Indian Historical Review* II, 1 (1975), pp.105-65.

[52] Patna Resolution for 1878-9, quoted in M[ackenzie], 'History of the rent question'.

[53] MacDonnell's views arose out of his work on famine relief, as a district officer in Bihar, and in preparing his *Report on the Foodgrains Supply* (Calcutta 1876). This particular remark was quoted by Sir R. Temple in 1874/5 and again in M[ackenzie], 'History of the rent question'.

starting-point and not the end-product of the changes under British rule. The partition of estates indicated the impact of regulations favouring individual property rights, but it also occurred more in some places than others, and meant different things in different places. In general, a proprietor was now being secured in his position by the state, substituting for the weight of the clan. With rising agricultural returns, it was inevitable that advantage would be taken of the mechanism provided in the revenue law to separate individual shares from collective property. There was a general incentive to several property in the economic advantages of undivided management and of recording an enhanced rent-roll during the pre-partition survey and settlement. Similar impulses would work on tenants, once occupancy right was secure. On the other hand, the consequences were not general at all: the incidence of partition was far greater in Bihar than elsewhere, and most of all in some parts north of the Ganges. In much of north Bihar it was appropriate or necessary to slice up dominant and proprietorial interests vertically. In Bengal proper and where there were very large estates in Bihar, such interests were more likely to be divided horizontally. Tenants faced different pressures and opportunities in both cases, and according to their caste, size of holdings, competence and independence. The resulting society was always a mix between pre-existing conditions or long-term trends, and the changing pressures of and chances under British rule.

This account has emphasised defects of understanding which had practical consequences. It does not, however, argue that a distant and arrogant colonial machine ground on unseeing through indigenous norms and values. Though there was a mismatch between different conceptions of society and classes or rights, there was also a diversity and complexity in colonial interpretations, which continually engaged with perceptions of Indian reality. Contrary to what is sometimes suggested, the British never focused only on the particular and intrinsic disabilities of the Indian 'other'. They valued aspects of the Indian past and of indigenous knowledge. Thus the notion of peasants' property was couched in historical terms, derived from notions of cause and effect, and of precedent. It privileged Western rationality *and* an Indian inheritance. The village community ideal too, while retaining the ambivalence about progress and modern knowledge which had characterised neo-classicism and other·'golden age' theories, clearly encapsulated the now-familiar sentimental vision of a past that had once been more humane, communitarian and ecologically-friendly than was the present. This again gave a moral superiority to some aspects of the Indian experience. What is more, at the same time there were arguments backwards from what was observed of contemporary poverty and oppression in India. As those conditions were illegitimate, they were assumed to be new, in a reversal of the usual historicist and evolutionary explanations. As well, this argument accorded not only an inferiority to the Indian present (attributed in part to Indian 'character') but also a kind of superiority to an original Indian way, in line with other assertions of the need for special or appropriate policies—that is, of the inadequacy of European theory.

But of course these attitudes and techniques did not remove the desire to progress (along Western lines) or the tendency to distort and generalise. Though the past gave legitimacy, to identities as to land rights, it was also made problematic because of a colonial discourse in which India was seen as a kind of living fossil, and evolution towards the 'modern' was thought a necessary improvement. It was this combination of attitudes, also appropriated by Indians, which implied that a selection had to be made from the past, or that it had to be re-interpreted; thus 'objective' public standards had to be agreed and then policed. From literary taste to religious belief to land rights, the outcome was new law of one kind of another. In the case of the tenancy debate the core disagreements were about the nature and rights of agrarian classes; and so land law participated in the major project of colonial policy, to create classes out of Indian 'disorder' (or order on different principles). The reformers' most basic arguments depended upon treating the raiyats in uniform categories. In the present they were uniformly downtrodden, even though the tenancy-reform movement had originated in concern at violent combinations of tenants, and at evidence of peasant differentiation. In the past, equally uniformly, the peasants were supposed to have had quasi-property rights from *khud-kashta* status. Providing an occupancy right meant once again defining homogeneous types of rural property-holders. Though classification and enumeration are *not* in themselves colonial innovations, contrary to some recent interpretations, yet in this case and others like it they represent significant new kinds of, and means for enforcing, standardisation and structures.

Much of the colonial intent was to remedy other suppposed Indian defects, and this permitted a greater degree of state intervention than was favoured by the current orthodoxies of political theory. The Tenancy Act continued the British (and Indian) attack on forests, 'primitive tribes', migrants, and concealed or unruly classes beyond the law. It expressed a countervailing preference for settled agriculture, with its supposedly greater openness and certainty. Such attitudes dominated official thinking, though they were opposed by some at the time, as by most environmentalists since. Applying an evolutionary model, the vagrant, the uncultivated and the unknown represented the past in a different light—as a 'waste' literally, and a danger. By the same account, the boon of certain and stable property was the future. What was this effort for? Why this expansion of the state? Because administrative reforms allocated definite duties, they imparted to the officials (if only for career advancement and job satisfaction, and by bureaucratic logic) a sense of responsibility for particular spheres, for people, or regions. A professedly Christian or more specifically a Protestant-inspired morality led the officials to emphasise their own duty to promote Indian well-being, and to place high value on some kinds of activity—on useful works, on cultivation (of fields and talents). Thus the British claimed the main object and justification of state policy to be the advancement of 'civilised' features, meaning settled and standardised or categorised populations within fixed, specific territories.

The process was paternalistic, no doubt, with its 'scientific' reformations of knowledge and its definite views of proper conduct. It sought to reduce independence of action. On the other hand, in that respect it was not peculiarly colonial, for such interference and control were featured in the growth of the state wherever it occurred. Moreover, even when emphasising India's difference, and its backwardness and division, as in the 1880s, British officials searched for elements compatible with 'modern' societies—such as the rule of law, individual rights, private property and even egalitarian or representative institutions. Such values were perhaps Western in form, and linked to ideas of Western superiority, but they were also universal in potential, and readily if selectively appropriated by Indians, along with some of the criticisms of India. In particular, a consensus on the rights to property was potentially liberal, in that private property was considered an essential attribute of nations. On one hand, to focus on 1793, with the landlords, was to reinforce ideas of a pre-colonial India without individual rights, a despotic India without history, an India which was therefore an inchoate congeries of tribes and castes. On the other hand if this India had been newly created by Western laws and government, as the pro-landlord arguments insisted, then it too now permitted individual property and hence national attributes, in the European sense; this some zamindars and intellectuals asserted. Henry Cotton, writing to Ripon of the inevitability of greater Indian participation in their own government, stressed the difficulty of advance 'in a country where the solidarity of classes is so broken up as in India'.[54]

B.H. Baden-Powell took the view, attributed to John Strachey and relevant to a discussion of the contribution of the Tenancy Act, that 'India' was merely a geographical and not a national term, and that therefore institutions took different forms in different places.[55] Nonetheless he made many generalisations. In doing so, he shared the general willingness of the period to revert to Hindu texts, including *Manusmrti*, as evidence of original and thus legitimate forms of landright. Though Mughal precedents remained important, the final arbiter seems to have become a notional Hindu past. It is an interesting preference, marking the 'communalisation' of historical periods, the mid-century repudiation of Mughal legitimacy, and the post-census recognition of the 'Hindu' majority of 'India'. To create property, similarly, in the 1885 Act, a fictional history was constructed which met the needs of the present, and also of theory, in that many argued that independent peasant proprietors were economically more efficient than landlords. Because of this fictional history—in which India was perceived as a *single* social entity—the ancient divisions of property rights were taken as generating rules for the proper disposition of land-rights in the present. But, if ancient rights existed so as to legitimise legislation, then it follows that India was not an arena in which European ideas were uncritically imposed, as for example were the ideas of individual property and other Westernisations that were being forced at just this time on Native Americans. The ideology was available to do likewise in India, as was the greed, but the confidence and power were insufficient. Instead there were alternative ideologies and objectives. These gave a value to indigenous forms, to the special character of individual places. The ancient land-rights gave India a national identity, as Britain had, thus returning to the comparative project started in the Indo-European studies of William Jones and the Asiatic Society of Bengal.

By this combination of elements, 'modern' and general categorisation was tempered (that is, hardened *and* modified) by the power and authority of the 'ancient' or specific. As early as 1810, Francis Buchanan, also had noted India's 'perplexing' local variety, which he blamed on successive rulers and their inferior officers who acted for 'temporary convenience' and on 'discordant principles'. He warned therefore against excessive standardisation:

We almost everywhere find the same terms employed in the customs, finance

---

[54] Cotton to Ripon, 10 September 1893, Add.Mss.43618.

[55] B.H. Baden Powell, *The Land Systems of British India* (Oxford 1892), vol. 1, p.5. The reference is to Sir John Strachey, *India* (London 1888).

and government of the people; and superficial observers have done infinite harm by representing the people as everywhere guided by the same laws and customs. Now I will confidently assert that many of the terms expressive of points of the most essential consequence...are taken in meanings essentially different, not only in different remote provinces but even in neighbouring districts, divisions and estates. The use therefore of any such terms in a general legislative view, without a most accurate definition of the sense in which it is to be taken, may prove in some cases highly prejudicial, while with a proper definition the regulation might have proved universally beneficial.[56]

This warning was often repeated but ultimately unheeded. The effect *was* often prejudicial, but standardisation could also be positive.

In the end, categorisation plus property, as in the Tenancy Act, implied individual rather than collective rights. That kind of interest, and its reflection in broad classes, was necessary to the construction of the 'modern' society and state. Altogether, in its appeal to historical and geographical unities, its emphasis on origins, precedents and classes, tenancy reform was also located within a broader project, that of constituting the countryside and the peasant as the 'real India'. The officials who endorsed the Tenancy Act, like the French painters of the Salon in the later nineteenth century, imagined an agrarian order, a 'profound' and symbolic landscape, which was a marker of shared history and common identity. The idealised peasant struck a chord with the reformers as part of a search for stability in the countryside. It was a conservative response to economic, political and social upheavals. But it was not necessarily altogether reactionary in impact: an identification or construction of what was 'Indian' was implied, since it was ancient rights, alongside common interests and goals, that legitimised the gift of property; and such properties defined the nation.

[56] Francis Buchanan, *An Account of the District of Purnea in 1809-1810* (ed. V.H. Jackson; Patna 1928), p.161.

## Chapter Seven

# *The politics of land*

Land questions were deeply political, in British minds, because of the debates of political economists, the enclosures and Luddites, the corn laws, the Irish question, and advocacy of land nationalisation. Ripon's interfering radicalism was intolerable to some precisely because it aped that of Gladstone; the supposed confiscation of property in Bengal produced an avid alliance of opponents in Britain partly because it was supposed to repeat a confiscation which had just occurred in Ireland. The Indian reformers' hands were tied, indeed, partly for fear of political upheavals in Britain. But land and politics had long been entwined in India too. In colonial times, land policies were particularly significant in determining the competing styles of Indian administration. The decisions of the 1880s were political because they represented a victory largely for officials of one persuasion, were achieved by political rather than bureaucratic means, and were about styles and purposes of government. They were political too because they reflected a choice of government allies, created potentially political constituencies and classes, and engendered habits of political action and debate in defence of such positions and interests. Put another way, each aspect in the rent law debate required political decisions—they were indicators of officials in ascendancy and styles of administration; they revealed preferred supporters and the interests of individuals and classes; they were about goals of government.

The most apparent political change, in Indian agrarian policy late in the nineteenth century, was the rise in the credit of the paternalist Punjabi model of Indian society and government, alongside the defeat of an extended permanent settlement. The Punjab success was associated partly with a Benthamite zeal for reform, regulation and improvement, and partly with the overwhelming regard paid at this time to the ideas of Henry Maine and to the village community as the original or natural form of Indian society. The 1859 Act had already marked this influence by giving exclusive jurisdiction in rent cases to the revenue officers. In the great rent law debate, the adoption of ideals and assumptions associated with the Punjab was deliberate though hotly argued. It married a sentimental espousal of traditional Indian forms (or ancient rights) with a professedly hard-headed appreciation of the

214

current laws of political economy (producing future comfort). It meant that differential benefits were welcomed as a means of securing capital investment, but that rights would nonetheless be provided and recorded at all the different levels of the economic hierarchy. The peasant proprietor embodied the twin approaches. Those who favoured peasant proprietors (and also praised the independent experience and judgment of the local revenue officer) were attempting to export to Bengal certain Punjab ideals; this was reflected in the antagonism between these advocates and the pro-landlord, pro-regulation parties. The victory of the former chiefly explained major features of the Bengal Tenancy Act of 1885, especially the emphasis upon peasant-proprietary rights.

British officials in India did have, unsurprisingly, 'a political view of reality whose structure promoted the difference between the familiar ...and the strange',[1] but more interesting they were also in a position analogous to the stereotype of mediæval Europe eloquently recapped by Michel Foucault, when, he claims:

The great institutions of power...rose up on the basis of a multiplicity of prior powers, and to a certain extent in opposition to them: dense, entangled, conflicting powers, powers tied to the direct or indirect dominion over land.... If these institutions were able to implant themselves..., this was because they represented themslves as agencies of regulation, arbitration, and demarcation, as a way of introducing order.... Faced with a myriad of clashing forces, these great forms of power functioned as a principle of right that transcended all the heterogenous claims, manifesting the triple distinction of forming a unitary regime, of identifying its will with the law, and of acting through mechanisms of interdiction and sanction....[2]

But also, in India, as surely in Europe, the prior powers lived on; they and new interests grew under the ægis of state sovereignty and regulation. Nor was the growth of modern institutions unilinear.

Also illustrated here and in the next chapter will be a lack of political will that restricted the effectiveness of the Tenancy Act as a charter for tenant rights, or a device of socio-economic reform, and instead contributed to bureaucratic incapacity, an inability to reshape the codes into a working system so as to approach the professed goals. A second point will be indicated without being pursued: the importance of the tenancy debate and law for the establishment of an organised representation of tenants and a language articulating their condition, needs and rights. A full study has yet to be made explaining this politicisation, connecting the nineteenth-century debates and the organisation

[1] Edward Said, *Orientalism* (London 1895), p.43.
[2] M. Foucault, *The History of Sexuality. An Introduction* (tr. Robert Hurley; London 1984), pp.86-7.

of pro-raiyat parties, to the campaigns against indigo planters in Bengal and Bihar (long before Gandhi), and to the well-known twentieth-century involvement of the Congress and other politicians in the countryside's legal and political issues and in mobilising 'peasant' supporters. A third point is implicit: the importance to the development of the state of this mobilisation of Indian 'classes' or interests, and of the profound agitation of public opinion through the tenancy debate.

It will be convenient at this point to recap some of the findings of earlier chapters. Each of two main systems of Indian administration (zamindari and raiyatwari) can be regarded as having been dominant at different times during British rule, just as analytical or pragmatic approaches held sway at some periods more than at others: Baden-Powell referred to the 'pendulum of general and official opinion' swinging between permanency and tenant right.[3] Policy took several forms, each with its own authoritarian streak, imposing a pattern of behaviour and a set of expectations even when the rhetoric of the policy-minutes extolled the virtues of *ad hoc* decisions by the man on the spot, the man who knew. The late eighteenth century in Bengal was characterised mainly by a distant and minimal executive and by imported theories of society and governance. A permanent settlement was designed in part to provide government by rule, under the scrutiny of an independent judiciary and through Indian intermediaries whose existence minimised the need for contact with large numbers of Indians. In the succeeding period the raiyatwari and temporary settlements were avowedly responsive to Indian conditions; they favoured direct, personal, even military rule. The system invented by Thomas Munro applied his interpretation of Indian society and customs in Madras presidency, but, like other systems, it embodied an emphasis on individual rights.[4] In the Punjab the administration, established on the remnants of the Sikh state, followed the design of Henry Lawrence, employing the argument that the province required special measures, given its frontier position (at the time), its military traditions and its warlike people. The officials developed and extended doctrines of the independent village

---

[3] B.H. Baden-Powell, *The Land Systems of British India*, vol.1 (Oxford 1892), p.342.

[4] See E.T Stokes, *The English Utilitarians and India* (Oxford 1959), W.J. Barber, *British Economic Thought and India, 1600-1858* (Oxford 1975), S. Ambirajan, *Classical Political Economy and British Policy in India* (Cambridge 1979), T.H. Beaglehole, *Thomas Munro and the Development of Administrative Policy in Madras* (Cambridge 1966), and Burton Stein, 'Idiom and ideology in early nineteenth-century South India', in P. Robb, ed. *Rural India* (London 1983; Delhi 1992).

community and the cultivating proprietor. A temporary settlement implied a personal and pragmatic system of government—that is, the combination (at least at the level of the revenue court) of executive and judicial functions in the person of the local British official, and a close involvement with the character and customs of the people as a whole. The Utilitarian gloss on this policy, its principles gradually refined in practice by political and economic experience, implied the addition of a hierarchy of duties and jurisdictions, and systems of fixed reports and returns, all of which were provided, in the 1830s and 1840s, as we have seen, to make the administration more answerable and effective. The post-Mutiny period was one in which regulation, legal codes and distant government, even a permanent settlement, were to the fore. The time of the great rent law debate saw a reaction, a renewed preference for the all-knowing paternalism of the local official, better acquainted with 'his' villagers and his horse than with his files and his clerks. At this time, custom was supposedly again supreme, and principles of political economy and ethics were qualified, or hitched to the cart of expediency.

Everywhere the strategy was to preserve what was seen as the old order on the land. But this naturally took several forms. In south India the key controller of the land has been shown to have been the village headman, on whom the local administration depended.[5] In the Punjab, of course, policy evolved into the preservation of so-called peasant rights. As the reforms in Bengal spread this approach to other parts of India, the long-term goal remained unchanged, but the beneficiaries of policy were changed—in Bengal, potentially from zamindars to peasant proprietors. The attitudes of the rulers to India were also always of two kinds, which oddly co-existed, appearing, for example, on both sides in debates over particular policies. On the one hand, there was a sense of superiority reflected in arguments from universal principle, a tendency which ranged from the Evangelical to the social Darwinist. On the other hand, there was a belief in the specificity of Indian institutions, an attitude which led to attempts to establish the origin of practices as a measure of the suitability of British proposals, and to restrict what was thought to be the inevitable encroachment of market and non-customary relations, of social and economic change. These differences also implied two opposing views of policy. The British favoured their own traditions of government and believed in the need to transform India both socially and economically. But they also considered it dangerous to make a frontal attack upon Indian customs and interests. By the same

[5] D.A. Washbrook, *The Emergence of Provincial Politics* (Cambridge 1976).

token, they set up, as appropriate to a civilised regime and a civilising mission, supposedly equitable but abstract administrative systems which depended upon regulation; but also, in order to match what they believed expected by India, they advocated the personal, pragmatic despotism of the district officer.

This meant—it facilitated the change in approach in Bengal—that in practice the difference between the two administrative styles was less than absolute. A temporary settlement involved some rules and some relatively powerful Indian allies—partly because it was sensitive to custom and political implications, partly because the British official was still too isolated and increasingly too overworked to offer a close personal attention to all aspects of his charge, and partly because bureaucratisation progressively affected even the most independent of the regional traditions. Conversely, the permanent settlement allowed some leeway for individual officers—even in this, as it was said, the man was to some extent the system. At times this regime too was concerned to search for measures affecting the welfare of the population at large or at least for potential allies beneath the level of the landlord. Both systems, moreover, involved a degree of distortion and standardisation of local practices and institutions. In consequence there was a tendency for opposing strands of policy to be reconciled at the margins, because of the need for continuity and to match central dictates with local practice. In the Punjab, for example, the 1860s and 1870s saw various measures of regulation which ran counter to the traditions of that province. The codification of law applied to the Punjab too, with a High Court to give it effect; this province too was subject to the bureaucratic revolution of mid nineteenth-century government and to the improving communications which brought its decisions under more immediate scrutiny. In the Punjab the old tradition had had to be incorporated in the new. By the same token, any contrary changes in Bengal would have been matters of emphasis and not absolute.

Yet some underlying principles were extended with the spread of Punjab influence. What the 1885 Act expressed—a new orthodoxy of tenant rights and the great value placed upon peasant proprietors in village communities—dated from at least 1812 and the Fifth Report, as confirmed by Munro's sytem and the Punjab tradition. But it had been contested by defenders of the permanent settlement, and by those who regarded Bengal as having long been (or as having become) a different case; it is interesting that Baden-Powell's book on the Indian village community hardly mentions Bengal.[6] The merits of peasant proprietors

[6] B.H. Baden-Powell, *The Indian Village Community* (London 1896). This

were generally and increasingly accepted, at least until 1857, and yet no effective steps were taken to help find or create them in Bengal. The Tenancy Act of 1859 provided jurisdiction in rent suits for revenue officials and thus a chance for paternalistic mediation between landlord and tenant (especially as, that same year, the offices of Magistrate and Collector were re-united once again). But, as we have seen, that Act was a measure whose most innovative features were introduced with very little discussion and under the impression (though also influenced by theoretical assumptions and experience in upper India) that they were no more than a codification of existing law and custom. The Act sought to simplify and standardise existing procedures and provisions rather than to redress what were considered imperfections of the agrarian and legal structure, and it did not remove the pro-landlord tendency of much Bengal policy, especially in decisions of the judiciary. It operated in a climate in which the prevalent view in Bengal was still that all land rights had been granted in perpetuity to the zamindars in 1793. The flavour of this view was apparent in the arguments already cited from the landowners in 1864. They claimed, in direct contradiction of Maine, that the permanent settlement was a contract to which the state had agreed 'for a valuable consideration', and which was 'not liable for alteration'. This meant the zamindar had power 'to deal as he likes with his own'.

On the other hand, even these landowners admitted that a concession was made in 1793 to allow certain established tenants to continue in their tenancies so long as they paid rents at the prevailing or market rate. In this version the government was entitled to intervene in order to insist upon that concession (but only to do so); Act X of 1859 had greatly extended it (to all those holding land for more than twelve years) and turned such tenants into proprietors at a fixed quit-rent. The alleged result was that raiyats, who all had once thought themselves liable to rent increases, now included a favoured exempt class, and others who were 'trying (through forgery and perjury) to get into it'.[7]

So much for the landlord view. In fact the 1859 Act had reflected the anti-landlord leanings of the previous generation of Company servants, without being supported by a coherent defence with regard to Bengal, with the result that, even in so far as it had clarified and protected tenant rights, it had been subverted to varying degrees by the

---

fact was related to the book's race theory (mentioned in chapter one) which attributed settlement in villages to the influence of 'Aryans'.

[7] H Judicial A 26-46 (18 June 1864). See chapter three, and Regulation I of 1793, s.7.

courts, the local government, the European planting and mercantile community, and the landed proprietors. Still needed were arguments which extended the conditionality of the permanent settlement, and justified the law's definitions of tenants and their rights. In a climate favouring a permanent settlement it was unremarkable that the fixing of rents should be seriously considered as an answer to this problem, as it was in the indigo debates of 1864. Later the same goals could be pursued by means of newly-defined legal rights in classes of property.

The debates in the 1880s thus sought to settle the unfinished business of Indian land policy. There is some debate about the origin of the pro-peasant resurgence. Van den Dungen attributed it to experience of Indian conditions; Barrier particularly to a fear of disorder as a result of British 'inability to defend the interests of several important classes'; and Dewey to a 'historicist-idealist' reaction to utilitarianism, which restored respectability to 'traditional land-based groups intermediate between the individual and the state', and recognised the political threat from 'anthropologically-inappropriate' policies. Barrier found government interference 'institutionalised into an active defence of peasant rights'. But the peasant and his economy also had first to be perceived. Dewey stressed that the new policy involved the abandonment of the free market philosophy, represented by James Fitzjames Stephen, and its replacement by deliberate conservation of rural interests: exemption from the full rigour of the law, seasonal adjustment of the revenue demand, and measures against land alienation or for the amelioration of rural credit.[8]

It will be apparent, from earlier chapters and in support of Dewey's position, that the 1885 Act marked an important if imperfect triumph for this new policy, and that the main mechanism for reaching decisions or for spreading ideas had been the harnessing of historical explanation

[8] A good short description of some aspects of the peasant strategy may be found in John R. McLane, *Indian Nationalism and the Early Congress* (Princeton 1977), ch. 8. The discussion in the above paragraph refers specifically to P.H.M. van den Dungen, *The Punjab Tradition* (London 1972); Norman G. Barrier, *The Punjab Alienation of Land Bill of 1900* (Durham 1966), especially pp.96-102; Clive Dewey, 'The Official Mind and the Problem of Agrarian Indebtedness in India, 1870-1910' (Cambridge PhD 1972), especially pp.1-21; and Eric Stokes, *The Peasant and the Raj* (Cambridge 1978), introduction and papers 4 and 11. Relevant published articles by Dewey are 'Images of the village community: a study in Anglo-Indian ideology', *MAS* 6, 3 (1972), and 'The education of a ruling caste: the Indian Civil Service in the era of competitive examination', *English Historical Review* (1973); see, for his definition of historicism, note 3 in 'Celtic agrarian legislation and the Celtic revival', *Past and Present* 64 (1974).

to policy debates. The later nineteenth century was a time of high administrative ambition, in ways that some other periods were not, and one in which intellectual considerations played a special part in policy-making. The construction of the reasoned minute and report was the mark of the successful official, even where the avowed tradition was of open-air paternalism. From the 1870s the temporary settlement system and the concomitant trust in close, personal administration were once again to the fore, but still the advocates of 'peasant rights' spread their influence upon policy by effective deployment of secretariat skills. They were politicians putting about a party line, even while they endorsed the potency of the semi-independent revenue officer, perennially touring his district, as the true representative of appropriate Indian government and the surest transmitter of the 'civilising' message.

In 1878, the Bengal government had advised the Bihar Rent Committee that 'the less radical the interference with the existing law the more chance there is of the proposals of the Committee being accepted'.[9] But soon afterwards the same government was adopting—albeit briefly—a fashion which was current elsewhere but extremely novel for Bengal. In defining agricultural classes, the 1885 Tenancy Act followed Punjab practice and was mainly concerned to support what were regarded as hereditary, resident cultivators in the villages. Again, they were defined by their property or rights; and again all possible classes were imagined to be subsumed in a complete schedule of tenurial forms. Let us consider again Field's suggestion, followed in the 1885 Act, that a presumption be provided that tenants had a right of occupancy in their land, with certain other privileges in regard to rent, unless it could be shown that they had held land in the village for less than twelve years. This turned the 1859 Act on its head, both in regard to the presumption of occupancy, and in deriving rights more or less from residence in a village, rather than from the long possession of specified plots of land. In law, one set of distinctions between tenants was removed, but room was left for the development of others. There was no longer any effective difference between 'original', 'full' or 'resident' raiyats on the one hand, and other, less privileged villagers on the other; anyone who had held or inherited any land in a village—unless they were patently newcomers—could claim occupancy rights in regard to all the land which they held there. Moreover, because the unit under consideration was not the estate (the lands of one owner or set of owners under one revenue head) but the village, as defined by govern-

[9] Proceedings of the Bihar Rent Committee, 9 November 1878, *RLC Report*, Appendices; see chapter three.

ment surveys (or historically by Metcalfe and Maine), it followed that rights gained under one landlord could be transferred to land held from another. What all this shows clearly is that the definition of occupancy right in 1885 reflected not so much an assessment of past conditions as the influence of Indian peasant-proprietary notions. The provision for survey, settlement and record of rights was an even more remarkable tribute to the persuasive powers of the Punjab school; its effects will be considered in the next chapter.

These abstractions and inexactitudes of policy do not mean that theory did not draw upon interpretations of Indian conditions; nor does the intellectual contribution make the policy changes any the less matters of political dispute. Grand theory altered over time, and drew policy along after it; but each step was doggedly fought, and each had implications for its protagonists and subjects. Also some fundamentals relating to the position of a colonial government proved inescapable. Almost invariably, for example, and with renewed force given the usual explanations for the North Indian revolt of 1857, British policies were avowedly conservative in social terms, even when 'progress' was held out as the rulers' main objective; where ideas were influential was in deciding the elements in society which were to be preserved. When those ideas favoured policies to boost the position of peasants, meaning in fact proprietary cultivators, this development too built equally upon three elements: first, the classical theories of political economy, the anti-landlord sentiment, and the individualist bias, introduced into official Indian circles by the Utilitarian employees and teachers of the East India Company; secondly the administrative precepts advocated first for the Madras presidency by Thomas Munro and his school; and finally the 'scientific' approach to government developed, alongside a critique of Utilitarian theory, in the course of census, settlement and famine work especially after the 1870s. All of these in the Indian context were both intellectual explanations and political strategies for ruling. For similarly mixed reasons, a regard for dominant peasant interests proved to be a continuing feature of public policy in India from the 1880s onwards, and indeed to the present day. In the twentieth century, of course, the British seemed to be facing the political consequences which had earlier been feared from social change: the nationalist struggle in the countryside could be taken to prove either that peasants were unable to provide a unified support base for the regime or that the strategies for maintaining their allegiance had failed. The same mixture of motives thus encouraged, yet again, the alternative strategy, to court landlords and present an aristocratic model as the indigenous and proper shape of Indian society. British colonial governments elsewhere also later assumed that the lesson of the Indian experience was that peasants were politically unreliable, a verdict arrived at by inegalitarian urban-based regimes in many parts of the world, and backed up by twentieth-century theories of politics and revolution.

For all these future vacillations, the debates of the 1870s and 1880s led to policies which were quite different, especially within Bengal, from those of the period which preceded the tenancy law of 1859. Turning from the hinterland of ideas to the foreground of debate, the immediate contest which we need to explain, therefore, remains that which, by 1885, produced the fundamental change in attitude towards the latest version of pro-peasant paternalism espoused in the Punjab. In all the criticisms and remedies then current, the implicit comparison was between the Lower Provinces of the Presidency and the Punjab—to the disadvantage of Bengal. When an extended permanent settlement was ruled out, the exception remained what many thought the ill-governed and ill-omened lower provinces of Bengal. The Punjab, with its canals, enterprising peasants and loyal soldiery, seemed the success story of British India; and naturally its officials thought they had the answers. The Punjab school advocated the establishment of a vigorous village agency, and active steps to protect what were seen as the uniformly down-trodden tenants of Bengal. The Punjab's 'manly' form of government and its supposedly loyal, independent and increasingly prosperous peasantry were what the tenancy reformers hoped to promote in soft seditious Bengal.

The caricature reminds us of some other special factors which allowed the Punjab model to flourish, and by stages turn a measure which was arguably once intended as a means of assisting zamindars to collect rents, into a Bill hailed as a charter for tenant rights. The Government of India played a powerful role. It advocated a pro-peasant line at different moments for reasons which related partly to personnel and geography. Punjab officials advanced notably in the central government in the 1870s and 1890s; many other success stories were of officials who shared much of their philosophy. Having the seat of government at Calcutta served to undermine the prestige of the local government in Bengal. The city's relatively active political life often proved less a stimulus than an irritant to the officials, who would blame it on the provincial government's weakness and the excessive influence of the courts. The central government's alternative summer seat at Simla, by contrast, seemed to put the departments in close and sympathetic touch with the Punjab, already important because of its strategic position, its role in 1857-8, its recruitment for the reformed army, and its growing significance for public works, trade and economic development. What is more, two main influences—the Punjab model and the Bihar example—combined when Charles Tupper, who in the 1870s had helped increase Punjabi influence in the Revenue and Agriculture Department of the Government of India, was placed on special duty in connection with the Bengal Rent Bill, and in the early 1880s produced an important report on Bihar. Tupper made it inevitable that the Bill would introduce a special set of provisions for that area, regarded as needing more and different measures from the remainder of the province.

Yet the 1885 Act was not forced on Bengal. The radical pro-raiyat proposals most evident in the early 1880s were not simply an import of Gladstonian liberalism under Ripon; as argued already, they were also the result of efforts by particular, mainly Bengal civilians. From the 'best' districts in Bengal—notably those in Bihar where the 'manly' virtues of the old-style district officer could still flourish—there emerged a programme to transform the conditions of tenancy. Bihar was economically backward, and, except for some huge mostly absentee landlords, could be characterised as containing a great mass of idle and insolvent petty zamindars who refused to cultivate even tiny holdings themselves so long as they had tenants to oppress. Such a region seemed the perfect exemplum of the peasant school's arguments. In the 1870s and 1880s interpretations of Bihar were informed by a view of India which was historical and prescriptive and partial; protagonists in the rent law debate created a range of concepts, definitions and judgments. Alongside special pleading about eighteenth-century regulations and circumstances, a view was enunciated about the 'natural' or 'appropriate' conditions of society for the Bengal presidency. The very different actual conditions in late nineteenth-century Bihar provided the yardstick by which proposals were measured. Thus it was was held by some that Bihar in particular proved it was necessary to restore people's 'ancient rights' if their 'future comfort' were to be assured.

Various other factors made the Punjab model attractive to the Bengal officials in the later nineteenth century. We have already noticed one: the interpretations placed upon what was a genuine though arguably exaggerated fear of disorder and violence, a lesson drawn from the uprisings of 1857 that policies were dangerous if they cut across 'natural' or existing social ties; thus were explained both the revolt in Awadh and the quiescence of the Punjab. In Bengal too rural disturbances in the 1860s and 1870s were interpreted as symptoms of the social disruption caused by inappropriate laws, and as omens of future threats to British rule. The likelihood of agrarian revolt was often flourished as a clinching argument.[10] A particular gloss was added by the indigo question. Planters were thought to represent an intrusion in the countryside, supposedly introducing a radical mode of production; they siphoned off profits, often out of India altogether, and their relations with their suppliers and workers were described as oppressive. If they suffered from agrarian riots, this could be held to be very much their own fault. But it was also said that the excesses of the planters were common enough among Indian zamindars; the criticism was partly that indigo was being produced not in the manner expected of Englishmen but by taking advantage of typically Indian tyrannies—such was village life under the permanent settlement. Racial stereotypes thus allowed the poor example set by the European indigo planter to add to the condemnation of a whole category of Indians.[11] Such considerations made Bengal officials receptive to alternatives to their long-standing reliance upon landlords, and gave a boost to the picture of landlords as useless drones who had failed to create economic improvements in Bengal and elsewhere. Outside Bengal, the fact that the zamindars in Bengal had failed in their social and economic task had been recognised for fifty years; in the rural disturbances of the 1850s and 1860s, there were indications that they were failing in their political job as well.[12] Well before the more violent upsets of the present century, which put the seal on British disillusionment, the usefulness of the old compact with the zamindars was being questioned, with a view to finding alternatives. Such sentiments were increasingly reinforced by objections to the

[10] See for example MacDonnell on his defeat over the preservation of the land record (discussed below): 'Ten or fifteen years hence some other Bengal officer will take up the struggle, if indeed before that time a *Jacquerie* in Bihar does not precipitate an earlier *dénouement*'; note, 3 August 1894, R&A Rev A 17-20 (January 1895).

[11] By the 1880s, as shown in chapter five, planters had come under great pressure to regulate their conduct, and they were not universally opposed to pro-raiyati provisions. T.M. Gibbon, for example, advocated abandoning the right of distraint, or transferring its operation to the courts. Gibbon to Patna Commissioner, 22 February 1879, *RLC Report*, vol.2. W.B. Hudson, another stalwart of the Bihar Planters' Association, told S.C. Bayley that he supported occupancy rights and limits on enhancement and ejectment: his views were shared, he said, by all planters who could 'look further than the length of their noses', but Bayley feared 'most cannot look that distance'; Bayley to Ripon, 23 January [1883], Add.Mss.43615. Gibbon and Hudson were considered, accordingly, for appointment as members of the Legislative Council. Gibbon later opposed the clauses allowing commutation of produce rents; note, 28 October 1884, Add.Mss.43584.

[12] See PCR 338, 12/19 (1883/4); and compare ibid. 12/1.

political activism growing up in Bengal; landlords were sometimes held to blame because of their acts of commission or omission. Multitudes of idle, ambitious, disappointed, educated men had supposedly been spawned by the easy surpluses and the 'subinfeudation' of the Bengal system.

As in the early years of the century, the argument was again being made that, contrary to expectations, the advent of private property, as for zamindars under the regulations of the 1790s, had not contributed towards prosperity. The readiness to decry the receivers of rent, which prevailed in many parts of India in the later nineteenth century, was only temporarily subdued by the campaign for a permanent settlement and by Lytton's elaborate wooing of princes and zamindars. It was important, though, that this anti-landlord fashion was related to the claim, agreed by advocates of the aristocracy, that historical legitimacy was the key to social harmony; in the pro-peasant camp this connected with a version of India's past and its present institutions which, as already noted, traced them principally to Aryan tribes. It was the break-ing of these continuities which, according to such theories, produced the social dislocations which the British perceived.

In the 1880s many Bengal officials joined in this chorus. In particu-lar, as said, the British were beginning to doubt the supreme influence of the zamindars: could they still deliver a quiescent population for the colonial rulers? Those who were active for tenancy reform expressed such concerns. Mackenzie wrote in 1881 in a manner suggesting that the zamindars were too inactive and self-absorbed to be politically useful—to the effect that the British Indian Association, the vehicle for the zamindars, was wholly the mouthpiece of its president, Rajendra Lal Mitra, as the committee 'simply accept any draft he puts in front of them'; only on rent questions did they have any opinions of their own; and the same could said for the utterances of the Association's paper, the *Hindoo Patriot*.[13] Bayley commented, in 1885, that it was

worth noticing how strong the feeling of antagonism and contempt is between the older Hindus of good position, represented by the British Indian Associ-ation, & the younger & more noisy party, represented to a great extent by Surendranath [Banerjea] himself. I am afraid the power of influencing Bengali public opinion is slipping from the hands of the former in spite of the strong social & quasi-official support which Eden gave them, at the expense of their rivals.[14]

[13] A. M[ackenzie], note, 13 September 1881, from keep-withs to Home De-partment proceedings, Add.Mss.43612, p.289.
[14] S.C. Bayley to Primrose, 5 June 1885, Add.Mss.43612.

The advocacy of tenant rights was, in short, not innocent of political calculation. Thus, in the eyes of its advocates, was the special case of the Punjab turned into a panacea. It implied a view of the most appropriate and effective form of society for India, one in which cultivators, by nature and experience different from other men, worked on plots of land which they owned and for which, ideally, they were unbeholden to others. It was one also in which communal ties and traditional practices —the cement which held together a diverse and segregated set of castes and occupations—could once again be regarded with respect. The pro-peasant school considered itself profoundly conservative, but also produced a particular view of society as it should be, usually equating it with the society as it was, or, in the case of Bengal, as it had been. It could then argue (as Munro had too) that working with the grain of the society was the best way to ensure its long-term improvement.

According to the pro-peasant theory, the original landowning interests had proved unable to keep up with the innovations introduced by the British, especially the grant of alienable property rights. This failure was principally to be set down to incorrect policy: it was innovation as the 'ruling vice' of policy, as in Metcalfe's famous dictum.[15] The newcomers in the countryside were politically useless, or dangerous, because they did not maintain traditional links of social dominance. The old style had proved economically incompetent while the newcomers were politically objectionable. In such an atmosphere, characteristic of the Punjab-dominated pro-raiyat school of the century's end, there was no room either for an optimistic assessment of the achievements of the past, or for an objective analysis of the part played by property. The British critics curiously shifted their ground: their political concern for social conservatism qualified their enthusiasm for economic change; their desire for progress dampened their regard for the old order. It was to answer this conundrum that one party extolled the allegedly improving landlord. To the other party, the peasant proprietor as agricultural entrepreneur offered a partial solution. It was assumed that a pro-peasant reform would help with the fact that Bengal did not really pay its way because of the permanent settlement; it was a rich and populous region which made little contribution to solving the financial crises which had beset the empire. The peasants were already being taxed; independent and prosperous peasants and the trade they

---

[15] See E.T. Stokes, *The English Utilitarians and India* (Oxford 1959), p.19, and compare Henry Cotton, *New India or India in Transition* (London 1885; 1907), ch.4.

encouraged could be taxed some more.

In this we may see that Bengal tenancy legislation which favoured peasant proprietors was not a victory for the Punjab school as originally conceived, where individual initiative was valued over regulation; rather it was an extension of Punjab practice, in which a framework of rules was important, along with longer-term, even Utilitarian notions of the optimum forms of agrarian society. In the Punjab, legislation had preserved supposedly original principles; the Punjab Laws Act (IV of 1872) declared the supremacy of custom. The strongest argument for such distinctions was naturally one about difference, even though the concepts underlying personalised government were general ones about Indian or even Asiatic tendencies. When the Punjab methods were on the defensive, their supporters fell back on the suggestion that they should be retained in those areas to which they were, supposedly, most appropriate. The argument could work both ways, and defend other traditions when the Punjab approach was dominant. It was ironic for example that in the 1890s Denzil Ibbetson, who was urging the extension of the Punjab approach to the administration of revenue law and the maintenance of a land record in Bengal, should have had to rely on the 'special case' argument to save his favourite project, the Alienation of Land Act, from the criticisms of other provinces; only by this expedient could he entrench this piece of 'custom' against the bias of the law in general towards contract and the market. Perhaps a greater irony still was to be found when the Punjab ideas *were* endorsed. Ibbetson regarded the 1872 Act as having 'saved us [in the Punjab] from the wholesale application by bookmen and lawyers, of the local law of a Bengal community whose social unit was the joint family, and still worse, of the law which Mahomed laid down for a people of herdmasters, to a province where the land is held in tribal occupation, and the unit is the village community.'[16] Yet, in the Bengal Tenancy Act, that spirit of the village community and of collective property ownership was supposedly being imposed where (by Ibbetson's own intelligent distinctions) it did not obviously apply, and it was imposed by bookmen and lawyers. There, however, as in the Punjab too, the victory was partial, again because of the bias towards contract and the market.

This point brings us back to the ideas. The history evoked in the policy debates was a special kind of history. It could justify particular policies, and give certain social formations a glow of historical justification. The decision about which to favour depended upon other theo-

[16] Ibbetson note, 31 April 1898, R&A Rev A 3-22 (November 1898), part IV (19-22).

ries and on fashion. Hence the importance of the fact that in the later nineteenth century the proprietary cultivator was made the ideal, a view which did not always prevail but gained in popularity among officials, a view which history and the comparative method appeared to endorse but did not wholly explain. It is sometimes said, on the contrary, that imperial policy in India was governed by pragmatism but not by ideas. The assertion gains no support from a serious study of any decision or legislative measure. Indeed two kinds of idea can always be found: first, *a priori* assumptions, and second, interpretations of what was supposedly reality in India, or in other words, both 'theory' and 'knowledge'.

But here we find an arbiter which continued to outrank even the advice of the Punjab. Knowledge divided into what was imported and learned, and that which was indigenous and practical. Intellectually-acquired knowledge tended to be regarded as superior. Thus attempts to improve the society rested upon the conversion of 'primitive' into 'civilised' values and practices, whether in social relations or methods of production. The science of the expert was valued above the experience of the practitioner. Part of the Punjab way was the enhanced authority of the expert on tenancy, indeed on India (we have noted how the revenue officer was preferred to the jurist); but by the same token even he had to submit to a superior wisdom—the very one embodied in the constitutional structures of the British raj. In the end it was the Secretary of State who decided, or at least had to be convinced; and hence it was the politics and judgments in Britain which prevailed. In consequence even changes in agriculture, trade and finance, in spite of repeated evidence that imported remedies were seldom appropriate, were generally expected to conform to those which had occurred in Britain.

In government too there was seen to be an Oriental and a Western way; and, though many professed to prefer the former, transition towards the latter was felt to be inevitable, a consequence—indeed a benefit—of British rule. So too the officials' explanations of institutions followed a logic based upon or judged in terms of European experience and ideas of progress. Definitions, and especially the legal ones in regulation and statute, imposed an external, 'objective' categorisation upon a subjective multiplicity, as in distinctions between religions, communities and 'castes'; between landlords and tenants, peasants and labourers, agriculturists and moneylenders or traders; and between state and subject, ownership and dominance, private property and corporate rights. So it was (as said) that the victory in Bengal was not of a Punjab way but of a supposed Punjab style, suborned to produce the optimum economic and political dividends in the colonial era.

## II

Because the Tenancy Act of 1885 was political in the broad sense that it related to ideas of ordering India, it had to reflect—or indeed modify —the range of allies and agents upon which British rule depended.[17] It is true that one of the strategies of the British was to create a kind of civil society that would be sympathetic to their rule, by being formed in the image of that existing in Europe. Roper Lethbridge's involvement in the tenancy debate points to the importance of the press and public opinion for tenancy and other issues in the 1880s, and also (contrary to the usual assumption—imperialist Briton pitted against nationalist Indian, autocracy against free speech) to the closeness between British official or commercial interests and some Indian journalists or classes, in this case conservative in opinion. But in rousing a public outcry over tenancy Ripon's government was producing an effect beyond what it had intended. The prominence of public opinion was growing as governments tried first to provide, and then to manage information, to create 'informed' support. As Press Commissioner, before he became a pro-zamindar polemicist, Lethbridge's job had been to collect material from secretariats and, after the Vernacular Press Act (1878), also to prevent the press from publishing 'falsehoods'. Madras had been first to provide information deliberately to the 'public', a policy commended to others in 1855; government gazettes superseded press rooms containing papers in 1864, and various ways of providing a précis of information continued in the 1860s; in 1876 'authentic news'—that is, news management—had gained importance. But under Ripon, Lethbridge's functions were returned to the Home Department. Though the Press Act repeal is often regarded as a retreat from conservative interference with freedom of speech and though Ripon did not find the Indian press as 'scurrilous' as expected, chiefly he wanted press and government to be separate, the latter not officially concerned to supply information. Many Liberals, from experience in Britain, felt estranged from the cosy relationship with the press which Lethbridge's appointment had implied.[18]

[17] I have discussed this at length in *The Evolution of British Policy towards Indian Politics*, especially pp.28-85.
[18] See keep-withs to General Proceedings A 43 (August 1882), Add.Mss. 43575.

Aspects of the political underpinning and impact of the 1885 reforms mirrored this timidity, and a preference for older indirect methods of government, a pretence that it was above politics. Ripon, despite his popularity among some Indians and with a coterie of like-minded civilians, was deeply upset by the upsurge of European opposition, especially to the Ilbert Bill and the Tenancy Act. His education policy was designed to produce a public, to which appeals might be made, but results could only be expected in the long term. Publicity was therefore eschewed in favour of strategies based upon compliant leaders or privileged classes, even in regard to education (notably with *ashraf* Muslims). Ripon's local self-government policy and the Tenancy Act exemplified this, and Dalhousie confirmed it, after toying with educated opinion and the Indian National Congress. Curiously, in this respect the strategy of Lytton was recast rather than reversed. The approach was not seriously challenged until the first world war, and even after then continued to be very important in British political policy.

That the British chose their collaborators in several different and watertight categories is well enough known. Petty administration could not have been carried on without a horde of Indian clerks and functionaries, the army could not have managed even its internal tasks without the Indian sepoys, and the very pax Britannica rested on the co-operation of those many Indians who, despite the panoply of the raj, were still a power in the land. A fundamental axiom of British policy was that the clerks, the sepoys and the powerful were and should be kept apart; but also there was a hierarchy of collaborators in British eyes. It rested on a definite idea of what was important in India. At the turn of the century Denzil Ibbetson, then Secretary of the Revenue and Agriculture Department, set out the principle when he wrote: 'Influence, in this country, goes with land, not with money; and it is influence that we want to preserve'.[19] Thus the rent law was particularly sensitive, in that it impinged upon the apex of the colonial system of supporters. We will now consider two aspects of this policy: the limitations of all appeasements of supporters, in the British system, as they affected pro-landlord strategies quite apart from the Tenancy Act; and secondly, the resurgence of concern for zamindari interests during the 1890s, as a reaction to the Act and a qualification of its impact. Together these may be seen, paradoxically, as reinforcing the general message of this chapter—that the Tenancy Act politicised land questions.[20]

[19] 12 May 1902, R&A Rev B51-2 (August 1903).

[20] The obvious general point here is that institutions, ideologies and laws

In dismissing the moneyed classes, as he would have the educated, Ibbetson was espousing a view of India that was quintessentially rural and traditional, at its extreme an India without history. Control of territory and its resources was what mattered; control of towns and opinions was less significant. The decision in 1885 to irritate the land-lords of Bengal was therefore a serious one; a countervailing appeal to peasant proprietors and to tradition was a necessary element in making it plausible. At the same time the decision reflected the erosion of the old certainties, as land ceased to be the only important source of reve-nue, and as supposedly localised life and economy in India's villages were invaded by the pull of cosmopolitan cities, by long-distance trade, by markets in land and labour, by inter-regional and inter-class com-munication and solidarities. Such developments underpinned Ripon's search for an Indian 'civil society', and made Ibbetson's principle vulnerable. Hence it was important for the 1885 Act to accommodate forces of change, or gesture towards supposedly Westernised elements of law, individuality, public responsibility and commercial production.

Marking the transitional nature of the Tenancy Act, however, great care continued to be shown for the landlords' position. Very noticeable is the caution with which the government began its direct involvement in rural affairs.[21] Every move the Bengal government made, any deci-sion on public policy, was softened by concern for the zamindars. The tendency of interference was contrary to the zamindars' wishes and interests, but at least their representatives were always consulted and listened to; at times they even seemed to exercise a veto. The standard procedure when a new measure was under consideration included dis-cussions with zamindars, not only because they were organised but also because they were recognised as having, in the nineteenth-century poli-tical sense, a legitimate interest. Thus, when it was still at a provisional stage, the scheme for patwaris drawn up under the 1885 Act (and to be discussed below) was submitted to the Bihar Indigo Planters' and the Bihar Landholders' Associations, which held a joint meeting under the auspices of the Maharaja of Darbhanga in order to discuss it. The same procedure was adopted in 1892 when the question came up again.[22]

---

shape politics; thus political interests and associations grew up around the de-bates and interventions of the Tenancy Act, as of other policies. But this does not show that state or colonial influence alone determined the political culture. Rather it was formed also out of indigenous connections and norms: politics occurred in the interstices of state and society.

[21] See also P. Robb, 'Hierarchy and Resources', *MAS* 13, 1 (1979).

[22] PCR 337, 26/5 (1882/3)—wrongly filed; properly file 64 (1885)—and R&A Rev A 3 (August 1892).

Such early consultation goes some way to explaining the intransigence of the local government on the issue of patwaris, and their repeated preference for schemes which the central government rightly considered doomed to failure. Earlier, by contrast, it had been to escape what was expected to be irresistible pressure that the Bengal government had been eager for the rent Bill to be introduced in the imperial and not the local legislature; they feared the Bengal landowners.[23] Earlier still (if we are to believe one of the interminable memoranda of the radical and bankrupt planter, D.N. Reid), a meeting at Sonpur in 1878, called by the Patna Commissioner to discuss the Bill, had caused the abandonment of the idea of a separate rent law for Bihar because of the wide differences of opinion it revealed: the result was that the 1885 Act applied to greater Bengal and, as Reid put it, 'favoured the zamindar interest'.[24] Certainly it went less far than many Bihar officials had wished.

By the later nineteenth century, Bengal's alliance with the zamindars took the form above all of a working partnership in the districts—the officials provided some assistance, for example with enforcing rents, and occasional supervision or control through the Court of Wards of encumbered or minors' estates; the zamindars entertained officials on tour, and gave them support and advice during public disturbances and disasters. Spectacular instances may be found of the alliance in operation. In 1908, for example, the estate of Sir P.C. Tagore was granted a huge loan in order to purchase property, and in 1909 the Bengal government proposed allowing a delay in the repayments in order that Tagore should continue to enjoy his full allowance. So great was the assistance that on this occasion the lower echelons of the central secretariat were distinctly flustered, and thought the family might be expected to manage on less than the Rs.15,000 a month which it was to be guaranteed. At higher levels there was criticism of the laxity of the Bengal procedures—the government had entered into an exceptional and sizeable financial commitment without even having checked the figures. But the political considerations were thoroughly appreciated. The loan had been granted in order that the public position of the Tagore family should be unimpaired, and its loyalty enhanced. It was immaterial that the estates had been grossly mismanaged, and that Tagore may have been merely using the government as a cheap banker; it was of first importance that his income should not be reduced or he

---

[23] See R&A Rev A 16-46A (July 1883).
[24] R&A Agric C 3-4 (January 1904).

himself left 'sore and discontented'.[25] The particular situation was extremely unusual—the government simply did not have the funds to enter into many such transactions—but it represents a kind of policy, one which the pro-tenant legislation violated.

In this context the ideological elements in policy-making, and their political superstructure, are important also because they emphasise the fragility of Bengal's conversion to a pro-peasant strategy. Conservatism was always less thoroughgoing in Bengal than elsewhere; even its Lieutenant-Governors could be notoriously 'unreliable'—that is, sensitive to Indian opinion. They were also closer to commerce than the military consuls of the Punjab.[26] The permanent settlement itself (as we have seen) had not precluded a transference of the landlord role into the most productive hands, and Lord Cornwallis, at least, recognised that successful merchants might apply their capital to land, and was as much in hope of economic advancement as in favour of an aristocratic social system. A familiar argument nowadays links the opportunities thus secured by zamindars, and also in government service and the professions, with the subsequent isolation of the 'middle classes' in Bengal from commerce and trade. But an economic partnership with urban dwellers was not ruled out by the Bengal system, as it was in the fully-fledged peasant strategies of late nineteenth-century Punjab.[27] Similarly, therefore, when the peasant-proprietary model, in a slightly earlier version, was imported into Bengal, it envisaged 'men of substance' who would benefit from it.

For similar reasons the long saga whereby the zamindars were favoured in Bengal was also diverted by several other political calculations, including the interests of trade and even Indian opinion. To an extent, these implied a concern for government within the law. The pro-zamindari policy may thus be compared but also contrasted with the concern with tenant rights that developed from mid-century. First, a recognition of the ruler's responsibility to his subjects—traced to the indigo disputes of 1859-62—implied the adoption of a goal of social justice, which was also the basis of the Indian challenge for political

[25] R&A Rev A 1-4 (April 1908), A 1-2 (July 1909), and A 22 (October 1909). Cf. PCR 367, 6/2 (1897/8) on management of the Dumraon estate.

[26] Note Cotton's criticism of growing commercial and non-official European influence on the government in India, in private correspondence (Add.Mss. 43618) and *New India*, pp.63-6.

[27] See R. Guha, *A Rule of Property for Bengal* ('S. Gravenhage 1963), pp. 171-3; Blair B. Kling, *The Blue Mutiny* (Calcutta 1977), especially the Conclusion; Sumit Sarkar, 'Rammohun Roy and the break with the past' in V.C. Joshi, ed., *Rammohun Roy and the Process of Modernization in India* (Delhi 1975.)

rights. In the original context, indigo disputes, this marked a transfer of rural power from planter to moneylender. But, second, the British government in India was no monolith; the terms 'policy' and 'strategy' may be misleading. Therefore the strong advocacy of a pro-zamindari line, as we have seen, bore the weight of British assumptions about Indian society—its hierarchies and deference—but on the other hand government by a bureaucracy was necessarily based on rules, and that meant that the balance would be redressed in favour of tenants. Equally it meant that zamindars' rights too were entrenched, and to a point would have been, even if colonial self-interest had been unequivocally ranged against them. In practice the bureaucracy, particularly in Bengal with its regulations, courts, newspapers and Calcutta public, was too committed to old assumptions and patterns, or insufficiently cynical, or too afraid of hostile scrutiny, to violate entrenched rights (at least powerful ones) as readily as its constitutional autocracy and its rhetoric would seem to have permitted. This both defended and restricted the alliance with the zamindars. Part of the problem with any pro-peasant calculations was how to communicate them to the subordinates responsible for carrying out policies. The pro-zamindar policy in Bengal was based on the permanent settlement and cemented by mutual support, but also institutionalised in codes of procedure, legislative acts, orders from government, and inculcated moral and theoretical principles, all of which limited the possibilities for change.

Let us take the restrictions first. Even in operating a self-interested compact with the zamindars, the British had been impeded, not only by principles in the way the Mughals had been (to some extent) by the dictates of religion,[28] but *institutionally*—by checks, balances and ideologies—within the structures of government they had created. They were naggingly aware of this in their preference for methods 'suitable to the East', believing, as they did, that India did not understand the toleration of dissent. But they could never completely follow their idea of the Asiatic mode; in practice they constantly interrupted themselves with the impulse to move in the contrary direction. The British were in their own eyes administrators under rule, and rulers whose justification was, in the Burkean sense, their responsibility for the well-being of the people.

This predicament constituted a grave impediment to any policy of seeking and securing collaborators. It was not that policies did not emerge, but that they were not imposed single-mindedly—and this

---

[28] See P. Hardy, 'The treatment of violence in Indo-Muslim Persian writing on history and polity', paper given at SOAS, London, May 1978.

quite apart from the well-known problems of competence and supervision which beset the administrative system. All alliances were conditional upon abstract and moral as well as practical notions. Already,
such scruples limited what could be offered to the zamindars, for much
the same reason that, according to Clive Dewey, differences between
British and Indian conceptions of friendship wrecked Malcolm Dar-
ling's hopes for racial harmony.[29] In both cases, the British obligation
was limited, in the abstract and by rule. A Bihar example will reinforce
the point. The Maharaja of Dumraon had been having trouble obtaining
rents from raiyats who were cultivating the flood-lands on his estates in
Shahabad. He took them to court, received judgment, and then (as the
boundaries were being surveyed officially) began to worry that the
court orders would be invalid if the area should be deemed to be in the
North-Western Provinces. He asked the government for a statement that
the villages had been in Shahabad since 1867. Dumraon was the leading landlord in the district and there was sympathy for his difficulties,
but the government declined to help him out. The law stated that the
midstream point had to be taken as the boundary, and officials could
not and would not overlook the law in such a case, even to consolidate
a political alliance.[30]

Moreover, if the law was not an obstacle, there was always the
public interest. Certainly, its outline was drawn in ambiguous shadows
which allowed room for rewards and favours. Thus, in Gaya, the Raja
of Deo enjoyed remission of revenue, the authority for which could not
be traced. G.A. Grierson, the Collector, a man not known for his
zamindari sympathies, concluded that the remission had been personal
to the present Raja's father, and therefore favoured resumption and
steps to recover the arrears. His superior, the Commissioner at Patna,
disagreed: an indulgence should not be withdrawn simply because
orders could not be traced. The public interest demanded protection for
the revenues, even if it meant making an enemy of a maharaja; and yet
government allies or potential allies could be given the benefit of the
doubt, where the rights of a matter were uncertain.[31]

But such discretion was sparingly used. We have already noticed, in

---

[29] See Clive Dewey, *Anglo-Indian Attitudes. The Mind of the Indian Civil
Service* (London 1993): if an Englishman was asked for help by a friend, he had
'a host of countervailing considerations to take into account; loyalty to the institutions of which he was a member; respect for abstract moral principles' (p.
196). The term 'friendship' here is intended to include all forms of alliance and
mutual obligation between individuals or groups.

[30] PCR 338, 12/19 (1883/4); and cf. ibid. 12/1.

[31] PCR 350, 12/1 (1889/90); 3,36, 12/1 (1881/2).

passing, criticisms of conditions in the estates of the Maharaja of Darbhanga, in North Bihar. The government held a tenancy (an escheated jagir) called Malinaggar from the estate. The Maharaja was one of the most important landowners in British India. The administrative saving on his vast estates alone was enough to make him important to government, quite apart from the political weight he carried in Calcutta and the social focus he provided for Hindus from (at least) Banaras to Purnea. Eden had described him as 'very sharp and well-informed', and recommended him for appointment to the Viceroy's legislative council, along with the Nawab of Dhaka and the Maharaja of Hathwa (in Saran district), as a useful representative of the landed interests, a man of high rank and social position.[32] His significance may be appreciated when we see him, a landlord whose wealth lay in North Bihar, asking questions on the council about the conduct of the local municipality towards Hindu temples in Banaras, where he was a public benefactor: clearly he could transcend the regional and hierarchical barriers by which the British divided their empire into manageable portions.[33] Yet when his estate demanded an enhanced rent or the relinquishing of Malinaggar, on the ground of change of use, the government defended the tenancy before the Magistrate, then on appeal in the High Court, and finally before the Privy Council. The point was not the possible loss to government—Malinaggar was notorious for its refractory tenants and probably more trouble than it was worth, while the legal issues were not such as to create any very dangerous precedents. The point was above all the duty, as officials saw it, of protecting to the utmost, in principle and in the name of the people, all the rights, interests and revenues of the government.[34]

But what of the sense in which these habits of government protected the zamindari alliance? The 1885 Act implied the rise of the rich peasant at the expense of the zamindar. Were rich peasants likely allies of British rule? Would they show gratitude, and could their goodwill be harnessed? Even more to the point, did the British have the courage to support them wholeheartedly, at the risk of completely alienating the landlords? The compromises of 1885 showed that they did not. What was true of zamindars, where the alliance was old and habitual, was more true of raiyats, where a new compact was on offer. The emerging arrangement suffered from all the inbuilt disabilities of political policy,

[32] Eden to Ripon, 10 February [1881], Add.Mss.43592.
[33] See R&A Rev C 36, March 1894.
[34] PCR 344, 5/61 (1886/7). On Malinaggar, see PC to Board of Revenue, 24 October 1887, PCR 345-6, 10/110 (1887/8).

and also from its novelty in the context of Bengal. Of course there were calculations of political interest, especially at the highest levels of government, which came for a time to favour the peasants and the 'real' India they embodied. But, as with the zamindars, there were again many instances from day to day when rule-book, precedent or principle led to actions which were counter-productive from the purely political point of view. This was rationalised in the argument (which was probably not objectively true) that the even-handedness of British rule was one of its best defences—a part of the argument for giving support to the raiyats in the first place. Plainly no alliance could be complete or exclusive.

The implications were potentially serious. There could be no absolute conversion in Bengal to a reliance upon proprietary peasants, because solid political reality still favoured the status quo, in Calcutta eyes at least, for the zamindars were concentrated in the capital, and long the best organised, most articulate and best connected of Indian pressure groups. Rather there was gradual attrition: belated and insufficient measures to assist the tenants and to improve the revenues of the province slowly eroded the goodwill which many zamindars had felt for the raj. Unsurprisingly, then, policies of the 1890s made more apparent the slippage from the proprietary-peasant ideal, already evident in late modifications of the 1885 Act, and from the supposed village-community tradition—anyway betrayed from the first in the inherent endorsement of individual transferable property and market-oriented production. This was a reassertion not merely of a pro-zamindar preference but of a deeper spirit of Bengal administration and Western legal practice. Increasingly the tenancy policy of Bengal revealed itself as a hybrid. It was illustrative of ambiguities and complexities within British political and economic policies as a whole.

Tenancy policy continued to evolve, and even the principles and attitudes of the reformers of the 1880s were modified. Three points were apparent. First, the pro-tenant emphasis was reduced by reassertions of the need to appease the landlords. Second, pro-tenant measures themselves came to be mediated by political considerations. Third, the increasing politicisation reduced the likelihood of decisive interventions on principle (for example, to reduce the poverty and dependence of actual cultivators): after all, the main limits on expediency had been law and the public interest—the *perception* of official duty—rather than an effective understanding of Indian conditions and the means of rendering them more equitable. A vivid illustration will be given in the next chapter, on the making and preserving of a record of land rights.

## III

The later adjustments which we shall see occurred in the 1890s and 1900s, and the original concessions of the 1885 Act, had the effect of further distancing the benefits of state intervention from the poor and the 'actual cultivators'. Also, as a struggle emerged between the Government of India believing that tenant rights were essential for peace and prosperity, and the Bengal government unwilling to antagonise the landlords, then the effect was more thoroughly to politicise the question of agrarian laws and conditions. This was a token of the future, when such issues would be intensely political, and in which rewards would go inevitably to those with most political clout. The context was one in which 'modern' features—the development of markets, the shift in emphasis from custom to contract, the political involvement of outsiders—were beginning to bite in India's villages. Any effort to monitor the changes and prevent excessive dislocation and distortion of the rural community was likely to be overtaken by stronger forces. Steps could be taken in the direction of restoring the 'natural' order, as in Bengal with tenancy legislation, or elsewhere with measures against moneylenders and the alienation of land. But external economic forces were ever more likely to be added to the political in determining outcomes.

The net effect of the measures of the last fifteen years of the nineteenth century was, according to the zamindars, a decline in their power and influence over their tenants; consequently they felt that the British had betrayed their mutual interest. This reaction and, in addition, political unrest in Bengal, early in the new century, certainly encouraged some officials to wonder if matters had not gone too far. The landlord policy might seem to have enjoyed an Indian summer. But the definite steps which were taken locally were in fact somewhat of a new departure. They were intended not so much to encourage landlords as they were, as to help create a new kind of landlord or at least a new attitude among them, as a counterweight to disloyal politicians. The Settled Estates Act of 1903 was one fruit of this policy; it was on this occasion that Ibbetson wrote his motto on the preservation of the influence of land, quoted earlier.[35] His view was (ominously for the Bengal zamindars) that 'exceptional treatment should be restricted to men who possess some political influence'; and it seems as if there had been a shift in the sense of 'political', that the compact was no longer

[35] See above, note 19.

mainly a matter of local order and good government, but rather what had previously been a relatively minor aspect, the control of public opinion. In general, with the political advantages in mind, Ibbetson welcomed the idea of being able to reward loyalty and good services by allowing the settlement of family estates.

It remained true too that the central government was reluctant to give Bengal full support in its wooing of the landlords. When the draft Settled Estates Act reached the Executive Council (six weeks after Ibbetson's note) almost the first suggestion was that appreciable stamp duties should be levied on settlements under the new law. Bengal resisted the idea. It was particularly embarrassing as the Bill had been framed in consultation with leading landholders who had been given copies and who would definitely not like the charge. J.A. Bourdillon, officiating Lieutenant-Governor (and a former Commissioner at Patna), would later duck the blame for the duty and advise the landlords to accept the whole package as it was that or nothing; at first, however, he pleaded with Ibbetson, privately, not to seem to be giving a boon with one hand and taking a fee with the other. (Oddly enough, H.H. Risley had indeed spoken of making 'a substantial charge for the concession'.) Bourdillon argued that to do this was to encourage, by example, 'a growing tendency in Bengal...for the rich and the charitable who render services to the state or the public, to consider what they will receive in return'. The bargain, it seems, should be unspoken and the rewards unspecific. Ibbetson was unimpressed, and thought Bengal were opposing merely 'as a matter of course'. Ibbetson was indeed a moderate on the subject, for some of his colleagues wanted to go further and stiffen the charges—their reasons went beyond the idea that it would be unfair to exempt a rich class from a tax which the majority would have to pay in similar circumstances, and on to the consideration that 'land in Bengal...pays far less...than land in other parts of India. It is bare justice to the rest of the country that when a legitimate opportunity occurs, we should...make it contribute a little more.' At the end only H.G. Stokes suggested that the question should be weighed with reference to the intention of preserving a 'permanent landed interest as a counter-poise to disloyalty in Bengal'.

By this stage the devastation wrought by the 'public interest' on the political motive was plain to see: what the despatch to the Secretary of State had called 'important land-owning families' (the phrase came from T. Raleigh) were now, in the words of Risley, not old families at all but merely 'successful banyas or promoted sheristadars' who wanted the Act to acquire rather than preserve status. Risley's now much-criticised theories of caste and race gave a kind of historical and ethnological authority to multiple levels and categories of society within supposedly indigenous hierarchies, in contradistinction from 'modern' economic or political interests or classes. In such a context, officials were ready to believe that, far from benefiting the British by giving a boon to useful supporters, the Settled Estates Act would merely revive the dwindling influence of the British Indian Association (which was really made up of journalists or lawyers, and not zamindars at all). The boon of a settled estate, therefore, should cost these parvenus one quarter of a year's revenue—and that was letting them off lightly.[36] Were landlords now too irrelevant to be worth reviving?

The problem with this, if one turns to 'actual cultivators', is that exactly the same ruthlessness was likely to apply. It already existed when Mackenzie had looked for 'men of substance' to whom the occupancy right should be secured. We have noticed that the colonial categorisations were not of indigenous forms, but inventions accommodated to a 'modern' agenda: in particular, the landed proprietor. Who should benefit from public policy, then? It should not be, we may recall Ashutosh Mookerjea arguing, any particular individual or class, at the expense of others. In 1907, when the Bengal government proposed to earmark revenue from the Road and Public Works cesses for their ostensible purposes (roads and public works), Risley objected that this was inconvenient, wrong in principle and supported only through an agitation engineered by Peary Mohun Mookerjea (who was still arguing that the cesses breached the permanent settlement). But Andrew Fraser, Lieutenant-Governor of Bengal, had announced his approval of the earmarking principle, and been greeted with 'hysterical gratitude in the Native Press'. The announcement was out of turn, given the contrary orders of the central government; that government none the less had to give way. Political expediency prevailed, in order to avoid a revival of agitation. On the other hand, this was not a thorough strategy of refurbishing the alliance with the zamindars. On the merits of the case, without Fraser's intervention, the Bengal proposal would certainly have been turned down.[37] But in such circumstances and given the political realities of the day, who was to ensure the protection of the *poor* 'unfriended peasants'?—not Mackenzie (whose phrase it was) or his successors, it seemed, though he had seemed to argue for the peasants, on principle, in the heated atmosphere of the 1880s.

[36] R&A Rev B 51-2 (August 1903) or Legislative A 7-11 (June 1903), and B 35 (December 1903) or Legislative A 1-7 (November 1903).
[37] H. Local Boards A 2-4 (September 1907).

This should not surprise us, for it was inherent in the terms of the reforms. The categories were always instrumentalist; they had political purpose. The same currents of thought and argument which arose over tenancy policy had been aired equally in the other great debates of the period, for example, those over indebtedness and the alienation of land. First came pedigree; second status; third effective power; and fourth loyal support. Of the malguzars of the Central Provinces, for example, Denzil Ibbetson had written in 1898, drawing on a report by Charles Lyall, that they were 'of no great importance from any point of view'. They were, he argued, 'of very miscellaneous origin'; and even those 'of genuine agricultural stock, were mere village headmen whom the accident of our policy...elevated to the position of great landlords'. Being 'mere headmen' (at best), they had fallen victim to their new wealth. They had also been infected by the 'habit of organised agitation'. In this regard the history of the Central Provinces was 'curiously like that of Bengal', except that in the former area, the development of which was at an earlier stage, there was still a substantial residuum which might have been 'well worth saving'. Unfortunately, Ibbetson concluded, there was nothing to be done for them. Unless they were prevented from transferring their land they were lost; yet the 'agitators' amongst them would resist such restrictions. Ibbetson was sifting through the proceedings, quoting James Meston when settlement officer at Badaon, the collector in the same district, the Commissioner at Lucknow and the deputy commissioner at Kangra. He concluded that it was among new men that agitation obtained a hold. Of course, declining 'traditional' elites were also a focus for discontent. Even in the Punjab the landowners realised they were ruining themselves and their children, but 'have no stamina and cannot resist temptation', whether it be to please their womenfolk or gratify their neighbours. The likely outcome could be seen in the North-Western Provinces. The great landlords of the past had 'gone to the wall', except in Awadh where they had been specially protected, and old landlords were sullen because dispossessed. In Meston's words, they lingered on in their villages 'as bad tenants and cultivators, as centres of disaffection, and in the last stage as hungry and unscrupulous tools for the dakait-leader'. But the class the British had installed on the land regarded it as a mere investment.

We see here the contradiction between the definition of effective collaborators and modernisers, and the fearful attachment to 'legitimate', past, Indian forms. An evident though unspoken orthodoxy is the view of there having been a natural order which had been distorted under British rule, but which was best preserved in the Punjab and other parts of North India; the distortion, moreover, was the long-term cause of disaffection and agitation. There was a belief that in the remnants of the old order lay true political power. The new men, in Ibbetson's view, 'might be probably be neglected with advantage. The native who shouts is not the man who matters.' The new men were, in the words of the North-Western Provinces' Chief Secretary (quoted by Ibbetson), 'the classes whose hostility can be most safely disregarded'. The only reason they were a danger was either by their infecting the more important agricultural classes, or in a negative sense by replacing them on the land, viewing it as a 'mere investment', and thus detracting from the security of British rule. In all this great landlords were of minor importance, except in a few areas such as Awadh; the problem was essentially small-scale—the emphasis was on village elites. There are of course many complex strands and differences of opinion in such controversies as these. But the constant ideas were of an old order which had changed, of some people 'worth saving', of soil ready for disaffection, of good (that is, loyal and conservative) sections infected by bad: so often the imagery was of agriculture or disease.[38]

We have already noted that a pro-peasant strategy was intended to widen the base of the government's support. The 1880s also saw some more ambitious gestures, particularly in Ripon's local self-government reforms and education policies. On the latter, E. Baring wrote interestingly in 1881:

The time cannot be far distant when the Natives of India will have to be associated with us to a greater extent than at present in the government of the country; and when the time for considering that great question arrives, we shall, unless I am much mistaken, find that our main difficulty is this, that the Native agency on which we shall have to fall back is for the most part such as we have created through our exotic system of high education; that the Natives bred under this system generally represent purely class interests; whilst the comparative stagnation of primary education will have resulted in the absence of any Native public opinion, properly so called, to act as a guiding and controlling power.[39]

Cotton, a radical thinker in terms of constitutional experiment, believed that the Indian call for Home Rule at this time was merely an accidental analogy with Ireland. What Indian politicians really wanted, he argued, was power, building on existing structures and norms. Surendranath Banerjea, he remarked, was the most conservative town councillor in

[38] Ibbetson, 31 January 1898, R&A Rev A 3-22 (November 1898), Part IV & kw.
[39] Baring note, 14 April 1881, in keep-withs to Home Department proceedings, Add.Mss.43575, p.295.

Calcutta.[40] One aspect, then, of the creation of a propertied class of raiyats was an attempt to widen the numbers of the power-seekers, the basis for an informed and involved public.

Thus it was also the case that the tenancy debate itself, and the legal identification and recording of socio-economic classes, had to contribute to the building of interest-groups. These (whatever Baring or Cotton might suppose, in their ideal of a post-colonial polity) were necessary pre-requisites for political life and constitutional advance. The agrarian emphasis of British political policies depended on a degree of rural isolation. It would not be possible indefinitely to claim that the man who shouted did not matter. Already there were signs that new tactics would need to be developed to meet changing political conditions, as the articulate increased the significance of their own spheres of influence and began to break down the isolation of the countryside. The nineteenth-century political policies would leave an important legacy for this new age.

In the case of Bengal, the pro-landlord policy was out of step with the prevailing currents of thought. Hostility to the province undoubtedly played a part in all these exchanges, but substantive, almost doctrinal differences were the main cause of the dissension. The peasant strategy carried most conviction. Even in its later versions in Bengal, or as tried by Harcourt Butler and others in the United Provinces,[41] landlordism was the exception not the rule. This meant of course, as the peasant strategy could hardly apply to Bengal, that the central government was left virtually without a political approach for that region. On the other hand, the pro-zamindari backlash in Bengal, such as it was, did not fundamentally alter the realities set out in 1885. To favour the supposedly entrepreneurial peasant over the allegedly rapacious and idle landlord might well enforce adjustments at some levels of the agrarian structure. It might influence the resources which were most useful to rural power-struggles. But it would not transform the distribution of resources throughout the society, and was not intended to do so. Nor would encroaching economic change necessarily alter this picture. The valuable people at whom policy was directed, and around whom politics came to revolve, were not the poor cultivators. Political influence, whatever Ibbetson might have wished, increasingly went to those who could organise themselves around recognised interests or causes.

Bengal intellectuals, social reformers and landlords had been aware

---

[40] Cotton to Ripon, 9 October 1888, Add.Mss.43618.

[41] See P.D. Reeves, 'The politics of order', *Journal of Asian Studies* XXV (1966).

of this fact since at least the 1830s. They deployed both 'traditional' and 'modern' means to organise social and political interests, including the establishment of the Bengal Landholders' Society of 1838;[42] and such mixed methods were the model also for subsequent political activity. But many new classes of interest—castes and communities, landlords, professionals, tenants, workers—were devised or re-defined under colonial influence. As in the 1870s and 1880s, new rules, categories and disputes encouraged ever more elaborate mobilisations and articulations of interest groups. Because state interventions helped politicise relations and classes of people, they had the potential not only to change the terms and means of politics, but also to advantage or disadvantage different groups within Indian society. How far they would do so in practice depended on the type and effectiveness of the intervention. The next chapters continue this story with consideration of the introduction, imperfect perpetuation, and impact of the settlement and record of rights.

[42] See S.N. Mukherjee, 'Class, caste and politics in Calcutta, 1815-1838', in Edmund Leach and Mukherjee, eds., *Elites in South Asia* (Cambridge 1970), especially pp.70-8.

## Chapter Eight

## *Keeping the record*

In considering the introduction and implementation of chapter X of the Bengal Tenancy Act, one purpose will be to explore how it was that officialdom was persuaded to go further down the road to intervention; another to assess the limits. The very inclusion of survey and settlement proceedings in the Act was remarkable—partly because in Bengal there had been no tradition of survey work of this kind and for such purposes. It was remarkable also because the tide of opinion, at least in London, was strongly against the cost of the full reports which had marked the second generation of settlements in the Punjab and north India. The work was, administratively, a logical deployment of the skills developed in an earlier generation. Officials as Goldsmid and Wingate had set up separate and hence specialist teams of map and assessment makers, to effect economic change by relating demand, according to principles of political economy, precisely to the character and ability to pay of holdings, villages and districts. The later Bengal tenancy reformers shared their view (still often heard in the later nineteenth century, though it contradicted some of the protective and paternalist impulses of the same colonial officials who espoused it), to the effect that thrift and enterprise would be encouraged by high, definite, appropriate and stable rates of revenue and rent. However, (as said) the intention in Bengal was to record and entrench rights. Appropriate taxation was but one ground for a renewed search for information: an attempt to tap concealed wealth (an old motive) led on to the use of fiscal policy to achieve economic ends (a rather newer one). Thus survey and settlement work, and the keeping of records of land rights, reflected a practical impulse for reform, in a region where lack of information had repeatedly been identified as an impediment to government. From famine relief to taxation, from social equity to economic efficiency, Bengal and Bihar were allegedly impeded by official ignorance.

Intellectually, the settlement work was a consequence of a range of ideas about government and society, in which an awareness of distinctive characteristics, believed to reflect different stages of social evolution, gave importance to the obtaining of knowledge about India. In turn this cult of knowledge promoted the idea that government was good in proportion to its understanding of the nature and origins of

246

social conditions, matters which could and should be elucidated in India by the efforts of Victorian Englishmen.[1] Practically, the survey and settlement work was justified for their supposed effect as a tool of state management. Without this double justification from the pretensions of scientific government, the expense would have seemed out of all proportion.

An interest in local data and land records started with the first land revenue investigations after the Company's acquisition of the *diwani* of Bengal *subah* in 1765. During the early nineteenth century, it produced inconclusive discussions and reforms of village agency—patwaris and chaukidars—and of inferior levels of administration (for example kanungos). In the early nineteenth century an attempt was made to revive and re-deploy the village agency. In 1812 Francis Buchanan reported an efficient system of local police only in Shahabad where 1,419 watchmen (*pasbans*) had been appointed by zamindars and registered by the Magistrate, who also appointed chaukidars paid by the raiyats. In 1841 the Board ordered that village chaukidars everywhere should be awarded a standard three acres of average land or Rs.3 per month. But just as Shahabad was an exception, so too this rule was only applied at settlement, and its general influence seems to have been slight.[2] Similarly Buchanan found patwaris being appointed by Collectors from the most able members of families claiming hereditary rights to the post, and it is true that patwaris, regarded with kanungos as virtually useless in 1772, and impervious to attempts to revive them in 1783, do seem to have been more frequent and effective in Bihar than elsewhere under the permanent settlement. But even in Bihar they were unsatisfactory as a government agency. Their records were reported in 1787 in Tirhut as nowhere complete or regularly kept, nor always honest, and in Bihar as much as anywhere patwaris were identified as zamindar's servants. Thus the state was left without effective local representatives since it had abolished the kanungos in 1793. The Court of Directors called for revival of both kanungos and patwaris, in 1813, 1814, 1815 and 1819. After an inquiry in 1815, kanungos were 'restored' in Bihar (Regulation

---

[1] See Richard Saumarez Smith, 'Rule-by-records and rule-by-reports: complementary aspects of the British imperial rule of law', *Contributions to Indian Sociology* 19, 1 (1985).

[2] Buchanan, *Shahabad*, p.345; CO, 9 June 1841. In 1808 and 1812 heavy penalties were provided for chaukidars who failed to carry out their duties; from 1837-54, equally ineffectively, control of all local police was transferred from the Commissioners to a Superintendent in Calcutta—Bengal District Gazetteer, L.S.S. O'Malley, *Patna* (Calcutta 1907). See also Palit, *Tensions*, pp.62-95. See chapter two for full references to these and following sources.

II of 1816) and government control, jointly with the zamindars, was
formally established over the patwaris (Regulation XII of 1817). But, as
early as 1821, the Collector of Tirhut reported that patwaris did not
submit genuine accounts to the kanungos, who were generally useless
to the Collector and ignored by the courts; the kanungos made no
contribution to raiyati interests. Their abolition was recommended in
1827.[3] Similarly under Regulation IX of 1833 patwaris' accounts were
supposed to be filed with the Collector, but the penalty, of denying the
zamindars the use of the law when accounts were not filed, depended
on the government's promulgating the necessary rule (which it did not
do).[4]

In this absence of effective local agency, the official experience of
information-gathering was restricted very largely to three main areas,
already mentioned: government or Court of Wards estates, the partition
of landed property-rights, and land-revenue resumption proceedings.
Each of these provided systems and precedents for the measurement,
establishment and presentation of land and land-rights—that is, in these
matters the making and keeping of a record became the major instrument of policy. Each of them also proved a severe strain on the
officials, and was in various ways inadequate or unsatisfactory.

For government and Wards estates, as was noted briefly in chapter
two, it was decided by the 1830s to concentrate on the improvement of
*khas* management. The chief problem was that the management was
generally 'so negligently and summarily performed as to leave great
scope for extortion'; hence reform was signalled by a call for *jamabandis* (rent-rolls, recording rights and dues) to be made 'absolutely
indispensable'.[5] In 1833 too the Board of Revenue ordered registration
of every *khas mahal* in sufficient detail to check abuses. They admitted
with surprise what they had found out about the scale of the problem—
some estates had outstanding balances from before 1793—and also the
difficulty of reform when the interests of the Collectors' subordinates
were pitted so strongly and uniformly against those of the government.
Collectors were warned to ignore protestations from the *amla* about
how difficult it would be to prepare the registers.[6] Four years later the
Board was still patiently calling for information so as to prepare rules
for the reform of *khas* management, and in 1838 further new
procedures were ordered, asking for professional or at least a minimal

[3] Buchanan, *Shahabad*, p.349; Hunter, *Records*; Muzaffarpur SR.
[4] CO, 16 January 1837.
[5] CO, 21 October 1831 and 25 August 1832.
[6] CO, 20 August 1832.

survey as soon as possible, and a complete record of the number and rent-history of holdings and occupants. Each holding was to be let in farm to its occupant for a definite period, advances were to be made to free the cultivators from the moneylenders, a liberally-paid patwari was to collect rents, and the whole was to be under the supervision of a Deputy Collector with no other responsibilities.[7] The scheme was optimistic to the point of being fanciful, in terms of what was, and indeed what the government must have known to be, practicable.

Early attempts were made to compile registers of these lands for Bihar—in 1784 (following Shore's recommendation), and also in 1791, 1795 and 1802. Some of the revenue-free tenures, for example those dating from before 1765, could be confirmed under Regulations XIX and XXXVII of 1793; but little advantage was taken of this opportunity (a mark of the unimportance of unenforced laws). All the early attempts at regularising the position failed. Francis Buchanan, describing conditions in Shahabad in 1809/10, concluded that no documents in the Collectorate were entirely satisfactory on the subject of free estates, 'by much the greater part of the lands having never been measured even by conjecture'. After 1822 (Regulation VII), the requirement of a cadastral survey changed the basis of the operations; and efforts began to be made to examine the tenures in detail. The procedures were slow, each estate at first involving the completion of no less than fourteen forms, and there was little progress until Regulation III of 1828 allowed officers to be placed on special duty for resumption work, and until, after 1833, professional survey parties and appeal procedures were provided to relieve the Collectors of the main burden.[8]

Even then special measures had repeatedly to be applied to the worst-affected areas, including almost all of the districts of Bihar—the secondment of extra European and Indian officers, and the formulation of a special plan after 1834 to enforce the resumption laws in that province. Earlier, in 1832, faced with delays and consequent corruption in the proceedings, the Patna Commissioner ensured that the revenue sheristadar was made personally responsible for keeping a register and preparing six-monthly reports, on the argument that duties not given to one individual quickly fell into disuse; the proposal was generally recommended in 1834. In 1838 the Board of Revenue itself admitted that it could not cope with the increase of work; it had to be relieved of some other duties by the revival of the office of Superintendent and Remembrancer of Legal Affairs. In 1837 it had ordered that attention

[7] CO, 23 January 1838.
[8] Muzaffarpur SR.

be focused on lands actually claimed as rent-free, and not on 'towfer', lands attached to permanently-settled estates—this to sweeten the zamindars and to reduce the workload.[9]

In 1839 improved procedure, devised for Purnea and Malda and recommended to the Collectors, involved the subtraction of revenue-paying lands (according to the patwari's records) from the area of the whole village (established by measurement), the remainder being investigated as if it were rent-free land. The advantage of the method was that it resulted, even counting larger holdings alone, in the retention of very much less *lakhiraj* land than measurements by the amins—in four villages 4,637 acres instead of 13,891, and in six villages (or 259 holdings) 32 holdings of over a hundred bighas instead of 83. From the official view, this was a devastating comment on the accuracy of the *amini* procedure adopted elsewhere, and was only obtained because the covenanted superintending Deputy Collector had remained camped on site.[10] Well might the Board exhort its officers to local investigations and vigilant supervision.

Partition was another area in which the British officials found themselves out of their depth. In the absence of any accurate records and because of obstruction by some or all of the co-sharers, *batwara* proceedings tended to be unduly protracted and hence liable to favour the corrupt. In 1828 government dispensed with detailed internal surveys unless asked for by the parties—as long as the total revenue was secured, the proprietors could adjust the shares among themselves. But such a withdrawal, while helping in one direction, could worsen the situation in another: as the British were well aware, *batwara* proceedings were often fraudulent, marred by collusion which allowed, in the interests of the estate as a whole, the gross over-assessment of one part, later to be relinquished and usually left on the government's hands. (Buchanan claimed that patwaris under the control of the Collectors were the only check on the fraudulent apportionment of revenue at *batwara*—and such patwaris did not exist generally in the 1830s even if they had done in the past.) In 1828, in proposals for dealing with fraudulent *batwara*, the Board disagreed among itself, a majority favouring automatic attachment by government during partition, but the acting President arguing that this, as well as unpopular, would be ineffective because of the extra duties (and opportunities) which would devolve

---

[9] CO, 21 January, 17 June, 5 and 26 August 1834 and 16 May 1837; Bengal Revenue Letter, 12 September 1838, L/E/3/42.

[10] CO, 14 March 1839.

upon the amin charged with collecting from the attached land.[11] In short, the government reached the stage of defining problems, but did not have the means of ensuring final solutions. It floundered about, finding that one cure seemed merely to uncover new problems, and that desirable measures were cancelled out by undesirable consequences. Thus, in 1829 the Board had sought the views of the 'most intelligent zamindars'; in 1835 they called for their opinions once more. On the one hand they saw the need to protect the interests of the more 'honest or less powerful' co-parceners, a realisation which not only preserved the *batwara* law but even gave rise to consideration (as in 1836) of whether or not the process should be made easier. Yet, on the other hand, the difficulty of collection and the outstanding balances increased between 1830 and 1831, and clearly partitions added to the work of the revenue authorities without reducing the pressure on the land. The government blamed the revenue shortfalls on the growth in the number of proprietors through inheritance. In fact the growth in the number of estates was far more significant. As early as 1827 Collectors had been forbidden to sell portions of estates for arrears in order to avoid unnecessarily swelling the size of the roll, and it was just such an increase which later made collections more difficult. In 1835 too, as if to make partition more suspect, the Board announced their belief that it was being used to avoid sales for arrears.[12]

A feature of early attempts at reform was the emphasis on at least trying to put right those things which actually came into direct contact with the government. Thus in 1840 came the suggestion that *khas mahals* might serve both as sources of information for the government and as models for the surrounding countryside—apparently the start of the pilot schemes which were to be a common (and apparently ineffective) device later in the century. In this case the project involved the reform of the local police, making village watchmen paid servants of government. The same year education had been provided for minors under the Court of Wards, after a dispute on the Board of Revenue on whether or not the government should make such 'authoritative interference'.[13] But as a general rule, beyond the points of direct control, capacity and not scruples limited what was done.

We see this conclusively by consideration of the survey and settle-

[11] CO, 7 July 1829 (orders, 18 August 1828, Board of Revenue, 25 July 1828, Acting President, 23 August 1828); Buchanan, *Shahabad*, p.349.
[12] CO, 22 May 1827, 17 September 1833 and 25 May 1835; Bengal Revenue Letter, 11 August 1837, L/E/3/40, IOL.
[13] CO, 22 December 1840; Bengal Revenue Letters, 2 April and 7 May 1840, L/E/3/1, IOL.

ment as a weapon in the official arsenal for the defence of the tenants in Bengal—the most important of the nineteenth century. Even in the earlier years, it is clear that a survey could make the hand of the government felt. In Chittagong in 1837, to take one example, some disturbances during survey were attributed to a 'small body of malcontents, connected with the existing or former Judicial and Revenue Establishments of Government', who had abused their power in order to gain possession of untaxed land.[14] In general there must have been some effect from operations running at a rate of nearly 5,000 cases a year in the late 1830s, particularly in areas (such as Bihar) which had more than their share.[15] In 1837 the government appointed a committee to examine ways of improving survey procedures, satisfied (as the Resolution put it) that the cost of surveys for 'the larger estates and more particularly, of extensive tracts of country open to assessment, will be abundantly repaid by more accurate knowledge of their extent and value...', and that 'advantage should be taken of every opportunity to increase the stock and secure the exactness of the Geographical and Topographical information at the command of Government', not least in order to facilitate the work of the courts in suits over landed property.[16] This represented the current orthodoxy, originally established through the efforts of Colin Mackenzie, and foreshadowed the thinking which was to lead to Bengal surveys from the 1890s.

However, the ambitions after 1837, though wider than at some other times were still very limited. The proposed changes coincided with a stream-lining of the process under the influence of developments in the North Western Provinces. There the government had abandoned the full internal survey of estates, extending instead the land-use records made by native agency.[17] In Bengal this reversed the previous situation, in which non-professionals (that is, revenue officers) had sketched in the externals, while professional surveyors had recorded the details, and instead placed most weight on the professional survey of external boundaries. Thus only in the most peripheral sense could the survey be said to have increased the stock and accuracy of the government's information. Reinforcing the point were the facts that in Bengal the work was supervised not by local Commissioners but directly by the Board, and that it was of inferior standard—or thus the senior member of the Board described it in 1838, contrasting it with that of the 'able

[14] Bengal Revenue Letter, 3 October 1837, L/E/3/40, IOL.
[15] Ibid., and see 5 September 1837, for Patna Division.
[16] Bengal Revenue Letter, 3 August 1837, L/E/3/40, IOL.
[17] India Revenue Letter, 18 August 1838, L/E/3/42, IOL.

and experienced' settlement officers of the North-Western Provinces.[18] Indeed even the simplest parts of the operation were not invariably carried out—in 1838 the Board had to insist that every *mahal* and *mauza* be recorded during a survey (sometimes two or three had been lumped together)—and in general the Indian Deputy Collectors who were chiefly responsible for the work were considered unreliable and 'deficient in activity'.[19]

What applied to individual surveys (for resumption and so on) was carried over, when a survey of the whole of Bihar and Bengal was proposed (1841) and the first overall British survey of Bihar conducted (between 1842 and 1849). A professional agency recorded boundaries and non-professionals prepared field maps showing estates (not holdings) within each village. Such general surveys and investigations, from James Rennell (1766-72) to the revenue survey maps of 1847-63, had always been designed mainly to fix external borders, as in the most elaborate example, the *thakbast* surveys of the 1820s to 1840s, which contained population and other details but no information on subordinate rights. The settling of estate boundaries—though perhaps encouraging land transfers to non-agriculturalists—was undoubtedly a boon, at a time when proprietors were generally in dispute with their neighbours. But the accuracy of even this much of the work was later called in question because of a confusion between villages and estates. More important, as details were kept to the minimum (to reduce popular suspicion, extortion by subordinates, and delays in the work), the results were useless in respect of landlord-tenant relations, and virtually so for general statistical purposes.[20] Much the same could said of an even more refined surveying system, introduced in 1850/1, which combined internal and external marking prior to survey with internal plotting by chain and compass to show the part of each *mahal* belonging to each estate: what it gained in accuracy compared with the eye-sketches which had previously been the basis of the internal surveys, it lost in completeness because of the abandonment of field-by-field measurements.[21] In short effectiveness could be increased in the main only by compromise, by limiting what was attempted.

Into this history of failure came the reformers of 1885. They could not promise immediate benefits to the state treasury. In temporarily-

[18] Bengal Revenue Letter, 22 March 1838, L/E/3/41, IOL.

[19] CO, 20 March 1838.

[20] Muzaffarpur SR.

[21] *Report on the Survey Operations of the Lower Provinces, 1st October 1851 to 30th September 1852* (Calcutta 1854).

settled areas, settlement officers tended to argue for limited increases in revenue, and even for reductions in real terms. As we have seen, the discussions of the benefits of a permanent settlement for temporarily-settled areas were couched, between the 1860s and 1880s, partly in terms of the chance to avoid these expensive and vexatious operations. In the instance of Bengal, there was obviously no financial case to be made for the provisions under the 1885 Act. Nor was there much experience of the use of surveys, except on individual estates, so as to improve returns. As said, there was some experience of surveys to reduce boundary disputes. But in the permanently-settled areas, no law provided for revenue surveys (of *rights*) before 1875 (Bengal Act V). The *diara* (alluvia) survey instituted after 1847 (Act IX) applied only to Dhaka Division, and to the special and repeated need there to re-establish boundaries affected by fluvial action. There was compulsory registration of landed interests for those in possession, but even under the consolidated Act VII of 1876 the purpose was to identify the responsible revenue-payer for each estate. Under the Sales Law and other regulations, there were voluntary provisions for the registration of co-sharers, of mortgages and of protected tenancies, but no subordinate rights *had* to be recorded, until they began to be listed, on a summary valuation, because of the tenants' liability for road and public works cesses (Act IX of 1880, superseding Acts of 1871 and 1877).

Bengal surveys thus identified the responsible revenue or tax-payer; they were used to facilitate resumption and partition; and they regularised the running of government estates or those under the Court of Wards. Their public purposes were limited, as was commitment from the public purse; for government or Wards estates the expense was approved by the officials on the unimpeachable but essentially private ground that the result would increase the income and secure the future of the landlord. This reminds us of our earlier finding that, although the British claimed that they had established a legal hegemony in India, their writ reaching to every subject, who was equal in the eyes of the law, yet in practice they had to come to terms with the residue of a multiplicity of local jurisdictions, and thus intervened mostly to assist allies. Their predecessors had been even more powerless to penetrate such barriers; under the British, interventions remained infrequent, and surveys tended to be regarded as no more than a means of resolving troublesome disputes over boundaries, or of serving, at the users' expense, certain specific administrative needs, as with revenue sales or the partition of estates. A public good could be invoked, even the wish to intervene against a particularly rapacious landlord, but generally this was seen only from the point of view of taking prudent measures to avoid public disorder.

By contrast, C.L. Tupper, in his report on Bihar, had insisted that a full survey was essential to the social and economic well-being of a whole community. His Punjab expectations meant that this rationale raised no questions in his mind, but he was aware that there was no similar expectation in Bengal. Therefore he checked his proposals with T.W. Holderness, and, on his advice, set out the NWP procedures as a model for Bengal. He wanted settlement officers who would start by correcting the patwaris' papers, and raising rents that seemed too low, on the basis of field measurement and soil classification. He argued that such a system already worked well in the permanently-settled areas of Banaras division, and that 'even an imperfect record of rights may be a source of great strength and stability to the tenants' interest'.[22] Holderness agreed: though the record would annoy the zamindars and any raiyats concealing excess holdings, for most people it would be 'a great relief to be freed from the perpetual struggle in which their hitherto undefined and indefinite counterclaims have involved them'. Tupper supported the need for records in another note of 10 August 1880, written in the Revenue and Agriculture Department. Buck had drawn the moral, and Holderness again elaborated the point. In 1840, he remarked, Thomason had made a 'fair and moderate assessment' of Azamgarh district, but neglected 'to draw up and record an accurate record of rights'. The result, according to J.R. Reid's settlement report, was twenty years' warfare between landlords and tenants, and 'numberless abuses' of raiyats' rights. Patwaris became instruments of fraud; even the Court of Wards was inconvenienced for want of accurate *jamabandis*.[23]

A far more general set of considerations came into play in Bengal after the 1885 Act. Landlords and tenants were still expected to pay towards the survey operations, a legacy of the past and another example of the creeping additions to state dues which zamindars claimed to be violations of the permanent settlement. The Bengal government, of course, continued to worry about the political unpopularity of such charges, and to try to make savings by invoking local Indian agency for record-keeping and surveying. But the thrust of the work was for an avowed public purpose and the bulk of the costs rested upon government. Why was the Bengal government persuaded that survey and

---

[22] Notes, 14 December 1881 and 19 January 1882, Add.Mss.43584.
[23] Notes on G/Be to G/I, 15 July 1880, R&A Rev A 16-46 (July 1882) in Add.Mss.43584.

settlement were needed? The decision may be regarded as another in the long series whereby additional state costs and responsibilities were admitted to replace earlier local or collective arrangements, and to establish instead definite, general categories of rights.

An earlier example was the involvement of the state in embankments and drainage policy. The permanent settlement had removed the various payments which had been allowed to zamindars for irrigation and protective works (by deductions from their revenue dues), while supposing that such tasks would still be performed. The inevitable consequences were neglect, official complaints, local disputes, and various enactments and procedures allowing or requiring the state to intervene in water management (summarised in Bengal Act II of 1882). Similarly, the main reason for surveys and records of rights under the 1885 Act was that they were accepted as a remedy for the evils against which the Act was designed. If the permanent settlement had erred, according to the new orthodoxy recorded by Baden-Powell, it was partly because it was not preceded by a survey: it had been made for named estates with persons deemed to be in possession and willing to accept the terms, with measurement, mapping and records of rights ruled out for reasons of time, capacity and doctrine.[24] Similarly, if the problem was famine and poverty, then the received wisdom was that Bengal had proved woefully unprepared over the preceding decades because of its administrative tradition. The permanent settlement had left it with inadequate knowledge of its subjects, and without the village agency to remedy this defect. And finally, by 1884 when the settlement and record of rights provisions were secured in the Bill, the advocates of the reform had experienced some set-backs, under Rivers Thompson, to their more radical proposals, and were ready to espouse a method of regulating rents and protecting tenant rights which was not open to theoretical objections. At least they were ready to do so when convinced that there were no insuperable financial or political objections: Tupper's example of the permanently-settled areas of Banaras division was the important one here.[25]

II

Yet this decision too had its limits. Another motive raised in discussion of the advantages of a survey was that accurate village records would

[24] Baden-Powell, *Land Systems*, vol.1, pp.407-9.
[25] C.L. Tupper, 'Memorandum on the rent question in Behar', 20 October 1881, R&A Rev A 16-46 (July 1883), with letters and notes by NWP Collectors, December 1881 to January 1882.

be helpful in 'disclosing the agricultural condition of the country'. This implied the further agenda already mentioned, and thus raised all the doubts which surrounded the institution of a state agricultural corps. The decision to embark on a survey and settlement was also a *limitation* of the goals of government, because it restricted interference to the recording of agrarian structure. In the politicisation of the rent question, as occurred in Bengal in the 1870s and 1880s, the issues included the appropriate types and role of government, as well as the competing interests in the countryside. A survey too raised such questions.

It was an instrument which met ideas and needs we have already identified. Seeming altruism, especially ideas about the purpose of British rule appropriate to the Victorian age, was again an important part of the motivation, though of course political and economic self-interest was also involved. A survey and settlement explicitly expressed the new willingness to intervene on behalf of raiyats, at least in order to define rights and reduce agrarian disputes. It too was required largely because earlier government measures and legal decisions were at last beginning to bite. It too suggested a renewed belief that the government was capable of acting to affect agrarian relations at lower levels. It too was regarded as a particular response to outbreaks of famine, in a context in which, by the last quarter of the nineteenth century, the government thought it at last had the capacity to begin improving the condition of the rural population. A survey, settlement and record of rights provided the basis and means of that improvement, a possible culmination, as has been argued in earlier chapters, for a kind of interventionist progression—from the permanent settlement and its focus on zamindars, through the patnidari regulations which recognised equivalent land-owning rights for large intermediary tenure-holders, on to attempts to protect the 'contract' interests of tenants at land sales, and then to the measures designed to 'restore' the ancient privileges of settled raiyats, in the guise of the 'actual cultivators'. In the twentieth-century the search for actual cultivators went still further, with measures directed at under-tenants, share-croppers and bonded labour.

More radical still were arguments for direct state interventions in agricultural production and in the development of the economy. A survey might or might not be intended as a step towards this further role. There was doubt because prevailing theories influenced policies, but did not wholly prescribe their trajectory. As said, in the argument over any link between tenant rights and future prosperity, both sides depended upon deductive rather than empirical reasoning. The officials did not generally debate the details of economic advance in the presidency, in the sense of trying to relate the expansion of cultivation or the development and marketing of new crops to specific social or political innovations. Almost the only exception was that they considered that the tea industry had depended upon European enterprise backed up by government. Nowhere, for example, was there any extensive analysis of the relationship between property-ownership and commercialisation, any more than there was a firmly established causal connection between limited, individual property-ownership and mass poverty. Historians too have tended to take the connection or the lack of it from *a priori* reasoning. The divisions between officials—and between historians— were thus partly a matter of preference, as between landlords and peasant proprietors. Where observation backed up these attitudes it provided ammunition rather than explanation. This absence of scrutiny was, as said, not universal; careful attention to detail was shown, for example, in examining indigenous types of tenancy, as in many other spheres. The selective lack of exact observation indicated a reluctance, in some quarters, to treat seriously any questions of actual production. For some officials the reliance upon structure, one with a long pedigree in India, was quite deliberate.

What this implies is that the extent of state intervention continued to be contested, as an ideological question as well as a political one. Here we reach a divide, among the reformers, which is also the division between this volume and its successor. We can capture a flavour of the debates by reconsidering briefly the issue of state's involvement in agricultural production, as the step beyond its regulation of agrarian relations. S.C. Bayley, ever seeking historical legitimacy, traced such involvement back to Akbar and to the importance of the land revenue in Indian finances. For the British, as mentioned in chapter three, the question was raised by Mayo in 1870 when he formed an Agricultural Department 'to take cognizance of all matters connected with the practical improvement of the agricultural resources of the country'. In 1871 local governments were urged to set up model farms in every district; in Bengal seven were established in 1873, some proving short-lived, and an Economic Museum was founded in Calcutta. In 1873 weekly agricultural returns were instituted from the localities. The 1880 Famine Commission revived the subject; it too proposed both the *diffusion* of agricultural knowledge, and the *collection* of information about agricultural conditions. Ripon's government suggested starting at the centre with a new Director of Agriculture, to help devise further programmes, and by way of example to the provinces. The Secretary of State's Council generally preferred provincial to central appointments in agriculture

—for example rebuffing Ripon's request for an agricultural chemist in 1883—but it was agreed that E.C. Buck should be appointed Agricultural Secretary in 1881. Elliott commented: 'he must not try too many things at once: he is in danger of putting so many irons into his fire that he puts out the fire'. Elliott saw the tasks of the Secretary as reactive: touring India, collecting statistics, setting up teams to gather them, and being able to predict output, import needs and so on. But Rivers Thompson hoped for expert appointments and that 'a real and active policy of agricultural development is contemplated'.

Buck wanted to be very active. He proposed, for example, that government should 'assist in maintaining a more satisfactory relation between agricultural capital and agricultural expenditure'—in regard not only to government loans but also agricultural banks, following an experiment in NWP by Crosthwaite. Cotton was appalled. He warned that even an expanded system of government loans would be positively mischievous because 'antagonistic to private enterprise'. G.E. Ward thought government credit schemes 'calculated to retard the growth of intelligence and self-dependance'. Rivers Thompson had argued the opposite: that the government, as effective joint owner of revenue-paying land, and in the interests of the 'prosperity of the cultivating classes', had an 'immense responsibility in developing its vast estate'. Bayley, echoing him and playing another favourite card of reformers, wrote that the need for state intervention was now recognised in 'every civilised country in the world' in matters formerly left 'entirely to private enterprise'.[26] But in 1883, when Thompson proposed a training school for record-keepers, Bayley did not oppose this but thought it premature. Thompson was starting at the 'wrong end', he claimed. Thompson thought of record-keeping as a means of improving agriculture; Bayley saw it primarily as a device for maintaining rights.[27]

Later a tension continued between those like Eden who believed that agrarian structure (once reformed) would act unaided, and those like Buck who believed in direct intervention (agricultural colleges, experimental farms, state-sponsored credit, and so on) to promote improvements in productivity and the value of output. Eden, following an established Bengal line, had regarded the Agricultural Department as a

[26] See Bayley to Primrose, 16 June [1883], Add.Mss.43612; G/I (H) to S/S, no.19, 13 March 1881, and notes by A.R. T[hompson], 17 October 1881, E.C. Buck, 26 February 1882, C. Crosthwaite, 16 March 1882, H.J.S. Cotton, 13 April 1882, and G.E. Ward, 15 May 1882, Add.Mss.43584; Kimberley to Ripon, 24 January and 8 February 1883, Add.Mss.43523; Elliott to Ripon, 26 June and 7 July 1881, Add.Mss.43605.
[27] Bayley to Primrose, 16 June [1883], Add.Mss.43612.

'sham' and favoured its abolition. Taking up Elliott's position he suggested that a roving agricultural commissioner to investigate and advise would suffice; moreover: 'if Buck had only had an experience of three months in each province before he began instructing others, he would not have written the reams of nonsense which first created a most unfavourable opinion of the department in the public mind'.[28]

Marking a similar divide, the 1880 Famine Commission had even recommended a system of supervised village accountants under a Deputy Collector, but the Government of India thought such a parallel establishment for agriculture and statistics would undermine the district officer. The 'economic condition and well-being of the people', they explained, was 'one of the highest and most essential functions of the chief district officer', embracing, 'directly or indirectly, almost every branch if the executive authority'; to transfer such functions was to run the risk of 'divided government'. This, though interesting for its endorsement of state responsibility, was more remarkable as a defence of the generalist role of the district officer: it amounted to a refusal to embark on close or extensive state activity in order to meet the professed goal.[29] Predictably Eden too was opposed to a local agency for such purposes; his preference was to rely instead on the rent Bill—that is, on the improvement of agrarian structure rather than of agricultural production. But nine months later, following Buck's apppointment and a despatch from London asking for proposals relating to agricultural departments, district administration and research, the Revenue and Agriculture Department had changed its view: it resolved that a 'systematic prosecution of agricultural *inquiry*', as the Famine Commission proposed, must 'precede any attempt at agricultural improvement', and that for this purpose the provinces needed a 'permanent organization for the maintenance of a thorough system'. They proposed not only the collection of statistics, but also investigation to check any causes of agricultural decline and to urge upon cultivators the greatest possible efficiency; the 'Native community' should also be involved, so as to tap 'local reasons which justify practices that may seem strange and illogical to an European observer'.[30]

The debates over agricultural policy show that the 1885 Act was a transitional stage on the way towards whole-society remedies; it pro-

---

[28] C.H.T. Crosthwaite and E.C. Buck, memorandum printed 17 May 1882, Add.Mss.43584, and Eden to Ripon, 13 November 1882, Add.Mss. 43592.

[29] G/I (H, R&A) to S/S, no.19, 14 March 1881, with Add.Mss.43584.

[30] S/S to G/I, no.55, 16 June 1881, and Resolution of G/I, R&A, 8 December 1881, with Add.Mss.43584.

vided concrete categories within given politico-economic theories. It seems that the first intervention, through law and settlement, was bound to promote a second, the direct involvement in conditions of production —as indeed was already being advocated before the 1880s. The next stage was to seek practical remedies in terms of credit, improved crops, scientific methods of production, and marketing. But these further steps required renewed policy-debates, and bore even greater political implications. Agricultural bureaucracies and government credit were too much for some officials to stomach, and the same could be said of a record of rights, and more generally of the collection of information as part of a project of agricultural improvement. All these questions were potentially related, as also was the issue of local agency. What was highly controversial was the extent to which the potential should be admitted; the question of how far to intervene was in dispute not only before 1885, but again from the moment the Tenancy Act was passed.

One key problem was that local records could be efficiently collected only by a responsible local agency, which did not exist in Bengal. To introduce one raised difficult political issues: could the government interpose itself in each village and estate between the zamindars and their tenants? A letter in 1883 from the Bengal government, signed by MacDonnell, on the subject of statistics and agricultural improvement, left no doubt as to the hackles raised and the confrontation required by such an intervention. True to the habitual emphasis on precedent, the letter recalled that (as we have seen) the government had long struggled to reinstate a local agency in Bengal, starting with Regulations I and VIII of 1793. MacDonnell claimed it had not succeeded because 'it was not in the interests of the zemindars that the Government should acquire information which might justify interference between them and their ryots'. The opposition was so effective that in 1827 kanungos were abolished except in Orissa. Patwaris were still supposed to exist, and Regulation IX of 1833 required duplicates of their records to be filed in the collectorate; but investigations in 1837 found that patwaris too had almost disappeared. Their formal abolition was considered in 1849 though not carried through. In 1863 the Commissioner of Patna noted the disorganised state of the register that was supposed to be kept of patwaris, and asked about improvements; George Campbell took up the question in 1871, freshly impressed by the need for information after his work on the Orissa famine commission. Various attempts at reform were made, but to no avail. Though a local branch for statistics was set up within its Finance Department, and weekly district returns were made from the 1870s, the

Bengal government continued to have to rely on the subordinate police for information which was collected elsewhere by junior revenue officials; the local knowledge of the district officials was held even to be declining as their burdens increased, and because of the transfer of rent suits to the civil courts. Again, except for the reorganisation of kanungos which had taken place in 1869 in Orissa, the government was thwarted by the zamindars, who 'loved darkness better than light, not so much because their deeds were evil, but because the casting of any light upon the internal economy of their estates was an interference with the exercise of a power which they claimed to be absolute'—a claim the government had not had the courage to resist until 1859. Seldom were the zamindars more clearly painted as the opponents of progress and justice than in this compact and selective history of the failure of local agency in Bengal.

Following Baird Smith's famine report in 1861, the Bengal letter went on, a statistical committee had been set up. Its report in 1866 called for elaborate sets of statistics; but (wrote MacDonnell), in Bengal, where there were 'no means of ascertaining facts', the exhibition of facts 'could be of no great value' and 'there were no facts worth the name to exhibit'. The implication seemed to be that information was an end in itself; but the point of the complaint was really that a lack of information indicated how no one in Bengal was responsible for the supervision of the agricultural condition of the country. Rivers Thompson's conclusion was that, though action would have to await the passage of the Tenancy Act, Bengal needed a very large increase in facilities for administration; agricultural statistics must underlie all real information on the condition of the people, and 'without a field survey, there can hardly be agricultural statistics worth the name'. He saw that survey as an 'essential preliminary to the revivification of the patwari system', the intention being to turn the village officers into government servants. He remained worried that the zamindars would resent any reform as trespassing upon their rights.[31]

On instructions from the Government of India, the Bengal 'Canoongoes and Patwaris' Act was introduced in 1885. It provided for qualified patwaris organised in circles and supported by a cess. It was designed, particularly for Bihar, to keep the record of rights up to date, once it had been prepared in a survey and settlement. Zamindars would be required to file their accounts, which the patwaris would verify. Introducing the Bill, MacDonnell explained that the registration of land rights was the true remedy for agrarian troubles. Repeating the argu-

[31] G/Be (Rev) to G/I, no.309T-R, 1 June 1883, Add.Mss.43615.

ments of the Bengal letter, he claimed that the local officers had originally been state servants and (quoting the Board of Commissioners in
1815) 'the means of defining the rights of the peasantry and adjusting
with facility such differences as may arise between landlord and
tenant'. He concluded: 'We have been engaged for ninety years in a
futile struggle to obtain...the elementary facts of rural economy...
essential to all efficient administration.'[32]

The establishment of such a system—given the sorry history of
efforts within Bihar to improve the standing and training of patwaris—
was considered essential to the success of the survey policy provided in
the 1885 Tenancy Act. But the zamindars, as MacDonnell later recalled, having 'failed in their efforts to defeat the Bengal Tenancy Act,
...redoubled their exertions, both in England and in India, to prevent
the Government from giving effect to the settlement (chapter X) provisions of the Act and from creating an agency in Behar to maintain the
record-of-rights'. The Governments of India and Bengal, at this stage,
were agreed that 'an elaborate survey and record-of-rights are a pure
waste of money, unless due provision is made to keep the information
they furnish up to date'. The Secretary of State decided to share this
view, in the midst of the controversy, but by the unexpected expedient
of stopping both the Patwaris Act and the experimental Bihar survey
promised by Dufferin's government as the first step towards a general
record of rights. The survey of Bihar was not approved, therefore, until
1892.

III

The keeping of the record was even more difficult than the procedures
for creating it. A retreat from pro-peasant policies started even as the
Tenancy Act and the surveys were being enacted. We may foreshadow
that discussion—and note other changes in individual officials' commitments and perceptions—by considering some Bengal measures just
before and after the turn of the century, chiefly from the perspective of
the Government of India. In the mid-1890s the meaning of the 1885
Act was undergoing radical change, as the procedures for survey,
settlement and record of rights were brought into operation. At the
same time the Bengal government introduced a range of measures as
palliatives for the zamindars. The local government's appeasement was
resisted by the Government of India. For example, when an amendment

---

[32] R&A Rev A 6 (April 1885) and 8 (August 1885), and Proceedings of the
Lieutenant-Governor of Bengal's Legislative Council, 31 January 1885.

to the Public Lands Recovery Act made 'concessions to the landed interest', not only were the concessions rigorously scrutinised, but it was proposed that the Bill should be transferred to the imperial legislature, where it would be 'less amenable to local influences'. Events proved that this would indeed have been wise, from a pro-tenant perspective. In particular Bengal proposed to extend to the zamindars the right to use the certificate procedure (whereby the aid of the courts could be invoked to ensure payment of dues) to recover, for example, a raiyat's share of the road cess. In practice this power might be used indirectly to recover rents. When the Bill had first come to the Revenue and Agriculture Department of the Government of India, in 1893, the local government had reported a difference of opinion with the High Court, which favoured restricting the certificate procedure to the recovery of purely public demands which could be ascertained from government registers; the local government had argued that this would preclude its use for government and Wards' estates, and instead advocated allowing it except in any case 'involving a question of right or title'. In the Government of India Sir Philip Hutchins had had some doubts about the suitability of this restriction but was ready to leave the question to the local Council where 'its intricacies' would be 'thoroughly understood'. But when the Bill came back from Bengal, the restrictions on the certificate power had been entirely removed (in committee, in response to non-official opinion) to the great surprise and alarm of the Revenue and Agriculture Department. The Bill now seemed to contravene a ruling of 1892 that the certificate procedure was not suitable for private individuals except where no question was at issue 'save the mere fact of payment or non-payment of a definite and admitted sum'. A.E. Miller tried to use this to put a stop to the Bill, but the Governor-General's hands were tied, in that great and public resentment would have been caused if he had vetoed the Bill on this point, especially considering the discretion allowed by Hutchins. Later Miller tried to sabotage the provision by proposing that any private use should be paid for by the government, but this offended against habits of financial caution and did not find support. Thus the centre lost this round. It was a peripheral confrontation, but illustrates the nature of the wider campaign, the issues and the weapons involved.[33]

Bengal had had an ally on this issue in Alexander Mackenzie, now a member of the central government; he thought it enough to tell the local officials that the centre would have preferred the principle of 1892 to

[33] R&A Rev B 11 (August 1895), containing Legislative A (May 1895); see also A 12-14 (April 1896).

have been embodied in the Act. Elgin had followed this advice. Almost immediately afterwards, Sir Charles Elliot, now Lieutenant-Governor of Bengal, approached Mackenzie again, privately, seeking support for a proposal to allow landlords to use a summary certificate procedure for the recovery of rents in any areas to which the Land Records Maintenance Act applied. This Act, supposedly designed to provide for the perpetuation of a correct record of agrarian rights and ownership, after the main survey was completed—and the subject of the next section of this chapter—had resulted from enormous pressure by the centre on the local government; as we shall see, it was generally agreed, outside Bengal, that it had been deprived of what few teeth it had had, in response to the complaints of the zamindars in the legislature. If Elliot's new proposal were to be accepted, therefore, the position would be that, even though the zamindars effectively controlled the government's records under the new Act, the onus of proof (that money was not payable) would rest on the tenant. The intention was avowedly to provide landlords with such facilities for recovery of rent as were consistent with the interests of tenants, a sentiment which provoked repeated exclamation marks on the central files and no doubt some snorts of derision in the office. That the idea should have come from Elliot or with his support, when he was regarded in Bengal as the centre's emissary sent to impose North Indian tenancy policies on the province, emphasised the political motive which was involved. 'This', replied Ibbetson when Mackenzie asked for his views, 'is another of the sops ...offered to the Bengal landlords in order to bribe them to accept the survey and settlement of rights'. Indeed, as the Under-Secretary (F.G. Sly) noted, Bengal had made no attempt to justify their proposals in terms of need, such as by statistics showing the unusual difficulty of rent collection in Bengal, where in fact landlords had far wider powers than elsewhere in India, but had been content to demonstrate that the changes were desired. Moreover, Bengal had had to blur the distinction between public and private purposes by seeming to imply that it was only fair, if government had powers to extract revenue from zamindars, that zamindars should have the same powers to extract rent from tenants. The local government was being disingenuous. The implication that the proposed powers met the usual criterion (no dispute about rights) because they would be available only where there was a record kept up to date under the Maintenance Act, rested on what was seen at the centre as a deliberate pretence that that Act had a chance of being effective. It was thought on the contrary that there was very little chance of the records being properly maintained, even if correct at the time of preparation, and that certainly they could not be relied on as proof that definite amounts were due in particular cases, for the information would have come from the zamindars and would record transfers of interest and not changes in rent. Accordingly Mackenzie warned Elliot that the Government of India would never sanction his scheme.[34]

The survey proceedings themselves and the long struggle over how the record was to be subsequently maintained, constituted of course the major front along which the centre tried to change the policies of the Government of Bengal. A peripheral theatre of this war was the wrangle over the amendment of the 1885 Act, which accompanied the first of the district surveys in North Bihar. We will first take up the latter story, in the cold weather of 1894/5. The government at the centre was convinced that existing procedures in Bengal would make nonsense of the survey—there was no way they could be used to carry out a settlement of the whole province with reasonable speed and efficiency. MacDonnell, acting as Lieutenant-Governor in November 1894, retorted by stressing the differences between Bengal and North India. Though convinced by his experience in Bihar of the need for tenancy reform, as acting Lieutenant-Governor he also championed the cause of Bengali methods against some aspects of the peasant school's remedies. In particular he argued that the courts must be left to deal with rent suits, as they had for a hundred years; he resisted the 'restlessness of men trained up in a school where the executive officer counts and the judicial officer is at a discount'. The moves which were favoured by Elliot, a man 'trained....where the village agency is reliable and under the control of village opinion', would not work (MacDonnell claimed) in the different circumstances of Bengal; the involvement of the civil courts was essential if the province were to develop 'on its own lines and in accordance with the spirit of its people'.[35]

Returning to this minute eighteen months later, Ibbetson, secure in his Punjab experience, was to scrawl in the margin that the Bengal system, 'Now that it is tried for the first time on a large scale, ...break[s] down hopelessly'. To Ibbetson and his department it was axiomatic that a settlement officer could not proceed judicially if he was to complete his work satisfactorily. Ibbetson did not mean (and thought that here MacDonnell misunderstood him) that there would be no recourse to the

[34] R&A Rev C 15, December 1895.
[35] R&A Rev A 10-14 (November 1894). For the discussion in the following paragraphs, see also R&A Rev A 8-15 (March 1898), A 15-30 (January 1897), and A 21-2 (February 1896).

civil courts on appeal against decisions, or that summary procedure would be used to fix fair—that is, future—rents. Rather he envisaged the settlement officer's drawing up a draft record of the existing situation without judicial inquiry, dealing at that stage with the thousand-and-one objections, most of them 'never intended to be seriously pressed, or...based on a misunderstanding which a little explanation removes'. Two great advantages of this method were that government could issue general instructions to settlement officers, and that each objection and dispute could lawfully be decided in part on the basis of the officer's experience and knowledge of other cases, evidence which he would be bound to suppress if acting judicially.

On a related matter Ibbetson expanded upon the advantages of the 'accumulated knowledge' the settlement officer was able to bring to bear. He wrote in favour of fixing rents as part of a general survey, and, though he accepted that the courts should deal with individual disputes, he did so out of no strong conviction of the courts' abilities, and merely to avoid overburdening the settlement officers—their knowledge, Ibbetson thought, would probably enable them to reach 'better' decisions than the courts even in individual cases. Later he went rather further, implying not only that the courts were less well-informed but also that they were liable to be unjust by favouring the zamindars who, being 'wealthy and intelligent', had an advantage in judicial procedure. His senior colleague, J. Woodburn, also dismissed the courts as adjudicators or protectors for the tenants: they did not discriminate enough in his view, with the result that 'rents under them stagnate which is not wholesome even for the tenant'.

It is obvious that the disagreement here was not just on matters of detail in connection with settlement procedure. Rather it reflected two different ideas of government—on the one hand the North Indian tradition of direct, personal rule through one official, supposedly inherited from the Mughals or the Sikhs; on the other the Bengal experience of divided responsibility between executive and judiciary and between different executive levels all subject to laws and regulations, arising ultimately from the 'checks and balances' of the eighteenth-century constitution. It reflected moreover two different views of India—the 'real' one (as the British conceived it, in the terms discussed above) and the one which could emerge under the benevolent influence of the West. In so far as they existed, the 'own lines' and 'spirit of its people' in accordance with which Bengal should be left to develop, in the view of MacDonnell, were the product of a century of British rule.

In this context the political aspects of the controversy were debated, and MacDonnell felt he was defending the true spirit of the 1885 reforms. A touchstone was the question of the zamindars' powers over their tenants, particularly in regard to enhancement of rents. This became a heated issue particularly because price rises coincided with the gradual interpolation of the government and the laws between the landlords and the peasants. The Government of Bengal formulated new rules under the Bengal Tenancy Act in 1894, making considerable alterations, the tendency of which was considered in the Government of India to be of 'very doubtful character'. For example, the mere admission by a raiyat was to be sufficient proof that there was no occupancy right—'a most dangerous provision' which would defeat the purpose of the Act, because it failed to take account of the landlord's power of coercing his tenants. The Government of Bengal, moreover, as noted already, believed it desirable to improve the definition of the 'prevailing rate' to which reference could be made in order to raise low rents—in its view, the present rule on the subject was 'unworkable'.

To Ibbetson, however, this was as it should have been. The prevailing rate had been retained as a ground for enhancement mainly because it had existed previously, as the pargana rate, and landlords were unwilling to give it up. But it had been meant to be 'unworkable' in the sense of being inapplicable in most cases. The danger of a wider definition was that 'prevailing' would come to mean 'average'. In that case, as Sly explained in his note on the subject, 'The landlord by individual enhancement suits would be able to continually raise the average, until all the ryots paid at the highest rate paid by any tenant in the village'. By 1896, nonetheless, as we have seen, the Bengal government had come to favour defining the prevailing rate as the rate at or above which the majority paid in a given estate or village—even Mackenzie, now Lieutenant-Governor, agreed. The definition was proposed only for areas of low or moderate rents, but there would replace something which could hardly ever be known, namely what rate prevailed when rates could rarely be strictly comparable over even a modest area, with a new concept which could always be ascertained: rents might be raised for any tenant who paid less than most of his fellows. This might seem to avoid the dangers of an average rate, but in fact it would make it just as easy to raise rents, given, as Woodburn pointed out, 'the experience in Bengal and particularly Behar…that tenants are habitually cajoled or coerced into enhancements of their rents, which might be withstood at law'.

A similar difference of opinion arose over the use of excess area for enhancement. Mackenzie was content that its discovery at survey should justify an increase in the rent. The central officials, however, calculated that the excess depended not only on the survey, which might be presumed accurate, but also on what was shown on the *jamabandi* papers (rent-rolls), with which the survey was to be compared; thus Bengal seemed to be proposing an automatic right to enhance rents, without further proof or enquiry, as if they had forgotten that landlords' records were notoriously false and partial. Indeed the prospect of gaining extra rent in this way had been, as Ibbetson observed, 'one of the strongest reasons held out to the Bengal zamindars to reconcile them to the Behar survey'. Ibbetson insisted that the onus should be on the landlords to specify and prove excess lands even after measurement. He argued that two additional conditions had to be satisfied—the area would have to be of the essence of the rent agreement and in excess of what the parties believed it to be. No increase should be allowable, for example, if the raiyat rented a certain field at a specified rent rather than at so much per bigha.

Clearly confrontation on this issue too was not simply on the merits of the case. It was between those anxious to preserve the existing order by appeasement of the zamindars, and those seeking to impose a new order by giving the raiyats the power to resist and by creating an administration which could watch over them as they did so. M.D. Chalmers went so far as to suggest that, since the settlement system worked admirably in Northern India, the more they could 'approximate to it in Bengal, the better'; the further implication was that the political system ought to fall into line as well. By such an analysis, to offer liberal conditions for enhancement, say, so as to placate the zamindars over the survey and settlement, was to perpetuate outmoded and ineffective methods of control, just when they might have begun to be replaced.

The argument eventually crystallised around a point of strategy. The local government had prepared two Bills governing settlement procedure, one intended to make significant changes and the other involving a minimum of adjustments. It was inevitable that the first Bill would be preferred at the centre. As we shall see, the Revenue and Agriculture Department was convinced that the Bengal system had had 'a fair trial and...failed', that under it settlement officers (if they observed it fully) turned out too little work and 'that not of good quality'. The second Bill, in Ibbetson's view, would merely legalise what was already happening and under which work had 'come to a stand still'. In Bengal, however, the first Bill was opposed by both the zamindars and the High Court. During 1896 pressure to abandon it mounted from the local government. Mackenzie wrote privately to Woodburn that the second

Bill was the only one he thought he could get through his Council in time to be of use in Orissa, where settlement proceedings had begun.

Mackenzie blamed his difficulties partly on the High Court which 'never was so weak and bad as...now', and which was headed by a man (Petheram) who, near the end of his term in office, could not be made to push for a quick decision on the first Bill. The second Bill, however, the Court would probably accept. Moreover, later exchanges with Mackenzie suggested that the High Court was a secondary problem: 'We must recognise that in Bengal', he told Woodburn in August, 'there is an intense jealousy of the Executive; and even if the landlords agreed...we shall have Surendranath Banerjea and all the Congress and landless men howling'. Woodburn was at first inclined to abide with Mackenzie's decisions, but Ibbetson dissuaded him, arguing that they had to have something worth fighting for. He could not understand, for his part, why the landlords should be opposed, considering how much they had to gain through the reduction in delays and the relaxation of restrictions, which would result from the main proposal. Nor could he see why the first Bill should take longer to pass than the second; he suspected that Mackenzie's depression and reluctance had something to do with 'boils and blains', from which he was suffering (by his own account). Fears of Banerjea and a 'howling' Congress do not appear to have been thought worthy of comment in the secretariat; only the Viceroy, Elgin, mentioned the subject again.

In October 1896 the idea arose (as in 1885) that the measure had better be undertaken in the central legislature, lest the Bengal Council emasculate it as it had the Records Maintenance Act. Woodburn, however, preferred the provincial legislature so that there could be an outlet for opposition which otherwise might find more violent expression. The government accordingly supported the passage of the first Bill in the Bengal legislature, with an option to the local authorities to limit it in the first instance to Orissa if that would make its passage easier. By the end of 1897, however, the Bills having been published, Mackenzie was in a stronger position to argue about the dangers of opposition. He had a long talk with Ibbetson in December and finally convinced him that it would be impossible to make all the changes involved in the first Bill for permanently-settled estates. Ibbetson resigned himself to this conclusion: 'If the landlords...prefer to retain the present cumbrous and ineffective method of enhancement, I do not see that we need very strongly to object'; though the result would be to protract the survey operations, this cost too would fall largely on the zamindars.

Earlier Elgin had accurately characterised this conflict as one 'between Upper India and Bengal opinion'—he had objected to legislation at the centre because it would have had the appearance of imposing the views of the one on the other (as was in fact occurring in the secrecy of the files). The prime mover had been Ibbetson, keeping his superiors in line. He even noted at one point, on the question of enhancement, that 'The interests of the raiyat...are far more important to protect than those of the Government'; he meant that the administration's financial interests, in its role as a landlord, could be sacrificed in order to gain the social and political benefits of protecting the tenants. The outcome, after all his pressure, the eventual fate of the proposed legislation in 1898, was superficially a defeat for Ibbetson and the more uncompromising aspects of the peasant school of thought— but only superficially. At a deeper level what was happening in the 1890s was an adjustment whereby the interference of the state in agrarian relations was being qualified by political considerations and administrative preference. Interference continued all the same. The main affront to zamindari interests was the survey and settlement operation itself; the Bengal victory on points of law might therefore be dismissed as incidental to the underlying trend. The debates confirmed the centre in its determination to put Bengal right eventually; they did not convince it that Bengal must be allowed to find its own way.

During the 1890s those at the centre of government continued to stress the comparative worthlessness for British purposes of the zamindari interest. Ibbetson dismissed its opposition to the tenancy law as still incomprehensible and, though he admitted the landlords' influence in India and England, went on to echo Bayley from 1885 (quoted earlier): 'I believe that none of these zamindari associations really represent any body of reasonable opinion based on an understanding of the matter'. Similarly, in Bengal, Finucane, now Secretary to Government and formerly (as Director of Land Records and Agriculture) in the vanguard of Bengal's conversion to rural intervention, informed Ibbetson that some of the landlords privately regretted their opposition, and one had told him: 'Well, you see, we are not quite free in such matters. When Surendra Nath Banerji comes down and tells us that it will be unpatriotic for us to extend the powers of the executive what can we do?' Mackenzie too remarked to J. Westland, the Finance Member, that the landlords had said as much to him, and that he would not accept their change of front. Westland concluded the reason was 'that he had to meet a body of official opinions in favour of the Civil Court procedure, and finds it easier to change his policy in deference to the expressed opinion of the landlords, than to force his policy against High

Court opinion and the like'. Be that as it may, it is clear that even in Bengal the zamindars were being seen as acting not so much in defence of their legitimate interests as out of anti-executive sentiment; and in that case the victory in 1898 was for a new kind of opposition to British rule rather than for the old kind of alliance. Mackenzie had not after all won the battle for the zamindar policy, for even in the eyes of Bengal officials the landlords were tainted by the influence of politicians, a warning that pleasing the landlords might not always be such a major consideration of policies in the future.

IV

When the Bihar survey was starting in 1893, E.C. Buck regarded it merely 'as the first (and an imperfect) edition of the annual series', on which Bengal would need expert advice, as they had so little experience. The decision to go ahead with the surveys was therefore preceded by elaborate but abortive consultations on an accompanying measure for maintenance, drafted by Elliott, abandoned by him as unworkable, and then revised by MacDonnell when he went on leave. MacDonnell was now pessimistic about the chances of achieving any thorough scheme, but thought the minimum necessary to be a procedure for correcting the records, especially the village map, on the spot, and a cess to cover the costs. His scheme along these lines was submitted to a process of consultation with Bihar revenue officials, planters and zamindars, and then at a conference of experts from all provinces and representatives from Bihar. The plan was accepted. Elliott then returned to office, decided that it was too difficult to carry against opposition, and suggested that he would devise an alternative. Two rival schemes were sent to the Secretary of State in 1894, MacDonnell's which he described as 'admittedly adequate', and Elliott's which he called 'admittedly a doubtful experiment'. Ibbetson called it 'shadowy in the extreme'. The Secretary of State opted for the experiment, thus deferring, in MacDonnell's view, both a confrontation with the zamindari opposition and, probably, any effective remedy.

Elliott duly produced a Bill which further weakened his original scheme. Ibbetson savaged it:

The new machinery is now confined to tenants' rights, proprietary rights being left to the existing Registration Law, wh[ich] has proved to be wholly ineffective. The presumptive truth of the record, which would have offered a very strong inducement to registration, has been abolished. The landlord is no longer asked whether he accepts a transfer by a tenant, so that the mutation entries may all relate to invalid transfers; & the Collector will have two sets of records of tenant rights, one from the point of view of the tenant, and another from that of the landlord.... What he is going to do with them, we don't know.... We may safely predict that the scheme will fail.

MacDonnell then concentrated on saving what there was of an existing patwari system in Bihar:

In every province in India we are laboriously bringing our village organizations into efficiency, having recognized the truth that, unless we have a proper village agency, we cannot come into touch with facts, or appreciate the real neccessities or feelings of the people. Surely we ought not, in Behar of all places, and at the bidding of the classes who make our work there so difficult, to disband and abolish, without first providng an efficient substitute, the organization which has existed since we first took hold of the the Province and which we have turned to excellent account in various emergencies.

He argued that Elliott was coming under great pressure to abolish the patwaris altogether, as he himself had come while standing in as Lieutenant-Governor. He wanted the Government of India to strengthen Elliott's hands by instructing him to preserve the patwaris. J. Wilson supported this, entering a notable attack on the zamindars and Bengal:

The most glaring defect of our administration in Bengal is that after...we handed over the ryot body and soul to the zemindar, we took no measures to preserve the village organization, on which depended the strength of the ryot's position. We passed laws declaring that this or that part of it remained, and that the burden and duty of maintenance was part of the zemindar's obligation under the settlement, but we took no measures to see those obligations were in any way observed.

From that day to this it has been the one constant aim of the zemindar party to shirk these obligations. To their rights they hold with grim tenacity, and charge the Government with breach of faith the moment it talks of anything remotely resembling an intention to enforce even its reserved rights against them.... The patwari system is one of these obligations....

'In the face of these facts', he too saw 'the strongest objections to the abolition of the Patwari Regulations', and hoped to preserve them so that they might, one day, form the basis of a new system to enable the government to 'do its duty by its ryots'.[36]

The true voice of the zamindars could be heard in the local pro-

[36] For the preceding paragraphs, see R&A Rev A 16-46 (July 1883); E.C. Buck, 'Maintenance of records of rights in Bihar' and note, 10 October 1893, ibid. A 11-34 (November 1893); demi-official, C.E. Buckland to Buck, 24 January 1894, ibid. A 23-34 (January 1894); notes by A.P. M[acDonnell], 3 and 19 August 1894 and 7 January 1895, Elgin, 15 August, A.E. M[iller], 25 August, J. W[ilson], 28 August, and D. I[bbetson], 31 December 1894 and 4 January 1895, ibid. A 17-20 (January 1895); and notes by Ibbetson, 6 May, and Miller, 7 May 1895, ibid. B 17-19 (July 1895).

ceedings. From Muzaffarpur—that 'acknowledged capital of agricultural interests in Bihar' (to quote the Government of India)—it was
reported: 'On every side I have heard approval expressed of the proposed scheme. ...Europeans and natives...are unanimous in rejoicing that
the patwari's day is over and hope for good results...'. The manager of
Hathwa raj in Saran also agreed eagerly to patwari abolition, while
arguing that any official scrutiny of *jamabandis* would 'only serve to
strain the relations [of landlord and tenant] which have hitherto been
amicable on the whole'. The Tirhut Landholders' Association professed
themselves agreed on the need to maintain a record of rights, but
wanted it to be 'cheap and simple'—by which they meant that transfers
of tenancy should have to be registered to be valid, but not that zamindars' *jamabandis* should be filed, for that would be 'a very hard burden
and cause great harassment to zemindars'. Samastipur planters were
very strongly of the opinion that to re-institute kanungos would merely
be to provide another lever of oppression to the zamindars, who would
bribe them. The whole scheme of record-keeping would be 'irksome',
added Babu Gauri Shankar, the manager at Bachour, a notoriously ill-
managed estate belonging Rameshwar Singh of Rajnagar, brother of the
Maharaja of Darbhanga. Bell, the manager at Darbhanga raj, thought
the proposed scheme unworkable, and, having outlined his own difficulties in acquiring information, concluded that the 'only way in which
a record of rights in a village can be maintained is by information
supplied by the zemindar', in whose interest alone it was to have a
'correct record'! Otherwise the maintenance would 'be felt as a more
severe infliction than the cadastral survey itself'.

The official view from Muzaffarpur was different: 'experience of
the lethargy and habits of suspicion of the Indian ryot points to the conclusion that some years will have to elapse before he fully understands
the advantages offered to him'—that is, the chance of registering his
interest (for a fee). From the Collector at Darbhanga, with support from
Saran, came the advice that only compulsory registration *for tenants*
would bring home 'the fact that the Government is in earnest'.[37] Cotton

---

[37] See R&A Rev A 16-24 (January 1894), including Proceedings of General
Conference, Calcutta, 3, 4 and 6 January 1894, and G/I to S/S, no.8, 26 January
1894; Muzaffarpur Coll to PC, 13 and 21 October, Ram Dhany Sahay, secretary, Turhut Landholders' Association, to PC, 18 October, Samastipur subdivi-
sional officer to Darbhanga Coll, 22 August, Babu Gourishunker to Darbhanga
Coll, 29 October, Bell note, [7 July], Darbhanga Coll to PC, received 3 December, Manager, Hathwa raj, to PC, 17 October, Saran Coll to PC,12 December
1892, and L. Hare, 'Keeping up the Record of Rights', 14 February 1893, PCR
357, 17/5 (1892-3). Interestingly E. Macnaghton, general secretary of the Bihar

reported to Ripon that the 1885 Act was a good and beneficial law; but
that the Bihar survey was 'exciting a great deal of interest and irri-
tation' in the affected area, and was not only very unpopular with both
landlords and raiyats but likely to increase rents; and that 'the preponderance of opinion appears to be in favour of making no attempt to
undertake so vast a work' as to maintain the record in future. They
were, he concluded, 'already within measurable distance of a fiasco'.[38]

One of the issues around which the controversy settled concerned
the periodicity of the surveys, as a last resort for regular maintenance.
Early in the twentieth century the Government of India, which still
really wanted a scheme for continual updating, was asking for biennial
revisions, and Bengal was holding out for ten-yearly intervals. Ibbetson
had responded indignantly when that idea had first surfaced in 1896:
'We have always maintained that Sir Charles Elliott's scheme did *not*
provide for the maintenance of the record-of-rights; and here we have it
admittted. What is proposed is to prepare the record anew every ten
years! The proposal seems to me monstrous...'.[39] In 1903 it was still
recognised that a long gap meant, in effect, no revisions at all, or very
delayed and irregular ones at enormous cost; but by then the local
government was arguing that the settlement itself had achieved the
object of protecting the tenants (a matter which will be taken up in
chapter ten). On the other hand, whereas in 1894 it had been reported
that only about half of the *proprietary* mutations were registered in
Bihar, in 1902 an inquiry had concluded that two-thirds of the entries
from the original survey in Muzaffarpur were already obsolete, so that
the record was almost worthless. In the Government of India, Mac-
Donnell's limited scheme for patwaris was dusted off and re-costed.
There was a strong view that it should be introduced without further
ado, but Curzon, missing the point or thinking it a lost cause because of
the Secretary of State's likely intervention, insisted that they were
bound to consult Bengal, 'the more so as a cess is involved, which the

Indigo Planters' Association, while agreeing that there was no need for an *official* record of rights, argued (to PC, 26 September 1892) that it would be 'most
desirable that the existing law regarding the issue of rent receipts should be
strictly enforced'.

[38] Cotton to Ripon, 6 June and 10 September 1893, Add.Mss.43615. Cotton
had never favoured the survey: '*plectuntur Achivi* is always my experience', he
wrote, referring to Cicero and Horace: *quidquid delirant reges plectuntur
Achivi* (that is, whatever errors the kings commit, the people suffer for them).

[39] Ibbetson note, 29 August 1896, referring *inter alia* to P.C. Lyon, Director,
Bengal Land Revenue and Agriculture Department, to Secretary, Board of Revenue, 18 April 1896: 'It does not appear to me...that the Act provides for the
maintenance of records-of-right'; R&A Rev A 6 (September 1896).

zemindars will not like at all'.[40]

Miller had pointed the moral in 1903. Both Elliott, a former settlement officer 'of the old Northwest school with his sympathies probably in favour of the tenant or petty proprietor', and Sir John Woodburn, a one-time settlement officer from Awadh 'with some tenderness for the big landlord', had gone to Bengal, he noticed, favouring a permanent record, but had become 'genuinely convinced that revisions at long intervals of time' would be sufficient. Miller was all in favour of annual maintenance if it meant instituting an effective local agency, useful for other purposes, but he advanced the 'unorthodox' view that Bengal's objections should be respected. They should not be set down to ignorance or fear of unpopularity: 'It is difficult for us, who have been brought up under a system where the maintenance of records is an accepted feature of Indian administration, to realise the actual difficulties that may occur'. Ibbetson continued to insist on converting Bengal opinion, which he remarked had opposed the survey too but now recognised its value; but his case was yet again being lost.[41] The zamindars had their way.

The central government continued to urge that there should be some means of maintenance, and special revisions began in 1907 to facilitate the institution of a system of review. In due course, in 1908, the Bengal government sent in a proposal to postpone the revision of the record of rights in Bihar. By this time the Government of India (with the approval of the Secretary of State) was committed merely to a fifteen-year revision programme, and secretariat officials professed themselves surprised that anyone should have thought of diluting this arrangement still further. The usual worries were expressed that landlords would take advantage of a 'decayed record' to enhance rents and oppress their tenants.[42] Any pretence that there would be permanent maintenance

[40] Notes by R.E.V. Arbuthnot, 7 May, J.B. Fuller, 25 May and 5 July, C.M. R[ivaz], 6 June and 8 July, Finance Department, 18 June, H.J. McIntosh, 21 June, and Curzon, 17 July 1901, R&A Rev A 1-2 (August 1901).

[41] Notes by J.O. Miller, 10 December, J.P. Hewett, 24 December 1904, Ibbetson, 4 February, Curzon, 26 February, and Andrew Fraser, 17 May 1905, demi-official from Fraser to Hewett, 17 December 1904, and to J. Wilson, 24 July 1905, R&A Rev A 30-1 (August 1905). Interesting (though in Ibbetson's view 'almost meaningless') comparative statistics emerged in this debate: Bengal had one ICS officer per 1,574 square miles, 881,811 people, and 1,496,020 revenue payers; the equivalent figures for NWP were 1,128, 437,539 and 3,104,460. One suggestion was that the difference made a proper village agency impossible to supervise.

[42] Notes by J.H. Kerr, 6 December 1908, R.W. Carlyle, 16 January, and J.O. M[iller], 19 January and 2 February 1909, R&A Rev A 5 (April 1909),

was finally abandoned in 1911, but Bengal were ordered to start a revision in 1912 of the north Bihar survey, which had taken ten years and cost Rs.50 lakhs. Again in March 1912 the Bengal government made a plea for delay, which was supported by the new government of Bihar in May. Though revisions in fact did begin a little later, at this stage the Revenue and Agriculture Department—which had already proved reluctant to share the costs—decided to give up trying to force the pace; all attempts to insist on revisions were dropped even in regard to Orissa (where revision was also due). At first it had 'generally been recognised that a fresh agency must be created' to maintain the record, but in the 1890s a plan for special staff to visit the villages annually had quickly been scaled down, becoming a mere reinforcement of the existing registration department. By 1913 worries had been expressed about the powers any such staff should have in respect of 'contracts' under the 1885 Tenancy Act: any arrangements, after all, would 'involve constantly recurring interference between landlord and tenant, the advisability of which is open to serious question on political grounds'.[43]

This sounds like a complete abandonment of the policy of interference in response to political pressure. It was certainly a retreat from the 1880s and the heady days of pro-raiyat policies. The story, however, is more complex. Land questions had become ever more political, and the Bengal government, like all governments in colonial India, had had to become gradually more responsive to expressions of public opinion or political interest. The state had not abandoned its agenda of interference. Rather the accommodation of political pressure had forced that interference along certain lines. The survey and settlement proceedings *were* carried out, in all of Bihar. As will be discussed shortly, the institution of that record could and did increase the certainty and hence the transferability of tenant rights. The Bengal government was not merely discovering a convenient fiction when it reported that the very fact of survey had changed perceptions. The twentieth century wore on, and land rights *were* increasingly registered. But the British had created no more than a 'private enterprise' system for recording mutations. This meant that the state was not really present, in the maintenance of registers, to protect the weak. Rather it had provided machinery to record and entrench the successes of the strong.

---

[43] See R&A Rev A 26-31 (July 1913). This keep-with includes an office summary whose appendices, with references, sum up the entire case since 1885. The quotation is from J.H. Kerr, Secretary, G/Be, to G/I (R&A, Rev), 5 March 1912.

Chapter Nine

## *Colonial rule and agrarian structure*

Conditions in India, and the colonial impact upon them, have been a ground base to the main themes of the previous chapters. They now must make their own contribution, by means of a consideration of the history of agrarian structure in Bihar from the eighteenth century. The starting-point is made appropriate by the permanent settlement, but called into question by recent refinements of ideas about India before British rule. Partly the product of renewed empirical research, and partly an exercise in demystification, these serve to illustrate how unformed the parameters of modern Indian history still are, how narrow the consensus. They re-examine not just the cruder assertions about Indian backwardness or decadence, but also those old orthodoxies in the more subtle forms in which they persist today. What was the trajectory of the Indian political economy in the colonial period? A range of possibilities is now being suggested: that no radical break with the past accompanied the advent of British rule (fitting with a tendency altogether to play down British impact), that India had been incorporated within or at least influenced by broader economic and political systems long before the nineteenth century, and that situations and reactions differed markedly between regions over the period.

Historians such as Irfan Habib have illustrated dynamism in some aspects of the Mughal economy, and condemned Hegelian and Weberian conceptions of India and its past. But, by contrast, Habib has also characterised the society as socially cohesive, and, while tracing a differentiated agricultural sector, conceded that the era did not encourage capitalist relations of production. For Habib the major—almost the only—event of India's recent history appears to be its experience of colonial rule and modernity. The 'central issue of the Third World's modern history', he has written, '[is] whether, and in what ways, relations with the advanced industrialised world have promoted or handicapped development'. In effect the question is how non-European economies were subordinated to and distorted by those of the West.[1] In

[1] Irfan Habib, 'Studying a colonial economy—without perceiving colonialism', *MAS* 19, 3 (1985), and 'Potentialities of capitalistic development in the

278

that context have evolved theories of under-development and colonial distortion and misrepresentation which depend equally upon a break between the pre-colonial and colonial periods, and upon teleological expectations of a continuous universal evolution.

In the newer historiography, pre-colonial dynamisms are differently read. An old picture of declining empires superseded by vigorous European powers has been modified by an emphasis upon earlier developments in trade, class formation, even 'proto-capitalism'. According to one version, seventeenth- and eighteenth-century India shared, with a wide band of territories from north Africa to southeast Asia, the experience of increasing monetisation and commercial development. The impulse came from fiscal pressure, the growth of trade and the import of silver, a rise in population, and the extension of consumption due to the emergence of merchant and service elites. The decline of the old empires was related to their failure to accommodate these political and economic developments, which they and inter-regional trade had encouraged—that is, they could not manage local divergence and rivalries, and succumbed to more vigorous regional states involved with and encouraging merchants and commercial development, the growth of towns and urban control of the countryside, the settling of nomadic peoples, the creation of peasantries, the strengthening of local identities and ideologies.[2]

---

economy of Mughal India', *Journal of Economic History* 29 (1969); see also 'The peasant in Indian history', *Social Scientist* 11, 3 (1983), and 'Theories of social change', Riazul Islam memorial lecture, Dhaka, May 1986, for comments on Hegel; this lecture also criticises Dumont, like Ronald Inden in 'Orientalist constructions of colonial knowledge', *MAS* 20, 3 (1986), and stresses the economic role of the Brahmanical view of caste in supporting inequality. C.A. Bayly, 'State and economy in India over seven hundred years', *Economic History Review* 38, 4 (1985), comments on the extent to which Habib has not escaped the assumptions of W.H. Moreland's *Agrarian System of Moslem India* (Cambridge 1929).

[2] C.A. Bayly, *Rulers, Townsmen and Bazaars. North Indian Society in the Age of British Expansion, 1770-1870* (Cambridge 1983). Indian and Western scholars, rejecting any uniform eighteenth-century decline, are re-assessing the role of demand, of merchants and of money supply. See also Frank Perlin, 'Proto-industrialization and pre-colonial South Asia', *Past and Present* 98 (1983), Bayly, 'State and economy', and Sanjay Subrahmanyam, 'Commerce and state power in eighteenth-century India: some reflections', *South Asia Research* 8 (1988), and ed., *Merchants, Markets and the State in Early Modern India* (Delhi 1990). My own view of continuities, in the means of surplus extraction, has been presented in Peter Robb, 'Peasants choices? Indian agriculture and the limits of commercialization in nineteenth-century Bihar',

This new view of the eighteenth-century is important for the nineteenth-century too. Perhaps some common ground *is* beginning to appear. In the 1970s, inheriting a minimalist position on the impact of British rule (set out most starkly by Robert Frykenberg),[3] a large number of studies had already stressed the continuities of dominance in the Indian countryside over the last two or three hundred years.[4] More recently, the key work, among several contributing to revision, has been C.A. Bayly's *Rulers, Townsmen and Bazaars*: its reformed chronology sees Indian economic, political and social forms persisting several decades into the nineteenth. And yet, then, their dynamism was undermined or co-opted by Company rule.[5] Despite an emphasis on continuities, Bayly does not take a minimalist view of colonial impact. Particularly important is his identification of a range of intermediaries (gentry, merchants and agents) whose roles were disrupted or distorted by the developing suzerainty of the British, with their attempted monopoly of force and taxation, their wooing of collaborators, their legal and administrative structures, their withdrawals of patronage. The fate of such people, and their smaller equivalents in the villages, is a subject deserving much closer attention. These ideas raise the possibility (to be explored in this chapter) that the divide we seek, in agrarian conditions, may be located rather later in the nineteenth century than has been supposed.

In addition to this north Indian account, and the Bengal zamindari case to which we turn in a moment, there have been south Indian studies of continuity, in which change is vested in an extension of individual property rights, political organisation and commodity production.[6] Yet another model, most fully presented for Western India, is

---

*Economic History Review* XLV, 1 (1992).

[3] R.E. Frykenberg, *Guntur District, 1788-1848* (Oxford 1965).

[4] See, for example, Dharma Kumar, *Land and Caste in South India* (Cambridge 1965) and 'Landownership and inequality in Madras Presidency: 1853-4 to 1946-7', *IESHR* 12, 3 (1975) and also *CEHI*; Tom Kessinger, *Vilyatpur 1848-1968* (Berkeley 1974); Eric Stokes, *The Peasant and the Raj* (Cambridge 1978), especially ch. 9. Habib arguably traces the inequalities further, in 'The peasant in Indian history', and 'Social distribution of landed property in pre-British India: a historical survey' in *Essays in Indian History. Towards a Marxist Perception* (New Delhi 1995) (which also collects versions of some of the other essays mentioned here).

[5] For another early nineteenth-century undermining of the compact between state and peasant elites or village officials, see *inter alia* Neil Charlesworth, *Peasants and Imperial Rule* (Cambridge 1985), p.25.

[6] See David Ludden, *Peasant History in South India* (Princeton 1985). In

based on a persistence or rise of the 'rich peasant'.[7] More contro-
versially, according to some schools of thought (in this respect taking a
lead from Morris D. Morris), the nineteenth century did not see a
general impoverishment of the agricultural sector, due to excessive taxation, economic subordination and demographic increase, but rather,
until about 1920, the rise of new rural elites alongside extensions of
cultivation, profits from commercialisation, and sluggish population
growth—albeit because of periodically high death-rates.[8] Even such
partly optimistic views of the colonial period, too much for many to
stomach, suggest at least that there may have been a differential impact,
as also has been increasingly argued. That possibility too may be
explored in regard to the 1885 Tenancy Act.

In face of Habib's assertion that *colonialism* must be studied—
meaning that its evils should be pilloried—the reply is that it is
necessary first to appreciate what colonialism was. Historians of British
India still engage in controversies which parallel those of the administrators themselves: both arise from interpretations of Indian society
which tend to differ according to the region and the period of the
interpreter's first experience. Certain assumptions in these debates seem

---

comparison with Bayly's study, this may be thought to proceed from a different
model of local power, one derived less from office under the state, than from
function within the society (expressed as caste). The one stresses a new kind of
intermediary class; the other the persistence of old politico-cultural elites. The
models are however complementary, together offering a new perspective on
their period. See also C. J. Baker, *An Indian Rural Economy 1880-1955: The
Tamilnad Countryside* (Oxford 1984); Tsukasa Mizushima, 'The mirasi system
and local society in pre-colonial South India', in P. Robb, K. Sugihara and H.
Yanagisawa, eds., *Local Agrarian Societies in Colonial India. Japanese
Perspectives* (Richmond, Surrey 1996), and essays by Ludden, B. Hjelje and S.
& C. Sivakumar in Robb, ed., *Meanings of Agriculture. Essays in South Asian
History and Economics* (Delhi 1996).

[7] See Ravinder Kumar, *Western India in the Nineteenth Century* (London
1968), Sumit Guha, *The Agrarian Economy of the Bombay Deccan, 1818-1941*
(Delhi 1985), and Charlesworth, *Peasants and Imperial Rule.*

[8] See Morris D. Morris, 'Towards a reinterpretation of nineteenth-century
economic history', *IESHR* 5, 1 (1968) and Neil Charlesworth, *British Rule and
the Indian Economy, 1800-1914* (London 1982) and *Peasants and Imperial
Rule.* Contrast this, however, with the large literature on Indian famines—that
is, from Naoroji and Datta to B. M. Bhatia, *Famines in India* (London 1967),
though not the meliorist reinterpretations of Michele Burge McAlpin, *Subject to
Famine* (Princeton 1983)—or with the evidence of the worsening man:land ra-
tios from the 1870s; see, for example, Rajat K. Ray, 'The crisis of Bengal agriculture 1870-1927', *IESHR* 10, 3 (1973).

little improved upon those made by British administrators when they reflected upon the success of their 'civilising mission'. Our understanding has been impeded by the detritus of two hundred years' theorising. The historical revisions call for a new take on some of the old issues. How central and radical was the influence of foreign government? Or how 'British' was British rule? (This book has considered how far the state was 'rationalist' in its agrarian policies.) Did *classes* of people benefit or suffer? It seems that British interventions were complex and significant. The colonial state inherited and continued much; many of its policies were influenced by Indian demands or expectations; moreover, as it gained a fuller capacity to intervene, so it qualified its initial enthusiasm for the universal 'laws' of political economy. Nonetheless the Indian state operated, during the nineteenth century, in a new and unfamiliar world, one being created by generalised categories, world-wide markets, and state economic and social policies or developmental ambitions. Colonial representations matter because they indicate the direction of this change.

Let us apply some of this thinking to the land question in Bengal, a subject which has also seen recent revision. We have noted already that the zamindari settlement has undergone many bouleversements in popular esteem, being variously regarded as a damaging and fruitless application of aristocratic prejudice, or alternatively, in its creation of a moderately taxed landed interest in conformity with Indian custom, as a model which other revenue systems might copy. Ideas of its effects on zamindars have undergone some modification since Metcalfe's and Mill's ringing denunciations—it is now not thought that quite 'the whole of the landed property of the country' was 'transferred from the class of people entitled to it, to a set of Baboos who have made their wealth by bribery and corruption'.[9]

The long line of arguments and counter-arguments about Bengal land rights began when Philip Francis assumed state ownership but accepted that land was 'the hereditary property of the zemindar', or when the anti-feudal Thomas Law condemned the raiyat as a 'vassal' and hoped prosperity might flow from a fixed land-tax.[10] The common claim has been with Charles Grant in the Fifth Report, that zamindars were 'merely...farmers-general...for annual rents'; the reason given was that they had evolved, Darwinian fashion, by displacing or absorbing

[9] James Mill, *The History of British India* (5th edn., by H.H. Wilson; London 1858), vol.V. Book VI, ch.V.

[10] See Guha, *Rule of Property*, pp.175-86 and passim.

the privileges of original village communities, of 'the poor but lawful hereditary possessors of the land', in Metcalfe's memorable phrase.[11] Metcalfe's minute of 1815 is still probably the most influential view, though one transmitted to more recent times partly by the medium of the great rent law debate. With so many of his successors, Metcalfe rejected the permanent settlement and its 'applied English ideas', and recommended instead the interests of cultivators—in his case settlements with the peasant proprietors he had found in north-west India. So too historians have held that the permanent settlement confiscated the quasi-property rights of cultivators, and encouraged their exploitation by layer upon layer of rentier classes.

The recent, differentiated picture of eighteenth-century India contrasts with these ideas. In place of a picture of landlords newly created by Company fiat, it may be suggested that local elites, though long created from both inside and outside local communities, needed external connections even in pre-colonial times. Given relatively fluid social conditions and limited economic opportunities, elites persisted through office, revenue-collection, ritual status; as military chiefs, creditors, traders. By such alliances were larger polities and economies created. In the Company's India, too, similar local and middling people benefited, as agents and allies, proliferating as a kind of petite bourgeoisie— local zamindars, village heads, small traders, bankers and brokers, dispersed over the countryside—to the extent that there was no general concentration of power and wealth. Indian local communities, once continually negotiated, existing in present time, *were* increasingly riven by general classes, supposedly fixed, persistent, and also exclusive rather than inclusive. But the process was gradual, and should not be assumed in analysing the society. Otherwise we merely continue contemporary debates, examining some questions more thoroughly than others, and describe intellectual as much as social or economic history.

Ignoring continuities, the old arguments have infected assessments of the permanent settlement. In particular, ancient origins are supposed to define not only the justice but also the impact of a modern innovation. The origins of rights *do* have significance. Baden-Powell, for

---

[11] See the discussion in Arthur Philips, *The Law Relating to the Land Tenures of Lower Bengal* (Calcutta 1876), pp.95-6; John William Kaye, *Selections from the Papers of Lord Metcalfe* (London 1855): 'in India there never has been a body of private land-holders possessing great estates'; K.N. Venkatasubba Sastri, *The Munro System of British Statesmanship in India* (Mysore 1939), p.23.

example, insisted on the original distinction between the 'occupancy' tenure of the raiyatwari village, and the 'proprietary' tenure of the various kinds of joint-village and then provided an eloquent passage on the practical importance of these differences.[12] Probably colonialism created as much 'tradition' as 'modernity'. But the permanent settlement should not be assessed as if only such considerations mattered. General presumptions imply externally-constructed categories—fallible constructions, revealed when administrators found cultivators slower to respond to changes in economic conditions than Metcalfe had expected, or saw the political dangers in land transfer. Similarly, if the Company could do little for the raiyats for want of capacity as much as will, did it follow that the effect of British rule was to worsen the raiyats' lot? The accepted view—that it was—depends implicitly on inevitable evolution and on general but new socio-economic forces.

More recent refinement of ideas has taken into account other revisions of interpretation, and produced a corresponding shift in assessments of the Tenancy Acts. It is suggested that 1793 did not necessarily reduce old 'owner-peasants' uniformly to 'wretched tenants-at-will': a substantial body of opinion has found itself close to the modified verdict reached by W.W. Hunter from manuscript records and under the influence of the great rent law debates, a verdict taken up in large part also by Baden-Powell.[13] Hunter concluded that Regulation I of 1793 was part of a systematic attempt to select the best aspects of Indian custom and British law, and to sacrifice future direct revenue in order to bring the country under full cultivation. As we have seen, he criticised the system for trying to give legal precision to uncertain and conflicting rights, and for reducing the complex and varied status of the zamindar to one uniform rule. He argued that dislocation for zamindars was caused firstly by the need to pay the revenue punctually when they had difficulty collecting rents, and secondly (after new laws had streng-

[12] B.H. Baden-Powell, *The Indian Village Community* (London 1896), pp. 423-45. Sociological functionalism had Indian origins too!

[13] See *CEHI*, p.86 ff.; W.W. Hunter, 'A dissertation on landed property and land rights in Bengal at the end of the eighteenth century', in *Bengal Ms. Records*, vol.1 (London 1894); B.H. Baden-Powell, *Land-Systems of British India*, vol.1 (Oxford 1892), pp.398-442 and 500-640. The most original modern examination is Ratnalekha Ray, *Change in Bengal Agrarian Society* (New Delhi 1979). See also, for an account which tends rather to generalise change but which has useful details, not least on zamindari lifestyle, Sirajul Islam, *The Permanent Settlement in Bengal. A Study of its Operation, 1790-1819* (Dhaka 1979).

thened their hand and raised the value of their property) by the right to mortgage estates in circumstances in which the courts were bound to enforce the actual debt regardless of equity.

We may go further than Hunter's analysis; despite it, the pernicious influence of the zamindari settlement on tenant rights has not been seriously questioned. Reactions are still usually hostile, perhaps because of an intellectual and political legacy of rhetoric against landlords and aristocracy, and because the areas to which the settlement applied have recently remained stubbornly poor and 'backward' in agriculture. The hostility means that in some respects, despite much revisionist research, the balance is still tilted towards those who regard 1793 as a decisive break. This view supports in turn the contention that economic development was stifled in Bengal—on the one hand because (after an initial upheaval in which 'traditional' families were replaced) the rent-receivers had easy profits without having to invest in agricultural improvement or even to maintain productivity,[14] and on the other hand because the peasants were impoverished, at the mercy of their overlords or the mahajan, unable to stimulate either agriculture or effective demand. In this context the tenancy legislation of the later nineteenth century was initially treated as a belated redressing of the balance.

Other current views effectively relocate the discarded generalisations about 1793 on to the 1885 Act. The consensus is growing that the Act extended to a middling class the benefits originally provided to the landlords, and thus progressively impoverished the majority. This school of thought points in particular to transfers of raiyats' holdings and a supposedly consequential increase in the proportion of landless labourers. The result is described as 'depeasantisation', that is, a reduction in the proportion of the agriculturists engaged in family-farm production.[15] The implication, which we need to pursue, is that such

---

[14] See the similar argument in P. Robb, 'State, peasant and moneylender in late nineteenth-century Bihar' in Robb (ed.), *Rural India* (London, 1983; Delhi 1992). For the eighteenth century see Ranajit Guha, *A Rule of Property for Bengal* (Paris 1963; New Delhi 1982).

[15] See Binay Bishen Chaudhuri, 'The process of depeasantization in Bengal and Bihar, 1885-1947', *Indian Historical Review* 2 (1975). The argument is that some peasants but in the main non-cultivators gained the land lost by small-holders through indebtedness and land transfer. For a recent application of these ideas see Asok Sen, Partha Chatterjee and Saugata Mukherji, *Perspectives in Social Sciences 2. Three Studies on the Agrarian Structure of Bengal 1850-1947* (Delhi 1982), for example pp.10, 21, 28, 114-22, 146-63 and 231-3. See also *CEHI*, ch.VI.

conditions had not been created until after the 1880s. The analysis centres on land control, thus justifying and confirming the attention given to tenancy legislation, but it is also complementary to the trade and occupation-centred theories of 'forced commercialisation' and 'deindustrialisation', latterly associated with an earlier period.[16] The chronology implied in such accounts throws up some puzzles.

The processes allegedly swelled the ranks of agricultural workers. Thus, where once the product of British law and administration was a uniformly downtrodden peasantry, it is now being seen as a mass of bonded and landless labourers. This has to be reconciled with the picture of a strongly differentiated pre-colonial society. The extent of the nineteenth-century change also remains ambiguous—such polarisations as occurred cannot be measured on a statistical basis: in 1900 as in 1800 some of the agriculturists were landless and some, effectively without land, were technically tenants. The debate about the condition of the peasantry is difficult to resolve, as the evidence is contradictory and evenly divided. The factual miasma on which generalisations have been based is shown in two recent essays. One endorses the depeasantisation thesis while admitting that it is impossible to show any increase in the proportion of landless labourers in the rural population;[17] the other remarks on the imprecision of the familiar assertions about 'subinfeudation' in Bengal.[18]

The links between the great minutes and measures of state, and

---

[16] See notes 22 and 25 below; Daniel Thorner, 'De-industrialization in India, 1881-1931', in D. and A. Thorner, *Land and Labour in India* (Bombay 1962); A.K. Bagchi, 'De-industrialization in Gangetic Bihar, 1809-1901', in Barun De (ed.), *Essays in Honour of Professor S.C. Sarkar*, and 'De-industrialization in India in the nineteenth century', *Journal of Development Studies* 12 (1976); the debate in *IESHR* 16 (1979); Partha Chatterjee, 'Agrarian relations and politics in Bengal: some considerations on the making of the Tenancy Act Amendment 1928', Centre for Studies in Social Sciences Occasional Paper 30 (Calcutta 1980); Tirthankar Roy (ed.), *Cloth and Commerce. Textiles in Colonial India* (New Delhi 1996).

[17] Willem van Schendel and Aminul Haque Faraizi, *Rural Labourers in Bengal 1880-1980* (Rotterdam, 1984), pp.5-6, 21 and 27-40. At p.40: 'The proportion of labourers declined, if anything.' The unreality of some data on this subject is shown by the 1891 census which gives figures of around one per cent for field labourers in North Bihar; estimates at settlement show that between one-fifth and one-third of agriculturists had insufficient land to support themselves, and perhaps half of all families could not avoid some labour for others.

[18] M. Mafakharul Islam, 'Some aspects of the problem of subinfeudation in undivided Bengal', *IESHR* 20 (1983).

British understandings of Indian conditions, have had the most authoritative exegesis.[19] But the practical or empirical issues have not been as well examined as the intellectual. Here too the eighteenth-century background may be helpful. New interpretations make it clear that, in eighteenth-century Bengal, local power was derived both from below and from above—that is, from one's standing with followers or with the state—and that the relative importance of each support changed over time. In the Bengal region the role of the Mughal state, though stronger overall in the seventeenth than in the eighteenth centuries, also varied from place to place. It was generally stronger, for example, in south Bihar and weaker in the north. The increasing independence of Bengal *subah* during the eighteenth century may appear from outside to be an assertion of regional dynamism, but it depended itself on accommodation to varying degrees with more local forces, and sometimes (as Robert Clive understood only too well) with combinations which competed for control of the *subah* as a whole.

Secondly, the changes of the eighteenth century seem to have been attributable not so much to trade and urbanisation—which in any case in this area were latterly more associated with European intervention than endogenous development—as to two seemingly contradictory features: the entrenching of local power through the inheritance of offices, and the increase in land revenue mainly to meet military expenditure or tribute.[20] The latter was achieved in part through the increasing use of revenue farmers, which has been noticed in other regions, but the former was allowed for also in the fact that these farmers seem often to have been drawn from the same intermediate elites who had been consolidating their local position. Indeed, the inheritance of land rights was in one sense a reversion, in style and quite frequently in personnel as well, to a local power-brokerage, resting on control of followers, social prestige and so on, which had preceded and then co-existed with the Mughal system. The farming of revenue thus represents not so much the breakdown of the system as a new means of maintaining the old

[19] See N. Bhattacharya's useful discussion, 'Colonial state and agrarian society' in S. Bhattacharya, *et al.*, *Situating Indian History* (Delhi 1986), and E.T. Stokes, *The English Utilitarians and India* (Oxford 1959), and 'The land revenue system of the North-Western Provinces and Bombay Deccan (1830-1860): ideology and the official mind', in C.H. Philips and M.D. Wainwright, eds., *Indian Society and the Beginnings of Modernisation, c.1830-1860* (London 1976); and Guha, *Rule of Property*.

[20] Habib, 'Potentialities', refers to an economic transformed into a political crisis.

relationship between the local elites and the state, one in which the nature of the transaction, as a bargain between parties, had become overt, instead of being, as it once was, subsumed under codes of law and administration, an order apparently imposed on the countryside from outside. By a similar argument, evidently there were also elements of the indigenous and of continuity in the growing power of some nineteenth-century zamindars over their raiyats.

One aspect of common ground, between new interpretations of the eighteenth and nineteenth centuries, concerns production and consumption. It must be the case that more surplus was extracted and that this allowed the growth of expenditure upon warfare, government and items of trade, at all levels of power. It is clearly true too that this activity implied a greater interest of the state and other holders of power in commercial production and trade as a necessary part of maintaining and strengthening their position. Indeed, in Bengal, such activities—and special tenures and concessions to encourage forest clearance and land reclamation—may be traced much further back, to at least the end of the sixteenth century: the continual movement eastwards of the river systems enabled and attracted the endeavours of what Richard Eaton calls 'Muslim religious gentry', either independently or in alliance with Hindu bankers or with revenue officials.[21] The rivers continued to require adaptive developers, to the present day, though the primary motive gradually changed from revenue extraction in support of political interests towards the securing of commercial production for the profit of merchants. Other recent research on eighteenth-century Bengal has stressed a (consequential?) vitality of regional trade, especially in rice, in addition to the increased commercial production of export crops.[22] From mid-century too, Bengal had formed part of wider systems: tribute to the Marathas or to the East India Company assisted in increasing the wealth of new or old elites, and of military or administrative expansion, in areas far removed from Bengal. Perhaps it was for this reason, coupled with misfortunes of climate, that the late eigh-

[21] Richard M. Eaton, *The Rise of Islam and the Bengal Frontier* (Berkeley 1993), pp.xxiii-iv and ch.8, especially pp.219-26. He concludes that eastern Bengal experienced unprecedented growth, relating his findings to those of Muzaffar Alam, *The Crisis of Empire in Mughal North India. Awadh and the Punjab, 1707-48* (Delhi 1986) and, on Maharashtra, Andre Wink, *Land and Sovereignty in India* (Cambridge 1986).

[22] For recent accounts see the essays by B.B. Chaudhuri and Rajat Datta in P. Robb, ed., *Meanings of Agriculture. Essays in Indian History and Economics* (Delhi 1996).

teenth-century economic crisis proved so cataclysmic for Bengal and Bihar, in the great famine of 1769-70 and subsequent periods of distress. On the other hand the famine had devastating effects (in several, mainly western parts of the region) both in areas of close control and in those where central power was weak, testifying to the importance of surplus extraction by local elites, as well as that prompted by the state.

What then was new in colonial Bengal; and which elements were built upon old patterns and norms? In a recent study of the eighteenth century as an age of transition, John R. McLane has shown Bengal to have been a fragmented polity, characterised by hierarchical harmony and by conflict.[23] It was undergoing change, in the political sphere, and also socially, particularly among Hindus with the spread of Vaishnavism. The pivots of the political system were the zamindars, hereditary petty rulers, mostly Hindu, possibly non-Bengali, often oppressive, owing their position to the Mughal nawabs but also to local standing. Mughals attempted to penetrate this society, with doctrines of responsibility, accountability and mobilisation, but mostly failed to do so.[24] In Bengal only about one third of the land revenue was alienated to military and other officials as jagirs (compared with four-fifths in Aurangzib's empire as a whole); despite Mughal theory and nawabi efforts, almost all revenue-free and service lands were local and zamindari, not state-sanctioned. In setting the land-revenue demand too there was a paucity of actual measurement. Even Murshid Quli Khan's strong regime, that curbed local power and enforced revenue payment, worked with and through certain zamindars and weakened mansabdari control. Along with the practice of revenue farming this led to the consolidation of powerful zamindars in the mid to late eighteenth century.

The fate of these zamindars under early colonial rule provided an example of the expansion of the state's role. As already suggested, there are two main proposals against which McLane's picture may be compared: one of marked change in the eighteenth century and continuities in the early years of colonial rule, and another in which the

---

[23] John R. McLane, *Land and Local Kingship in Eighteenth-Century Bengal* (Cambridge 1993).

[24] This appears to differ from Eaton's account, but that may be a matter of the level and means of control. Eaton distinguishes between an integration of eastern Bengal into 'the Mughal bureaucracy and ideological framework' which he believes resulted, and an 'ability of officials in Delhi to elicit obedience on the political periphery' which he concedes did not (*Rise of Islam*, pp.311-12).

accession of the East India Company to power is regarded as a sharp break from a more equitable and prosperous past. Obviously assessments of the permanent settlement are one key to this difference. McLane offers an account of developments induced under Company rule from the 1790s, from a society which was already undergoing major change. Despite revenue rates which remained remarkably constant over long periods, there was clearly a rising demand, including nawabi and zamindari *abwabs* (additional cesses), over several decades before Company rule. On the other hand uncertainty and fluidity also seem to have been characteristic of the pre-colonial period, given the variable collections, the lack of land measurement, the uncertainty of records, the weakness of central management, and the incidence of village and intermediaries' fees. Revenue collection depended not so much upon regular system or definite dues as upon power. This situation British rule changed by its legal codes and administration.

McLane tells us that his zamindars had one face that was beneficent, ceremonial, paternal. Thus power rested partly upon legitimacy, reinforced by rituals and patronage, on symbolic, quasi-familial ties not yet replaced by contractual or impersonal relations. Much of this continued under colonial rule. It did not imply a more just, pre-existing society than would later develop. Gifts and reciprocity probably affected most of the rural community to some degree, but they were certainly not enjoyed evenly—or invariably, for we will hardly imagine that the same prominence was accorded to the patronage of religion and learning in reality as in the exhortations of religious and learned texts. The zamindars' other face was coercive and extractive. It seems likely that, even with the stresses and increasing revenue demands of the period, Bengal was relatively prosperous, and, with the probable exception of the period 1790 to 1820, its overall *state* taxation was still relatively low. At the same time, the majority of its cultivators and artisans were consistently poor and weak. Presumably the advances made to weavers and peasants were needed because of their want of capital. Patronage was not the end of the story therefore. Particularly over the lower classes of people, power was evoked as well through force and bodily suffering, which McLane again links interestingly to religious and legal practices, norms and texts. In revenue as in other contexts, pain was inflicted partly to test honour and probity (in this case the true capacity to pay). Similarly, though there were exceptions, trading intermediaries tended to secure produce for sale by coercive means, by debt bondage or socio-political dominance. Such measures imply high levels of surplus extraction, but also, in nawabs as in zamindars, institutional weakness. There were few if any curbs on the rulers' despotic powers, except that they lacked effective means of enforcing their will at a distance or generally (or of punishing the excesses of subordinates). Debt-bondage too, whether or not invented by colonial rule (which seems doubtful), certainly received a major fillip through the expansion of trade. To an extent reinforced by colonial policies, despite theoretical objections and occasional attempts to create 'free' markets, it also revealed the shallow penetration of Western laws and market relations.[25]

On the other hand, the political arrangements were already under strain, as revenue demands increased. Then British rule, which initially adopted many of the same measures, gradually began to revolutionise the basis of local power. As it established individualistic but depersonalised and certain property-rights after 1790, the Company was able to move towards confiscation through enforced land-sales as a means of ensuring revenue payment. The diagnostic role of punishment was replaced by theory, or investigation and measurement, or records. Private sanctions too turned more towards property than person, as the state claimed a monopoly of violent force; interestingly crimes against property also seem to have increased markedly, from a very low level. Similarly the role of patronage was reduced. Although religious and other charity continued to be offered and to bring social prestige, such gestures came, at least for a time, to be dissociated from the mainsprings of political authority. For example, the part played in rural life by revenue-free and service land-grants was curtailed, not least by the increased revenue-take, up to and including that in 1793. As we have seen, the East India Company first attempted to record and regularise such grants, and later sought to bring all land, like all coercion, within the purview of the state. On the other hand it also reduced the number and public role of state accountants and functionaries, through whom the nawabs had sought influence and information to check the zamindars. It interfered through law and the courts, and also by the direct administration of zamindari estates. The Company came to value, court and protect the rajas, and frequently intervened over their succession,

---

[25] Robb, 'Peasants choices?'. Since this chapter was written Bhaskar Mukhopadhyay has shown me his interesting 'Orientalism, genealogy and the writing of history: the idea of resistance to silk filature in eighteenth century Bengal', *Studies in History* 11, 2 n.s. (1995), which attributes the origin of debt-bondage to the Company but, in my view, is not bound to do so by his evidence or for his general argument.

conduct and finances. The Company raised rents, appointed supervisors and sometimes even managed the zamindari lands. It reduced the rajas' own complements of troops, and their village servants and agents.

Some of this marked a transfer of functions to the state. But it also represented, arguably, a concentration of estate management. Power, which had been dispersed, was being focused at fewer points (not necessarily at zamindari level). Its weapons were also changed, most strikingly in the case of the *patni* (or lease-holding) system introduced into some Bengal estates early in the nineteenth century as net rental values improved. By this means, without any need for direct zamindari involvement in production or management, definite rents could be readily collected through intermediaries, on agreements enforced by British courts. This undoubtedly new situation did not change all aspects of agrarian relations. The picture is one in which Bengal's petty rulers reacted with different overlords, including the British, with mixed success but often great ingenuity. As remarked, the Company needed those who survived what McLane calls the 'shake-out' of the period from 1790 to 1820. Their position was aided by new regulations designed to secure their collections, and later by protective interventions such as from the Court of Wards. In the 1830s and 1840s privilege seemed to be being attacked again when revenue-free lands were resumed on to the revenue rolls, but this was done usually at a reduced rate, and only provided the grants were not legitimised by age (by dating from before 1790). Thus, where previous rulers had been ineffective in securing the well-being of the population as a whole, the Company's government was often complicit in its oppression. It actively helped the recognised landholders to coerce the higher rungs of intermediaries, and it reinforced the rent-extracting capacity of its allies, thus infiltrating its power down to the level of the cultivators.

This would seem to reinforce the interpretations which treat the advent of colonial rule as heralding a marked deterioration in the conditions of the cultivators. On the other hand, contrary to several former interpretations, some continuity was also provided in the midst of change in the conditions of the tenantry. As will be discussed in more detail shortly, the new arrangements which depended upon property law clearly could not yet be applied to tenants, for whom modern property rights were not provided in the regulations. And among those who benefited from the changed conditions were certainly many *jotedars* and *mandals* (rich peasants and headmen), as others have noticed. McLane says much less about the lower orders of society than about the zamindars, but it is significant that he finds the peasants high-ly stratified, and also responding in a variety of ways to the changing circumstances. Clearly, a majority in the villages suffered under a long-standing differentiation, and remained subject to the older forms of control, despite the Company's attacks on zamindari courts and criti-cisms of local oppression. We have considered in this book the later extension across the population of the political changes implied for landowners in the permanent settlement, for *patnidars* by regulations of the 1820s, and so on.

Some understanding of the position of the peasants may emerge in regard to the Bengal famine of 1769-70, when there was relatively little violence, compared with the large numbers of *dakaits* (robber gangs) and the rural jacqueries later reported in Bengal, and the crime associ-ated with famines elsewhere in India.[26] First, this may well indicate a society in which powerful lords and intermediaries successfully coerced the population. Even in the nineteenth century very many instances of protest involved the mobilisation of local people by village or local leaders; such is the view of recent work by Shinkichi Taniguchi on this area and period.[27] Second, the relative lack of violence may be a reflection also of a society in which the overlords were able to secure a very large share of the surplus. (There is evidence of extremely high proportions taken as revenue elsewhere in eighteenth-century India too.) This, despite the indications of considerable trade in agricultural produce and the undoubted existence of local markets, as discussed in

[26] McLane (*Land and Local Kingship*) does not exactly dispute the fatalism, or at least the cultural and social expectations, which have often been held to account for a lack of violent protest by the dispossessed in Bengal. Such an assessment would follow from the importance he attributes to ritual and to reli-gious patronage in perpetuating local power, and to the evident creation, through land grants, alliances and appointments, of vested interests at many levels of a hierarchical society, one in which, as Paul Greenough suggested on the Bengal famine of 1943, violence would be internalised from above to those below (*Prosperity and Misery in Modern Bengal: the Famine of 1943-1944*, New York 1982). On the other hand, McLane is uneasy with this explanation because he notes the readiness of rural people to assert themselves and their rights in other contexts. There is room in his portrayal of Bengal to account for this apparent anomaly. In the 1769 famine it seems likely, as he suggests, that there was more variation between areas, a smaller loss of life, and also more migration, than has often been supposed.

[27] See Taniguchi, 'The peasantry of northern Bengal in the late eighteenth century' in Peter Robb, Kaoru Sugihara and Haruka Yanagisawa, eds., *Local Agrarian Societies in Colonial India: Japanese Perspectives* (London 1996).

recent work by Rajat Datta and others, would suggest local societies in which relatively little grain was stored and very few commodities purchased from outside. Even the families of dependants and landless labourers characteristically had tiny plots and local common or forest resources to provide or augment their food supply. Their concern was subsistence not profit. This implies a world in which brokers and coercion would be needed to extract the 'surplus', a world of local transactions that were but little monetised, despite the apparent collection of taxes and dues in cash (the necessary medium for the extraction and exchange of surplus outside the localities, for transfers from the many village to the few large urban markets). In such a world, with small local stocks and little experience of obtaining subsistence from outside, a lack of famine violence against local holders of power would not be surprising. In 1769 there may well have been incidents and *dakaiti* against outsiders or traders moving grain in boats or bullock-trains, as later in north Indian famines.

A further issue is how far the situation differed in Bihar from the more fully discussed case of Bengal. C.J. Stevenson-Moore, examining records in Muzaffarpur, concluded that the settlement there *prevented* a distortion of the zamindars' role. He argued that it was impossible to apply in north Bihar the orthodoxies that, in the permanent settlement,

the Government did not know what it gave nor the proprietors what they received; that...the assessment was very unequal; that settlements were largely made with persons who had no hereditary interest in the soil, that an enormous number of estates, especially the larger ones, changed hands owing to the stringency of the revenue sales law, and that the attempt to substitute 'contract' for 'status' failed, leaving the raiyats utterly unprotected.

On the contrary, and this is a view which must command respect, in north Bihar the assessment was fairly accurate, was worked out estate-by-estate from effective patwari records (therefore, we may think, conforming at least with the existing distribution of power), and was made with zamindars who had virtually abandoned their rights in favour of the government's amils. Thus it restored to the original proprietors what they had been about to lose.[28] Here Stevenson-Moore differs from

[28] See Muzaffarpur SR, pp.27-8. Though Bihar conditions were very varied, this able and intelligent Report set the pattern for others on Bihar and to that extent may be regarded as typical and even authoritative; therefore, in the interests of space, this chapter will focus on that district and, unless otherwise stated, that Report (without further references). See also Chittabrata Palit, *Tensions in Bengal Rural Society. Landlords, Planters and Colonial Rule* (Calcutta

Hunter's view on Bengal proper, previously discussed. However they agree that the failure to fix rents at the same time as revenue, and the destruction of the government's local agency, seriously prejudiced the rights of the tenants. Can this have been true both where old zamindars were preserved and where they were replaced?

Harmony replaced by repression leading to landlessness: this picture of two centuries of agrarian decline no longer quite fits, or helps us understand the 1885 Act. Key features must be tenure and rent, two means whereby patterns of land control could change. But most interpretations were linked to advocacy of policy; the peasantry 'suffers' in recent accounts just as in the rationale for the legislation of 1885. This is unsatisfactory. While the Act reduced complexities to a uniform rule, the record was much more ambiguous. In the 1820s the Tirhut Collector could not detect rights for any tenants in regard to rents; a little earlier in an estate in Shahabad only the intervention of the courts had debarred the raiyats' claim to fixed rents after five years' tenure. In Purnea, Buchanan thought tenants' (though not labourers') conditions improving.[29] Yet we can be given a picture, as by one writer, in which zamindars were both oppressive and inefficient, raiyats both downtrodden and evasive or even riotous, and government both trying to check abuses and causing them by the revenue demand; a picture in which the courts were ineffective and yet tenants suffered greatly as a result of the land laws, and in which the raiyats' lot 'rather worsened' while the 'great majority...remained as indigent and destitute as before'.[30]

---

1975), which concludes that zamindars were chosen for the settlement as the 'cheapest, the safest and the smallest' available agency, and minimises both its novelty and impact with regard to Bengal proper. Manoshi Mitra, *Agrarian Social Structure. Continuity and Change in Bihar, 1786-1820* (Delhi 1985) agrees that the settlement, though it led to change, did not involve drastic revisions of the landholding pattern. The return to local people is also noted by Girish Mishra, *Agrarian Problems of Permanent Settlement. A Case Study of Champaran* (New Delhi 1978).

[29] Francis Buchanan (Hamilton), *An Account of the District of Shahabad in 1812-1813* (Patna 1934), p.348, and *An Account of the District of Purnea in 1809-1810* (ed. V.H. Jackson, Patna 1928), p.436.

[30] Ram Narain Sinha, *Bihar Tenantry, 1783-1833* (Bombay 1968), pp.23-7, 29, 121, 147-9. (Quotations italicised in original.) The confusion, which extends to the patwaris (pp.73-4), occurs in spite of an unexceptionable conclusion, that 'the slowness of the administration, mistakes committed by the authorities, and the greater attention paid to other aspects of the land revenue policy, stood in the way of betterment of the raiyats' conditions' (pp.148-9).

The temptation obvious in much contemporary and more recent writing is to assume that change occurred. Thus we are told that after the permanent settlement there was an increase in the exploitation of the poor by the 'dishonest, unscrupulous' superior raiyats, the ashraf, and that the disappearance of the kunungos placed the cultivators almost entirely at 'the mercy of the zemindars'.[31] Similarly, Buchanan's journal, kept while writing his report on Shahabad, seems to paint a vivid picture of areas in decline. We find accounts of deserted villages, rapidly increasing plantations, neglected reservoirs, burnt-up thickets where rice once grew.[32] The account is riven through with an unspoken idea of a more prosperous past—not just a reflection of the immediate stress of several years of scarce rains. Yet there is nothing in Buchanan's account to indicate that partial and shifting land use was not the norm, or indeed to rule out the promise, in pockets of prosperity, of improvements to come. These difficulties of interpretation apply just as much over the nineteenth-century as a whole as for the immediate impact of the permanent settlement. However, having analysed some new views of pre-colonial conditions *and* the nineteenth-century debate on tenancy, we should be well placed to go beyond the conflicting positions adopted by its protagonists.

II

One of the conclusions of chapter two was that the capacity of the administration remained limited in the earlier nineteenth century. We may now apply that conclusion in more detail to the question of colonial influence on agrarian relations. A government which administered with difficulty was not very likely to make major changes in society even by inadvertence. Of course there were positive actions even at the start of the nineteenth century, but they tended to be isolated and their results not immediate—for example embankments were started, as in north Bihar on the Gandak in 1801 (re-aligned in 1830) or on the Bagmati after 1810. Perhaps physical engineering was bound to prove easier than social. Secondly, the ignorance of the ruler was a time-honoured defence of local interests in India. At this time it was not only jealously but rather easily preserved. Buchanan, looking at Arrah, esti-

[31] Ibid., pp.85, 146 and 148.
[32] Buchanan, *Journal Kept during the Survey of the District of Shahabad, 1812-1813* (ed. C.E.A.W. Oldham, Patna 1926), for example, 18, 23 and 29 November and 3, 26 and 28 December 1812.

mated that nearly 15 per cent of the holdings must be revenue-free, but the people had admitted to only ten per cent; in Behea he suspected eight per cent but had been told three. The people wanted to conceal as much as possible and of course had succeeded as far as the official record was concerned. The result was that government could move the society only at the points where it was willing to coerce, with violence if necessary, or where its measures coincided with Indian interests.

One of the issues, even in considering the evolution of agrarian conditions for the majority, must be the fate of the zamindars after 1793. If tenants were to be seriously affected by a settlement, it would have to have put a strain on landlords. Apart from dispossession at the outset, on which we have just considered Stevenson-Moore's testimony, pressure would mainly have been felt through the manner and rate of assessment. In north Bihar the charge of over-assessment can hardly be substantiated. The area had paid little since Mughal times and had only a third of Bihar's liability under Muhammad Reza Khan. The permanent settlement perpetuated the disparity, only about 40 per cent of Tirhut even being assessed. Four per cent of estates were advertised for sale in 1793, not very significantly more than in 1792, and the proportion remained about the same in later years; 54 estates were sold in 1801, 112 in 1802 and 19 in 1803, after which the numbers became insignificant. And very few of these early sales were even alleged to be due to over-assessment. By 1799 most of the arrears concerned farmed or *khas mahals*. Collectors, until forbidden to do so, tended to sell even tiny portions of estates to meet the actual arrears, thus increasing their own work but reducing its impact on society. Later there was some reduction in the *jama* (revenue demand; in Tirhut for example from Rs.1,310,611 in 1801-2 and Rs.1,357,426 in 1802-3, to Rs.1,258,828 in 1803-4), but it would be unwise to deduce a general over-assessment by the ten per cent the figures suggest, because the reductions were mainly on individual estates, many of which had lapsed to government for want of purchasers, and were probably carrying an artificially high assessment through fraud. Certainly the prices at sales were initially low, but by about 1825, as the value of land increased, they had levelled out at between twelve and sixteen times the *jama*, where they were to remain for some fifty years.

Even in south Bihar the burden of revenue does not seem to have been generally prohibitive. There too British control may be supposed to have arrested change to the extent that the country had fallen into 'predatory anarchy' after being plundered by Marathas.[33] Buchanan did report complaints that the rate was too high, but he concluded that the main cause of difficulty, in Shahabad for example, was once again that 'sufficient precautions were not taken to secure the public interest in divisions of property among heirs, or in cases of private sale'. He reported that many proprietors, 'under the guidance of two great bankers, procured unequal distributions of the revenue on different shares of their estates, and having alienated or separated the good parts, allowed those which thus became overassessed to be sold for arrears'.[34] Buchanan was hardly a neutral observer, believing as he did that too low a rate disadvantaged agriculture and even landlords; but he also discovered that any estates offered for sale were being avidly bought, even at an inflated *jama*. That is a surer indication, at least that any over-assessment was short-lived.

The complicated picture continues once we turn to smaller areas or individual estates. The detailed estimates of Buchanan on the large estates in Shahabad suggest that the revenue demand accounted for between a quarter and a half of the rentals, but this was after considerable extension of cultivation. Thus Arrah, which paid Rs.164,000, had rents which Buchanan estimated at Rs.430,000 with the land fully occupied. But rents had been raised, and changed from produce to money; in 1793 almost half the land was said to have been waste, and, if rents were also lower, the assessment must have been very high indeed. Also apparently over-assessed were the high lands of Sassaram and Chainpur, where many holdings had fallen to government for want of purchasers. It is more difficult to decide whether there was much over-assessment, however, from the point of view of what was likely to affect tenants. The impact of assessment rates was manifestly varied. Arrah and northern Sassaram were prospering in 1810; and in the high lands the estates acquired by government because of uneconomic revenue demands were farmed out again, in Sassaram at a loss of only about Rs.10,000 (or three per cent) on the original settlement. Another area, Danowar, on the other hand, with a low assessment, was in a distressing state, its reservoirs unrepaired, its rice crop lost, and some of its fields abandoned. Buchanan concluded that a high demand encouraged thrift; but at this time agrarian prosperity seems rather to have

---

[33] Francis Buchanan (Hamilton), *An Account of the Districts of Patna and Behar* (Patna n.d.), vol.I, p.269.

[34] Buchanan, *Shahabad*, pp.351-3. The following discussion of Shahabad also draws on this source.

followed the divide between high and low land. There were some individual problems, such as a family feud which led to the destruction of, and the failure to repair, a dam in Chainpur; but repeatedly in Arrah, Behea, Bhojpur, Sassaram and Chainpur neglect or under-utilisation was reported on the high ground dependent on reservoirs (*thikadars* were often blamed), while expansion of cultivation was as regularly discovered wherever land relied on periodic flooding for water and enrichment. Perhaps cultivation was merely shifting. The reason could have been the revenue demand, to the extent that a higher outlay would reduce funds for irrigation works and thus be more damaging where they were essential (though this was not the explanation in Danowar where the main family was that of old kanungos and 'very rich'). Or there may have been some local reduction of population, an incomplete recovery from the setbacks of the late eighteenth century, or (against the general trend) in this district the British may have increased alternative sources of income. Shahabad had a strong tradition of military service, and between 5,000 and 12,000 were involved at the time, remitting home 'as much money as pays the rent of a good farm, upon which their family lives in comfort'. Perhaps shifting cultivation had always been practised on the more marginal lands, or the relative certainty of the British revenue system may have reduced advantages of cultivating the higher estates, which had existed in days of more doubtful and incomplete collections and of more violent rivalry for property.

The picture is equally uncertain with regard to the transfer of property rights, which is usually considered second only to over-assessment as a cause of rural problems. Seldom can the revenue demand be clearly blamed for the sale of land. Buchanan encountered one notable apparently at crisis point—Sahebzada Singha, an important zamindar in the northern parts of Shahabad district. He was a 'great favourite' with his tenants and farmers, and, even though they were said to be 'deeply in arrears', would never extract money by force or legal process. But he had quarrelled with his high-caste *amla*. They had then put up a pretender to his estates and involved him in a protracted law suit. He had won, and afterwards employed only Kurmis and Dusadhs, but was supposed to owe Rs.350,000, which cost him about Rs.60,000 a year. His life-style did not change. He was still interested mainly in hunting, and maintained a personal staff of 350, feeding a hundred from his own kitchens. But obviously he was in danger of losing to his creditors the property he had defended in the courts.

The pressures on landlords may also be illustrated from the situation in Chainpur. The area had once been dominated by Chaubhan Rajputs, but was usurped by, in turn, military Brahmans (alleged to originate near Agra), Pathans from Sassaram, including Rajput converts, and the Rajkumars, an illegitimate line of the Chaubhan descendants, and the clan which provided the Rajas in the late eighteenth century. The family suffered from the encroachment by the Raja of Banaras, and also became indebted to a Muslim who gained possession of eleven of their seventeen revenue-free *mauzas* after suit before the Collector at Patna. The Rajkumars then fomented violence among their former tenants, the new proprietor was killed, the Raja fled, and, afraid that his son would be punished in his place, the family forged proof that he had had no heirs. Unfortunately this meant that the estate fell to the government. The rents were farmed out, and, when the lease came up for renewal after ten years, the son put in a claim but was dismissed as an imposter. The remaining six revenue-free *mauzas* were awarded to an official to pay his alleged costs in searching for the Raja, but the son later sued the heirs of the murdered man and recovered possession of the eleven *mauzas* which had been lost. By this time most of the Raja's kinsmen had alienated their lands to bankers, and the largest estate in Chainpur still in the hands of a long-established family was one of 55 *mauzas* belonging to the head of a clan of Parihar Rajputs (or Bhars). The chief proprietor of the area was now a banker from Patna, and another from Arrah also held considerable lands; both had obtained their property, it was said, as nominal transfers from others who had kept only over-assessed lands later to be sold for arrears. They had presumably adopted this ploy at a time when the British Collectors were still likely to sell several of a proprietor's estates to cover a deficit in one of them. It had subsequently turned sour because the bankers refused to give up the formal title which had been transferred to them and which had gained unexpected significance in the legalistic system of the new rulers. However this may be, at least one such proprietor still lived and was regarded as the owner of lands which ostensibly he farmed for one of the bankers. Thus a more probable explanation for the extent of the bankers' holdings may well be that they had foreclosed on favourably-assessed *mauzas* to meet the proprietors' debts. Buchanan was told that local landowners never paid revenue unless coerced by soldiers or the collector's presence on the threshing floor. The permanent settlement at first seemed to remove even these rare inconveniences; but when arrears built up and had to be cleared, the owners were forced to borrow and in the end lost their property.

This account reveals the complicated origins of any rural disloca-tion. Sahebzada Singha's problems were the creation of local and personal factors, and were influenced by British rule only to the extent of the existence of the courts and perhaps the inappropriateness of his easy-going ways. The Rajkumars stood at the end of a line of usurpers which greatly pre-dated the British, though their difficulties also derived partly from an attempt to work to their own advantage a new order which they imperfectly understood. The other Chainpur propri-etors may also have failed to adjust to the more rigid law and accoun-ting of the British, but it is difficult to see the bankers—who here, as also in north Bihar at this time, seem to have been investors rather than speculators in land—other than as the latest in a succession of outsiders who had gained an interest in the area. And the new weapons they used were not exclusive to them—the Raja of Chainpur's son also went to law to recover some of his family's land. It seems certain that over-assessment, however much the locals complained of it, and indeed the imposition of British rule, were not consistent or necessary factors in increasing pressure on landlords and indirectly on peasants.

Much of this would also ring true for other important government measures. The social effect of the partition law, for example, is extremely problematic. North Bihar was already known for its multi-tude of proprietors. Thus was a product of inheritance, exacerbated by the law (*mitakshara*) which shared property between father and sons in the father's lifetime, unlike in Bengal proper where the father remained sole proprietor. The widespread institution of *malikana*, or unalienable interests in land, is further evidence of a tradition of partition—at least it is if we may assume that it should be explained in the need to pre-serve residual rights in the family as a whole, for example for unborn sons. In south Bihar too the picture in 1810 is clearly already one of small estates. Buchanan described the 'ashraf', as he called it, as made up of Muslims and high-caste Hindus with 'an abundance of pride', but also such numbers that 'abstinence from manual labour is no longer practicable'. The majority had lands which they cultivated not only on their own account but with their own hands, even in some cases holding the plough; many families had to supplement their income.[35] It is true

[35] Buchanan, *Patna and Behar*, pp.265-6. Even that evil innovation of British rule, the absentee landlord, was manifestly a necessity in much of Bihar with its complexity of landholdings, and, if we are to believe Buchanan, was encouraged by fashion—in Barh Muslim families seemed 'to prefer towns, as they have all landed estates but seldom visit these': *Journal of Francis*

that partition increased as a result of British regulations. In Tirhut for example, whereas fifteen estates had been divided into 33 between 1803 and 1813, in 1815 alone thirteen estates became 75. The upsurge was due to the repeal of the regulation of 1807 which had forbidden partition on estates paying less than Rs.1,000. But, as this reminds us, the law created estates and not proprietors. It seems likely that in the early nineteenth century much of the increase by partition was statistical—that is, it was in the records rather than in the number of co-sharers or even in the arguments between them. In many cases it meant no more than that proprietors were realising the advantages of formalising any divisions of property to avoid continuing joint liability for the revenue. Thus though there were certainly important differences between shared and divided estates, the incidence of partition was probably of greater administrative than social significance in this period.

Perhaps the best test of dislocation under the settlement, particularly for our purposes, would be the demographic evidence. Bihar's population raises further difficult questions of fact. But there was certainly a recovery from the losses of the catastrophic famine of 1769-70 which struck particularly at northern and eastern Bihar as well as some areas of western Bengal. There was probably also a continual growth over the nineteenth century, even if totals cannot be given with any confidence. The first part of the period was one in which tenants were ready and still relatively able to migrate away from oppressive conditions. Even in the late 1830s, for example, in Hooghly, raiyats in *khas mahals* relinquished their lands immediately after a settlement which the government later severely criticised for over-assessment.[36] Buchanan reported that most parts of Patna and Behar were 'as fully occupied as possible';[37] but cultivation still seems to have been extending in the north. In the 1780s the Tirhut Collector had proposed registering *pattas* (the written leases supposed under new regulations to include all rents and *abwabs*) in the face of reports of raiyats fleeing to Nepal to escape the tyranny of the revenue farmers. In 1790, the Collector reported Tirhut (most of north Bihar) as depopulated and devoid of trade. But in 1847 the revenue survey found between 75 and 80 per cent of the land intensively cultivated. All the indications are that Tirhut's population increased steadily under the British: estimates in 1790 and at the per-

---

*Buchanan (Hamilton) Kept during the Survey of the Districts of Patna and Gaya in 1811-1812* (ed. V.H. Jackson, Patna 1925), p.3.

[36] Bengal Revenue Letter, 22 March 1838, L/E/3/41.

[37] Buchanan, *Patna and Behar*, vol.I, p.269.

manent settlement put it at 1,236,309 and 1,244,310, whereas others in 1846 and 1856 suggested 1,637,545 and 1,856,269. All were certainly too low, possibly by as much as a half, but the suggested increase, slightly over five per cent per decade, is a plausible one. It would seem to have applied throughout the century except for a major upsurge (15 per cent, some of it census error) in the 1870s when most of the remaining cultivable land was taken up.[38] By the last quarter of the nineteenth century, reports state that land use had been maximised in most Bihari districts. This was what Buchanan had already claimed for some villages; the fact that the verdict was untrue, in an absolute sense, is now demonstrable in the huge increase in rural population which occurred in the middle decades of the twentieth century. What was undoubtedly the case, however, was that by 1885 the availability of cultivable land had been sharply reduced, by objective demographic and economic factors, in addition to any socio-political restrictions.

This rising population and extending land use may indicate that conditions were not so severe in the earlier parts of the century as they have been painted; the corollary is the potential crisis already discussed in earlier chapters: pressure on the land is usually cited as allowing competitive rents. This suggests that any sharp decline in the conditions of Bihar raiyats should not be attributed to the permanent settlement and the early administration of the East India Company. It implies continuities. One reason for thinking this would be the administrative weakness already discussed. But (as also argued) this did not preclude successful collection of the revenue and gradual encroachments by the state, and therefore, above all, perhaps, the indigenous system may have been protected by its complexity. Thus would the interests of some of the people been maintained. For example, proprietorial rights were multiplied by overlayings from the past, by rival claimants over generations all retaining a stake. In Shahabad, in three neglected estates, the numerous heirs of maliks allegedly ejected just before the permanent settlement (the claim was not upheld in the courts), were still in possession of about one-third of the land, on low rents to 'keep them quiet', when Buchanan observed them. In Arrah, too, *malikana*

---

[38] There are good reasons for suspecting that even the 1871 census may underestimate the totals for North Bihar by as much as 15 or even 20 per cent, an error which would account for much of the presumptive increase of the following three decades. This argument extrapolates from the results of MacDonnell's checks on the census figures in Darbhanga. See W.W. Hunter (ed.), *A Statistical Account of Bengal*, vol.XIII (London 1877), pp.31-6.

was paid to the heirs of original proprietors on revenue-free land, and
the assessed land, divided into 105 lots, was held by feuding clans—in
pre-British days Ujayani Rajputs had seized most of the *mauzas* of the
chief of their old enemies, the Lotimiyas, but members of the latter
family still retained property. Under British rule the usurped lands had
been bought by the local *amil*, and many were still held by his
descendants, though the sales had been disputed and some reversed
after the arrival of the first European Collector. Management too was
extraordinarily complicated. In three-quarters of the cases in Arrah the
rents were farmed to thikadars in lots from Rs.400 to Rs.1,000, though
usually village by village (subsequent division between co-sharers
being made by hereditary patwaris). Sixty per cent of rents were fixed
amounts of money for a term of years, the remainder representing the
rice crops for which rents were calculated as a share of the produce,
though usually paid in cash. In Behea, an estate with 264 lots, mainly in
Ujayani hands, a similar arrangement prevailed, though the thikadari
leases ranged in value from Rs.50 to Rs.10,000, the larger ones being
sub-let. In Bhojpur again, with 78 lots divided between Ujayani and
Peramarka Rajputs and the Jagdispur and Buxar families, three-quarters
of the rents were farmed in leases from Rs.20 to Rs.40,000, though
there were more money rents than at Arrah, especially on high ground.
Different rates were fixed for different crops and no total was stipu-
lated; also, when there were produce rents, there was more actual division of the crop.

The complexity of such arrangements, not just in their details but
even in the more general features, was well known but perhaps not
always remembered in generalisations about the fate of the raiyats
under the permanent settlement. W.W. Hunter himself seems to have
forgotten his own apt phrase about 'the infinite gradation in the rights
of the various classes interested in the land'.[39] We have seen that he
held that the permanent settlement erred, because it was not made to
depend on proper leases for the tenants, and because it did away with
the kanungos, the only effective check on the zamindars. Hunter
supposed that patwaris and with them the village records *became* mere
servants of the zamindar, so that when tenants began to compete for
land they were at the zamindar's mercy. Perhaps this was so; but here
we reach a further point, that the possible continuities in agrarian
conditions in the first century of British rule in Bihar do not rule out a

[39] W.W. Hunter, *The Annals of Rural Bengal* (7th ed.; London 1897), p.373.

life of harsh oppression for many cultivators.

Had there been a golden age when, for example, patwaris behaved otherwise than at the behest of the maliks? In some areas there were consistent reports from the earliest British observation that patwaris were subservient to the landlords and oppressive of the raiyats. Elsewhere the system apparently worked moderately well even in the nineteenth century when reform was supposed to be needed everywhere. In Shahabad we saw patwaris in 1813 still paid wholly by the tenants and to some degree working under the Collector's supervision, at least for appointment or dismissal. The difference between areas may be better explained in the general resilience of local customs, than on one area's immunity from a general decline. Hunter believed that the abolition of kanungos and the subversion of patwaris had the twin result of reducing all raiyats to the position of tenants-at-will, and of perpetuating an unusually disadvantageous situation for resident cultivators, who had fared badly under the pressures of late Mughal rule and the subsequent population decline. Later tenant rights could not be determined; the *patta* system was rejected by the raiyats as merely recording oppressive rents.[40] But this analysis depends on a smoothing-out of the 'infinite gradation', and as such does not fit with the Shahabad conditions: they would seem to reinforce the idea of subtle adjustments in power between sections of the community. This is the impression too (though not the conclusion) given in Buchanan's own report on Purnea: there zamindars acted 'meanly and oppressively' but were also 'ignorant and slothful', apt to be 'grossly defrauded', and likely to 'maintain an enormous army of dependants'. Even the high-caste tenants, who enjoyed low rents, were put at a disadvantage through having to pay for labour and by being generally indolent.[41] This is a situation of checks and balances, not polarities. Here, as also in Tirhut, according to Stevenson-Moore, there would have been little of practical significance in government measures to assist zamindars to collect rents (Regulation VII of 1799) or indeed in measures to mitigate those powers (V of 1812). Much more important were pre-existing local differences and social accommodation and differentiation.[42] These seem to have pro-

[40] See also Sinha, *Bihar Tenantry*, pp.45-51.

[41] Buchanan, *Purnea*, pp.426-50.

[42] This stance is broadly in line with the procedures and conclusions in Ratnalekha Ray, *Change in Bengal Agrarian Society* (New Delhi 1979) and, most usefully for Bihar, Manoshi Mitra, *Agrarian Social Structure*, but differs from others which either adopt the rent-debate rhetoric or are content largely to des-

duced some raiyats who were well able to resist landlords, some landlords who were successful oppressors, and a mass of underprivileged
cultivators and labourers dependant upon such social superiors.

Though Bihari tenants were not generally in a position of strength, it
is uncertain that their position had seriously deteriorated as a consequence or incident of British rule by the middle of the nineteenth
century. It is important to remember how rhetorical was the assertion
that conditions had worsened, how dependent on notions of theoretical
wrongs done in 1793, and how instrumental in the rent-law reforms
being advocated. Even the worsening incidence of famine in the later
nineteenth century was not an objective argument among officials and
polemicists, and does not itself prove a deterioration in underlying poverty. The writer of the *East-India Gazetteer* considered the peasantry
of Behar district more prosperous in 1820 than at the permanent settlement. We need not accept that verdict. We can argue against clear benefits for the raiyats as readily as against their certain dispossession in
1793. Hunter thought that the courts put themselves on the side of the
raiyats from the 1820s, and, presumably for that reason, that large
numbers of tenants 'retained' occupancy rights in 1859. Even if we
could believe in a major role for the courts, with their shortcomings and
in particular their inordinate delays, it would be unconvincing to draw
conclusions from the numbers (however large) who were qualified for a
legal status not established until 1859. Since there had hitherto been
little reason for landlords to prevent the continuous occupation on
which the right depended, the fact that they did not do so says little
about their power over their tenants. On the other hand, we should
attend to the main point behind the verdict of the *Gazetteer* in the
1820s, that whatever the peasant's disabilities in theory or law, in
practice he need not have suffered proportionately at the hands of the
zamindar, since there existed 'reciprocal wants of the parties driving
them to something like an amicable compromise'.[43] It seems improba-
ble that British rule should have seriously altered the balance of those

---

cribe the legal framework; in the former category see several works by Arvind
Das, including *Agrarian Change and Socio-economic Change in Bihar, 1900-
1980* (New Delhi 1983), and in the latter Mishra, *Agrarian Problems*, for example pp.123-37, with which one might compare, say, S.C. Chatterjee, *Bengal
Ryots. Their Rights and Liabilities being an Elementary Treatise on the Law of
Landlord and Tenant* (Calcutta 1864; ed. A.C. Banerjee and B.M. Ghosh, Calcutta and Colombia, Missouri, 1977).

[43] Walter Hamilton, *The East-India Gazetteer...*, vol.I, (2nd edn.; London
[1828]), p.105.

'reciprocal wants', or the strengths and weaknesses of the parties, by 1820. But the 1870s and 1880s—and, even more, the decades after the 1885 Act—may offer quite another picture: the forces of reciprocity were surely being weakened.

## III

It is safe to suppose then that, at first, Bihar retained much of its agrarian structure under colonial rule; north Bihar, relatively little affected by Muslim rule except near the Ganges, was characterised before as well as during British times by the 'old Hindu system' with its strong *jajmani* relationships, its dominant Brahmans and Rajputs, and, controlling the villages, its *jeth raiyats* or patwaris. The south too had long had, and did not suddenly acquire, its proportion of more independent people and its dominant castes and families. It was at the beginning as well as the end of the century, as Buchanan testifies, that sections of the Shahabad tenantry were said to be high-spirited and the atmosphere rather violent; that the numerous Ahirs were thought prone to robbery, and the landlords 'inclined to use force against their neighbours'. Some of these features—it is important to remember—persist to this day, or certainly well into the twentieth century, and thus will qualify the extent not just of Company but of all colonial impact. For a long time continuing circumstances such as these decided relations between landlord and tenant, however great the apparent or legal changes introduced by the British. We will deal with some of these continuities first, before returning to the question of change.

The hallmarks of the society, and of its resilience in the face of external pressure, were the long-persisting complexity and variety already mentioned.[44] The organisation of great estates as productive rather than

[44] The following description draws inter alia on district gazetteers and settlement report for Champaran, Darbhanga, Muzaffarpur, Saran, Shahabad Patna and Gaya districts, on the relevant volumes of Hunter, *Statistical Account*, and the report and evidence volumes of the Bihar and Orissa Provincial Banking Enquiry Committee (Patna 1930) and of the Royal Commission on Agriculture (1928). A related attempt at an overview was included in P. Robb, 'Law and agrarian society', *MAS* 22, 2 (1988), and the subject will be taken up in the proposed second volume of the present study. Some features may be found also in Mitra, *Agrarian Social Structure*, though its time-limit prevents consideration of long-term change or any new situation emerging in the later nineteenth century. See also Jacques Pouchepadass, *Paysans de la plaine du Gange: le district de Champaran, 1860-1950* (Paris 1989), which is easily the most comprehensive and convincing account to date. For a local study, see Arvind Das,

extractive units, through the application of capital and the employment of hired labour, could have evened out the many locally-significant social differences into the wide bands of class. Some instances of this occurring were reported in Bihar. But elsewhere, in the absence of such conditions, and given that most estates and holdings in Bihar were small, large categories could be discerned by outside observers, applying theoretical principles, but they would have been less evident to the participants of the locality than more minute distinctions. Even in the purely economic sense, ecological reality alone enforced tiny and fluctuating variations of fortune. As late as the 1870s a linguistic survey of Bihar could list at least eighty different terms relating to shares in land, in a region with relatively little sub-tenancy. The same survey recorded three different bases for classifying soils, with the result that there were at least fourteen distinctions according to distance from the village, at least seventy according to quality and topography, and perhaps thirty according to use.[45] Many of these distinctions were real, and appreciated by the people: the richness and subtlety of their nomenclature were matched only by their perceptions of essential similarities, the blurring of all distinctions.

This circumstance is of the first importance in considering the impact of colonial tenancy legislation, whenever it was made locally effective. The society to which it was applied was hierarchical but not rigid. Its complexities and ambiguities of status seem to have derived from ecology, custom and time. In some places in Bihar, for example, irrigation works evidently helped decide the tenurial or rental regime, while in other, dry areas money rents prevailed. Some proprietors' control was located in surplus agriculture; and for others their role was rather in opening up new frontiers of cultivation. As a village could export people to farm in different villages, or be taken over by outsiders through fortune, conquest or even purchase, so too one layer of control could be imposed on others. One range of variations was socially-defined: rent might relate to the tenant and not the land, be decided (that is) by caste as well as by soil. There might be distinctions also between actual and ritual employment, and relative power and wealth might be ambiguously reflected in social standing. Great caste-leaders lorded over vast estates, but multitudes of equally high caste vied over

---

'Changel: three centuries of an Indian village', *Journal of Peasant Studies* 15 (1987).

[45] G.A. Grierson, *Behar Peasant Life* (Calcutta 1885), Divisions III and IX.

petty holdings. In addition different roles might be played by the same people simultaneously, or at different times. The web of customs and obligations, moreover, was seldom exclusive to one kind of transaction. All was conditional upon various levels and kinds of power and practice—systems of belief reinforcing subordination, but also rivalries and conflict demanding compromise. Thus the land encompassed multiple and indefinite roles, and rights conditional upon those of others. Above all, agricultural practice varied in response to climate and conditions, both from place to place and from time to time, and generally the differences between people were often small and variable, however much they were also sought to be rationalised and perpetuated. This is contrary to what would be expected if villages were either homogeneous or wholly subordinate and hence levelled down. A result, in economic as in social behaviour, was a high degree of pragmatism, an adjustment to circumstances, very unlike what was encoded in British interpretations with their preference for abstract, absolute principle and certainty.

The imperfections in British categories and statistics do not result solely from unreliable observation and calculation; they are also due to a more substantive difficulty, the genuine variations in Bihar between place and time. In one sense this is merely an argument about the lack of integration, for example in prices, but it is also a reflection of the extent to which in reality there was no fixity of practice. Non-standard and regional measures of land, weight or money are the symptom of a problem which did not simply go away as the nineteenth century progressed. Even the relative importance of the different harvests would vary from year to year, according to climatic exigencies. So too would the fortunes of individual families. There is evidence both of the extreme variability of ranking year-by-year according to any one criterion (outside, that is, of very broad categories), and the conditionality and changing fortunes of particular advantages over time.[46] Behind this idea, may be found an essential ambiguity and multiplicity of roles and functions, especially when they are conceived in European categories: different peoples have different pictures in their minds, and organise themselves according to idiosyncratic principles and concepts. The degree of fluctuation even in a single village should not be underestimated. Even what were apparently the most stable of conditions, the size and relative value of holdings, might be shown to vary markedly

[46] The following discussion is drawn from P. Robb, 'Hierarchy and resources: peasant stratification in late nineteenth-century Bihar', *MAS* 13, 1 (1979), which includes the charts and tables referred to again here.

from one year to the next. A study of one village on a government
estate proved this. Held on produce rents, it was apparently homogeneous in caste (most of the cultivators were named Singh or Jha) and
contained one relatively large landholder, probably the former zamindar
or thikadar. His rental varied from nearly triple to one and three-
quarters times the amount of that of his nearest rival; his area of
cultivation was greater than that of anyone else to similarly fluctuating
(though smaller) degrees. In addition, about twenty holdings were never
larger than five bighas, which was at the time the average area below
which a raiyat would have been very unlikely to have had an effective
surplus for sale. Most of these families must have supplemented their
incomes by service or labour. Outline stratification was straightforward, into 'landlord', 'raiyats' (income from surplus), and 'labourers' (income partly or largely from labour), though the divisions were
not reflected in rates of rent, except very broadly in a tendency for more
of the higher rates to be paid by holdings above the presumed subsistence level in cultivated area. But a similarly precise or stable stratification could not be imposed upon the body of peasants on the basis of
total land cultivated, and total rental paid, considering the more
substantial villagers. Real difficulties began when this 'raiyat' group
was examined more closely. Among this group one was clearly the
most substantial on average, but he was not the biggest rent-payer in all
years. All the other rankings were gradual, and the range very large
(from Rs.22 to Rs.77), so that if we were to identify the 'rich peasants',
say from two to ten in the average rankings, many in that 'group' would
have had more or at least equal affinity with others outside it. This
picture was reinforced by evidence of variations from one year to the
next: in no two years would the groups be the same, whatever the size
or method of division, except for the initial outline, of landowners,
raiyats and labourers. A line might have been drawn between 'surplus'
and 'subsistence' holdings; but there was nothing similar to help distinguish within the surplus group.[47]

Such variation virtually ruled out stratification as a basis for ana-

---

[47] Ibid. The charts were calculated from and the discussion based on enclosures to Stevenson-Moore, Settlement Officer, Muzaffarpur, to the Director of
the Bengal Revenue and Agriculture Department, 12 June 1896, PCR 366,
15/11 (1896/7). The village had 61 holdings, for 44 of which figures are available in full. The calculations discussed here took no account of income from
external or non-agricultural sources, but concentrated on the primary question,
surplus to sell.

lysis within the peasantry, and was not just a matter of occasional mavericks whose fortunes fluctuated wildly, though these too were in evidence. It suggested that different holdings were affected to widely different degrees by the forces which made for fluctations in the output and profitability of the estate as a whole. It must have related to different individual circumstances and decisions, including the allocation of land by village controllers or intermediaries. The same variability was indicated on a regional basis by the fact that the differences in prices between areas in ordinary years could be as great as the difference between the averages of those years and a year of scarcity: some areas had higher but more steady prices, while others, where grain was usually cheaper, suffered from large fluctuations.[48] Such variability does not illustrate the validity of the notion of the egalitarian peasant, as in the village just discussed the leading tenant— the presumably dominant, resident villager—would have been subsumed within the peasantry in most definitions. More importantly the picture presented was of great differentiation at a single time, as much as of a variety of fortunes over time. Statistical summaries would blur either kind of fluctuation. Such variety persisted because it was built into patterns of land-ownership and land-use, into ecology and custom and interests.

The argument here is for something other than random variation. There *were* specialisations. These were probably as old as agriculture itself, if only in what was demanded by the environment and the distinction between wet and dry crops, and by specialist, caste-related occupations and skills. But flexibility implied that labour often did not work rigidly at one occupation: artisans cultivated small patches of land, agriculturists processed crops, and all production reacted to fluctuating demand. Flexibility was reflected too in the complexities of land-holding and employment, and rested ultimately on the variety of the seasons and the range of cultivating possibilities. The consequences are hidden in the records. On the other hand, though practice was various, there were fine and definite distinctions of several kinds. It is sometimes said that before the British helped define and generalise exclusive, ranked and recorded categories in Bengal society, there were among Hindus effectively two categories of people, the Brahmans and the Sudras, priests and workers.[49] But this was to view the society from

[48] An illustration is provided in P. Robb, *Rural India* (1992), p.151.

[49] See Somendra Chandra Nandy, *Life and Times of Cantoo Baboo*, vol.II (Calcutta 1981), p.466.

only one point of view. From other perspectives, it is clear that there were small units defining ritual and occupational status; ranks and types associated with village and other functions; indigenous terms reflecting many different kinds of distinction. The usual word now used to describe these units is 'jati', which, significantly, may be translated as 'type' and used in various senses other than the one pertaining to social rank or sub-caste. Thus there were kinds as well as degrees of 'respectability', and different terms recording leading roles based upon heredity, wealth or personality. This is the sense in which we may understand that there were villagers who were 'resident' by status, and others who were 'non-resident' even though they might in fact live within the territories of the village. (The term 'village' was also misleading: not necessarily a unitary settlement, but a series of related, more or less scattered dwelling areas and fields, the access to which reflected status.)

In each of various aspects of life, a complex of different terms was available to record differences, many of which were only perceivable by insiders. Thus in rural Bihar could be found both a multiplicity of categories and a variety of practice—in land use, employment and income. The consequence being conditionality of status and custom, these had to be generalised by overarching traditions, often fiercely enforced, but also preserved through a range of different sanctions. Relations typically involved mixtures of several kinds—personal, productive and ritual, or social, tenurial and economic. The price of variability seems to have been a more complete or broadly-based control. The village head tended to be high caste, an agent of government or trade, chief employer, social arbiter, dispenser of resources of production, and so on, not only because these roles reinforced one another, but also because such a multiplicity was needed for success in face of the variety and complexity of village life.

We have considered new views of pre-colonial India that imply continuities, discovering in the eighteenth century aspects of agrarian structure and conditions that once were attributed to the impact of colonial rule and the international trade it supposedly first introduced. We have found similar continuities in early colonial Bihar, despite the application of Western property laws and taxation, and have attributed them partly to the complexities and resilience of rural life. But we have also suspected that greater changes *were* beginning to be apparent by the later nineteenth century. To that possibility we now turn—in particular to the impact on agrarian relations of the 1885 Act and the survey and record of rights.

Chapter Ten

*Rents and rights*

Into a milieu of variety and contingency were cast the hard categories
of Western law and government, and a range of external economic
forces associated with the internationalisation of trade and production.
It is the extent to which these forces changed the balance of the agrarian
structure which we have to consider. In particular, we are concerned
with the increased oppression of the raiyats, as shown for example in
greater insecurity of land-rights. The case for a deterioration (as explained already) rested largely on a supposed increase in the burden of
rent after 1793. Emotionally, as we have seen, its basis was that raiyats
had been deprived of property, expressed particularly as the privilege of
paying rent at a rate which the landlord could not change at will and
which was not affected by competition and contract. For some scholars
this seemed enough.[1] Empirically, however, an absolute change of this
nature was insupportable. There *were* customary ideas about rates of
rent, some of which were still evident at the end of the nineteenth century. But each agricultural plot was subject to a recognised 'field rate'
which varied from one plot to another whenever zamindari management was sufficiently close. (On large estates it tended to be merely the
average of the rate for an entire holding.)[2] The tendency of custom, as
this information shows, was towards specific rather than general rates
of rent—rents which changed in accordance with status, soil, crop, and
supply and demand too. Average rent rates certainly differed from place
to place and, less dramatically, between the different categories applied
by the British; but the greatest variations were from village to village
and holding to holding. As already discussed, there was no 'pargana
rate' at the end of the nineteenth century, nor was anyone able to
demonstrate one in existence at any previous period. Theory and even
state dictat may have called for it, but investigators repeatedly failed to

[1] See for example Upendra Narain Singh, *Some Aspects of Rural Life in Behar. An Economic Study, 1793-1833* (Patna 1980), and also Sen *et al.*, *Perspectives*, p.3. For full citations for this chapter, see chapters eight and nine.
[2] See PCR 357, 15/1 (1892/3). The plots were virtually invariable, unlike
holdings; hence the importance to the record of the *khesra*, the field number.

313

find it. To consider that custom reinforced it, is, moreover, a gross misunderstanding of the nature and effect of Indian social norms.

Rent and other payments by cultivators rose in the eighteenth century, and economic considerations played some part in fixing the amounts. Moreover, despite the special pleading of certain protagonists in the great rent law debate, the intention of Shore and Cornwallis in 1793 (so far as they considered the question) was that rents should result from contracts between landlords and tenants: this was the essence of the *patta-kabuliyat* system and the provisions relating to tenants in the sales laws.[3] It was therefore not a sufficient condemnation merely to show that rents rose after 1793. It was necessary to measure the increase in real terms, per acre and per person. Attempts to do so are fraught with difficulty. The *Cambridge Economic History* estimated that rents increased by between 60 and 200 per cent in the 50 years to 1890, and related this increase to the proportionately smaller enlargement of the cultivated area.[4] But this is not to say that real rents increased accordingly. Very many complications arise. There were changes in what constituted rent, in particular the consolidation of additional cesses (or *abwabs*) and varying abilities to reimpose them. There were changes in the manner of calculation or payment, as between produce and money rents, and within the former between *batai* (division) and *danabandi* (appraisement). Such changes might affect the real proportion of the crop made over by the cultivator. But in particular there were changes in the value of agricultural produce, and possibly in access to its benefits. Here polarisation becomes essential to the idea of progressive impoverishment, for the later nineteenth century saw a shift in production towards higher-value crops, and a progressive though patchy improvement in agricultural prices, alongside fairly steady prices for other commodities.[5] The agricultural sector benefited.

---

[3] As discussed above, see [R.H. Hollingbery], *The Zamindary Settlement*, 2 vols. (Calcutta, 1879), the Report of the Rent Law Commission (Calcutta, 1880), and Ripon's despatch of March 1882 in R&A Rev A 16-46 (July 1883).

[4] See *CEHI*, pp.124-43 (p.138 for estimates of rent). The following discussion will not seek to disentangle the large and separate question of produce rents which prevailed in south but not north Bihar, taking different forms with varying implications (*CEHI* at p.124 is possibly misleading and incomplete). By 1900 the main point is that zamindars preferred product rents often in effect to secure unregulated rather than regulated tenancies, and *zerat* rather than raiyati land.

[5] *CEHI*, chs.IV and XI. Sen claims that in eastern India rice was some 30 per cent dearer in 1900 than 1887; Sen *et al.*, *Perspectives*, p.111.

Questions of productivity, population and entitlement needed to be resolved before anything more precise can be said. With regard to rent, there is no way through such complexities, and we are unlikely to be able to generalise about the period as a whole. We can produce reasonably accurate averages, for the first time, only from the 1890s, and even these figures are open to interpretation. Some officials thought they vindicated the view that rents were intolerably high (the conclusion reached one hundred years before). In Bihar others professed themselves agreeably surprised to discover that rates in Bihar were after all moderate compared with those in neighbouring districts of Awadh.[6] Perhaps many observers considered the agricultural population of Bihar to be poor by Indian standards, and, aware of the wealth of a few great landowners, assumed that rack-renting was the cause.

This was to place a wrong emphasis on agrarian structure. Before returning to that issue, we should try a different approach. Why should real rents have risen? One reason might be demand. Elsewhere a high revenue with regular *kists* (instalments) exacted after 1793 may be a factor. But it will not explain the prominence of Bihar as an example of rural poverty—its landlords were thought less hard-pressed than their fellows in Bengal—nor the alleged increases in rent later in the century when the real value of revenue payments gradually declined. On all-India and for that matter international comparisons (except for the remainder of the Presidency), it would be easier to argue that Bihar was poor because its agriculture was *lightly* taxed.[7] Similarly, the beginning of extra taxation through government cesses from the 1870s, though a significant departure, was more the occasion than the cause of extra rent demands. Moreover, government demand must have been very patchy in effect: the proper criticism of it in Bihar was not that it was high but that it was carelessly made, and this may have been a perennial feature in the region.[8] Again, the resumption of 'invalid' revenue-free holdings, completed by about 1850, undoubtedly had an effect on specific holdings, but there is no reason why it should have led to a general enhancement of rents. It would naturally be related to a large

---

[6] See R&A Rev B 17-18 (January 1897).

[7] For a version of this argument see Robb, 'State, peasant and moneylender'. A contrary argument is that by acquiescing in rural stagnation, landlords became hard-pressed (see Sen *et al.*, *Perspectives*, p.111). How then is one to interpret the expansion of cultivated area and cash cropping? Eric Stokes' explanation is far more convincing; see *CEHI*, pp.36-68.

[8] See for example Buchanan, *Shahabad*, pp.351-2.

decline in the proportion of rent-free holdings, once suggested to account for as much as 30 per cent of the cultivated area and nowhere above a half of that by 1900. (The other influences here would be the desire to increase rental incomes as prices rose, as an alternative to *pro rata* increases on rent-paying holdings, and the availability of other sources of supply for the services which rent-free holdings provided.) The decline of rent-free lands—though its effects were sectionally specific—increased the general significance of the recorded enhancement in rents per acre; it decreased the relevance of district-wide calculations on the basis of cultivated area. Finally, the very large expansion in the number of estates, through partition, may have represented a real growth in the number of rent-receivers, the product of formal registration and generational increase. On the other hand, partitions seem to have resulted in fewer co-sharers per estate, and by the later nineteenth century they were concentrated on small zamindaris, suggesting that families were seeking to preserve the larger estates at a size which would allow incomes based on rent: the growing numbers of very small estates implied increasing involvement in direct cultivation rather than an explosion of rent-receivers or 'sub-infeudation'. Numerous though partitions were, they did not affect all estates or areas. Conversely, increased rents were also found on great estates which avoided partition and were not subject to division at succession.[9]

What then of the opportunity to secure higher rents? It increased on some large estates, when they were controlled by the Court of Wards and management systems were reformed. Closer undivided supervision could pay dividends also on partitioned estates. As already noted, the legal position strongly favoured the zamindar under the permanent settlement: measures such as the distraint of property for non-payment of rent weighed the balance heavily against the tenants, and official attempts to redress this balance were largely ineffectual before the present century. This is not to say that law was very important. The permanent settlement vested much in the zamindar, but by the same token removed most of the direct agency whereby the influence of

[9] This discussion is indicative not exhaustive. As will be shown below, the question is further complicated by the doubt over what constituted rent: another way of saying that it was often uncertain. For example, were illegal cesses less common because of the impact of official and legal bans, or more common due to increases in zamindari power and possibly some decrease in alternative income such as that from ground rents in markets or tolls on trade and communications?

European concepts and practice would be felt. Law was little used to increase rent. Landlords benefited from the assistance of the executive or the police *in extremis*, but were mostly dependent on their own resources.

Rising prices and increasing numbers of rent-receivers naturally generated pressure to increase cash rents, though for much of the later part of the nineteenth century this pressure would seem to have been mitigated by relative stability in outgoings, and not certainly to have created a general demand for a higher proportion of agricultural surplus. But the improvement in agricultural returns between 1860 and 1900 followed two or three decades of depressed prices for items of long-distance trade, and was interrupted by repeated crises of climate and production. The sequence of events would have increased zamindari appetites; and uncertainties of output would have damaged the resistance of raiyats. On the other hand periodic scarcities would also reduce the landlords' chance of actually receiving regular and general increases in rent. But above all, marketing for cash was still peripheral in terms of Bihari production and consumption. Those of whatever legal status who could sell their produce stood to gain in the later nineteenth century as prices rose; the zamindar dependent on rent had to exert additional pressure on such producers in order to enhance rents at comparable rates. Where payments were made in kind, the price inflation was disguised and even further efforts would be needed to increase the zamindar's portion or to reduce the share taken by labourers and artisans. In short, fortunes varied. Some zamindars made the attempt to increase real rents in response only to pressing financial difficulties. In Bettiah, for example, rents were supposed to have been little changed until 1869 when a shortage of funds forced an effort: in the following years, allegedly, the 'controlling influence' of the great Bhumihar clans was mobilised to extort rack-rents, *thikadari* leases were auctioned to the highest bidders, and by these means the ignorant cultivators were prevented from acquiring a permanent interest in the land.[10] Subsequent rent rates on the estate, only two-thirds of those elsewhere in north Bihar, show this assessment to have been exaggerated; but the moral is plain: when rent rises depend on incentive, they will occur only where landlords are especially eager and effective. And if rent increases depended upon both opportunity and incentive, for the landlord, then they were bound to have been selective and conditional

[10] Hunter, *Statistical Account*, vol.XIII, pp.256-7 and 283-4.

from the perspective of tenants.

Rent rates recorded in the 1890s cannot, in aggregate, reveal distinctions showing which social groups were benefiting and which were being oppressed. But they suggest that rents were higher where population was greatest, and even higher where zamindaris were small: they reflect the realities of demand and power. They show also that the legal categories of tenancy offered no uniform picture. So-called 'fixed-rate' tenancies were always more lightly rented than others, but not to the extent that would be expected given their supposed pedigree of having enjoyed unchanging rents since before 1793. Settled and occupancy rates were sometimes lower and sometimes higher than those of less privileged status. Sometimes non-occupancy and under-raiyats' rates were at a discount, because such people—little better than day-labourers, as one report had it—[11] needed to be attracted to under-populated areas, or held inferior lands, on the better part of which they paid produce rents. At other times such tenants paid significantly higher rents, most notably on the crowded lands of Muzaffarpur.[12] The differences imply that the strength of zamindars or thikadars on large estates may have evened out the average rates for tenancies of different kinds, whereas on petty estates the occupancy tenants' average was reduced by the fact that village elites and successful cultivators (whose holdings appear elsewhere among tenants' lands) were often returned as zamindars. The imperfections of the categories thus make the question of rents less amenable to analysis, as if it were not already complicated by the poor correlation between rents and productivity, and the fact that weaker raiyats could pay more than stronger for land of similar quality.

The picture offered in chapter two was of a hard-pressed government confronting a complex and entrenched society; that explained some of the preoccupations of the administration under the Crown. The

---

[11] Such was the Muzaffarpur Collector's view in 1891: almost all raiyats had occupancy rights, the exception being a few who were 'scarcely anything but day labourers'; PCR 355, 15/3 (1891/2).

[12] Almost complete figures for average rent rates in the Reports on Survey Operations by 1898 are produced in the previously published version of this part of this chapter, in Clive Dewey, ed., *Arrested Development in India* (New Delhi 1988), pp.188-222, as follows:

| | Muzaffarpur | | Saran | | Champaran | |
|---|---|---|---|---|---|---|
| Holding | Rs/acre | Rs/clt.acre | Rs/acre | Rs/clt.acre | Rs/acre | Rs/clt.acre |
| Fixed rate | 3/06/4 | 3/14/0 | 3/08/0 | 3/13/9 | 1/01/6 | 1/04/2 |
| Settled/occ. | 3/15/9 | 4/05/5 | 3/14/6 | 4/01/0 | 2/00/3 | 2/03/5 |
| Non-occ. | 4/13/9 | 5/01/6 | 3/10/7 | 3/13/2 | 1/15/5 | 2/3/11 |
| Under-ryts. | 4/15/9 | 5/04/5 | 3/15/6 | 4/0/11 | 1/09/2 | 1/10/8 |

position of tenants under such a regime was, we concluded, unlikely to have been quickly or profoundly affected by it. This did not mean that the condition of the cultivators was necessarily good—it is more likely to mean that existing disparities continued—but even then it might be argued that the crisis conjured up in support of the tenancy legislation of 1885 was as much as matter of new perception as of new problems. The progress of opinion in the nineteenth century was not necessarily a journey towards truth; it was also an evolution in accordance with ideas. It cannot be denied that there was an element of special pleading in descriptions of Bihari conditions.

Conversely, however, debates over policy did not decide British impact at the local level in the way that practicalities did. Reform had to wait not only for ideas but for opportunity, and opportunity was the child of necessity. One of the opportunities was administrative capacity. Was one of the needs a real decline in the condition of the poor, for example in Bihar? As argued already, there did seem to be a real basis for concern, both for the welfare of the cultivators and over the manner in which their position was being affected by legal, economic and demographic conditions. In 1894 MacDonnell recalled his and the government's impressions of 1874, a famine year:

> 2. ...It was then perceived...that the districts of north Behar, bordering on Nepal, are among the most, if not the most, poverty-stricken tracts of all India.
> 3. This has been attributed, not to any want of fertility in the soil, which is indeed most productive, but to insecurity of land tenure and its consequence, excessive rents, to the depressed scale of wages, to the general ignorance of the people, and to over-population. Be the causes what they may, there is no doubt at all as to the prevailing agrarian depression which deprives of energy those who ought to emigrate, and deadens the industry of those who stay at home.[13]

The situation may have been relatively recent, not least in north Bihar which was attracting population over the period in question. While not exaggerating the novelty of the problems of the poor in Bihar, we need to bear in mind a possible mid- to late-century deterioration when considering the impact of the 1885 Act. The timing would fit with the new interpretations of the early colonial period discussed at the outset of the preceding chapter.

Let us read off the complex of possible influences and changes rather differently. We find a very varied picture, both regionally and socially, and accordingly effects which could work differentially. But

[13] Note, 3 August 1894, R&A Rev A 17-20 (January 1895).

there were also generally rises in population, prices and rents; there were greater marketing of higher-value crops, and higher profits from the agricultural sector; such incentives, plus regular revenue demands, resumption and partition all encouraged closer management of landed estates and/or agriculture. In many respects, then, the first part of the nineteenth century might be viewed, as far as the peasants are concerned, not as a period of recovery from distortions introduced in 1793, but as a time for gradual evolution towards something new. In north Bihar, for example, there was a steady decline in the proportion of rents calculated in produce, which were virtually unknown by the 1890s, and also a gradual development in the sale of tenures, unheard of in 1825 but common five decades later (mainly because of tenancy legislation). Indeed the development of such a market, as also for estates, leases, rents, labour and produce, and the swallowing-up of waste lands, may be seen as the crucial events of the century. An important shift had occurred by the 1880s. In the eighteenth century, as Hunter alleged, there was a certain mobility of labour and tenantry because they were relatively scarce.[14] Those who were willing and able to move could colonise abandoned or previously uncultivated land, on favourable terms. This fact does not always explain the difference between 'settled' and other raiyats and the rent each paid; much needs to be added about cultural and political restraints on movement, especially for high-caste agriculturists.[15] Yet there was certainly a chance for malcontents to seek out zamindars who were asking for lower rents to attract cultivators; and this 'colonising' option was far less common in 1900 than 1800. It existed within Bihar mainly in Champaran, where it depended on a favourable man:land ratio but also on economic incentives. By 1900 another option was far more common than before: the situation in which zamindars sought raiyats who would pay higher than average rates. The reason was a less favourable man:land ratio, but also—and perhaps primarily, in the nineteenth century—the increasing opportunities to market higher-value crops. This option was expressed by filling in or dividing up under-utilised villages. It must be taken into account in connection both with emigration—arguably related partly to a proportionately reduced demand for non-family labour with a decline of high-caste in favour of agricultural-caste production (a process of peasantisation?)—and with the subdivision of holdings which represents in

[14] See Hunter, 'Dissertation'.
[15] See Aditee Nag Chaudhury-Zilly, *The Vagrant Peasant: Agrarian Distress and Desertion in Bengal, 1770 to 1830* (Wiesbaden, 1982).

part the alienation of land to higher-paying tenants, and indeed concentrations of land in such hands, rather than a straightforward response to population increase. To sum up, then, the mobile raiyat in 1800 might be one who paid a lower rent, for demographic and development reasons. In 1900, however, he was more likely to be one who paid a higher rent, the reasons being again demographic but also economic. The argument depends on a sufficiency rather than a rapid increase of population. It is very different from the idea of all tenants being rack-rented as their numbers inexorably grew, but it allows for a mounting crisis in the conditions of vulnerable cultivators from the mid-century.

## II

The setting for the impact of the 1885 Act on Bihar was one in which there was a weak and oppressed agricultural labour force, and possibly pressures building up further to strain agrarian relations. There were ambiguities and complexities, but some rural people were clearly stronger than others. Those who were strong did not always fit neatly into the British conceptions of agrarian structure. But the local ways were not uniformly inviolate, sometimes because of the specialisms they contained. Part of our concern must be to trace the ways in which they were challenged and reduced to more standard forms. The 1885 Act, in defining and protecting an occupancy right, certainly attempted such a standardisation. It concentrated on the need to avoid denials of occupancy right by manipulations of tenancy or records. However— and this is relevant to our consideration of the extent of early nineteenth-century changes in the conditions of tenants—the new basis of twelve-years' holding in any one village was a legal rather than a practical innovation: a tenant who held some land over a long period already had occupancy in practice; he was, in the terminology of 1885, 'settled'. The Act therefore sought to define the legal incidents of existing practice, and to make it defensible in law. But most significantly it allowed the status to be independently established and recorded in a private or district settlement. Unlike any previous survey or regulation of rights in land in Bengal, this latter record distributed holdings according to what it defined as 'cultivating' as well as proprietary possession: 'cultivating' possession meant in effect management of agricultural production, by personal or employed labour. Several types of possession were defined, according to the legal status of the 'cultivator': holdings for zamindars, permanent tenure-holders and temporary lessees, for tenants of several kinds, and for sub-tenants.

An important instrument for this change was the survey and record of rights. District-wide surveys started under the Act in the early 1890s in north Bihar.[16] Two broad configurations were revealed in these surveys, one in which rent-receivers held relatively little land in relatively large holdings, and another in which rent-receivers held a quarter or more of all land but in holdings more nearly of the average size for the area. In the first variety were places, such as most of Champaran, where very large majorities of all holdings were leased from intermediaries and not the zamindar. Both varieties contained settled and occupancy holdings covering between 60 and 80 per cent of the cultivated area, and accounting for similar proportions of all holdings. Wide variations were found within this pattern; on the other hand, the categories based on British legal terminology may well have overlain a social profile that was more similar across the region than it was made to appear.[17] The similarities suggest that there were throughout Bihar a small number of people who lived principally from rents, and many who were dependent on moderate to small holdings, some of them held as tenants and some as zamindars. This position was codified after 1885; it was not the stratification into landlord and tenant which was supposed to have resulted from the permanent settlement. Clearly, settled raiyats survived the inimical laws of the earlier decades of British rule.

The record of rights, nonetheless, created an alternative view of the rural order, in which raiyats' 'property', the right to cultivating possession, was elevated to consideration alongside landlord's property, land ownership. Settlement *amins*, however 'corrupt and venal', were not local men, and were under the control of officials and rules imbued with the spirit of tenancy reform. They expected to identify as occupancy right the position in which they found the great mass of resident raiyats, and they did so, it seems, to an extent that the local patwaris

---

[16] The origins of the inclusion of a settlement procedure in the Act have been discussed in chapters four and five; see R&A Rev A 16-46 (July 1883), especially C.L. Tupper, 'Memorandum on the rent question in Behar', 20 October 1881.

[17] Two principles of analysis are being contrasted here: the settlement and categories based on source of income. Some officials also referred to two main classes: rent-payers and rent-receivers including raiyats—see PCR 355, 15/3 (1891/2)—which might imply those who controlled production or distribution and those who provided the surplus or their labour. None of these categorisations was to be found uniformly.

would not.[18] The manager of Bettiah raj complained that the survey had assumed that raiyats held 'all the land measured to them as theirs of right', whereas (he said) hitherto occupancy rights had been unknown and the land was leased or cultivated at the zamindar's will.[19] The record of rights standardised the perceptions of the government and the law in a way which weakened the landlords' standing with these institutions and encouraged official intervention in rural life. The record of rights also provided a standard measure of lands, often the first exact measurement available. Compare Purnea in 1810, where rents were set at rates 'totally unconnected' with soil quality—by caste or influence, or at will at the point of harvest.[20]

At first sight it might seem that a survey and record would benefit the landlord, as the discovery of 'excess area' led to the enhancement of rents. But in the longer term certainty was a disadvantage to those whose incomes rested on the collection of rent from regular tenancies. There are three main reasons. First, government and other external interference became far easier, and intervention was most likely to encourage the 'cultivating' interest: despite the political vacillations of the 1890s, both officials and entrepreneurs considered the zamindari interest unproductive. Secondly, the zamindar's power rested in part on a monopoly of knowledge, which these changes breached. The best-run estates could formerly impose effective management over a multiplicity of subdivided tenant interests, because their complexity and ambiguity allowed them to be manipulated at will, with little hope of challenge or combination. (This may be one reason the relatively standardised indigo contracts could be successfully resisted.) Thirdly, rising agricultural prices imposed a continual pressure on landlord incomes wherever these were expressed in money terms, and one of the strategies adopted to combat this, in the later nineteenth century, was the attempt to extend the land which the zamindars kept 'in hand' (the *zerat*). The Hathwa raj made numerous such claims, even in respect of lands which had been passed down through several generations of intermediary leaseholders

---

[18] This argument, too complicated to detail here, is based mainly on a comparison of returns made by patwaris and those many *amins*. See also R&A Rev A 73-4 (October 1894) and B 3-4 (December 1898).

[19] Gibbon to Champaran Coll, 7 January 1892, PCR 355, 15/4 (1891/2).

[20] Buchanan, *Purnea*, pp.136-43. Just as the institution of landed property occurred in law more absolutely than in practice, and needed a variety of administrative acts to reinforce it, so tenant rights depended on such support in order to evolve outside the statute book.

(thikadars) or tenants. The beauty of *zerat*, for the landlord, was that it avoided outside interference, maximised any benefits from competition for land, and allowed for flexible strategies on an annual basis. Such lands might be cultivated directly using hired labour, but often they were let out on short leases or capitalised through usufructuary mort-gages. The government noticed the landlords' hostility to inquiries in the first quinquennial review of the 1885 Act. 'The effect of a survey and record', they predicted, '...would be to fix once and for all the area of the *zerats* and prevent extensions which are now wrongly made.'[21] At least such encroachment would be more difficult wherever it could be challenged, once relations in land were regularised and recorded.

As early as 1894, tenants as well as landlords were reported to be attending settlement proceedings patiently and the former to be keenly interested in receiving *parchas*, copies of the entries relating to differ-ent holdings. Often this eagerness succeeded a period of apathy, inspired partly by rumours sponsored by the zamindars. During Holi, in Muzaffarpur, new songs were sung celebrating the settlement.[22] Earlier intervention by the British had imposed an order from outside in the interests of proprietors, even when measures were gradually taken to protect tenants. This was true of the sale laws which encouraged the legal insecurity of most tenancies by treating agrarian relations on the basis of contracts between individuals; it was true of the partition of estates (or *batwara*) which, among the tenants, invariably raised rents as it divided holdings. The record of rights was more thoroughgoing and deliberately directed towards tenant rights. Its methods ensured that the influence brought to bear would be, locally, that established in the villages of settlement and cultivation, and not necessarily that which had previously been visible, the revenue-payers. The context was an attempt by rent-receivers to erode the security of tenure of settled rai-yats, a process aided by rising prices, increased population and, some argued, the provisions of the 1859 Tenancy Act. The record of rights reversed the law and in some situations also affected the practice, by strengthening the hand of the tenant. A pilot survey undertaken in Muzaffarpur in 1885-86 was found in the 1890s to have produced

[21] R&A Rev A 17 (February 1893).
[22] See for example Bengal Revenue Resolution, 30 May 1894, R&A Rev B 3-4 (May 1898), B 17-18 (January 1897), A 21-3 (July 1904). One result was that collections of contributions to costs were better than expected; see R&A Rev A 10, 11 and 14-15 (February 1897), A 15-18 (March 1896), B 36 (April 1897).

results that were incorporated in zamindars' *jamabandi* papers and then kept up-to-date, finding their way into the materials in use by the people to an extent not repeated in the records maintained by government.[23] This was the kind of evidence which gave some credence to the Bengal government's assertion, noted already, that regular revisions of the record were not crucial to its impact. The raiyat knew which holdings he cultivated; with a record he could produce evidence in a standard form which, at one time, had been admitted by all parties.

Many practical checks inhibit the impact of law and government in rural India, and the investment of official effort in the settlements did not influence behaviour uniformly. But the overall effect of the record of rights was to favour the tenant interest. Was there also a distortion between tenants? It seems likely. The basic unit of the survey was the true field or plot, held under a single title at a single rate of rent. This represented the probable unit of production, ranging in size from about one-third to one-half an acre. The unit of the record, however, was the holding, consisting on average of between three and seven plots. A judgment was required each time a holding was defined, in terms set by the 1885 Act. The holding was a collection of production units expressed through ownership and rent. Complexities of land use and land users may have been lost in this transition. Moreover, many individuals had more than one holding and holdings in different categories, effectively dissolving the British categories. Again, holdings within each category varied greatly in size.[24] Sub-tenancies too were likely to be under-recorded. The 1885 Act vested occupancy in the holder, not the holding, and this is likely to have encouraged the concealment of sub-

[23] In common with other arguments below, this qualifies the suggestion that even the record of rights had little result because ignored in the courts—in regard to rent, until legislation in 1906; see D. Rothermund, *Government, Landlord and Peasant in India* (Wiesbaden 1978), pp.104-5 and 107-8. The area contained a 'mass of involved coparcenary tenures' and changes in government records were numerous; in sixteen villages entirely new *khesras* were needed. Growing awareness and the importance of the record-making are perhaps indicated by the disputed entries, over 25,000 in Muzaffarpur in 1893-4, covering 241 out of 712 villages and 368,217 out of 487,099. For an investigation suggesting a lack of zamindari interference after the survey see R&A Rev A 1-2 (August 1901). These points also diminish the damage done by the failure of plans to maintain the records; see for example R&A Rev A 40-5 (March 1895) and A 26-31 (July 1913).

[24] In one Bettiah village 153 raiyats held 2.3 *bighas* on average, but 42 held less than one, 19 held 5 or more (8 of these 9 or more and one over 17); PCR 355 15/4 (1891/2). In Muzaffarpur the average raiyat had two holdings.

ordinate rights once the claim of a privileged raiyat was admitted, particularly where part holdings were sublet to someone who was not himself a substantial tenant. The record was after all still only of a legal
property, albeit supposedly that of cultivating possession. Conversely,
the occupancy category must include many tenants whose tiny holdings
were insufficient to allow them a surplus and who had to work for
richer villagers. The category presumably at the same time represented
a smaller proportion of the population than of those whose interests in
land were recorded. The tenancy legislation was intended to benefit
actual cultivators, but political accident or expediency had conflated
this cultivator with the resident raiyat and secured to the latter a part-
proprietary right. There remained the potential for the separation of cultivation and ownership, and yet the emphasis on giving rights to agricultural producers had obviated the need to scrutinise and regulate the
relations between one tenant and another or between the owner of a
cultivating right and the man who worked on the land. In the law these
relations were largely ignored; in the record of rights they were virtually invisible.[25] The effect of the record of rights on popular perceptions
in rural areas also altered the balance of power in agrarian conflict. For
the first time the government was seeking out a new alliance in the
Bengal Presidency, and it was presenting a view of the rural order
which was significantly different from that which existed. Less weight
should be given to the operations of the courts and specific acts by
district authorities; more weight should be given to generalising
activities of the executive, as in the creation of the record.[26] Expectations may well have been raised which affected transactions between
and indeed among zamindars and raiyats, in instances which never
came to the attention of the courts.

It has been argued that traditional forms of land control and land
tenure were multiple, various and ambiguous—to the extent that eighteenth-century states found it impossible to enforce uniformity and
tended to incorporate in outward form what was still semi-independent
in substance, and also that British power did not at once transform the
situation. Nonetheless multiplicity and ambiguity first began to be lost

[25] It was thus—in part a matter of terminology—that Ibbetson could state
that the proportion of protected tenants was very much greater and the protection much stronger in Bengal than elsewhere in India: R&A Rev A 28-9 (December 1902).

[26] Compare the 1920s when commutation of produce rents was sought not so
much for financial independence as for 'taming' the landlords; *CEHI*, p.130.

with the permanent settlement, the process slowly continued with the recording of ownership in revenue papers, sales or resumption proceedings, and surveys of estate boundaries, and eventually reached its most concentrated form in the field-by-field survey and settlement operations. Such activities, following decades of administrative and legal action, tended to make practice more regular, or rather in conformity with what was provided in regulations. Partition too had marked a readiness to use British forms to adjust and record ownership. The divisions of ownership consequent upon inheritance and transfer were hardened, under the influence of more effective machinery for making all formal control in land individual, recorded and of one kind. The larger estates adjusted by avoiding partition after 1850. The Act of 1885 and the record of rights mark an extension of this process to occupancy raiyats. If reports are to be believed, very few of the transfers and mortgages of their holdings were recorded in the 1880s but almost all of them were by the 1920s.[27] Again, the average size of the holdings transferred was greatly reduced, partly because the larger transactions were more likely to be recorded earlier, partly because the average holding was becoming smaller, but largely because bigger holdings apparently came to be divided less frequently. Arguably, a reason for tenancies as for estates was that weaker holders were less able to stand out against the tendency inspired by administration and law. The result, in the absence of any other factor, would be developing polarisation among landlords and raiyats. For the latter, the change would be most effective where one of the pressures for subdivision came from richer tenants, zamindars or creditors anxious to secure land.

Having said this, it is important to stress again how gradual the process was. Many features of the pre-existing, informal systems continued in existence after a century of British rule. In 1893/4 there were still almost 1,300 boundary disputes to be resolved among the petty maliks of Muzaffarpur, where zamindaris were numerous and tenancies small. In Patna division too, of the two thousand or so raiyati transfers recorded each year in the later 1880s, only about five were of succession: heirs still expected to succeed without the benefit of official regis-

---

[27] Inquiries in selected villages in Hajipur in 1898 showed 14 per cent of holdings transferred since settlement (6 per cent by succession); in another case, of 200 transfers, only 21 had been registered; R&A Rev B 3-4 (May 1898). For the later period see *Report of the Bihar and Orissa Provincial Banking Enquiry Committee 1929-30*, vol.1 (Patna, 1930). Figures on partitions are available in R&A in annual Revenue Administration Reports.

tration.[28] These differences in impact and the consequent survivals had major consequences, as will be shown later.

No doubt, as has been claimed, zamindars 'refined the existing machinery' in order to raise rents, and holdings became smaller and a section of the peasantry was forced into agricultural labour.[29] The 1885 Act could benefit landlords who sought to manage their own production. Codifying the occupancy right certainly also encouraged alienation and subletting, and thus contributed to a process whereby excessive demands in rent and especially debt led to higher proportions of *bargadars* (sharecroppers) and labourers in place of peasant-family farmers.[30] Both of these apparently contradictory interpretations seem to agree that the tenancy laws brought benefits to some tenants, those who avoided the loss of their land and privileges, even though it was these, confusingly, who had the mortgageable property which was at risk through debt. Again, rent is clearly important, and particularly the differences between that paid on formal tenancies and what was extracted in irregular ways. A weapon of the economically successful among tenants was arguably the rent control provided in the 1885 Act; by the same token the weakness of other tenants might be traced to the effective lack of such privileges.

But the 1885 Act, a compromise between pro-raiyat and pro-landlord pressure, was never a charter for low rents. Common wisdom was that rents should be high but 'fair' in order that the raiyats might (in Woodburn's prim phrase) have 'impulses to industry and be relieved of the temptation to subletting'; alternative arguments were regarded by Ibbetson as 'vicious' and 'abominable'.[31] The legislation provided for state regulation of disputed rents, a record, and restrictions on enhance-

[28] R&A Rev A 17 (February 1893) and B 17-18 (January 1897).

[29] *CEHI*, p.175.

[30] In *CEHI* the engine for change is unclear, and perhaps is intended to be merely demographic. Sen *et al., Perspectives* claims the role of the 1885 Act to be on one hand to provide raiyats with mortgageable property. Hence it disadvantaged those with occupancy by tempting them into debt and leading to the alienation of their land. On the other hand (it is said) the Act allowed subletting and unregulated rents or terms. Hence it disadvantaged 'true cultivators' who did not have occupancy, making those who did into a newly-secure class. The inter-regional variations in landholding, moreover, are explained by differences in the severity of debt, largely for ecological and marketing reasons, a view which further confuses the assessment of the Act and is in any case ahistorical—regional differences being of very long standing and not shown here to have arisen in the later nineteenth century.

[31] R&A Rev A 22-3 (November 1896).

ment, particularly for settled raiyats; it was not to be expected that it would have immediate or specific impact. Until 1906, indeed, the civil courts allegedly ignored its provisions, such as those restricting rent increases for occupancy holdings to 12.5 per cent at fifteen-year intervals.[32] The Act was irrelevant too in that its remedies for raiyats depended on their initiating civil actions, except for a few provisions whereby the aid of the executive could be invoked. We may recall that raiyats could deposit disputed rents with district officers, who could fine zamindars for refusal to issue receipts, and officials could be called in to divide or appraise crops where produce-rents prevailed. But we also know that British administration was ill-equipped for close and effective intervention, especially in the Bengal presidency. In the 1890s receipts were in evidence only on larger estates, and though officials were called in about 450 times a year over produce rents in the Patna Division, particularly in Gaya, they reported themselves pawns on the landlords' side in disputes little connected with rents, rather than instruments for securing fair rents for the raiyats.[33] In itself the Act was likely neither to raise rents nor progressively to lower them.

Nonetheless, 1885 does mark a stage in the gradual pressure of the law towards regulation of tenancy and rents, and in this respect, again, the survey and record of rights were more significant than the Act itself.[34] Settlements were not imposed on individual zamindars to curb oppression—the first such case was not until 1910.[35] Nor was the settlement of government estates generally to the advantage of tenants: in the absence of specialist survey teams, the work could be rough-and-ready and sometimes resulted in additional power for village elites along with

[32] Rothermund, *Government, Landlord and Peasant*, pp.104-5 and 107-8.

[33] R&A Rev A 17 (February 1893); see also 17-18 (January 1897). There were some differences in the use of the law: distraint by zamindars was most common in Bihar (Patna Division accounting for 48 per cent of all applications in the Presidency in 1889-90), whereas deposit of rents was used more by tenants in Bengal proper; see R&A Rev A 8 (November 1885). Such differences, which also occurred in the reactions to the record of rights, are indicative of regional and local variations, important in assessing change. The 'salience of diversity' has recently been developed into a major theme in a study of South India, and is as applicable elsewhere; see David Ludden, *Peasant History in South India* (Princeton 1985).

[34] J.H. Kerr told Minto: 'experience shows that this [record] is the only true remedy, and far more effective than isolated suits brought by individual raiyats or executive interference between landlord and tenant'; H Political A 33-5 (May 1908).

[35] R&A Rev A 15-16 (May 1910).

overall increases in rent.[36] The district-wide surveys, however, present what was for Bihar an unprecedented intervention in agrarian relations. Their effect too was at first sight to increase rents. On the great estates, initial hostility by the zamindars quickly gave way to attempts to use the occasion to increase rental incomes, and the demand per tenant. In Bettiah every raiyat was required, with the agreement of the settlement officer, to enter an agreement to pay in full at the existing rate per bigha for whatever land he was proved to hold, less ten per cent: thus half of all tenancies were subject to increased demands on the ground of 'excess area', though the net increase in the total rental was extremely small. In the Hathwa villages in Saran district a smaller proportion of the tenants were also subjected to more significant enhancement. In such areas too the recorded increases may have represented a small proportion of the additional influence which the operations provided to the landlord.[37] The overwhelming majority of the applications for the fixing of fair rents (section 104 of the Act) were lodged by zamindars and European planters—in Muzaffarpur in 1894/5 only 9 out of 406 were tenants—and in the case of the planters almost two-thirds of the claims were very small and withdrawn before judgment: clearly they were devices to secure the tenants' acquiescence in indigo leases or other agreements. In the same way, and particularly in Muzaffarpur with its mass of petty estates, disputes over entries (section 105 of the Act) allowed zamindars to contest issues which had never been contentious before.[38]

And yet the record of rights was not a straightforward invitation to increase rental incomes, let alone to increase rents per acre. In Muzaffarpur section 104 was used against just over one per cent of the tenancies; even under the influence of a large estate such as Hathwa the proportion reached only 20 per cent. (Champaran was a special case in that many tenants undoubtedly did hold larger areas of land than were

---

[36] Careless methods and rent increases are illustrated for Shahabad and Gaya in PCR 359, 17/9 and 30/9 and 12 (1893-4); 361, 30/1 (1894-5); and 366, 30/14 (1896-7). See also R&A Rev A15-18 (March 1896).

[37] On Hathwa see R&A Rev A 17 (February 1893) and B 17-18 (January 1897). Already in 1887-88 Saran accounted for 853 out of 874 applications for enhancement in Patna Division, including claims for wells built with Opium Department advances.

[38] A breakdown of over a thousand objections in 1898 showed just over half referred to possession and just under half to rent; of the former two-fifths were by landlords against raiyats, a quarter by raiyats against landlords and one-seventh by raiyats against raiyats; R&A Rev B 3-4 (May 1898).

recorded.)[39] Moreover, it was soon recognised that the means provided in the 1885 Act to justify increased rents were very nearly useless to the zamindars. Figures on prices were not available during the settlement; as already remarked, the power to enhance on the basis of 'prevailing rate' proved a dead letter (with the exception of some cases brought by the Hathwa raj) as the reformers had intended it to be; and if a zamindar went to court, there was the danger that the resulting rents would be declared fixed for a period of years.[40] Zamindars were generally better off using existing methods to enhance their rents.[41]

Very soon, however, the landlords and the local government in Bengal were complaining about the provisions of the law in regard to rent, as if they did indeed have practical consequences; and the number and vehemence of their representations imply that they were after all finding it desirable to use the courts.[42] Here too the settlement was important. The presumption of the operations was that existing rents were 'fair'. In the vast majority of cases the effect of the record was merely to establish what was payable. The effect on the future, however, was potentially to stabilise these rates. In a minority of cases, in which existing rents were disputed before the officials, the settlement established what should be paid. The prospective effect in these cases was apparently normative, particularly because in Bengal the rules provided for judicial procedure and not for the *ad hoc* and locally specific decision-making of the north Indian system.[43]

---

[39] This assessment allows for the confusion of earlier measurements and the use of a smaller *bigha* at the settlement. See R&A Rev B 17-18 (May 1897) and B 3-4 (May 1898). For other districts, which were similar, see R&A Rev A 21-3 (July 1904).

[40] See R&A Rev A 21-2 (February 1896), 15-30 (January 1897), and C 1 (December 1895). Ibbetson was here speaking for the framers of the 1885 Act, whose attitudes he did largely share. On prevailing rate see M.N. Gupta, *Land System of Bengal* (Calcutta 1940), p.207. Excess area was also interpreted restrictively at survey and proved difficult for landlords to prove in court because of the development of case law. A contrary argument was that the 1885 Act distinguished between fixed-rate and settled raiyats, allowing the latter's rents to be raised; see Board of Revenue to Government of Bengal, 30 April 1892, R&A Rev A 17 (February 1893). In practice it probably helped prevent the raising of 'fixed-rate' rents!

[41] The view of Peary Mohun Mukherji, R&A Rev A 17 (February 1893).

[42] Earlier, zamindars had objected to government scrutiny; see a petition against the record of rights, R&A Rev B 24-8 (May 1892).

[43] See chapter eight. On the other hand, before a draft record was formally published, disputes were dealt with summarily, though strictly this was illegal;

The newly-received *parcha* was thus, for the majority, a record of what they should pay, something which raiyats may not have generally known. The zamindars' *jamabandis* tended to be defective in this regard, as in distinguishing between dues of different kinds and payments of different years.[44] The position was worse in the case of joint proprietorships and joint tenancies. The uncertainty, except sometimes when co-sharers fell out amongst themselves, suited the landlords well, and particularly when they wanted surreptitiously to match their rents to rising prices. Real or notional arrears of rent were also useful, in the confusion of the estate records, for maintaining the zamindar's economic and social control. Loans advanced to cultivators and mixed in with the records of rent could serve the same purpose. By contrast, the visits of the settlement team were designed to establish what each tenant paid to each zamindar.

The British argued in the later nineteenth century, as some scholars do today, that custom had provided a check on zamindari power and extortions;[45] it is true at least that from the 1870s economic constraints on behaviour were changing and arguably were reducing the interdependence of each local community. In their place the British were seeking to introduce the protection of generalising law. The diminution of ambiguity in rents as in land rights was part of this process. Landlords were being edged, therefore, towards more formal means of control; twentieth-century reports remark on their acceptance of the tenants' right to transfer their holdings, subject to the tenant's payment of a transfer fee;[46] they also draw attention to the virtual disappearance in some areas of landlords who lent to their tenants. Such landlords were potentially vulnerable.

Certainty in rents would promote stability, but not necessarily standardisation. In the Hathwa case the estate did not achieve a general

---

R&A Rev A 21-2 (February 1896). Even so, the officials were applying the principles of the pro-peasant school, to the extent (the Government of India complained) of settling rather than recording rents: R&A Rev A 73-4 (October 1894), and see also A 22-3 (November 1896). These arguments undermine Rothermund's in *Government, Landlord and Peasant*.

[44] See for example records in one Bettiah village which did not show area, rates per plot, type of soil and so on, but only totals per holding; PCR 355, 15/4 (1891/2), including note by Finucane, 24 November 1891.

[45] For parallel explanations of the differing awareness of the 1885 Act in different districts, see R&A Rev A 17 (February 1893), report by PC.

[46] On landlords' earlier opposition to raiyati transfers see R&A Rev A 3-22 (November 1898), A 56-8 (November 1895) and A 17 (February 1893).

enhancement of rents, though the officials believed this would have been permissible in view of the rises in prices and their belief that rates had not been increased for twenty years.[47] Rather the estate raised certain rents and recognised others as exceptions: the claim was that low rents were being raised to the average unless a discount was justified, as where cultivation was new or the land inferior. The explanation was invited by the 1885 Act and need not be taken too literally. It is hard to believe that concessions operated wholly on such objective grounds, for all that settlement officers' judgments implied a notion of a standard rate: this would indeed have amounted in the longer run to rent control rather than selective enhancement. In practice, however, rates of rent between villages and raiyats remained diverse, particularly where there were many small estates, but also (no doubt because of equivalent local bases of power) on the great zamindaris. It is tempting to think that rents in comparable areas were becoming more similar; in fact divergences were being entrenched.

Rent after the record of rights was still an instrument of differentiation among the raiyats. There were any number of important variables. Many rent agreements solemnised at the settlement were the outcome of old-fashioned duress. Many disputes merely continued earlier quarrels in which the 'richer class' of raiyats—as the Muzaffarpur settlement officer called well-to-do Bhumihars and Kayasths—were 'perfectly able to hold their own' against the petty maliks.[48] A raiyat who paid a rent calculated in money terms benefited from the erosion of his rent by inflation, and the commutation of produce rents was one indicator of the impact of the legislation. In general, zamindari incomes from formal rents were limited rather than augmented by the record. Tenants with established privileges were protected from pressures tending to create tenants-at-will in practice as well as law, and able to maintain favourable (rather than low) rents. The Act was particularly obliging to middle-sized raiyats who encroached on their fellows: it gave them weapons against the zamindar which it denied to under-raiyats.

The 1885 Act proceeded ostensibly from the belief that Indian society needed to be protected rather than reconstructed, and conse-

[47] The comparison was with records made under the Court of Wards.

[48] Though in Patna Division total applications rose from 5 in 1886/7 to 154 in 1889/90, there was little commutation in the earlier period; see R&A Rev A 17 (February 1893) and *CEHI*, pp.142-3. Of course produce rents might not be wholly immune to the impact of regulation on cultivators' ideas of their 'rights'; see also *CEHI*, pp.128-9.

quently that it was acceptable to attach occupancy right to raiyats rather than to the land and hence to those who actually worked it. This distorted its impact; understanding the record of rights makes this verdict even more plausible for Bihar. However, the impact was further qualified by pre-existing conditions. As explained, the society was one in which the larger social categories (of rent-receivers, surplus cultivators and those with insufficient land for subsistence) were fairly rigid and contained, while at the same time there was remarkable flexibility, in terms of land use, in the relative strength of families within the surplus category and the labourers, apparently because of rapid, even annual fluctuations of fortune (rather than Chayanovian family cycles). Though the society was (as said) complex and various, it was also integrated and interdependent and hierarchical. The changes discerned in the late nineteenth century seem, as a result, to have been unable to take either of two extreme forms. They could not produce a society wholly dominated by a few land controllers and traders leading to large-scale capitalist production; but nor could they transform the conditions and opportunities of the majority of the population. Rather, benefits were captured by relatively large numbers of dominant peasants and brokers of various kinds, who already commanded appropriate resources and the existing points of exchange. By contrast, the 1885 Tenancy Act postulated essentially two classes, landlords and tenants. Being applied to a society made up of a multiplicity of linked sections, it had the result of encouraging only those of the tenants who were already advantaged. More extended marketing of crops, too, in a stratified society, did not open up general opportunities, but increasingly locked already subordinate people into systems of control. Thus the influence of both the state and economic change reinforced the same tendencies in the society. It was hardly remarkable, therefore, that the record of rights tended to make definite and defensible the differences in status and privilege between the raiyats, and to benefit some of them against some of the zamindars, rather than to secure the supposed rights and well-being of the body of 'actual cultivators'.

III

Some indication of the raiyats who benefited, and the means and circumstances of their doing so, can be gleaned from a comparative study of thirteen villages in Muzaffarpur which were surveyed in both

1886 and a decade or so later during the district-wide settlement.[49] The sample is small but the data are interesting and relatively rare. The thirteen villages differed markedly in size, holdings per acre and so on. They ranged from those in which a body of maliks held a large share, to others where a single proprietor occupied relatively little land. Once again British terminology ignores similarities and conceals distinctions. The ten years between the surveys witnessed some remarkable change, but also strikingly different fortunes.

In aggregate, the number of zamindari holdings was greatly reduced; only two villages stood out against the trend, one because of a large increase in the area of *zerat* and the other due to subdivision among a large number of proprietors. At the same time there was an increase in the number of raiyati holdings, amounting to twelve per cent, along with a small decline in the area covered. The increase was unevenly distributed, though roughly related to villages in which the proportion of *zerat* had declined. There is no correlation to suggest that zamindars were dividing holdings in order to raise rents; nor is there any connection with the size of the average holding in 1885 or with stricter official definitions at survey. The explanation is that zamindars were consoli-. dating holdings, and that raiyats were not. The increase in the area of *zerat* and in the average size of zamindari holdings bore this out.

More detailed examination, however, undermines these generalisations. Most of the increase in *zerat* in aggregate was achieved in only two villages, which in 1885 had stood at the bottom and in the middle of the range in regard to the landlord's share of the land. The former was the smallest of the villages; the latter one of the largest. The only other significant increase in *zerat* was in a third village which already had the highest proportion of proprietary land. The fortunes of different villages in fact reveal different management strategies: on the one hand increasing reliance on *zerat*, and on the other increasing dependence on rents. *Zerat*, as noted already, could be let out on short-term leases or cultivated directly; the latter was more likely where there was a large number of zamindari families. The letting put the land with raiyats whom the British categories ignored; cultivation might make for zamindars hardly to be distinguished from raiyats. Villages of both types were included among the thirteen. The alternative strategy, to increase the amount of raiyati land, was also to be found, and in some cases

[49] This section is based on the Annual Report on the Settlement Operations in Bengal, 1896/7.

resulted in significant increases in income.

In aggregate too rents rose considerably over the ten years. These figures present the usual difficulties of interpretation, and do not show real outgoings. It is impossible to judge or explain variations in the absence of information about soils, cropping, irrigation and so on. The comparison is in each case merely with the recorded figures of ten years before. In detail, moreover, the picture is very different. In nine villages the raiyats paid more per acre. One very highly-rated village apparently experienced great pressure; it was perhaps engaged in profitable agriculture, even market gardening, in 1885. This and one other village with a large increase had been subject, moreover, to *batwara*; their rents bear out the reputation of such proceedings. Conversely villages with a multiplicity of zamindars tended to be little disturbed; least affected were four owned by more than one estate. And indeed several villages actually paid less per acre, or experienced very small increases. The decade was on the whole a good one for north Bihar, and prices rose. It is arguable therefore that about half the villages were paying a lower proportion of their crops by value to the landlord in 1895 than they were in 1885. It is tempting to believe that the record was holding down rents—at a time when on subjective evidence revenue officers were reporting a general and extortionate enhancement—but more probably the figures reveal the expected stickiness of rents. The main conclusion from the figures is that, in real terms, zamindars in these villages were not after all being very successful with rents, even though, in terms of the land they held, the proprietary interest was overwhelmingly strong.

It is interesting that the fortunes of villages varied. Most instructive, however, is that the fate of raiyats varied within each village. *In toto* nearly half of the holdings were enlarged, about one-third experienced no change in size, and the remainder lost land. The first of these categories accounted for 67 per cent of holdings and a greater proportion of raiyati land in one village; in another it was as little as 25 per cent. This evidence testifies to the effective security of tenure experienced by a majority of raiyats in respect of most of the land; the same could be said of the group experiencing no change. It is unfortunately impossible to break down these categories into the legal heads employed at the settlement, but whether or not the two are identical it seems reasonable to call this majority 'settled', in that they had occupancy in practice. Their advantage was also expressed in one of two ways: either they held their land and resisted rent rises, or they enlarged their holdings and—without exception—on average paid higher rents. The latter group is of the greatest significance.

Except in one village, raiyats in this group had paid below the average rate in 1885; in some villages they continued to do so in 1895. Those who lost land had very often paid more originally but paid less per acre in 1895. The category may conflate some who paid at a higher rate for the same land with others who paid at the same rate for more land, but it does very strongly suggest that in many villages there were raiyats ready and able to take on increased area at higher rates of rent, and others who could or would not do so and who lost land as a consequence. As their rent rates were then reduced, it seems probable too that it was their better land which had been taken over. Moreover, turning to the average size of holdings, one finds once again that the group paying higher rents enjoyed fortunes quite against the trend. In some villages average holdings were becoming smaller; in others they were increasing or remaining unchanged. But the larger-than-average holdings, in almost all villages, were in the hands of raiyats whose rents were either raised or maintained. These raiyats thus were able to follow the example of the zamindars. There was one village where the so-called raiyats' holdings were mere pockets presumably allocated to servants and labourers, and where the maliks' interests were on average almost as small; but even in this village the average size of holding was doubled in the period. There were other, true exceptions, associated with *batwara* or increases in *zerat* (and presumably re-letting to cultivators or sharecroppers). But most zamindars were consolidating their holdings, on average, without much affecting the size of the raiyats'. It is possible that this indicates an increase in direct cultivation. It implies a benefit. It was one some but not all raiyats shared.

The conclusion for the thirteen villages is that only a minority of zamindars was able to gain land and to raise rents significantly in real terms. Most, however, were able to increase the average size of their holdings. The majority, then, may have been embarking on different, more direct means of tapping agricultural surplus, as rental incomes proved less elastic than those from production. One result was that a majority of raiyats experienced little change, except those in the minority of villages whose zamindars had the power to increase their *zerat*. In some villages raiyats whose position was unchanged constituted a majority; and in some, but not all, these people were apparently privileged, judging from rent rates and average sizes of holdings. A more clearly advantaged group was those raiyats who gained land at the cost of paying higher rents. This section seems likely to have included successful agriculturists but also those managers and brokers of surplus within the village, the dominant peasants.

There is no way of knowing, from these data, whether the changes were cyclical or secular; they are likely to have been both. The advantaged group may have been composed of different families at different times; changes in the average size of holdings may subsume temporary circumstances and family cycles. On the other hand, within the averages, there were bound to be even larger or stronger raiyats—with the kinds of variation visible between zamindars—for whom the changes represented a progressive strategy of commanding the most valuable resources, in this case larger holdings because of the increasing value of agricultural production. We have already identified such people at the theoretical level, and there is ample evidence of their existence in reality. Some of them enjoyed collective advantage, as when raiyats were known for resisting their landlord, even the government; more significant, however, were others who, often by their outside contacts, were able to assume control over fellow villagers. Details of maladministration on government estates in this period offer many instances in which enterprising, opportunist individuals or families succeeded in dominating villages. Such people were typical, not perhaps in their opportunism, but in filling a role which was to be found in villages throughout Bihar.

The officials concluded that the answer, on government estates and generally, was a record of rights, to secure that 'artificial thing', tenant right.[50] But if its effect was at all to harden and perpetuate the differences in society, then it must have worked to the further benefit of those who, in the thirteen villages, were taking progressive advantage of the changes in landholding, the hidden category as it were within the section of raiyats who were gaining lands at higher rents. The mechanism was not purchase at this stage, and indeed the statistical evidence for an increasing number of sales, even in the twentieth century, does not entirely justify the emphasis which has been placed upon it.[51] (Much of the increase was in registration; in any case numbers as a proportion of holdings were always small.) In the villages discussed in this section many transfers of property were at the initiative of the

[50] R&A Rev A 9-11 (June 1909); the phrase is J.H. Kerr's (one-time Settlement Officer in Darbhanga). He assumed, that is, that tenancy was created by British law.
[51] See Chaudhuri, 'The process of depeasantization'.

landlord, and the most common transaction recorded was of mortgage with possession; few were sales despite signs that the price paid for occupancy holdings was increasing. Of the mortgages 89 were to lawyers, 746 to moneylenders and 6,153 to raiyats; the moneylenders were likely to be most often raiyats too, as mahajans from bazaars tried to avoid taking over land for cultivation. In Champaran a survey of 391 villages showed in addition migration from one to another, when a raiyat took up a small-holding to escape his debts. Proprietary rights were also sold: a study of 194 villages in Muzaffarpur showed 607 transfers affecting 7 per cent of the area: 72 per cent to landlords, 16 per cent to raiyats, 10 per cent to moneylenders and 2 per cent to lawyers. The price paid was remarkably uniform. Most interesting of all perhaps was another study of 1,269 villages in the same district, which showed 8,083 transfers, 14 per cent by sale, 85 per cent by mortgage (representing about 4 per cent of all holdings—again only mortgages with possession were recorded), but of these very many were of part-holdings only: in the case of sales this was true for over half, and with mortgages for over 70 per cent. In the light of the thirteen villages discussed here in detail, the changes seem thus to be largely by mortgages of parts of holdings, or by landlords who were able to oust one tenant in favour of another. Changes in holdings were not new. It was normal for under-raiyats to hold land for short periods at high rents (except in Champaran where low cash rents were common in such circumstances) and for occupancy raiyats to cultivate for a year or two the lands of a neighbour who had more land than he wished to cultivate directly. The pattern of the thirteen villages and the corroboration from other studies may however have represented a secular trend whereby the advantages of the well-to-do section, to be found everywhere, were increased. The weapon was apparently a willingness to pay higher rent, at least during the nineteenth century. The suggestion is that the holdings of petty raiyats were being subdivided, and amalgamated with those of the more successful. If a record of rights made tenancies more definite, moreover, this process would gradually be accelerated, but subdivision would have been encouraged through the normal pattern of inheritance and partition; only the strong would be able to resist this impoverishment, and the gap between them and the remainder, widening already as they retained a larger share of the profits from marketing crops, would be further increased.

Such polarisation was not of course produced by the Tenancy Act or any single official policy. The Act and particularly the record of rights, as they came to have some effect, worked on existing inequalities, which they did nothing to reduce, and which they allowed to harden. The influence of economic change on persistent institutions and attitudes was another potent factor in the equation. The society was extremely various in detail, but also had certain prevalent and resilient features. Thus tenancy laws could modify without transforming. British rule was not applied to a *tabula rasa*; Bihari society was neither egalitarian before 1793 nor uniformly depressed by the permanent settlement. European concepts of class and property, in the latter case particularly arguments about value, combined with notions of moral economy and village community to obscure the inherently divided and stratified nature of Bihar, where structures ensured redistribution of resources, and hierarchies were buttressed by complex concepts of differentiation. Thus, in 1885, when the 'boon of property' was extended, in theory, from landlords to cultivators, in practice it proved an additional benefit to individuals who were already well-placed. It revolutionised neither property nor production, but helped produce and then fix the kinds of changes visible in the thirteen villages.

Trade offers a metaphor for the continuities contained within the process of change in the later nineteenth century, a process in which it was of course a most important factor. Cultivators had always been involved in exchange: between rich and poor in villages, between wet and dry lands, between rent-payers and receivers, between areas of specialist production, between country and town. In Bihar, as in many other places, such exchanges, when not between superiors and subordinates and hence subsumed under the dominant culture's preference for gifts, tended to be mediated through a variety of hands or separated over time. The payment of advances of cash, food or seed was a characteristic means of stimulating production for sale; the tendency was to capture the producer rather than to compete for production. A *jajmani* system is a similar mechanism for services and labour. In Bihar these features were still very apparent in the later nineteenth century, and as much in the new industries based on European capital, such as opium and indigo, as in the predominant rice trade or for oilseeds and other long-traded commodities. It is extremely hard to establish the extent to which the substance as well as the form of such institutions persisted over time, but that is immaterial to our present purpose of establishing the existence of controllers and intermediaries and their continued role under conditions of growing trade and commercial agriculture. It may be of course that they were the more secure because much of Bihar and a majority of Biharis did not attract large inward trade although providing commodities for export: methods appropriate to the extraction of 'surplus' thus continued to be preferred to methods appropriate to the generation of consumption. In such a case, it is inevitable that as the volume of trade increased, its benefits grew but continued to be concentrated on those who were strategically placed within existing systems. And as the number and range of exchanges grew, without transforming the manner in which they were conducted, it follows that the role of exchange in reinforcing control and in promoting hierarchies would be, if anything, enhanced. On the one hand one has, therefore, the *jeth raiyats* of Champaran who became indigo planters' *amins*; on the other hand one has the chorus of allegations about the burgeoning exactions based on debt, which indeed was often substituted for money from the point of view of the cultivator at the end of a line of intermediaries who delivered his crop into the market.[52] So it was also, as the property right was individualised and made more secure.

There were some interlopers, but mostly the hierarchies and intermediaries worked within village society. Thus a numerous section of the rural population benefited as opportunities grew; the section can be described by caste, tenure or some other particular resource but can only only be defined as those who commanded their own production and controlled others. The British did not identify them, except occasionally to record some indigenous term, such as 'malik', meaning in effect a dominant one. Hence tenancy laws were but clumsily directed. However, as the dominant were themselves of diverse kinds it was possible to give advantages to one role over others, as the record of rights did in shifting the balance in favour of tenants over landlords.[53]

[52] This is discussed more fully in Robb, 'Peasants choices?'.

[53] See also Sugata Bose, *Agrarian Bengal: Economy, Social Structure and Politics, 1919-1947* (Cambridge, 1986), which argues that credit was the key to agrarian structure and change, but also that rent was *becoming* less important than the management of cultivation as a means of extracting surplus. This paper finds the latter also true for Bihar from the later nineteenth century, but assumes that, though credit always mattered for social control, its importance grew in the twentieth century, after the weakening of state and legal support for rent-receivers (other than raiyats), improving of the hand of settled tenants, shifts in land control, and the differential benefits of expanding trade. See also Partha Chatterjee, *Bengal, 1920-1947. The Land Question* (Bengal 1984). Another recent study of connections between British law and socio-economic conditions, in deltaic Bengal, is Sirajul Islam, *Bengal Land Tenure. The Origins and Growth of Intermediate Interests in the 19th Century* (Rotterdam 1985).

## Chapter Eleven

# *Peasants, property and nation*

The fallacy of a homogeneous peasantry distorted the 1885 Tenancy Act, and allowed it to ignore the poor. Similar generalisations have affected subsequent interpretations of agrarian structure. In Bihar, categories of advantaged families already existed—a mixed bunch of landlords, petty maliks, rich tenants, *ashraf* and high-castes, service elites, moneylenders and skilled agriculturists. The Tenancy Act, the record of rights and commercial production helped change the balance of advantage among these families and between them and the rest of the population, especially by favouring the direct management of cultivation on *zerat* or secure tenancies. The Act and the survey also demonstrated the importance of articulating 'rights', or properties (in several senses), by appeals to external arbiters, the officials and the courts. They generalised a need formerly experienced by fewer, isolated agents and allies of the state, and helped consolidate disparate local groups into competing political interests. Such broad classes are necessary to modern politics and national identities. This last chapter reflects on such issues.

One difference which has underlain this study is that between structure and chronology: the intention was to seek a morphology of ideas. By trying to explain both the past and earlier perceptions of it, we have been looking for the hidden agenda in colonial depictions of the Bihari countryside, searching not for neutral ground, but for the fullest possible awareness of colonial and current prejudices. We have done so also in the hope of locating epistemological imperatives which have gone untested or even unobserved—the elements of data (in a literal sense), which Bihar had given to the record rather than what the record had imposed on Bihar. We found that the contribution of indigenous ideas and practices was large and independent, but remained, in regard to state policy, one of establishing conditions upon which imported concepts had to work. That much was colonial in character. The fundamental ideas of the tenancy debate were foreign; the historical rhetoric and the superstructure of detail referred to Indian realities.

A key point was that the reformers' conflation of the proprietary tenant with the occupancy raiyat and the 'actual cultivator' in Bengal produced a case of mistaken identity which is in many respects identical with that which still persists in modern concepts of the peasants. In the midst of the grand theories, a perennial puzzle of Indian history has been how to relate the social superstructures to the base. In the theories (as opposed to some of the descriptions) the gap between elements is rarely filled. So unclear is it how things worked as a whole that it is often concluded that they did not: the polity was segmentary, the trade fragmented and marginal, the production subsistence in character, the culture localised. Such starting-points determined the definition of change, for, by contrast, the story of more recent times tells of progressive connections between and generalisations of the different social elements, through the growth of the state and trade. The gaps are filled by law, politics, or technology, which disturb what had long prevailed. Thus the same assumptions about the Indian past and the course (or the lack) of its history have kept reappearing, in different time-frames and within opposing ideologies—whether to emphasise an autochthonous modernisation with peripherial European interventions, or a thwarted development, or a transformation under powerful colonial stimulus. Recent accounts of British rule or of modernisation cast out this view of India with one hand but slip it back with the other. Nowadays few admit to the old assumptions about the organic nature of Indian society —that on the whole it embodied a Brahmanical tyranny over the mind, but isolated and 'socialistic' village republics, the two combining to produce an intellectual and economic stagnation. Yet, despite the revised historiography of the eighteenth century, despite also a new interest in low-class solidarities and populist movements, the Indian village community lives on; and the traditions, hierarchies and economies of India's peoples are often still perceived as having once been stable over time and discontinuous across space.

In nineteenth-century Bihar, the middling groups between cultivator and state, long important for linking the different levels of society, were again active in the legal and commercial changes fostered by colonial rule.[1] To understand this requires a reassessment of the meaning of

[1] See A.A. Abdullah, 'Landlord and rich peasant under the permanent settlement', *Calcutta Historical Journal* 4, 2 and 5, 1 (1979-80), the first part on the permanent settlement and zamindars (akin to some points in this book), and the second on the role of long-term middlemen and village elites, and the exaggeration of their dominance, as rich peasants and petty zamindars, through subletting, moneylending and the employment of wage labour, especially after 1885. (It may be significant that my similar conclusions for Bihar were reached quite

'peasant' as well as 'state'. The former concept, flourishing in the scho-larly or emotional demesne that has come to surround it, proposes that there is a kind of person or society common to many parts of the world and conforming more or less with certain characteristics.[2] The operative part of the definition conceives of the peasant as an individual small-holder using family labour, concentrating on subsistence, and (though subordinate to external elites) living among others of his own kind. Its omissions and elisions provide a supreme example of the missing levels of the historiography: the 'peasant' world is composed almost entirely of barons and underlings, lords and farmers; a vast majority of the lower orders possess some land and are more or less undifferentiated.

A Western theory invented a common category, in our version the resident raiyat, and equated it with the mass of the population. It con-cluded that it needed protection from distorting pressures of external law and capital, but ultimately so that it might resume its inevitable march towards dissolution, in individual enterprise and modernity. In Bihar, the result was further benefit for certain groups within that supposed peasantry. In addition the practical denial of collectivity—the imagined peasantry being composed of individual productive family-

---

independently.) More generally, the discussion in this chapter has been influ-enced by B.B. Chowdhury [Chaudhuri], *Growth of Commercial Agriculture in Bengal, 1757-1900* (Calcutta 1964), 'Rural credit in Bengal, 1859-1885', *IESHR* 6, 3 (1969), and 'Growth of commercial agriculture in Bengal, 1859-1885', *IESHR* 7, 1-2 (1970); A. Siddiqi, *Agrarian Change in a Northern Indian State* (Oxford 1973); articles by Neil Charlesworth, Colin Fisher, P.J. Mus-grave, and D.A. Washbrook, in Clive Dewey and A.G. Hopkins, eds., *The Imperial Impact* (London 1978); C.A. Bayly, 'The age of hiatus: the north Ind-ian economy and society, 1830-50' in C.H. Philips and M.D. Wainwright, eds., *Indian Society and the Beginnings of Modernisation, c.1830-1850* (London 1976); and Shahid Amin, *Sugarcane and Sugar in Gorakhpur* (Delhi 1984), especially pp.1-12 and ch.3.

[2] My dissatisfaction with the term 'peasant', expressed here and in earlier publications, led to a draft of this chapter after which, thanks to Walter Hauser, I was directed to Victor V. Magagna, *Communities of Grain. Rural Rebellion in Comparative Perspective* (Ithaca and London 1991), where I found many cogent statements which accord with my own conclusions. I have added some notes drawing attention to these similarities. Though methodologically I may appear to differ from Magagna by arguing that one can approach the 'standpoint of the dominated' by means of a critical analysis of 'macrostructures and elite power' (see ibid., p.ix), generally Magagna's work has the effect of reinforcing and broadening my arguments (not least through his lengthy references, espe-cially in ch.1), and also of showing (contrary to his own apparent doubts on p.257) that many of his arguments may indeed be applied to India.

units—allowed the efficient landlord and the privileged peasant proprietor to pursue their individual interests according to a newly exclusive legal and economic rationale, less and less constrained by communal norms. This was not a simple slide from collectivity to individualism; it was a change in the character of both these aspects of society.

An extreme conclusion from their pre-existing differentiation might have been that Indian villages never operated as communities, and that dominant classes always exercised power over subordinates. But it is not necessary to go so far. In one of his wide-ranging essays, Eric Stokes also described the traditional view of the village community as one based on a discontinuity between the rural base and the political superstructure.[3] From this, he explained, followed the idea that modernisation was inimical to peasant communities, an idea depending to some degree upon the stability not just of peasant production but of the old order as a whole in India. On a similar basis, as Stokes described it, a whole literature treated Indian politics as a 'middle-class' activity exclusive of the peasantry, and economic change as the capitalist exploitation of stagnant rural producers. When these ideas came to be challenged, it was first by regarding Indian elites as brokers mediating between Western trade or foreign rule and a passive rural base, and then by identifying sections within a changing peasantry which had some contact with and benefits from the outside world. A rich peasantry was found, and later, following the dictates of theory, discontented middle peasants who were the more radical for being incompletely involved with market or state and hence uncommitted to the status quo. At this point Stokes discovered the 'ghost of the village community' in the descriptions of sociologists and others. He denied that there was a firm class structure in India, or at least that it could be clearly articulated; he cited the multiplicity of occupational roles generally performed by individuals, the range of wealth within various legal or social categories (for example land tenure or caste), and the evidence of vertical cross-class connections between dominant villagers and their followers. He seems to have believed in the persistence of local pre-capitalist formations, but also in extended lineage or caste groups, and perhaps in political linkages, and therefore in a peasantry which was neither dis-

---

[3] 'The return of the peasant to South Asian history' in Stokes, *The Peasant and the Raj* (Cambridge 1978); also published in *South Asia* 6 (1976). Parts of the following discussion are adapted from P. Robb, 'Ideas in agrarian history', *Journal of the Royal Asiatic Society* 1 (1990), and 'Law and agrarian society in India', *MAS* 22, 2 (1988).

associated from market and state, nor divided internally into conflicting classes. In unusually acerbic prose, he attributed attempts to find a class structure to 'the force of modern political slogan-mongering'. Thus he believed in the village community in a fundamental way. The 'ghost' which he welcomed was, he thought, the true spirit of India.

He may be read as proposing a more than usually radical revision. Three points seem to be central to his vision and to be true. First, the localities in India were deeply involved with the outside world. The old notion of isolated village republics was patently wrong. Secondly, the Western concept of class as a necessary condition of humankind was positively unhelpful to the analysis of Indian society. All the new attempts at discussion in these terms did violence to what actually happened. Thirdly, at least in the nineteenth century, there remained village cultures which were distinct from that purveyed by the state or through long-distance exchange: that is to say, modern trade and government did not necessarily dissolve the village community, and Indian society did not move inexorably from status to contract. It was this culture and evolution which could be violated by the individualism and market-orientation of British rural policies.

Together these points redefined the village community. It was not unchanging or passive, but nor was it inevitably transformed by capital or colonialism. It was not isolated, but nor was it integrated. It had elements in which it was autonomous or resilient, but it was not homo-geneous. As with other concepts, too, this one has to be defined and re-defined as a host of specifics, and not as an unchanging set, or as a pre-diction. If we picture the supposed characteristics of pre-capitalist and capitalist societies as representing two parallel lines a long way apart, then we can imagine the Indian village as occupying (at any one time) a jagged range of positions all over the ground between them. What this means in practice is that the two opposing lines are not always parallel but are sometimes convergent. Therefore there were often strong collec-tive elements operating within villages as a whole, but the villages were often also highly differentiated. There were powerful intermediaries between villages and the surrounding world, but they did not form a class, an economic identity which subsumed all others: they recognised other loyalties and were divided by castes and lineages. Nor did their dependants and subordinates form a class: they too were divided.

In general several distinct and persistent roles could be distin-guished, but these merely delineated the possible elements and limits of agrarian structure. They have been implicit in these discussions. First, there was control over people, land and other resources, which may be called the primary zamindari or, as in Bihar, the malik role, but which could be played equally by a clan, lineage or 'brotherhood' as by an individual and his family. Then there was a separate role of collecting land-revenue, at least in Mughal times; it was known as *malguzari*. The holder is sometimes described as a secondary zamindar because he could operate from an area or regional base. But, though *malguzari* was distinct in law, it had at some stage to be combined or allied with the malik role. Just as central rulers, including the British, found it wise to accommodate and partially to incorporate regional magnates and chiefs into their state systems, so those regional powers in turn recruited or were linked with the controllers at village level.[4] Thirdly, below these superior roles, there was another distinction between, on the one hand, resident or original, hereditary villagers and, on the other hand, non-residents or outsiders. The difference was expressed in varying ways, but, as we have noted, the *khudkashta* raiyats were taken to have enhanced responsibility and claims within the village, while *pahikashta* raiyats included all families (including actual residents) who were not treated as original or full members of the community. It is safe to assume that before state law intervened (mainly under the British) the distinction was definite but not absolute over time. Finally, though this has been a vexed issue, there were landless labourers: it was misleading of some early accounts to treat village society as comprised only of the land-holders, large and small. Labourers existed in the villages, among those with insufficient land as well as those with none—artisans, servants and field workers. Their existence, as in Bihar, was not merely a factor of the man:land ratio, but attributable to the command system and the exigencies of production. However, even these underprivileged people observed minute differences in status.

Within the Bihari village, as opposed to a view from the wider world, the combination of fine distinctions and variations implied integration and interdependence. Each status was particular, but described in comparative terms, for what was intrinsic to one was extrinsic to others, as Brahmans implied non-Brahmans, and castes outcastes: together they constituted a whole. Production depended upon a division of labour which offered position and protection at the expense of 'efficiency'. Some high castes in north Bihar, for example, sold their stand-

---

[4] Compare Stephen Henningham, 'The Raj Darbhanga and the Court of Wards, 1860-1879: managerial reorganisation and elite education', *IESHR* 13, 3 & 4 (1982), on the shift from thikadari to bureaucratic control.

ing tobacco crops to the agriculturist Koiris in order to avoid the effort, and the social stigma, of harvesting and preparation, at the cost of some redistribution of profit. Many occupations—the multitude of agents and brokers, for example, or some specialists such as ploughmen—seemed to exist mainly in order to delineate more exactly the status of the principals (their employers: the rulers, landowners or merchants), and to incorporate at the same time a range of people who were seen to be otherwise distinct. If a high-caste member employed labourers or refrained from marketing produce, he was at once separating himself out from the mass and sharing himself with it. He merged aspects of his activities, by combining social and economic relationships. He expressed his involvement in the whole while asserting his separate identity.

This brings us to a second main proposition. The village was not one corporate unit of production; but comprised many individual units that performed cooperatively. This point of congruence with 'modern' theory meant that the British laws did after all find a target. A distinguishing attribute of rural life in Bihar was that the most common relationships were of dominance and dependence, concepts repeated endlessly in the state, the region, the village, the family, even with reference to the human body. In the village the existence of difference also necessarily implied that poorer families worked for richer—notably (though this was not an invariable or solitary instance) the socially-inferior for the ritually-pure. The theory might propose that each person served the whole according to his dharma. The practice was that resources, such as water or land, were distributed by those who were locally powerful, admittedly within differing limits imposed by custom or latterly by law, and usually in alliance with some outside authority—a clan or state—capable of influence over wider areas. Such was the case with the pyne and ahara irrigation systems of south Bihar.[5] But the differentiation should not be thought of as originating from outside; it was apparent in the very ecology of the village. Nor in itself should it be related to a particular type of trading relationship or external control. Where division of labour occurs without the stimulus of specific technology, it is hardly surprising that it should express internal political factors. Nor it is surprising that locally-generated difference should

[5] Among many sources on these are G.A. Grierson, *Notes on the District of Gaya* (Calcutta 1893)—drawn on for P. Robb, 'Peasants' choices? Indian agriculture and the limits of commercialiation in nineteenth-century Bihar', *Economic History Review* XLV, 1 (1992)—and Nirmal Sengupta, 'The indigenous irrigation organization in South Bihar', *IESHR* 17, 2 (1980).

result in a system that was dispersed, risk-averting, redistributive and incorporating. It is tempting to attribute it in Bihar to a rich but not entirely secure agriculture in conditions of dense population.

These descriptions re-work rather than refute the old notions of hierarchy and stability. Underlying them is a sense of the village as responsive or of behaviour as interconnected. In addition, as Stokes reminded us, we cannot merely jettison the idea that the village was isolated. Rather we need to describe the nature of its insulation from the outside world. Though the village was not disconnected from its surroundings, its involvement was channelled and controlled. Caste itself was an expression and a vehicle of the exchanges, each jati being a regulator of behaviour in the village and of outside relations through kinship and marriage. Superior castes too acted for and gained from associating with the great caste lords who dominated regional social life, as from echoes of the Brahmanical tradition which were incorporated in village mores. But more than this, intermediaries were as characteristic in the society as 'big men' and dependants. In almost any transaction they institutionalised the distance between parties. This was apparent politically and administratively, and in the world of trade. It serves to remind us that many of the indigenous socio-economic limits were restrictive, for example in the case of caste barriers which confined the lowest people to menial occupations. Therefore breachings of barriers, or conflations of category, or new bases of distinction—as in colonial legislation—were not necessarily equally disadvantageous to all.

## II

The thesis advanced in this book is that there was no single 'peasant' identity.[6] The rural producers of Bihar were not in the position of having no property, even in their own labour, like a Marxian proletariat,

[6] This is also the view of Magagna, *Communities*. He argues that none of the elements of classification—property, relations of production, life-style or beliefs—are uniform among peasants or exclusive to them; and that therefore the category is often inappropriate or counterproductive. Instead he offers 'community' in a hard definition based on space (territory, social function) and order (hierarchy, rules of conduct, ritual, material relations), and geared to 'producing and distributing the means of life' (p.12-19). Nonetheless—and less clearly or convincingly, though the point about hierarchy is well-taken—Magagna also offers as 'peasant' society one which displays a certain 'mode of domination' (though contested and incomplete), the peasantry representing 'a determinate relation of power that binds supralocal elites and local communities' (pp.45-6).

and nor did they enjoy only one kind of property; they were not all petty proprietors, like the middle peasants of Eric Wolf,[7] though they were imagined to be so by the British architects of the Bengal Tenancy Act of 1885. Property was indeed a key, both to the idea of the peasant and to the official perspectives of Indian society in the nineteenth century. The evolution was supposed to be from group to individual rights, from overlapping to exclusive possession.[8] Given, however, that 'exclusive' property is produced by power and sanctions and subject to rules, custom and other limits of coercion, it is plain that the progression or distinctions cannot be absolute.

This study has applied, first, the well-known discovery that the several communities had been subject to external influences over the millenia—from beliefs, government and trade—and the certainty that India was no mere conglomeration of isolated, unchanging cells, awaiting unification by an external agent, British rule or international capitalism. In pre-colonial India there was evidence both for division, derived from birth and marriage, reinforced by residence and behaviour, and for co-operation, even for common culture. The conflict between specifics and generality, locality and centre, is a major theme of pre-colonial as of colonial history. The objective great community is not necessarily a later or better development than the local, subjective one; both were implicit in Brahmanism itself. Hence, in these respects, the British period could do no more than intensify a process of the *longue durée*.

Second this book has insisted on the concomitant recognition that the forces of change were equally as mixed in character as the forms of continuity. It is necessary to contrast social multiplicity and standardisation, as ideal types, but the one should not be attributed to India and the other to the West. As the boundaries of the general were extended, so the armies of the particular began to be overrun. But the forces for uniformity were not—perhaps one could say, are never—all pervasive. In India, even by the end of the nineteenth century, they were only beginning to bite, with the developments in state intervention, communications and markets. One school of thought held that the Bihar tenant

---

[7] Eric Wolf, *Peasants* (Englewood Cliffs 1966).

[8] Magagna, *Communities*, defines property in terms of relations (rather differently from the material, production-related definition of the Indian tenancy reformers), that is, 'the performance of people in daily life when they claim rights and enforce responsibilities'; there is elite property, either privileged (rights from status) or exclusive (control over use), and 'community' property (trusteeship) (pp.39-45).

had already been reduced in mid-century to a common misery by the overweening power of the landlords. On the contrary, it seems that a range of social and ecological distinctions persisted in Bihar far longer than is sometimes supposed. The very multiplicity of categories, and the separation but interdependence of social, economic and political differences, are likely to have made them resilient. As mentioned already, a multitude of terms for land and tenures persisted in Bihar; they did so despite the tendency in British legislation to restrict and regulate the types and incidents of landholding and tenancy according to Western notions. It is true that none of the terms—indigenous or exotic—necessarily retained a constant meaning over time; and of course isolation is a major preserver of local difference: the one may be said to be an indicator for the other. Our earlier counts of the different agrarian terms in Bihar would have had to be multiplied perhaps sevenfold if we had included the huge lists of synonyms and local variants. In many cases, though the broader distinctions (as between rent-paying and rent-receiving roles, or cultivated and non-cultivated land) were expressed in terms with a regional distribution, the words for more precise distinctions would perhaps be understood only within areas of a hundred square miles or less. Thus is illustrated the difficulty—and also the process—of generalisation in reality. But in the case of Bihar the explanation of agrarian conditions cannot depend only upon isolation being broken down or maintained. The argument is not that isolation and other pecularities in Bihar slowed down developments that were otherwise relentless; the argument is that our understanding of the nature of these processes has been imperfect.

An insistence upon India's diversity and localism would have sounded familiar to the colonial rulers, for whom it was a favourite argument; but their's is the very argument rejected here. The British were concerned with the supposed disunity of Indian races, regions and classes. They believed in the essential sameness of everything contained within the categories they constructed. But the situation described in rural Bihar was one of variety alongside linkages, not of similarity plus isolation. We have needed therefore to find an alternative description of India's diversity, one which does not depend on the products of 'modernisation' with its overarching organisation of belief, class and government. Here too rival paradigms have been contending in the literature, some depending on extended horizontal links (or factions) and others on broad horizontal groupings (or class). It is possible to combine elements of both these models, and to view rural

Bihar as made up of different, overlapping components (or points-of-view). The first component is the mass of local communities which, because they were hierarchical, may be pictured as small triangles. The second is the range of horizontal groupings, either cutting through some of the triangles or operating above them—for example, merchant communities in various towns, and family and clan ties across regions. In the main they were of a similarly circumscribed character to the village communities. Third were the networks, linking parts of these components; they could be representative sets, or arranged across a vertical scale, and they performed specific political, social or economic functions. In this category came the connections recognised among themselves by village headmen (one drawn out of each local community), and on the other hand the structures of administration, ritual and trade, stretching between localities and over space and time. It follows that processes of change could influence any or all of the components. The local triangles could be hardened, enlarged or broken down. The horizontal groups could split or unite into larger units. The networks could weaken or become larger, stronger and more general. Such changes were affected by ideas, by needs and by efforts, and particularly by states and other leadership. On the other hand each component could resist change, even though it was occurring in others, while the existence of a range of relations implied that new kinds of social and economic linkage could often be formed by adaptation rather than revolution. Both points stress continuities.

Certainly the alternative supposition (that Indian agriculturists were mainly and originally 'peasants') had consequences in the nineteenth century. In Bihar, in the aftermath of the 1885 Tenancy Act, it seemed that some of the poor were yet further dispossessed. But the suffering did not happen to a 'peasantry'. The unconscious assumptions of that ideal would lead us to claim that the Act 'made' rich peasants and landless labourers, as the permanent settlement was alleged to have 'made' landlords. The evidence tells a less dramatic story. The measure of the importance of this question of the peasantry and peasant societies, is thus that it can help or hinder us in the quest for those who benefited and those who suffered under colonial changes, and indeed in understanding the nature of those changes. The beneficiaries of the tenancy legislation were groups of people with the skills and resources to become protected producers within the framework of the law and the system of records, whether as landowners directly managing production or as tenants able to tap the labour of others. The opportunities which they were given derived in part from their absence in the imagination of the law-makers. They represented confusions of category which could not be perceived within the basic framework of lord and peasant, or trader and cultivator. Hence our attention to agrarian structure, the categorisation itself. In assessing the influence of particular forms of category, one is also considering the impact of language upon thought and practice. A concept implies a norm, which therefore defines what is deviant. Could there be any 'tenants' in pre-colonial India? Certainly there could not be land relations conceived and expressed in terms of that particular standard of agrarian relations and landholding. Did tenancy then suddenly appear? It could not until what was provided in colonial law and policy was localised and indigenised in practice and understanding. We also have to take the argument further. Some supposed influences of category are distinctions without a difference. Could there not have been, under pre-colonial regimes, agrarian relations which approximated to the tenurial, though conceived and expressed in different terms? Similarly one could ask if a 'bonded' labourer really became more oppressed with the advent of a Western legal concept defining his oppression, considering that comparable myths and justifications for it had long existed.[9] An additional question therefore is: was it material that, in law and eventually in practice, generalised types of tenancy replaced a multitude of more ambiguous and contingent relationships? It seems it was, because indigenous conduct and understanding were changed. A tenancy law made it harder for some kinds of relationship or right to prosper, because they became contrary to the supposed norm; on the other hand it helped some landholders by giving them a vocabulary and mechanism for expressing and defending 'rights'. Finally, such influence took particular forms and direction, because this tenancy law was a categorisation with a message: it assumed landholders held property not only as a portmanteau of legal and economic rights, but also for an economic purpose. The terms 'landlord' and 'tenant', or 'proprietary peasant', like their antonyms 'nomad', 'pastoralist', 'tribal' or 'subsistence cultivator', represented a value-judgment, a Eurocentric evolutionist view of the world, based around environment-for-profitable-use and agricul-

[9] See Gyan Prakash, *Bonded Histories: Genealogies of Labor Servitude in Colonial India* (Cambridge 1990), and the discussion of it in P. Robb, *Dalit Movements and the Meanings of Labour in India* (Delhi 1993), pp.26-45; the rejection of 'hegemonic' influence in that essay does not preclude the *influence* for colonial law and administration proposed in the present analysis.

ture-for-exchange.[10]

Because thus based on imposed classifications which were seriously flawed, the tenancy laws made poverty invisible in policy terms, even while it was being admitted in a host of reports and studies. Two explanations for this indifference are related to different aspects of our present discussion. One was the kind of ideological myopia which allowed officials who were appalled at the condition of the poor to be satisfied with remedies which were directed towards occupancy raiyats. The mismatch was typical of British categorisation. The officials consistently under-researched economic difference. Indeed any official who laid too much stress on the horror of rural conditions in Bihar was in danger of being ignored;[11] efforts were made to demonstrate that the population did have enough food on which to live. Above all, when seeking to make more precise distinctions the British fell back upon caste, which certainly may have economic implications, but which is not derived from them (at least in theory); indeed, given that any caste was presumed to have a distinct function, and could include a range of wealth, there was a sense in which the concept could mask or even justify the number and condition of the poor. Nor, as noted in chapter one, were the developmental beliefs of the reformers appropriate; the British understanding of the means of economic change altered little over the period. The pro-peasant lobby did not dissent from the prevailing belief in the instrumentality of property, capital and trade.

But a second reason for indifference to the poor was the continuing British preoccupation with control. The debates of the period were not after all between sympathisers of the rich and supporters of the poor; they were between advocates of alternative modes of social dominance, by zamindars or by peasant proprietors. The British had little choice but to acquiesce in local command systems because of their vested interest in 'order'. It was partly by political calculation that, in nineteenth-century India, British laws never contemplated anything less than exclusive property in land (except belatedly to reduce its transferability), and that when they tried to preserve a tenant right it too was regarded as a kind of real estate. The British idea and need were for such rights to subsume all other rights. Land ownership became *the*

---

[10] Compare Pierre Clastres, 'Copernicus and the savages' in his *Society against the State* (1974; tr. Robert Hurley with Abe Stein, New York 1989).

[11] This point is frequently illustrated in this book. It is also mentioned in Burton Stein, ed., *The Making of Agrarian Policy in British India, 1770-1900* (Delhi 1992), pp.1-25.

resource in terms of the law, as in political policy. Non-proprietors had at best an inferior right. They were tenants by actual or implied contract between the parties.

Thus, for all the efforts of the pro-peasant reformers, most subordinate land rights were ignored throughout the nineteenth century. In the landlord areas, the cause of the tenants was taken up from time to time under pro-peasant influence, and yet the so-called tenancy legislation was effectively a charter for occupancy rather than a regulation of tenancy. In peasant-proprietary areas, tenants were hardly supposed to exist and were scarcely an issue before the twentieth century; indeed if tenancy legislation was intended to produce peasant-proprietors, it is hardly surprising that it was little favoured where they were believed to prevail already. An insistence upon property obscured the need to attend to actual units of production, and worries about fragmentation of holdings took a higher profile than attempts to improve the independence of farming households. The importance accorded to capital investments which would replace labour defied the realities of agricultural employment—and credit—and hence the priorities of agrarian society in many parts of India. By contrast, the neglect of other possible elements may have distorted or prevented change. Little concern was shown for the wide transmission of information (for example through education) or for the improvement of internal demand through the fairer distribution of wealth. There was limited understanding of agricultural decision-making and the relations of production, and in particular of the role of intermediaries. [12]

Within these limitations the British debated whether to favour rent-receivers or controllers of cultivation. The choice was not peculiar to Bihar or the 1885 Act; these were the two main strategies adopted before 1914 to protect and extend British power and revenues. All these strategies changed the pre-existing legal framework; they contravened the complexities of agrarian relations through their uniformity of regulation; and they had some impact on behaviour and expectations, given the relatively stable administration, especially as the nineteenth century wore on. This increased capacity meant that it mattered that there was

[12] See also ibid., which concludes (as also explained and elaborated above) that 'the legacy of colonial subjugation for the agrarian order was that it hastened a process which pre-dated foreign rule', partly through the degradation of communitarian institutions. However, Stein (contrary to his own example in the case of Munro) also advocates a 'new' study of class relations in place of the 'old' study of agrarian law, as if the two were distinct in practice or effect.

an imperfection in the official definition of tenancy.

The outcome of legislation was progressively to create a legal category of protected tenancies which became, in effect, sub-proprietary. The impact of the Bengal Tenancy Act, and indeed of the permanent settlement and of zamindari abolition in the 1950s, differed from what the promoters intended, and in each case this owed much to the distortions of theory and perception. The permanent settlement sought property rights under the physiocratic assumption that Bengali zamindars were or could become improving landlords. The result in law was the replacement by a single legal identity, the landed proprietor, of a multitude of roles associated with local power and with representing the state, especially in revenue collection. The nineteenth-century tenancy laws were supposed to safeguard the 'actual cultivator', and zamindari abolition was intended to provide an equitable redistribution of land to tenants; but arguably both benefited middle-level landholders and agricultural entrepreneurs, people already rich in resources. Consistently the target was missed because of a mixture of erroneous assumptions about how the society worked, or what it was which was being tackled: in particular there was a continuing insistence upon private property, and at the same time, paradoxically, from the early nineteenth century, upon the Indian village community.

This framework helped explain the changing fortunes of raiyats over the century. The evidence proved just as conflicting for the later period as for the earlier; much of it had been fodder for the tenancy debate itself. But it was not impossible to draw conclusions. A good example might be drawn from an article which appeared in the *Calcutta Review* in 1883, commenting on the surveys of rent-rates in Bihar, by Finucane in the north and Tobin in the south. The latter was conducted in four villages in Bhojpur in Shahabad, a choice to which P. Nolan, the Collector, a supporter of rent-law reform, had objected as untypical, in that the villages were 'cultivated by ryots, of whom a considerable proportion have...*guzashta* rights, while nearly all have occupancy rights, and that the same leniency of the landlord which permitted such privileges to grow up and continue, has prevented him from generally enhancing rents on other lands'. But Nolan went on:

It is the object of some of the framers of the present Bill to secure for the ryots of Bengal as a body rights of occupancy at moderate rents, which they contend would insure superior cultivation through the improvements to be expected from those who enjoy security of title, a certain prosperity in ordinary times, with the credit necessary to enable cultivators to tide over periods of famine without becoming a burden on the taxes, and which would also, it is urged, tend to give to the tenants the independence and manliness of character generally found among peasant-proprietors. On the other hand, there are many who believe that low rents and security end in sloth, the sale of land to speculators, and in the end to sub-letting at a rack-rent. It would be most important to ascertain whether in the selected tract the conditions which it is proposed to create eleswhere, have led to the results anticipated by the one school or the other:

I think that there can be no doubt in such a question. Sub-letting is not unknown in Bhojpur, and some of the cultivators are in debt; but these are exceptional cases. The general rule is, that the ryots cultivate their own lands with their own small capital, and when they sell their holdings, it is to others of their own class. Their industry is marked, and has resulted in the clearing of the jungle with which much of the land was covered 50 years ago, and the creation of a cultivated area as well planted with fruit trees, as well irrigated from wells, and as well fenced as any I have seen in India. No one can encamp for a day in the tract without being struck with its exceptional prosperity, which contrasts strongly with the backward state of those parts of the district in which rents are high, and occupancy rights unknown.

Nolan's is a testimony to the contemporary recognition of the policy whose features have been described in this book, with the exception perhaps of his endorsement of low rents. But the account carries its own caveat. The area in question *was* exceptional, and not only in the comfortable condition of its raiyats. It was also an area of relatively recent reclamation, often associated with favourable terms of occupancy, and one inhabited by people renowned (at best) for their independence, for being if anything (in Nolan's words) 'too manly and independent': 'The Bhojpur wrestlers have a name throughout the country, and every man carries the large Bhojpur *latti* which he can use with great skill. They are equally ready to defend themselves in law courts with which the complication of rights, inseparable from any system where the majority possess interest in land, has rendered them familiar.' Nolan believed that these characteristics had developed from their conditions of tenure, but if we are seeking determinist explanations then the reverse is at least as likely to be true. The large bodies of high-caste land-controlling peasants of parts of Shahabad, notoriously belligerent and litigious, made their own good fortune in constant conflict with their landlords, often caste-fellows. Buchanan, seventy years before, had reported that the 'great proportion of the tenantry' of this area were 'too high spirited to submit to the most trifling abuse and...willing to fight with any one for a cowrie'.[13] Tobin's report, while agreeing about the independence

[13] Francis Buchanan [Hamilton], *An Account of the District of Shahabad, 1812-13* (Patna 1934), p.339.

and prosperity of these villagers, demurred over their 'industry and good cultivation': 'They have in past years', he wrote, 'held more land than they could cultivate properly; they generally select the crop that requires least cultivation, *viz.*, peas, although it commands a very low price, and does not yield a greater outturn than other crops. In those lands, where Brahmins, Rajputs and Bhunbaes [Babhans; Bhumihar or 'military' Brahmans] have been superseded by more industrious castes, I notice a marked difference in the care with which the land is culti-vated.'[14] The article quoting these findings was anxious to attack the pro-tenant camp, and argued that 'low rents and security of tenure... have ended in sloth, and...sub-letting, at rack-rents'. Our conclusion must be that the Tenancy Act of 1885 assisted the rent-receiving peas-ants without necessarily providing the incentives to enterprise which Nolan expected. Where other groups were able to gain in independence and economic power, it could also help them. But it was not, and could not be, a cure for poverty, in households or region.

## III

The Bengal Tenancy Act of 1885 marked a point around which to locate a discussion of agricultural property in nineteenth-century Bihar, the region for which much of the Act was originally intended. The Act worked against a background of economic change whereby the formal rent-receiving roles were losing out in comparison with more direct means of securing agricultural surplus—that is, through cultivation or non-regulated tenancies and share-cropping. The benefits of the Act were also not shared equally among landlords or among tenants because these economic changes also took place within the context of persistent norms and institutions, which marched with weaknesses in the Act. Two broader assertions also may command widespread assent. One is that the institution of landed property, as a commodity, acted to some extent as a social solvent and a sump for capital. The other is that concentrations of agrarian power dispossessed and impoverished large sections of the rural population. In other circumstances such changes might have been regarded as painful but necessary accompaniments of

---

[14] G. –, 'Is Behar rack-rented? An enquiry into the condition of the Behar ryots', *Calcutta Review* LXXVIII, CLV (1883), quoting correspondence from No-lan, and from Tobin's report (para.18, *Government of India Gazette*, 20 October 1883, p.1,758). On the improvements noted by Nolan the article commented that the wells and fruit-trees had been provided at the expense of the Dumraon raj, and the 'fencing' was merely the usual *aals* (ridges of earth).

industrialisation, increasing agricultural productivity per capita and creating an industrial labour force. In colonial India, however, the wider economic transformation did not occur, and changes in the agricultural sector have been seen as an additional impediment to development. Not only was the economy 'arrested' in terms of manufacturing and trade, it was also 'distorted' in terms of agriculture and rural life. This discussion has tried to provide some clarity about the processes involved.

The story of the nineteenth century in Bihar is thus of two great interventions—one bureaucratic and one commercial—but interventions affecting a resilient society. A professed desire to preserve the past did not necessarily impede the state's interventions to alter the present. And it was in the nature of these interventions to grow. The devices of British government may be described as demarcation, surveillance, and incorporation. The process was partly one of measurement, and measurement implies definite margins. Such mapping, whether literal or metaphorical, has to choose some categories, and to confront others. Its impact lay in the reduction of allowable alternatives and variants. Take the case of common land. There is a great difference between that which is freely available for use, that which is open to the members of a community, and that which (though still common) is owned by a collective institution, whether community or state. In India, all three kinds existed in 1800: there were legally 'unclaimed' lands available for settlement, lands used at will by villagers, and lands whose use was regulated by village or other elites—though in all cases access was complicated by considerations relating to the status of the user. The British at least pretended formally to ignore these social and ritual distinctions, but their law certainly recognised no waste land and no land which was not owned; in default of valid claimants, land belonged to the state. Thus they lumped common land into a single category, and also of course went much further and encouraged private ownership in the lands controlled by the elites. This amounted to an attempted redefinition of society as well.

The measurement of landed property and the resumption of revenue-free lands had removed elements of choice in agricultural practice. The more fixed and pervasive ownership became, the more difficult it was, for example, to use land as part-payment for services or labour, something which continued throughout the nineteenth century at many different social levels; the danger of ownership was that it rigidified these arrangements, with varied consequences for rich and poor. Payment in land was one of the features which mixed the categories in

India, as between landlord and official, or peasant and labourer; state policy was tending slowly to disentangle these complexities. Thus too the identification of 'criminal' or 'agricultural' castes, for legal purposes, reinforced the character and restricted the mobility of all groups. Nor did such measures act singly: their impact was cumulative.

On the other hand, to argue that imperial rule distorted the society by confiscating the rights of non-proprietors, is to suggest that a pre-colonial system with definite features—a moral economy, the village community and so on—was being superseded by a new system which really mirrored what was provided by law. We have seen that it was only historical interpretations of resident villagers as the original owners of the cultivation which convinced officials that a mass of would-be proprietary peasants was held down by zamindars. The 'village republic' was an idea. It follows that there could not be a 'natural' and even progression under British rule, towards several property and social differentiation, not only because of the weakness and confusion of forces for change, but also because of the lack of any pristine or isolated condition from which a linear development could begin. Even as the doctrine of the village community was being devised, observers recognised an existing stratification: land, manpower, cattle, water and other resources were not evenly shared, but distributed according to 'ancestral rights', or by caste and power, which were anyway needed to make rights effective. Rights depended, that is, on economic and political forces as well as on custom and expectations, so that they were bound to be were distributed differentially, and (later) not precisely as legislation provided.

Nonetheless at several points in this discussion the supposed certainties of rights under Western law have been compared with the complexity and variability of Indian custom. The contrast was related to long-term change, which was not just colonial in origin, but which accelerated during the nineteenth century. It is unsafe to generalise about pre-colonial, let alone original modes of agrarian structure in India. But it is possible to outline the elements of an ideal 'customary' form. Its chief feature, as Maine proposed, would be the allocation of shares according to status; over time this was being replaced by contract or market relations. A village operating on a system of shares could certainly be hierarchical and oppressive for many of its people. But it would not be dominated by private property. Though land could be held and cultivated separately, its output—the grain heap—would not be 'owned', but would be subject to division among co-sharers, retrospectively at harvest *and* subsequently through provision of seed and of food for work. As these distributions were not exactly wages or payments directly linked to tasks, there might be an expectation that they would continue in times of hardship: the shares were a form of risk-distribution. Hoarding or speculation in grain would be morally as well as politically outlawed. It was thus that private property and growing markets, as in the later nineteenth century, implied greater social differentiation and vulnerability. For the wealthy they would allow greater profits and lower costs (less redistribution to appease or protect the workforce). For the poor, they would imply the reverse. The poor might also have fewer alternatives as waste or forest-lands and other resources were privatised, and as alternative employment and food-sources narrowed, especially if mobility were insufficient or no improvement, and if state provision were misguided or inadequate.

Within this general framework, a more specific conclusion about the impact of colonial rule is that it changed the fortunes of many individuals and some groups, and increasingly became the arbiter of such categories and their fortunes. It did not newly create the undoubted suffering of underprivileged cultivators, any more than it wholly dispossessed an ancient aristocracy. It did not render religious and social allegiances irrelevant. It did not wholly create or standardise classes of people and the divisions between them. But it modified the basis of group identities and power relations in the countryside, reducing some features and exaggerating others. The Tenancy Acts too were no unprecedented imposition upon a region with no experience of state power; but they *were* an enhancement of an influence long weakly felt and readily accommodated. Moreover, the law did not work in isolation. The existing society reflected economic and political forces in tandem; so too, if the 1885 Act influenced the local disposition of power and wealth, it did so in harness with economic change. The law also worked upon a complex society, one that was already differentiated. Thus, when the 1885 Act insisted on the category of occupancy raiyat, on the assumption that there was no important difference between resident villagers, the outcome was enhanced security and certainty for the majority recognised as 'settled' raiyats, who had hitherto enjoyed continuity of residence and landholding *de facto* rather than *de jure*. But the outcome was also increased advantages for a minority of the rural population who were already privileged and strategically-placed. These could be landlords on their 'own' holdings, or substantial tenants able to maintain independence. People in villages who held most village resources, including capital, and who were helped by expanding trade to capture petty producers, were likely to be the same people who could manipulate the opportunities offered by British laws. Indeed, this was all the more likely because of the law's standardising impulses and its offer of state protection to the few who could seek its support.

## IV

We return now to our opening theme, the connection between land, law and the growth of the state. We have seen that for some of the time the rulers thought they were respecting custom. 'India' was not a void to which the British gave form—though in another sense the name itself *was* another essentialism—and it contained its own jurisdictions, norms and processes; these existed before and during the efforts whereby, little by little, the British set out their view of arenas, conduct and values. But the colonial state was overwhelmed by practicalities and prejudices. In declaring one matter to be illegal and another to be lawful, it established or formalised boundaries which were inevitably different from those which existed already. Sometimes Indians were ready to adopt the changes, for example in deciding where and on what basis a dispute should be adjudicated. They readily colonised the institutions and frameworks provided to them, as in the use of the courts or the bureaucracy—a factor which should not be underestimated. In these ways Indians admitted extensions of the areas which the state defined. At other times, however, Indians declined to accept the standards of behaviour or the role for the state which their rulers advanced; such quarrels over jurisdiction helped inflame the uprisings of 1857, or the later controversies over the standing of general, secular law in regard to marriage or women's rights. In such cases, the state might assume its opponent to be a transgressor who had taken upon himself the role (in the practice and mythology of British rule) of the tiger or the Pathan: as an outlaw, he risked reprisals for violating the supposedly 'civilised' arena established by rule. Thus, the same pattern was followed in social and religious life, as over territory—where border disputes or supposed violations of Western-style treaties had encouraged further annexations. Allies in particular were expected to conform to the norms set by the colonial state; legislation would coerce them where they were thought not to have done so. In such a way did the tenancy reformers regard the zamindars of Bengal; but they had expectations too of the raiyats.

Above all, an incompatibility of opposing standards—British crossings of an Indian boundary, or Indian of a British—could lead to further state interventions, even when the rulers sought to preserve or make use of the indigenous, in the manner of recruiting the Pathans or the Gurkhas for the army. Even the attempt to recover ground for Indian practice was accomplished by further, if different state regulation, as in the Bengal Tenancy Act. Old institutions were restored but for new purposes: peasant proprietors in order to spearhead capitalist agriculture, or the village community as the agent of the state. Thus is explained that odd circumstance that British interventions really began to grow in India at the very time when historicist caution was at its height, and relativism beginning to gain hold.

Revenue gave us one illustration of state intervention, of the pushing back of the frontier between public and private. Clearly two elements pervaded from the later nineteenth century. The first was the ever-expanding delineation of public roles and hence also of private rights, conceived as matters of rule and precedent. This had lasting consequences: it was significant that at zamindari abolition in the 1950s it was thought necessary to compensate the landlords to some extent for the loss of property, the legitimacy of which the abolitionists otherwise repudiated. The second element, also long-lived, was the idealisation of 'community'. From the 1870s it appeared in fields as diverse as schemes for local policing and strategies of national economic policy or political development. The two elements appear to conflict, in theory and practice. It was a curiosity that a Westernising state should to a large extent have privileged what it perceived to be indigenous. But the indigenous was favoured only by various sleights of hand. Consider the idea of 'restoring rights'. The notion of rights-as-property is inherently conservative, but in this case the garb of history was put on so as to conceal a reform; it was a pretence of tradition while espousing change. When the tenancy reformers talked of 'ancient rights' they were according a special status to Indian-ness, and at the same time attempting to modify it. The expression sought to establish, retrospectively, a British view of sovereignty and law, of the public and private, and of the nature of rights. According to the idea of India which these officials also accepted, 'ancient' and 'rights' were contradictory or mutually exclusive. It was thought that only Western law could so confine the arbitrary and personal exercise of power as to permit the growth of individual property. In practice, before British rule, there do seem to have been general concepts of law and localised notions of propriety which restricted the absolutism of states and overlords. And yet the

'ancient rights' of 1885 were new: they were encapsulated in statute
and interpreted by courts.

In India as elsewhere the evident prospects of conflict, suffering and
injustice had required strategies of social management and some means
of establishing proprieties. A mediation between 'rights' and 'duties'
was at the heart of the colonial state's programme. Among the
resources to hand was, on one side, the tradition developed in J.S.
Mill's concept of liberty. Its demerit was that, by emphasising individual rights rather than collective obligations, it was bound to strengthen
those able to defend rights (or property) as individuals—that is, the
strong. Doctrines of autonomous rights invited assertions of self-
interest at the expense of others, and such rights, endorsed or curbed by
definite rules, might also justify authoritarianism: the new rules
enforced behaviour of advantage to the law-makers and their allies. On
the other side, contrasting with these selfish liberties, were those traditions which advocated the surrender of self as a means of discovering
or protecting self; notable instances existed in India. In social terms,
such ideas supposed communal norms or heteronomous obligations.
Their drawback was that they did not necessarily benefit the weak
either: they might demand conformism, and lead ultimately to that
subordination of the individual to the collective good which produces
social oppression, communalism, terrorism and war. Neither individualism nor communitarianism is exclusively Indian or European. But
both are reflected differently in different local institutions and norms, in
India differently from in Europe. Thus, whether deciding between these
modes or failing to do so (often both were confusingly on offer at once,
as in 1885), the colonial government could not avoid meddling with
India. To build new kinds of institution and law, and to support existing
'custom', it focused on legalistic privileges rather than collective
duties, and enunciated rights, both against the state itself and in order to
resolve conflicts between its citizens. In the process it forced a competition between norms, for the institutions which it introduced did not
operate with the same vocabulary as the pre-existing order. Inevitably a
tension was created within the society, as people struggled to negotiate
between incompatible understandings and expectations.

## V

This book has argued that the colonial state in India embarked, in
effect, upon social engineering, especially from the later nineteenth

century. Its understanding of categories and of the state's responsibilities provided the theoretical side to a revolution in government. This shows that there was a strong instrumentality in the colonial attitude to law and society. There was very little recognition, even in the desire to preserve what was ancient or pre-existing, of the importance of what has been called non-event causation—that is, of intrinsic qualities, of effects that could not be traced to some prior means, or of social forces that (like gravity) exerted a continuous influence. The assumption was that old rights *caused* new ones; new laws *created* social change. On this basis of instrumentality the Bengal Tenancy Act partook of the broader aspects of state expansion set out in the opening chapters of this book; thus it took on distinctive forms. The ideas which informed and shaped the Act focused on definite categories, and on rights located in them, because the rights were conceived as a species of property. Moreover, the Act interfered to regulate and encourage this categorisation, especially with regard to occupancy raiyats, because of the sway of related doctrines of the state's proper role. The intervention marked an important step towards active socio-economic management, but it misunderstood and distorted aspects of the structure of Indian rural society, for example in Bihar. What is more, the tenancy reform then had actual impact, because it was given practical bureaucratic form, especially through survey and settlement proceedings. Such expansions of administrative capacity constituted the operational aspect of the revolution in government. They could also have been considered in relation to agricultural production; the extent to which agricultural policy too was based upon an inappropriate conspectus will be examined in a further volume on agriculture and improvement.

In view of their evolutionary and instrumentalist framework, the colonial state's interventions helped produce a decline of the rural community—for example, the replacement of a moral economy by market relations. Victor Magagna has proposed that communal institutions, once 'redistributive' (deciding property rights) or 'regulative' (prescribing land or labour use for owner-households), may have become 'residual' (marginal to the distribution of property and the organisation of production). The change would occur with the supra-local definition and enforcement of property rights, and the development of representative institutions, reducing the autonomy and increasing the accountability of local elites.[15] Nineteenth-century British

---

[15] Magagna, *Communities*, pp.252-3; one might call this a change from sta-

officials, having read their Henry Maine, knew this, and keenly debated the desirability of allowing the rural communities to decline under an onslaught from law and the market. The officials resisted, but also permitted and encouraged, such change.[16] Thus the Bengal Tenancy Act of 1885 encouraged the exercise of individual rights or oppressions. It also curbed the freedom of and increased the public scrutiny upon landlords, while seeking (for a generation at least) to remove the control by landlord or state over a cultivating or 'peasant' elite which sublet or gave employment to others.

What were the wider consequences? Neither dispossession nor advantage were complete, because the state and legal controls were relatively weak—there was, for example, supralocal definition of rights through survey and settlement, but no proper maintenance of the record. Indeed, we have seen that the distortions in the intended outcome occurred in part because of the *weakness* of subsequent policy—as over the survey and record of rights, a bureaucratic and political inability to adjust state practice as the results of earlier errors became apparent. But landlords and their supporters complained bitterly, and questioned their collaboration with the colonial state. They also sought new means of control over their subordinates. Together these effects contributed to socio-religious movements and to nationalism and political change. Arguably, the response to external pressure included peasant rebellions and broader social revolutions, such as occurred in early modern Europe and in Asia in the twentieth century.[17] Fundamentally these imply an imperative of institutional and cultural survival: that rural communities rejected the challenge of outside political or economic forces or (on other arguments) internally of demography. Thus were

---

tus to contract. Note also Magagna's recognition of the importance of bureaucratic interference, pp.33-6.

[16] See also Thomas R. Metcalf, *Ideologies of the Raj* (Cambridge 1994), but note that he considers Maine's contribution as have been chiefly to help establish a myth of 'difference', an India that was medieval and feudal. Perhaps for that reason, Metcalf presents only the aristocratic model among the 'created constituencies' of the British raj (pp.66-80 and 186-99).

[17] A general argument along these lines is also made by Magagna, *Communities*, ch.2 and passim. Many accounts of India have stressed such rural protest, perhaps exhibiting a desire to exhibit popular assertiveness (in the face of theories of Indian passivity) vaguely reminiscent of the physical training favoured by nineteenth-century Bengalis to counter the colonial stereotype that they were 'effeminate'. That there was more protest than used to be realised cannot be denied, though much of it is also continual and within rural society, rather than occasional and directed against external pressure.

continuities important.[18] There was also another possible reaction: one of accommodation. We have stressed institutional adaptability: in the case of nineteenth-century Bihar, the co-optation of the colonial state and capitalist trade by the rural elites. And disappointed accommodators could also be rebels.

There are in short two models of the results of intervention. The first is analogous to instances when an indigenous population succumbed to new, imported diseases. The second is more like the action of a well-placed opportunist farmer in bringing in an improved strain of wheat—or it might be like the New Zealand Maori deploying the firepower of the musket in customary tribal warfare, the new adopted by the old with tragic results. In Bihar, given prior experience of external contacts, and extensive subordination and dependence of sections of the population, the result of the two great interventions of the nineteenth century were thus special exaggerations of both entitlement and dispossession, in other words relative enrichment of the few and impoverishment of the many.

What can be said of legal roles may be applied, *pari passu*, to social institutions. We can see caste similarly as an aspect of social control which developed in particular circumstances, and changed its role continually as the circumstances changed. In the later nineteenth century, economic and legal developments opened up the possibility for dominance or at least independence to be derived in new ways. A window was provided, for example, for successful agricultural castes, well-equipped to pay higher rents and to operate in the market-place. Undoubtedly, in favourable circumstances the independent household may be an important force for agricultural improvement: the spread of independence amongst producers is an important yardstick to establish. Thus the expansion of marketing could lead slowly to consequent changes in the basis for wealth; so too—slowly—could some measures of British administration and law. There are many documented instances of upward social mobility for groups who found a new niche in a changing situation; though it had always been possible to do so, the type and extent of the opportunities varied. And yet what was still most

---

[18] This was the argument of an article on rural protest written in the 1970s; see Robb, *Emergence of British Policy towards Indian Politics* (New Delhi 1992), ch.10. It has been criticised as 'elitist'; but the problem of the alternative explanations of unrest from the perspective of 'Subaltern Studies' (see the volumes edited by Ranajit Guha and others; Delhi 1982-95) is the singularity, uniformity and egalitarianism it supposes in the peasantry.

evident in many areas in the nineteenth and twentieth centuries was the continuing dominance of upper-caste lineages. One reason is presumably that the forces for change, in government or the economy, were very far from overwhelming. Just as important, however, is once again the fact that circumstances were not entirely new. The more one regards each society as *sui generis*—in the case of India the more one appreciates the antiquity of state interference and of systems of exchange—the less one is surprised if the old social forms can adjust to meet apparently new conditions. By such arguments, a 'rich peasant', say, can be taken to illustrate either continuity or change. An earlier premise of this book was that a stable rural world should not be contrasted with the dynamic one of 'modernity'.

## VI

The political and ideological impact of the British also can be described as significant. They were altering the terms of a perennial dialogue between the particular and the general—though the diffusion of broader identities, like the construction of national interest, depends very closely upon economic as well as politico-legal changes. Again, the first pole of the state's influence concerned the individual. The British described the impact of their rule as if there were a unified progression, unique to the West, towards independence of choice and equality before the law. Property right was equated with the West and with progress. It led to citizenship, which, combined with race, produced a nation, as if, in the 'modern', Westernised future, the objective sum of individuals' will and rights would supersede the more personal and involuntary collectivity of the Indian past. We do find the appearance (when conditions were right) of broader connections chosen by individuals. Hence the second pole of British influence concerned the nature of community. At heart it was a question of identity.

There is a range of different perceptions of himself possible for, say, a Bihari Kurmi: first as a member of a particular village and as part of a certain set of family and other relations, influenced by the external connections of headmen, priests and traders; or second, as a member of a caste with shared interests and characteristics across a region, made up of people with whom there was no actual or feasible contact, but among whom there was an idea of 'Kurmi' as a category; and thirdly, as a member of some still broader and more abstract grouping, as cultivator, as member of a Kisan Sabha (peasant association) or a co-operative society, as Hindu, as Bihari, as Indian. These identities are not necessarily mutually exclusive, but together they may be seen as a widening range of possibilities. They situate the individual differently within the community from the old village forms of society described earlier; they define the private and the public differently. Similarly a distinction may be made between a group enhancing its *varna* status, and a number of groups coalescing into one regional caste organisation. The British tried at times to protect the local communities and to restrict the expansion of both horizontal identities and the networks between them, but the tendency of their rule was in the opposite direction. The government attempted to use the structures they observed in India; and when nationalists opposed them they too had to mobilise or develop local issues and hierarchies, horizontal interest groups and various kinds of linkages—in a socio-political equivalent of increasing market relations.

There has been no complete triumph of the individual or the nation in India; there has been no even transition from structure to culture, to adopt Ernest Gellner's terms. On the contrary, elements of 'structure' have been strengthened, even while shared cultures also spread. Many of the British efforts failed: some pre-existing linkages became stronger, even while larger and more objective identities were enhanced. Small, local, inherited allegiances continued to be important. The interdependent character of village life and production was perpetuated, for all the British efforts to recreate a society dominated by property-owning individuals. The puzzle which this outcome represents, when assessed in conventional terms, called for a different understanding both of pre-colonial India and of the processes of change.

However, there *has* obviously been a development of broader allegiances, and of nationalist rhetoric and even national identities, in India. Broad parameters were set particularly by ideologies, by perceptions of political, fiscal and economic imperatives, and by personal and official ambition and self-interest. The idea of state responsibility helped shape and decide the direction of particular decisions. Also, so it has been argued, '...national history secures for the contested and contingent nation the false unity of a self-same, national subject evolving through time. This reified history derives from the linear, teleological model of Enlightenment History....'[19] Undoubtedly, in India, such a narrative of

[19] Prasenjit Duara, *Rescuing History from the Nation: Questioning Narratives of Modern China* (Chicago 1995), p.4. Similar ideas have been explored by Benedict Anderson, *Imagined Communities* (London 1983), Partha Chatter-

history helped identify this self-aware subject, as do rules of (especially female) conduct, or 'national' norms, ethics and characteristics, or a discourse of common interests and of geographical, ethnic and linguistic limits. All might be represented (as is commonly recognised) in maps, flags, currency, uniforms, museums, textbooks, codes, rituals, and so on: the signs and symbols of the nation. They evolved, but (like the 1885 Tenancy Act) supposedly only in order to express an essence, *what always was.* Such are the visible and rhetorical instruments, the overtly national texts and ideas. But—what may be overlooked in analyses of discourse, and perhaps more important—there are also evolutions in indirectly influential processes and institutions, which deploy these same means for immediate practical ends, in the way that history, custom, category and state (ancient rights and future progress) were all marshalled in the tenancy debates. They too produced public arena, civil acts, and common understandings. Land law could become an important frame of nationality, once it embodied 'rational' features, specifically individual property regulated within legal classes as economic and political interests. Actions speak at least as loudly as words in nation-building. This book has been concerned to elucidate such indirect, unconscious influences, which accompanied the growth of the state in India.

Colonial policies had many motives, certainly including exploitation of various kinds. They included job satisfaction, the search for legitimacy and support, the concern with legal 'rights', and the fears of bad publicity in India, Britain and elsewhere. The relative influence of various goals differed. Opinions as to the proper means of achieving the ends varied. But there was also, in the colonial period, a continual and

---

jee, *The Nation and its Fragments* (Delhi 1994), and Eric Hobsbawm and Terence Ranger, eds., *The Invention of Tradition* (Cambridge 1983). But see also Duara, pp.51-6 and 61-5. My account regards the nationalist identity as modern (requiring print, state and market) but also as containing earlier representations and narratives. However, the latter do not imply a single 'Hindu' political community with effective awareness of its descent or transmission over time and region, producing a non-linear or pre-modern 'culture', *dharma* versus state. The problem with that formula lies in its positing the separate and continuous existence and opposition of such constructs, as Duara seems to acknowledge when finding it hard to choose between Jawaharlal Nehru and Gandhi as his model for India (p.212), but to forget when (like the acolytes of Hindutva) he contrasts a supposedly unconstructed traditional self-image of the Indian populace, with a supposedly reconstructed modern image of the Westernised intelligentsia (p.226). Indian identity has been constructed from both aspects.

fairly constant concern in India with state responsibility and with improvement, a concern which seemed to derive partly from general (modern) notions of states and sovereignty, and of public and private spheres. A concept of duty (as this may be described) explained many policy decisions and developments of the state. Here this improving impulse has been incapsulated in the goal of 'future comfort'. That concern was qualified by others, such as a desire for continuity or appropriateness, represented here as a concept of 'ancient rights' and more generally by the importance accorded to precedent. The combination of influences distorted some of the British policy-measures, or made them confused and contradictory. But overall, during the nineteenth century, the capacity as well as the ambition of the colonial state grew, largely by expressing the positive goals of government. Beyond the ideological changes, one saw the growth in bureaucratic developments and particular policies. At the core was the establishment of discrete spheres and functions for the state or for private enterprise. This was true even of laissez faire and other ideas which minimised the role of the state: they still defined proper public or private roles, a categorisation which fostered a professionalisation of the state, through departments, career structures, and specialised skills and knowledge.

The Bengal Tenancy Act also helped expand the state's roles. In particular it marked an attempt to regulate social and economic categories, by means of the central and defining concept of property, which was also the accepted, mechanistic basis of other current binary schemes of classification and enumeration. That is to say, categories were constructed from individual components which shared characteristics; each was distinguished by its different properties, which also defined its capacity and function. Thus landholding or tenancy was divided into classes by virtue of incidents or 'rights', which in turn were supposed to determine how each category performed economically and which social goods it would produce. Surveys and courts and Indian usage gradually gave effect to the classifications. These processes coincided with the nation-making agenda.

There were benefits and disadvantages associated with the *growth* of the state and its role, which should be regarded as a distinct issue. Considering the state itself may provide different conclusions from discussions of, say, the impact of colonial trade, or of education policy, or of tenancy law. Here we have found that, like other major acts of policy and law, the tenancy debate, the legislation, its categories, and the survey, merging with local conditions and concepts, helped invent a kind of economy and revised sets of agrarian rights and interests. They provided weapons and torments. They would be vigorously defended and sometimes resisted. Thus grew up interest groups which broadened the range of possible types of political and social organisation in India. The same measures, by developing the scope of government, also significantly moved colonial and Indian expectations of the state and of politics. All this, not entirely inadvertently, helped prepare the way for the nation, as a new, composite India.[20]

The defects of the 1885 Bengal Tenancy Act resulted from faulty diagnosis and understanding rather than the distorting priorities of an exploitative colonial state—although those priorities certainly supported an emphasis on individual rights and property, and the Act erred in particular when it extended individual rights in a society whose dispositions were in large part collective. At the outset it was noted that this represented an incongruity between 'public sphere' laws or assumptions, and the realities of Indian society. The effect was to make of individual rights a lever to exaggerate the inequalities of the collective system. Such defects were very real and serious. But they were also qualified by some possible gains, as in the protection of individuals under law. The problem tended to be that the gains were differentially provided and only partially enjoyed. In these respects the Act provides a metaphor for the impact of colonial rule.

Roberto Calasso has written:

Jacob Burckhardt came close to the secret of Sparta. With typical sobriety he comments: '...the power of Sparta seems to have come into being almost entirely for itself and for its own self-assertion, and its constant pathos was the enslavement of subject peoples and the extension of its own dominion as an end unto itself.'

...The Spartan state subjected every form to itself, subordinated every usage to its own existence. This was the ancient and thoroughly modern philosophy that the Spartans tried so determinedly to hide by passing themselves off as ignorant warmongers. ...The philosophy turned out to be the most effective weapon of war and self-preservation. And it was not discovered by the Athenians, as always too garrulous, vain, and distracted for that kind of thing.[21]

After all the British in India were not quite Spartan.

---

[20] This is an argument against essentialised or communalist definitions of India and Indian polity; that, as they exist today, they were also built on colonial laws and institutions, themselves in part adapted for and adopted by India.

[21] Roberto Calasso, *The Marriage of Cadmus and Harmony* (tr. Tim Parks; London 1994), pp.247-8.

# Index

This index lists proper names and significant discussions of certain topics, in the main text only. Indian names are listed according to usage.